The United States
and the End
of the Cold War

The United States and the End of the Cold War

Implications, Reconsiderations, Provocations

John Lewis Gaddis

New York Oxford □ OXFORD UNIVERSITY PRESS □ 1992

Oxford University Press

Oxford   New York   Toronto
Delhi   Bombay   Calcutta   Madras   Karachi
Petaling Jaya   Singapore   Hong Kong   Tokyo
Nairobi   Dar es Salaam   Cape Town
Melbourne   Auckland

and associated companies in
Berlin   Ibadan

Published by Oxford University Press, Inc.,
200 Madison Avenue, New York, New York 10016

Oxford is a registered trademark of Oxford University Press

Library of Congress Cataloging-in-Publication Data
Gaddis, John Lewis.
The United States and the end of the cold war : implications,
reconsiderations, provocations / John Lewis Gaddis.
p. cm.   Includes index.
ISBN 0-19-505201-3
1. United States—Foreign relations—Soviet Union.
2. Soviet Union—Foreign relations—United States.
3. United States—Foreign relations—1945–
4. Soviet Union—Foreign relations—1945–
5. Cold War.   I. Title.
E183.8.S65G345   1992
327.73047—dc20   91-17992

9 8 7 6 5 4 3 2 1

Printed in the United States of America
on acid-free paper

For Charles and Claire Ping

Who rebuilt a university

Preface

Early in 1985, a Washington foreign policy institute which shall remain nameless invited me to join a group of "experts" who were to meet periodically, under its sponsorship, to draft recommendations on United States policy toward the Soviet Union through the remainder of the decade. Flattered to have been asked—and not realizing, at the time, how frequent and forgettable such exercises tend to be—I promptly accepted. Having dutifully read the background material for the first meeting, I flew to Washington on the appointed day, looking forward to a series of wide-ranging and far-reaching discussions. At a minimum, I expected that the group would want to consider the likelihood of new leadership emerging soon in the Kremlin, the growing evidence that Ronald Reagan was moderating the hard line he had taken toward Moscow during his first term, and the prospect that the future of Soviet-American relations might not simply replicate its past.

The meeting, as it turned out, was a disappointment. The participants seemed unable to focus on anything beyond the next few months, and their comments amounted to little more than reiterations of the need to continue existing policies. After listening to several hours of discussion along these lines, I very tentatively raised my hand and asked whether we should not be looking ahead to the possibility that the Cold War might someday end: should we not give at least some thought to how we would like it to do so, and to what might then replace it? An embarrassed silence ensued, broken finally by this observation from a highly-respected senior diplomat: "Oh, it hadn't occurred to any of us that it ever would end."

An appreciative titter went around the room, after which the group quickly turned its attention back to the conventional wisdom my question had so ineffectually challenged. I went home in something of a funk, and subsequently found excuses—an important advantage of living in Athens, Ohio, is, at times, its distance from Washington—not to return. The group's policy paper, when it finally came out, proved no more imaginative than its first day of discussion had been, and as far as I could tell it made no impression whatever on anyone inside or outside of the government.

But the experience, for some reason, stayed with me. It had something to do with the fact that the John and Elizabeth Baker Peace Studies Program hosted a conference at Ohio University in April, 1986, on "How the Cold War Might End." It led me to write an article for *The Atlantic*, published under the same title in November, 1987, and included in this volume as an illustration of why historians are not very good at prediction. And it certainly came to mind on a damp and dreary November afternoon two years after that, when the phone rang in my office and a student reporter asked whether I would like to comment. "On what?" I inquired. "Europe," she replied, unhelpfully. "No, I wouldn't," I'm afraid I snapped—it had been a bad day, what with a long series of interruptions, a stack of unanswered correspondence and ungraded papers on my desk, an overdue manuscript to complete, and a malevolent computer that seemed bent on putting all the footnotes in the wrong places. It was not until I got home that evening, turned on the television, and saw Berliners dancing deliriously on top of their Wall that I realized what the phone call had been about, and how far things had come since my abortive contribution to the Washington policy-making process four and a half years earlier.

This book too, I suppose, is a delayed response to that meeting in Washington in what now seems a very distant past. Like one of its predecessors, it is a collection of essays prepared at different times and for different purposes; they all relate in one way or another, though, to the end of the Cold War. Chapters One through Seven are reconsiderations of Cold War history in the light of the fact that we can now view that history as a whole, from its beginning to its end. Chapters Eight through Eleven (and, to some extent, Chapters Six and Seven) represent very preliminary attempts, from several different analytical perspectives, to deal with how the end of the Cold War came about and what the implications of that development might be for the future. And all of the chapters, I hope, are "provocations," in the sense that they are meant to question conventional wisdom with regard to the topics they address. The distinguished senior diplomat could have had no idea what an elaborate response his flip remark on that day in 1985 would eventually elict. But then none of us have foreseen the future very clearly these past few years; this book is also about our failure to do that.

Most of these essays have appeared elsewhere in print; the locations are duly noted in footnotes. I have revised them all, however, and have substantially rewritten most of them; I have also updated bibliographical references wherever appropriate. There is no disguising the fact, though, that this is yet another "retread" book: surely it is a sign of advancing age when authors begin turning them out one after another. I promise that this will be the last one for a while, or at least until I am provoked into doing another.

Many people have contributed, in a variety of ways, to the researching, writing, and revision of these essays. I have tried to acknowledge them individually in the notes for each chapter, but I probably have missed some and so herewith extend both apologies and generic thanks. Through their reactions to most of the arguments it contains, students and colleagues in the Ohio University Contemporary History Institute have had a very considerable influence over the shaping of this book; that is not to say, though, that they will necessarily approve of its contents, as I am sure they will find opportunities to remind me. Without the efficiency, good humor, and extraordinary management skills of Hallie Willard, the Institute's senior secretary, I would never have had the time to complete this manuscript. My favorite copy-editor, Leona Capeless of the Oxford University Press, put up patiently with my stylistic eccentricities, and Judith Hancock prepared the index with admirable efficiency. It was also a pleasure once again—for the third time now—to work with Sheldon Meyer.

It is easy, but foolish, to take for granted the role that family, friends, and environment play in sustaining one's life and career. Barbara, Michael, and David have long since learned how to be there when needed—but also how to stay out of the way—when a book is being written, and I am as always grateful to them for that. Knowing the care with which people read them, they have also aspired, so far unsuccessfully, to stay out of my prefaces.

Friends, whether in Athens or elsewhere, have already heard the substance of this book so many times, and in so many different ways, that they are hereby absolved—as an act of friendship—from the duty of reading it. (This absolution does not extend, however, to friends who also happen to be my students.)

Under the exemplary leadership of Charles and Claire Ping, Ohio University has become a remarkable, if still insufficiently known and appreciated, institution. Since one of the arguments of this book is that individuals do still make a difference in history, I thought it appropriate to use its dedication as a way of expressing my gratitude to these particular individuals for the very many differences, extending over more than a decade and a half now, that their presence on our campus has made.

Athens, Ohio   J. L. G.
July, 1991

Contents

The United States
and the End
of the Cold War

## ONE

# The American Foreign Policy Style in the Twentieth Century

At the beginning of his 1895 novel, *The Time Machine*, H. G. Wells has his main character, the otherwise unnamed "Time Traveller," point out to his friends that any physical object has to have four dimensions: "It must have Length, Breadth, Thickness, and—Duration." The first three were obvious, but, "through a natural infirmity of the flesh," most people tended to overlook the fourth.[1]

Infirmities of the flesh—and of the intellect—are real enough, and one of their effects is to limit the capacity of individuals and nations for self-analysis. It is never easy, whether in the realm of interpersonal or international relations, to "see ourselves as others see us." Just as individuals (at least those who can afford it) expand self-awareness through psychoanalysis, so nations tend to rely on perceptive outsiders for the clinical detachment that produces insights into their own character.[2] Infirmities—whether of energy, imagination, or honesty—keep them from achieving this themselves.

The problem has been greater for Americans than for most other people, because the very pervasiveness of this country's influence throughout the world has prohibited the use of distance—the great advantage of foreign observers—to gain detachment. One liability of living in the "American century"[3] is that Americans who move through space so often encounter their own culture in its transplanted forms. And, whether for better or for worse, American culture has, rather like kudzu, transplanted very well indeed.

Movement through time, though, is another matter. Studying the past has a way of inducing humility—a first stage toward gaining detachment—because it suggests the continuity of the problems we confront, and the unoriginality of most of our solutions for them. It is a good way of putting things in perspective, of stepping back to take in a wider view. There is nothing to prevent us, though, at least as a thought experiment, from moving through time in the opposite direction: from imagining ourselves at some point in the future—in what may *not* be an "American century"—looking back on the present, and on the sequence of events that led to it. Were we to attempt this exercise, we might find an equally effective way of stepping back from the periodic outbursts of pride or chagrin with which we regard our current national conduct. We might gain insights into our present condition from the detachment of temporal distance; we could then test the suggestion of Wells's Time Traveller that measurement in all four dimensions is necessary if one really wants to understand where one is, and where one is going.

My own favorite method for doing this is to imagine myself in the familiar role of a history professor, but one suddenly transported a hundred years into the future with the responsibility of lecturing to a large class of fidgety undergraduates on the subject of the American foreign policy style in the twentieth century.[4] (This exercise proceeds on the pessimistic assumption that students will still be bored a hundred years from now, but also on the optimistic assumption that there will still be professors around to bore them.) Were I to undertake that task, I would concentrate on the way in which Americans have dealt with three particular problems: power, interests, and threats. I would strive for at least some of the detachment we admire in the best foreign observers of the United States, past and present. I would conclude with a few observations on what the United States accomplished in the world during "its" century; and I would then dismiss the class, on the assumption that attention-spans will be no longer a hundred years hence than they are today. This essay is a rough first draft of that lecture. It is always a good idea to prepare one's presentations well in advance.

Power

Let us begin by considering how Americans in the twentieth century thought about that most basic requirement for being a great power, which is—not surprisingly—power itself. I mean by this nothing more complicated than the capacity to make things happen in the world, whether in the military, political, economic, ideological, or cultural realms of human activity. The United States certainly had that capacity during the twentieth century; indeed, the possession of power, more than anything else, distinguished the American experience from that of other states during that epoch, and from the experiences of Americans themselves in the more distant past.

The power the United States had came to it partly through inheritance: the nation's founders had the good sense to establish themselves and the state they created on land that was not only isolated and uncrowded but also enormously productive in both agricultural and mineral resources. One need only compare the experience of Russia, which also expanded into isolated and uncrowded regions at about the same time, to see what a difference climate and geology made.[5] But environmental circumstances provided only the potential for power. Its actual attainment required sweeping away the competition, and this the Europeans obligingly did for the Americans during the first half of the twentieth century.

It makes more and more sense, the farther in time we are from them, to view World Wars I and II as a single European civil war, in which the nations that had dominated world politics for the preceding five centuries managed to transform themselves, through their own fratricidal behavior, into second-class powers. Geopolitical influence shifted, as a result, from Europe to its peripheries, with the United States and the Soviet Union—or so it seemed—as joint beneficiaries.[6]

But that migration of power away from Europe produced concentrations of power of unequal magnitude, for although the Soviet Union would, in time, develop military strength roughly comparable to that of the United States, it did so only as its influence was diminishing in economics, politics, culture, and even the ideological arena of competition Lenin himself had created when he launched the Bolshevik Revolution in 1917. By the 1980s no one would have voluntarily chosen to follow the Soviet model. Moscow's power had come to rest upon a monodimensional military base, while that of the United States and its allies remained multidimensional;[7] the resulting situation determined which side finally prevailed in the Cold War that had dominated international relations throughout most of the last half of the twentieth century.

Less clear than the fact that Americans accumulated great power is the extent to which they consciously sought it. It is too easy to infer, from the reality of power, a coherent strategy aimed at acquiring it. It is too simple to conclude that, because a nation has gained influence over much of the rest of the world, it set out deliberately to produce this result. The gap between what nations seek to do and what they wind up doing is often as wide as it is for individuals; that fact alone ought to make us suspicious of causal chains that too rigidly link consequences with the intentions that lie behind them.

For Americans were never very comfortable with power they accumulated; witness the extremes to which they went to fragment it in their own domestic constitutional arrangements. Nor were they always confident of their ability to wield power wisely—that is, in ways that would promote their own interests—in the world at large. The possession of great power was indeed a dominant theme of United States foreign policy in the twentieth century, but so too was a deep and abiding suspicion of it.

It is worth remembering, in this connection, that the United States could have become an international power of consequence long before it actually did. As early as the 1860s, Americans had impressed the world with a striking demonstration of what industrial strength combined with military purpose could bring about. In the decades that followed the Civil War, foreign observers monitored the progress of economic development and technological innovation inside the United States with a keener sense than the Americans themselves had of implications for the future.[8] But the actual policies Washington adopted during those years were curiously unassertive for a nation whose population and industrial strength were so rapidly expanding. Certainly no single-minded "drive for world power" animated the thinking of a Grover Cleveland, or a Benjamin Harrison, or even the most hyperactive political figure of his day, James G. Blaine.[9]

Even when Americans did shift to a more assertive role, in the mid-1890s, their hesitancy about wielding power remained. They passed up the opportunity to make Cuba a colony after taking it, by force, from Spain. They did create a colony in the Philippines, but decided almost at once that this had been a mistake and began slowly preparing the Filipinos for independence. They maintained and even strengthened their traditional sphere of economic and strategic influence in Central America and the Caribbean, but made only half-hearted and ineffectual efforts to expand that sphere to East Asia. And despite the fact that a historical accident had brought to the White House, in the person of Theodore Roosevelt, one of the twentieth century's most sophisticated practioners of power politics, Americans played almost no role in European affairs during the years that preceded World War I. The outbreak of that conflict was one of the last great European events with which the United States had nothing whatever to do.

World War I was, of course, as a historian long ago labeled it, "the great departure."[10] The armies the United States dispatched to Europe in 1918 shaped the outcome of that struggle more decisively than did the larger forces it sent back to the Continent in 1944; certainly no one would deny Woodrow Wilson's extraordinary personal influence on wartime diplomacy, or on the drafting of the peace settlement that followed. But even here the American distrust of power overcame the American appetite for it, for the United States dismantled its military forces almost at once and then rejected participation in the League of Nations, Wilson's chosen instrument for managing the post-war world. This was not the behavior of a nation eager to impose its authority over the rest of the planet.

The effects of American participation in World War I came to lie primarily in the emergence of the United States as Europe's chief creditor and source of investment capital. It took historians years to begin to grasp the critical role Americans played in the rehabilitation and stabilization of Europe during the 1920s, one that now seems comparable in importance to their better-known activities there after 1945.[11] But unlike the Marshall Plan of a generation later, United States involvement in post-World War I European reconstruction took the form of private initiatives carried out with tacit government support. Given the strength of isolationist sentiment—in itself an indication of how much Americans distrusted their own power— this was the only way the United States could play any role at all.

What happened after 1929 made it clear, nonetheless, how important that role had been. The American depression spread to Europe even faster than American prosperity had, thereby demonstrating the extent to which the health of the European economy—and indeed the economies of most of the rest of the world—had come to depend upon that of the United States. But Americans made only minimal (and then only grudging) efforts to use their economic influence to promote recovery beyond their borders during the first half of the 1930s;[12] they made no effort at all, during that decade, to assert any comparable military or political influence. There was a striking contradiction between the American capacity to shape the world economy and the almost petulant refusal of Americans to have anything to do with world politics; as a result, the United States had little more to do with the events that led to World War II in Europe than it had had with those that produced World War I.[13]

It took the fall of France and the attack on Pearl Harbor to overcome this persistent insularity, and even then remnants of isolationism remained. Franklin D. Roosevelt himself, it is true, had few if any reservations about participation in world politics, but having been an appalled witness to Wilson's failure a quarter of a century earlier, he harbored real doubts as to whether the American people were prepared to share his view. He was careful not to get too far ahead of public opinion as the United States edged toward active belligerency between 1939 and 1941, so much so that his friend Winston Churchill began to despair of the United States ever entering the European conflict.[14] Roosevelt's wartime strategy, which critics would subsequently deride as naïve, in fact had the entirely practical objective of achieving victory at minimal cost; the president hoped to provide to the maximum extent possible the *weapons* with which to defeat Germany and Japan, but to leave principally to allies—chiefly Russians and Chinese—the expenditure of *manpower* that would be necessary to do this. It would not do, Roosevelt thought, to have the war be too painful an experience for an American public still not fully reconciled to global responsibility.[15]

The Roosevelt strategy worked better in Europe than in the Pacific, where the United States did have to assume the main burden of fighting. Nevertheless, victory came with remarkably few casualties given the scale and duration of the fighting. It also brought important compensations. The United States emerged from World War II with an industrial plant far larger and more advanced than it had been in 1939; gross national product had roughly doubled by 1945. American military strength at the moment of victory appeared unchallengeable, especially after the successful development of the atomic bomb. And the prestige the United States had accumulated by that time was immense: one indication of it was the surprising absence (at least in retrospect) of any significant opposition when the League of Nations' successor organization, the United Nations, voted to locate itself permanently in New York City.[16] "Of the great men at the top, Roosevelt was the only one who knew what he was doing," the British historian A. J. P. Taylor once commented, "he made the United States the greatest power in the world at virtually no cost."[17]

Whether Americans would pay the price necessary to retain such power, however, was still not clear. The United States did accept, after 1945, political responsibilities it had shunned after 1918, but at the same time it dismantled its military forces almost as thoroughly as it had done a quarter of a century earlier. Gaps between commitments and capabilities became painfully evident as President Harry S. Truman launched the effort in 1947 to contain the

Soviet Union's expansionism, while attempting to hold military spending within limits only slightly above prewar levels. It took not just Moscow's emergence as a rival in Europe but also the appearance of a perceived communist threat on a global scale—something that did not develop until after the victory of that ideology in China and the onset of the Korean War—to convince the nation of the need for a permanently large military establishment, and for the levels of spending that would be necessary to sustain it.[18]

Not until mid-century, then, did the United States reconcile itself once and for all to its status as a superpower, and even then Americans retained mixed feelings about the exercise of power itself. Consider the haste, for example, with which those responsible for administering the postwar occupations of Germany and Japan sought to end them. Even Americans as imperious as Generals Lucius Clay and Douglas MacArthur did not find the role of overlord a permanently congenial one.[19] Winning Congressional approval for overseas economic assistance—which in the form of the Marshall Plan had proven to be such a potent instrument of American influence—became more, not less, difficult as the Cold War wore on. The United States severely limited its own freedom of action in fighting the Korean and Vietnam wars; and even as the nation was engaging in those conflicts, its citizens were conducting searching debates among themselves over just what their responsibilities in the world ought to be.

When abuses of power occurred, or appeared to be occurring, the Congress investigated them thoroughly, relentlessly, and before the eyes of the world. No other country subjected its leadership to the kind of public grilling President Truman and his advisers received after the sacking of General MacArthur in 1951, or to the scrutiny President Nixon and the White House staff underwent in the aftermath of the 1972 Watergate break-in. No other intelligence organizations would find their most secret activities over a quarter of a century abruptly exposed to public view, as happened to the Central Intelligence Agency and the Federal Bureau of Investigation during the Ford administration.[20]

And when the United States confronted, in the 1990 Iraqi seizure of Kuwait, the most obvious case of outright aggression since the Korean War, the nation insisted upon a careful, protracted, and thoughtful debate before using military force, despite the clear probability that the coalition it led would win, that it would do so at reasonable cost, and that it would have not only United Nations approval but also the fervent applause of most of the world for having done so.

The American ambivalence about power came through most strikingly, though, with respect to nuclear weapons. The United States had exclusive possession of the atomic bomb for only four years, but Soviet stockpiles and delivery capabilities remained at such primitive levels that Washington's monopoly for all practical purposes extended well into the 1950s. The Eisenhower administration had proclaimed itself ready to use nuclear weapons wherever American interests were threatened. Nor were opportunities lacking for such use: the possibility was seriously contemplated in Korea just prior to the armistice agreement in 1953, in Indochina in 1954, and in the Taiwan Strait crisis of 1954–55. And yet, the president and his advisers failed to employ the awesome military power they had accumulated and publicly threatened to use, largely because they thought it would look bad—in the eyes of allies and the non-aligned world—to do so. In effect, Americans deterred themselves, for fear of what the use of such great power might imply about themselves.[21]

It is, then, this self-consciousness about the wielding of power that distinguishes the United States' possession of it from that of most other great nations in the twentieth century, and in the centuries that preceded it. It was not that Americans had no appetite for power, although it was thrust upon them about as often as they actively sought it. It is not that they consistently tried to divest themselves of power once they got it, although there were instances in which they did just that, whether through design or incompetence. It is simply that Americans were never wholly comfortable in the role of a great power. They tended to worry more about playing that role than other great powers have done in the past; they tended to look, more actively than most other great powers do, or have done, for ways to justify the power they had not in terms of power itself, but of some quite separate end.

Interests

That brings us to the subject of interests. Like the British, from whom they inherited the tendency, Americans had traditionally associated their security with the balancing of power in the world. Just as they worried about their own ability to wield power wisely and equitably, so too—and to a much greater extent—they distrusted the ability of others to do the same thing. When others threatened to accumulate power in sufficient quantity to upset the international equilibrium, Americans were prepared, if reluctantly, to build up their own power to counterbalance the threat, or to form combinations of power with those who shared their perception of the danger at hand.

Woodrow Wilson was thinking in balance of power terms when he decided that American interests could not tolerate a German victory in World War I: the combination of Continental land power with the naval power of a defeated Britain would be too great. Roosevelt took precisely the same view regarding Nazi Germany a quarter-century later. And the Truman administration saw the Soviet Union's expansion into Europe after 1945 as yet another threat to international stability; its response represented the third projection of American countervailing strength across the Atlantic in the twentieth century, although this time without a war. That same concern with potentially hostile aggregations of power shifted to the world at large as the Cold War intensified, so that by the 1950s and 1960s any disturbance in the global status quo, however minor, could seem to threaten what American leaders now perceived as their global security interests.

But the Americans' distrust of power prevented them from justifying their interest in the balancing of power for what it really was; there was always something too amoral, too cynical, too "European" about that kind of thinking. Instead Americans sought ways to link their concern with stability to some entirely different concern, whether of a self-interested or a disinterested nature. Quite frequently, in fact, they managed to do both: Americans were uniquely adept among the peoples of the world at combining appeals to both immediate and ultimate interests.

Take, as an illustration, the principle of open markets. The United States had long called for a reduction of barriers to trade and investment throughout the world, on the grounds that humanity at large would benefit if individual producers were free to concentrate on what they could most efficiently produce. Indeed, Americans went farther than that. Wars, they tended to believe, grew out of rivalries resulting from economic nationalism; if nations could become economically interdependent, war itself might become obsolete.[22] (Never mind that their own tariffs had remained high throughout most of their history, or that the connection between trade, investment, and economic development was less than clear, or that the historical record suggested little correlation between extensive economic interchange and the avoidance of war.) And yet, as has often been pointed out,[23] the doctrine of "free" trade brings disproportionate benefits to the most efficient producer, and the United States happened to find itself in that fortunate position throughout most of the twentieth century. Americans' disinterested endorsement of the "open door," therefore, served their self-interested ambition to expand markets, investment opportunities, and profits.

This same integration of self-interest and disinterest showed up in the concept of self-determination, one of the most frequently avowed American interests in the twentieth century. It was difficult to argue against the proposition that people throughout the world ought to choose their own governments. In fact, Americans tended to see in the idea of self-determination, as in the idea of open markets, a way of abolishing war: if everyone lived under regimes of which they approved, then what would there be to fight about? But Washington's support for self-determination coincided noticeably, over the years, with the requirements of geopolitics. Wilson invoked the principle as a means of breaking up Germany's major ally in World War I, the Austro-Hungarian Empire; he was less keen, though, on applying the same idea to the colonial empires of Great Britain or France.[24] Roosevelt endorsed self-determination, along with Churchill, in the Atlantic Charter; but efforts to encourage it in Eastern Europe, at a time when the Soviet Union's cooperation in the war against Germany and Japan was still thought necessary, were at best half-hearted.[25] The United States called regularly during the Cold War for self-determination within the Soviet Union's sphere of influence; it was much less ardent, however, in insisting that anti-communist allies and associates respect that principle in places like Indochina, Central America, the Middle East, or South Africa. Despite surface appearances, there were no real inconsistencies here. These policies were all aimed in one way or another—and whether wisely or not—at preserving a favorable balance of power in the world. But by refusing to acknowledge that reality, by seeking to cloak the balancing of power behind an idealistic façade, the United States not only created the appearance of inconsistency; it also gave rise to expectations that lay well beyond its capacity to fulfill.

The United States was, of course, hardly the only nation in the world to link immediate with ultimate interests. All nations do that to some extent, and in this they are not much different from most individuals. But the efforts Americans made to construct such linkages, and the persistence with which they adhered to them, did go beyond what most other nations have done. What went even farther—and what surely must constitute a distinctive characteristic in the conduct of international affairs—was the extent to which Americans in the twentieth century actually believed in these linkages.

Threats

Closely related to the definition of interests is the perception of threats, and here too there was a distinctively American approach to the problem. The United States was noteworthy for the extent to which it allowed *forms* of government to shape expectations about the *behavior* of governments; for its tendency to deduce intentions from organization, to assume that once one had understood the way in which another government was put together, one would then know fairly clearly what to expect from it.

Woodrow Wilson bears much of the responsibility for this, as for so much else that was characteristic of American foreign policy in the twentieth century. It was Wilson who publicly defined the nation's objective in entering World War I as making the world "safe for democracy"; it followed that Germany was the enemy because it was not democratic. Prior to April, 1917, Wilson's attitude toward the German government had been one of analytical detachment: he had not held Germany exclusively responsible for the outbreak of the fighting; he had been patient, some said to the point of weakness, with that country's reliance on submarine warfare; he had called, only weeks before the final rupture of diplomatic relations, for a "peace without victory."[26] But once the United States became an active belligerent, Wilson's view shifted dramatically. He now differentiated between the German people and the German government, portraying the latter as the embodiment of autocracy, as a regime with which one could have no dealings if one was to build the foundations for a lasting peace. He demanded its overthrow as a condition for a ceasefire. He thereby saddled the successor republican government with responsibility for an unpopular peace; but, more than that, he created in the minds of Americans an unfortunate association between the form and the behavior of governments. He portrayed autocracy itself the enemy, rather than the uses to which autocracy was put.[27]

Think, for a moment, about the implications. The United States had coexisted throughout much of its history with autocratic governments. It would not have occurred to American statesmen in the eighteenth or early nineteenth century to claim that because other states did not adhere to democratic principles—few states did at that time—there could be no interests in common with them. Interests were assumed to take precedence over ideology. Yet Wilson had now reversed that order: henceforth ideological differences would claim priority, from the official perspective of the United States government, even over the existence of shared interests.

The new approach became clear in Wilson's response to the Bolshevik Revolution. He concentrated on the ideological orientation of the new Russian regime—which was not only autocratic but revolutionary as well—and as a result neglected the possibility that the United States might still share certain interests with it, notably the need to restrain Germany. There followed the abortive American intervention, alongside major World War I allies, in Siberia and North Russia, from any viewpoint one of the least productive political-military enterprises of the century. No one can say what would have happened if the United States had made a more careful effort to separate the interests of Lenin's government from its rhetoric; what is clear is that Lenin himself never subordinated interests to ideology, and that possibilities existed which Wilson's preoccupation with form rather than behavior kept him from exploring. It is ironic that in this situation Americans more than the Russians appear to have been the prisoners of ideology.[28]

It is even more ironic, therefore, that the United States was as slow as it was to react to the clearest example in this century of a link between form and behavior—the rise of Adolf Hitler. The delay can be explained partly by Americans' distrust of their own power and the isolationism that resulted from that distrust; it is also the case, to be fair, that most Europeans failed to grasp the significance of Hitler's movement until it was too late. When it came, though—in the aftermath of Munich—the realization of a connection between internal repression and external aggression burned itself deeply into the American mind; it would take more than a generation for the nation to learn that not all dictatorships carried with them the same appetite for violent expansionism, and the destruction it brings.

The first real application of the "lessons of Munich" took place, only shortly thereafter, in East Asia. Despite its ostensible commitment to the Open Door policy, the United States for four decades had witnessed, without effective protest, the growth of Japanese power on the Asian mainland. Not until 1941, when the nation stood on the verge of war with Germany, did it take a firm stand against Japan. The reason was not, as conspiracy theorists would have it, that Roosevelt was looking for a way into the European war by the "back door"; he could have had no prior assurance that the outbreak of war with Japan would elicit a German declaration of war, as it so conveniently did. Rather, the United States took a tough line with Japan because Munich had taught that aggression anywhere, left unresisted, threatened the interests of stability everywhere. The United States equated the Japanese effort to dominate Asia with the Nazi attempt to dominate Europe, and decided—quite apart from any effort to rank its own interests or to assess its capabilities to defend them—that it could not put up with either one.²⁹

But the most egregious example of this American tendency to confuse forms of government with the behavior of governments was the nation's long-standing misunderstanding of international communism. For decades after the onset of the Cold War the United States officially took the view that adherence to Marxism-Leninism not only made governments internally repressive but also—through their presumed subservience to Moscow—a threat to the global balance of power. There was never very good evidence to support these claims. Even at the height of the Cold War, few Soviet specialists or intelligence analysts accepted the view that communism was monolithic; as early as 1948 strategies existed within the United States government to exploit divisive tendencies that were known to exist inside the international communist movement. A vigorous proponent of these, at least with respect to the Soviet Union and China, was no less ardent an anti-communist than John Foster Dulles himself.³⁰

And yet, American leaders failed, in most cases, to apply these insights in their actual dealings with the communist world. The Truman administration blundered into a disastrous conflict with China on the Korean peninsula because it interpreted that country's concern about the security of its own boundaries as ideologically motivated aggression. The inability to understand that in certain parts of the world one could be a communist and a nationalist at the same time contributed to an even more disastrous American involvement in Indochina a decade and a half later. Even well into the 1980s—and despite the fact that by that time some of its best foreign friends were communists—the Reagan administration was still assuming the worst about Marxism in the third world; indeed, its fixation was so great as to cause it to excuse equally distasteful non-Marxist autocracies on the basis of a tenuous semantic distinction between "authoritarian" and "totalitarian" regimes.³¹

There was, in all of this, a curious myopia. Whether in dealing with the Kaiser's Germany, Lenin's Russia, Nazi Germany, Imperial Japan, Stalinist Russia, Communist China, North Vietnam, Castro's Cuba, or even Nicaragua under the Sandinistas, the United States tended to equate internal form with external behavior. It assumed an "inner-directed" quality to these regimes that neglected the impact of external circumstances on what they actually did. It failed to take into account the fact that, just because a nation embraces what one considers to be a repugnant ideology, it does not cease from that time forward to have state interests; those interests may, at times, diverge significantly from what ideology would appear to require. There were not, in the twentieth century, very many national leaders who proved themselves so zealous as to place ideological interests consistently above state interests—indeed, Hitler himself may be the only clear example of this. And yet, the United States, which was so slow to recognize Hitler for what he was, sought to atone for that error by assuming ideological zealotry on the part of all of its major adversaries for decades afterwards.

A balance of power need not depend upon the ideological homogeneity of the states that make it up. Nations possessing radically different forms of government can and often do share common interests, as the United States would discover in its relationship with both the Soviet Union and the People's Republic of China. And yet, Washington persisted in the assumption that form governs behavior; the result was an imprecision in the identification of threats that caused repeated misunderstandings, and often gross exaggerations, of the dangers the nation actually faced.

Consequences

But what were the consequences, for the rest of the world, of the way Americans dealt with power, interests, and threats? What difference, if any, did it all make? Any discussion of these questions should proceed from the assumption that the United States was neither wholly innocent of, nor wholly to blame for, the things that happened beyond its borders. The point would appear unexceptionable, and yet assumptions of almost total innocence or almost total culpability figured prominently—if oddly juxtaposed with one another—in the American view of the world in the twentieth century.

During much of it, their leaders encouraged Americans to believe that the nation was above such sinister trappings of the "old diplomacy" as power politics, or espionage, or covert action. It took revelations like the Yalta Conference, the U-2 incident, the Bay of Pigs, and the existence of Henry Kissinger to alert most people to the fact that this was not the case; even then their the shock over the exposure of CIA activities in the mid-1970s showed how deeply rooted assumptions of innocence still were.

Among intellectuals, though, the tendency was more often to assume guilt than innocence: the exposure of *some* instances in which power was abused led to the suspicion that power had been abused in virtually *all* of the instances in which it had been wielded.[32] This line of reasoning in turn produced the curious belief that where evil existed in the world, it must be because some American put it there. The anguished debates that took place over alleged American involvement in the overthrow of the Allende government in Chile in 1973, or alleged responsibility for the Khmer Rouge massacres after 1975, or alleged complicity in the maintenance of *apartheid* in South Africa in the early 1980s, or alleged perpetuation of the nuclear arms race during the same period, all illustrate the point.

Americans in the twentieth century were prone to a curious absolutism regarding the effects of their actions on the rest of the world. They either had no responsibility whatever for them, or they were completely responsible; there seemed to be no middle ground. But of course the middle ground is where the truth, as usual, resided. Americans did cause certain things to happen in the world, good and bad, and for these they should indeed be held responsible. But it was stretching things a bit to imply, as many critics did, that a sparrow could not fall to earth anywhere in the world without that event having been orchestrated by the American military/industrial/intelligence complex.

There is no way to prove that the world is better or worse off because the United States became the dominant power in twentieth-century world politics: one can hardly re-run the experiment with different variables to assess the alternatives. One can, though, invoke the principle of accountability: Did the United States in fact enhance its stated interests? Did it contain real threats? And did it do these things in such a way as to preserve rather than degrade the quality of the international environment within which it operated?

If one defines the most vital American interest as that of counteracting potentially hostile power—as most American leaders did ultimately define it—then the United States was indeed successful. Despite the fact that the twentieth century was an exceptionally violent one, aggression did not often pay off during it, and the United States played a vital role, certainly in the two world wars but also in Korea and Kuwait, in bringing about that result. By 1991 no major nation or group of nations seemed prepared to use force to challenge the international status quo;[33] that statement could not have been made during most of the twentieth century. If maintaining a balance of power was the fundamental American interest, then the United States must have done something right.

Threats to the balance remained, to be sure. They always will, as long as there are interests. But the world was fortunate in that the twentieth century's greatest danger—an all-out nuclear war between the superpowers—proved to be a manageable one, while the disruptions that were more difficult to manage—revolutions, guerilla wars, terrorism, economic rivalries, and the like—posed far less of a threat than a Soviet-American nuclear confrontation would have. This benign asymmetry, in which the world learned to control big dangers and to live with uncontrollable smaller ones, allowed the Cold War to become the longest period of great power peace in modern history.[34] The behavior of the United States, along with that of its long-time rival, the Soviet Union, largely brought this about.

But the "long peace" was not without its costs. Adversaries do not pose the only danger that comes with world responsibility; there is also the danger that a nation poses to itself through the ever-present temptation to misuse the power it has. One can, in the process of containing aggression, become an aggressor; one can, in the determination to resist imperialism, turn into an imperialist. How well did the United States guard itself against these self-generated evils?[35]

The record here, one must conclude, was mixed. Certainly the United States was more tolerant of diversity within its various spheres of influence than was its chief rival, the Soviet Union. There was something about the openness and flexibility of American society—and the corresponding absence of these things in the U.S.S.R.—that made it easier for Washington to put up with imperious allies, unpredictable clients and unruly associates. It was no accident that Franco-American friendship survived Charles de Gaulle, but that Sino-Soviet friendship did not survive Mao Ze-dong. It is also the case that where Americans set out fundamentally to restructure another society—as they did in Germany and Japan after World War II—they accomplished that task with surprising effectiveness, and with a remarkable sensitivity to the local cultures involved.[36] It was no small achievement to have turned two very different societies upside down, creating two solid democracies in the process, and still to retain the gratitude of the inhabitants for having done so.

But there was, unfortunately, a darker side to this question of how the United States used its power. There were instances where the sheer weight and mass of the Americans' presence crippled a country, even though those who brought about that presence had intended no such effect. Where this happened, the result was ultimately to the considerable disadvantage of the United States, as the examples of Cuba, Iran, and most tragically South Vietnam clearly show. The power of the United States too often extended beyond the nation's own awareness of it, with social and political consequences that are appalling, even now, to contemplate.

They are not as appalling, though, as what the competition inflicted upon its victims. The authoritarian alternative that was fascism produced not only the most devastating war but also the most horrifying example of genocide in modern history. The authoritarian alternative that was communism produced, in Russia, the virtual annihilation of two entire classes—the peasantry and the intellectuals[37]—and, when projected beyond Russia, an array of ossified political institutions, inadequate living standards, degraded environments, and blighted lives so vast and so obvious that one wonders how those who suffered these tribulations put up with them for as long as they did.[38] If the experiences of the twentieth century demonstrated anything at all, it was the arrogance of the assumption that one could create a "science" of human behavior that would somehow improve the human condition. Americans asserted no comparable claim;[39] whatever their other deficiencies as a global superpower, in this respect their modesty—a characteristic not often associated with Americans—served the world well.

It requires no great insight to note that the world is a diverse place. But it required a rather remarkable combination of both luck and skill to maintain a political system that was comfortable with diversity at home, and hence prepared, for the most part, to tolerate it in the world at large. The success with which Americans accomplished this task, the extent to which they were able to reconcile the appeal of spontaneity with the fact of power, may well have been, more than anything else, the key to the influence they were able to bring to bear over the rest of the world during the twentieth century.

Prediction?

The future is, of course, unknowable, and will remain so until it gets around to becoming the present and the past. But nothing in the above lecture requires knowledge of what is to come; its conclusions, I think, are defensible on the basis of what we can see now, provided we make the effort. The detachment that characterizes wise foreign observation of the United States, like the detachment that characterizes good historical analysis, need not require fore-sight; it is a matter, more, of separating out what is important from what is not, of overcoming the passions and prejudices that distort our view of what is happening, and of trying to think about the relationship of all of the parts of the present to the whole. It is a matter of gaining calm in the midst of turmoil, and from that calmness, perspective.

The difficulty is that the world in which we live so rarely allows that kind of reflection. Just as one thinks one is getting into the appropriate frame of mind, the afternoon mail arrives, or the fax machine faxes, or some reporter calls up wanting an instant comment on whatever instant event has just taken place, even if one had not been aware, until that moment, that it actually had. One is hurled back into the messy, cacophonous, and relent-lessly ahistorical present; and one's analytical insights—such as they are, or might have been—suffer grievously therefrom. H. G. Wells had a point about the need to transport ourselves, at least intellectually, beyond the confusions of this time and this place, if we are ever to make much sense out of what is going on in this time and in this place.

TWO

The Objectives
of Containment

Containing the Soviet Union, together with the ambitious ideology it created, has been the most durable foreign policy priority of the United States in the twentieth century. Each presidential administration since Woodrow Wilson's has devoted itself in one way or another to this task, and during the Cold War containment became a national fixation. Historians, political scientists, and journalists have hardly neglected the subject either; entire forests have become victims of their successive attempts to explain on paper what containment "really meant."[1]

But the end of the Cold War is raising new questions about containment, as about so many other aspects of Cold War history. One of these has to do with the oddly neglected issue of just what it was that containment was supposed to accomplish. Containment, after all, was never intended as an end in itself; rather, it was supposed to lead to a new kind of relationship with the Soviet Union that would remove, or at least render irrelevant, the reasons for having embarked on that task in the first place. Both practitioners and scholars of containment have remained vague, however, about exactly what that relationship was to have been. What kind of Soviet Union was containment to have produced? How was one to know when the strategy had accomplished its objectives? What *were* the objectives of containment, anyway?

The foreign policy goals of most great nations are rarely immediately apparent. It is not at all unusual to find them concealed behind the same façades of self-deception, over-simplification, bias, myth, and legend that impede the diagnosis of individual psychoses in a clinical setting. Further complicating the issue is the fact that when the behavior of governments is under examination, it is normally multiple clinicians who are doing the examining. Then, too, there is the difficulty that what one intends is not what one always winds up doing. That is a problem for individuals but even more so for governments, obliged as they are to filter policy through complex and often discordant bureaucracies without losing the support of vociferous but often clashing constituencies.

Nor have those who write about foreign policy done all that much to clarify such matters: the problem here is the academic propensity for methodological compartmentalization. Political scientists tend to focus on the *processes* by which policy is made; but they give little attention to the effects those processes are supposed to produce, or to whether we would even recognize those effects if we were ever to achieve them. Historians concern themselves with the *evolution* of policy over time; but they rarely make explicit the assumptions underlying it at any point, or the manner in which these differ from what has gone before and from what is to follow. Most journalists, when they write about such matters at all, do so in an anecdotal style that leaves tasks of generalization almost entirely to their entertained but not always profoundly enlightened readers.

If we are to resolve the question of what the United States has really wanted in its relationship with the Soviet Union over the years—if we are to overcome the official reluctance to define objectives, the methodological bog with which scholars have surrounded it, and the tendency of journalists cheerfully to assume that "truth will out" if only enough "facts" are assembled—we will need an approach that combines generalization with a careful examination of the historical record. One way to accomplish this is to identify a range of *possible* objectives for containment, and then to match them up against history to see which among them Washington actually sought, when, and for what reasons.

There are, of course, problems with this kind of approach. It proceeds deductively rather than inductively, thus running the risk of imposing upon the past an analytical structure that exists only in the mind of the analyst. It can distort and, at times, even reverse chronology, thereby obscuring relationships between cause and effect. But chronological narratives, too, have their weaknesses, not the least of which is the difficulty of attempting to generalize from them in any meaningful way. Departing from chronology allows comparison to take place; and as long as one does this with careful attention to historical context, then it should be possible to make a certain amount of progress toward clarifying the nature of the Soviet-American relationship that containment was supposed to bring about.

I have organized the following essay around five conceivable objectives for a strategy of containment: (1) overthrowing the Soviet regime altogether; (2) confining Soviet influence within the boundaries of the U.S.S.R.; (3) competing selectively within a framework of overall coexistence; (4) cooperating generally within a framework of shared interests; and (5) producing a fundamental change in the Soviet Union's internal structure. I will then compare these alternatives against the historical record of American policy toward the Soviet Union since 1917, with a view to determining which of them were seriously pursued, by whom, for how long, and with what results.

Overthrowing the Regime

The United States could have sought, as an objective of containment, to reverse the consequences of the Bolshevik Revolution altogether: to overthrow the Soviet government, to remove the Communist Party of the Soviet Union from its position of authority inside that country, and even to break up the U.S.S.R. itself into its constituent parts. The assumptions underlying such a policy would have been: (1) that the government which came to power in 1917 was and had always been illegitimate; (2) that the United States could have no interests in common with such a government; (3) that Washington was obliged, because of American national interests and the interests of legitimate states elsewhere in the world, to take the lead in eliminating that government; and (4) that there could be no stability in world politics until that goal had been accomplished.

The abstract formulation is clear enough. But what historical evidence is there that the United States government—or even isolated officials within it—ever regarded overthrowing the Soviet regime as a serious objective? Has there ever been a time when all of the assumptions required to inspire such an ambition have been in place?

It was the administration of Woodrow Wilson that came closest to seeking the overthrow of the Soviet government as a deliberate objective. The year 1917 witnessed not only the triumph of Bolshevism in Russia but also the abrupt—if temporary—emergence of the United States from its long-standing tradition of non-involvement in European affairs. What happened in Petrograd in November of that year appeared to threaten a conception of American interests that had abruptly and dramatically expanded. Washington's response, in turn, appeared to threaten Bolshevism itself as President Wilson refused to extend diplomatic recognition to the new regime, initiated an elaborate ideological campaign against it, and in the summer of 1918 actually authorized military intervention by the United States—alongside that of its wartime allies—in Siberia and North Russia.

But the fact that Wilson considered the new Soviet government illegitimate and saw the United States as having no interests in common with it does not mean that he was prepared to regard that government's elimination as an overriding priority. Intervention took place, it is important to remember, within the much larger context of a world war. The Bolsheviks' separate peace had endangered prospects for an Allied victory, and Wilson, like the British and the French, was determined to prevent Germany from taking advantage of what had happened by transferring troops and supplies to the Western Front. Painful experience in Mexico had made the President sensitive to the danger that foreign intervention might actually *strengthen* a revolutionary regime by conferring the legitimacy of nationalism on it; significantly one of his motives for authorizing American participation in the Siberia and North Russia operations was to ensure— or to attempt to ensure—that they did not become so overtly anti-Bolshevik as to produce that effect.[2]

What Wilson really wanted was a "nonpartisan" intervention. He hoped to keep German troops tied down in the east while at the same time creating a political arena in which the various forces in Russian society—Reds as well as Whites—could compete democratically for the favor of the Russian people.[3] It was to be intervention *on behalf* of self-determination, not intervention to *crush* revolution. Admittedly, this may have been a naive approach. Certainly it reflected little sense of Russian historical realities, or of the conditions that existed inside that country at the time. The Bolsheviks themselves regarded it as a scheme aimed at their destruction, and with good reason, for as their own actions in dissolving the freely elected Constituent Assembly had already shown, they were incapable of winning popular support and had no intention of trying to do so.[4]

But there is a difference between hoping that something will happen as a serendipitous by-product of a praiseworthy effort, and resolving to do whatever is necessary—however unpraiseworthy—to bring about the intended consequence. Wilson's policy fell into the first rather than the second category. He hoped that the Russian people, given the opportunity, would overthrow Bolshevism; but he was at no point willing to commit his own or his country's energies single-mindedly to that purpose. Victory over Germany and the creation of a stable postwar order were his overriding priorities; with the American people yearning for a return to their normal state of disengagement from world affairs, the possibility of engineering anything as purposeful, costly, or *internationalist* as an anti-Bolshevik crusade was simply out of the question. And even if that had been possible, there is reason to believe that Wilson himself would have regarded such a crusade with profound misgivings. He had used force to promote democracy in unprecedented ways—that had been his avowed objective in getting into the war in the first place—but he never ceased to agonize over the contradictions involved in resorting to coercion to bring about freedom from it.[5]

"The existing regime in Russia is based upon the negation of every principle of honor and good faith, and every usage and convention, underlying the whole structure of international law; the negation, in short, of every principle upon which it is possible to base harmonious and trustful relations, whether of nations or of individuals." That is how Bainbridge Colby, Wilson's last Secretary of State, justified making "non-recognition" the official policy of the United States toward Soviet Russia in 1920.[6] But although this statement emphasized in the strongest possible terms the illegitimacy of the Soviet regime and the impossibility of having normal relations with it, the Colby note also reflected Washington's quiet acknowledgment that Bolshevism was now soundly entrenched and not likely soon to go away. One rarely proclaims policies toward governments one does not expect to survive.

Non-recognition had evolved, under Wilson, as a means by which the United States could make clear its dislike for what was happening beyond its borders without at the same time feeling obliged to do anything about it.[7] Colby made this point clearly enough: American officials would welcome

the overthrow of Bolshevism, but they were not prepared to take active measures—beyond denying normal diplomatic relations—to bring that event
about. Instead they would rely upon the effects of isolation and the passage
of time to produce the desired results.

As it happened, events proceeded in just the opposite direction. Most
other nations had established diplomatic ties with Moscow by the mid-1920s;
even more remarkably, American trade, investment, and—at a critical moment in 1921–22—famine relief, had by that time played a major role in
stabilizing the new Soviet government. Far from overthrowing Bolshevism,
the Republican administrations of the 1920s inadvertently helped to stabilize
it through their own commitment to the idea—based on the principles of
limited government and free enterprise—that they had no authority to force
private individuals and corporations into compliance with official policy.[8]
The contradictions of capitalism, as Lenin would have been the first to acknowledge, can move in mysterious ways.

Another opportunity to seek the overthrow of the Soviet government
came during the first two years of World War II. There was nothing automatic about the Roosevelt administration's forbearance toward Moscow
in the early months of that conflict. Good will generated by the establishment of diplomatic relations six years earlier had largely dissipated by
1939; the Nazi-Soviet Pact and the invasion of Finland caused it to disappear
altogether.[9] Given the persistence of isolationism in the United States
together with the consequent political dangers of aiding Britain and France,
it would not have been inconceivable for Roosevelt to have accepted what
some historians have alleged were the geopolitical assumptions of Neville
Chamberlain and Joseph P. Kennedy: that the Soviet Union posed the greater
ultimate danger than Germany, and that the Western democracies should
accordingly seek to channel Hitler's aggressive tendencies toward the east,
thereby turning one repugnant adversary against another while sparing
themselves.[10]

What Roosevelt actually did, of course, could hardly have been more
different. He took the consistent position that Germany posed the greater
threat to world order than did the Soviet Union; he resisted pressures to break
diplomatic relations with Moscow following the pact with Germany and the
attack on Finland; he ran considerable risks both politically and constitu-
tionally to get military assistance to Britain for use against the Germans; he
went out of his way to share with Stalin intelligence pointing to the likelihood
of a German attack; and when that attack finally came, in June, 1941, he
immediately embraced the Russians as allies and within months made them
eligible for Lend Lease, on the grounds that defense of the Soviet Union was
now vital to the security of the United States.[11] These were not the actions
of a nation determined to exploit the vulnerabilities of another.

To be sure, once the United States itself had entered the war, it was
content to allow the Red Army to bear the main burden of ground fighting
in Europe, a strategy that carried with it the obvious danger—some Soviet

scholars have suggested the deliberate intent[12]—of exhausting Stalin's regime, or even bringing about its collapse. But it is not at all clear that the United States and Great Britain could have created a successful Second Front much earlier than they did; a failed Second Front would only have helped Germany. It is worth recalling, as well, that the United States at this time was carrying virtually the entire weight of a not insubstantial war against Japan, a war from which the Soviet Union—for its own good reasons—had remained aloof. Nor should one forget the simple fact that Roosevelt expected the anti-Hitler coalition to win. He knew full well that victory would ensure even a severely weakened Russia a significant expansion of political influence over postwar Europe, especially if the United States reverted to isolationism thereafter, as the President thought it might.[13]

There is simply no evidence, then, that the Roosevelt administration at any point contemplated taking advantage of what in retrospect was the most obvious opportunity since 1917 to eliminate the Soviet regime: alignment, whether openly or surreptitiously, with the geopolitical objectives of Adolf Hitler.

Hitler's demise, of course, changed things drastically. The attainment of victory not only dissolved the chief bond that had held the Grand Alliance together; it also created a power vacuum in Central Europe with increasingly suspicious super-powers glaring at each other from opposite sides of it. The condition of those two great states would appear, at least on the surface, to have been very different. Whatever gains it had made in political influence as a result of the war, the Soviet Union was a crippled giant in 1945. It was in no condition to engage in any kind of protracted economic or military competition with its American rival. The United States, in contrast, was at the apex of its strength. Its participation in the war had been, by comparison, relatively painless in terms of casualties suffered or civilian dislocation sustained; it had emerged from that conflict with an undamaged industrial plant twice the size of what it had been five years earlier; and it now possessed, as impressive products of that capacity, a monopoly over atomic weapons and the means to deliver them.

The question therefore arises: why did the United States not exploit these advantages to eliminate, or at least to neutralize, its only possible competitor for influence in the postwar world? With a succession of crises in Iran, Turkey, Greece, Czechoslovakia, and Berlin between 1946 and 1948, there was no absence of provocations that could have justified such a policy. Stalin's totalitarianism was no less objectionable in American eyes than Hitler's had been; was not one of the "lessons" of the war just ended that internal repression breeds external aggression? The wartime strategy of "unconditional surrender" had emphatically reinforced the principle of eliminating adversaries, not compromising with them. And there were a number of prominent individuals—both within and outside the government—who urged preventive war against the Soviet Union before it had had time to recover its strength.[14]

As had been the case with its predecessor, though, the Truman administration never seriously considered taking advantage of Soviet vulnerabilities in so cold-blooded a way. There were several reasons for this:

First, however things may have appeared in retrospect, it was not all that clear *at the time* that the United States enjoyed so decisive a military edge over the Soviet Union. Both nations had demobilized substantially after the war, but American demobilization proceeded at twice the pace, leaving the Soviet Union with at least the appearance of conventional force superiority in Europe.[15] Atomic bombs provided only a partial counter-balance; there were so few as late as 1949 that American military planners were expressing serious doubt as to whether the United States could prevail in a war with the Soviet Union, even if it used all available weapons.[16] There also existed within the Truman administration, at least until the summer of 1950, the strong if misguided conviction that further increases in military spending would almost certainly bankrupt the country.[17]

Second, moral considerations—and their very realistic political implications—also discouraged any serious thought of initiating military action against the Soviet Union. Advocates of that alternative had to overcome the deeply engrained and widely held presumption that "Americans don't start wars."[18] It was a simple-minded and, in the light of history, at least a debatable proposition, but the political reality that lay behind it was inescapable: the American people would not support what they perceived to be aggression. For statesmen who had just fought a war that had commanded almost universal approbation—but who remembered another war two decades earlier that had not—the need to ensure public support was critical. And, at least for strict constructionists, there was also an interesting constitutional dilemma. How could a democracy plan—and secure necessary Congressional authorization for—a preventive war without giving away the fact that it was doing so?[19]

Third, there was the growing realization that the total elimination of adversaries can cause more problems than it solves. The geopolitical consequences of having insisted on "unconditional surrender" during World War II had not been happy ones.[20] The capitulation of Germany and Japan had imposed upon Americans and their allies the complex and often distasteful burdens of military occupation. It had also left power vacuums in Europe and Northeast Asia that the United States had been obliged, within three years of victory, to attempt to fill. Given the size of the territory that would have to be occupied, forcing "unconditional surrender" upon the Soviet Union in the event of a future war appeared to be a wildly unrealistic option. Nor could there be any certainty, as George F. Kennan pointed out, that a successor regime in Russia, following in the wake of a defeated or discredited Soviet government, would be any easier to deal with. As a result, contingency plans for war with the U.S.S.R. made no automatic provision for overthrowing the regime, but rather assumed, as Kennan put it, "a *political* settlement, *politically* negotiated."[21]

Underlying these arguments against preventive war and unconditional surrender was the sense that the Soviet government— unlike the adversaries of World War II—was not irredeemable. The whole idea of "containment" was based, after all, on the assumption that it is sometimes better to live with adversaries than to seek to destroy them. It is significant that this viewpoint existed *prior* to the Soviet Union's acquisition of atomic weapons and of a retaliatory capacity that could be used directly against the United States. Even before the threat of nuclear annihilation had forced Americans to acknowledge the stake they had in the survival of their adversary, the idea of trying to overthrow the Soviet government had been discarded—if it had ever seriously considered in the first place.

But international relations are not just a matter of what nations *plan;* they involve as well what nations *perceive.* Soviet leaders over the years apparently *perceived* an intention on the part of the West to overthrow their regime, even though that intention—at least in the case of the United States— was not in fact there. Given the conspiratorial background from which Bolshevism emerged, the existence of such suspicions should hardly seem surprising. We even have Khrushchev's account of Stalin's warnings that his successors would "never be able to stand up to the forces of imperialism, that the first time we came into contact with the outside world our enemies would smash us to pieces; we would get confused and be unable to defend our land."[22] The fact that Soviet fears were exaggerated does not make them any less significant, nor did it lessen the Soviet government's deep and persistent preoccupation with the question of its own legitimacy.

Rarely if ever has a regime required such constant acknowledgement by others of its right to rule. It was vital to the Soviet leaders, not only to have won the war and to have gained enormous influence thereby, but also to have that victory and that influence explicitly *recognized* by the United States and the other Western powers. Hence, the Soviet Union's long and curious campaign, sustained over two decades, to persuade the international community officially to confirm World War II boundary changes in Central and Eastern Europe; it was as if the Russians had inherited the same propensity for "legalism" once thought to be characteristic of the American approach to international affairs.[23]

The great irony of the 1975 Helsinki agreements—which did at last recognize the "inviolability" of the World War II European settlement—is that they reinforced as much as they relieved Moscow's anxieties by introducing into the dialogue on "security and cooperation" in Europe the issue of human rights. This happened for a simple enough reason: the West's price for acknowledging the legitimacy of boundaries was Moscow's acknowledgment that concerns about human rights were also legitimate, not only in Europe but within the Soviet Union itself. What the Russians had not anticipated was the persistence with which these concerns would manifest themselves over the next several years. The Carter administration would make human rights a central issue in its relations with the U.S.S.R., and the Reagan administration during its first three years in office appeared to expand this indictment into an attack on the legitimacy of the Soviet regime itself. From

Moscow's perspective, the path from Helsinki to the "evil empire" speech was straight, and all downhill.[24]

But from an American perspective, one can only be struck by the extent of the misunderstanding that was involved here. Even without access to still classified documents, it seems quite safe to insist that at no point did either the Carter or the Reagan administration give anything like serious attention to how they might actually overthrow the Soviet regime, or to what they would do in the unlikely event that such a thing should come about.[25] What the Russians perceived to be challenges to legitimacy were in fact calls for liberalizing the *existing* system in the Soviet Union, or, equally often, bids for domestic political support within the United States through the easy tactic of exaggerating an adversary's iniquity.[26] If one wanted to test the extent to which any real enthusiasm for overthrowing the Soviet system has existed within this country during the past decade and a half, there could be no better way than to contrast the acclaim with which Americans received Alexander Solzhenitsyn's eloquent accounts of the horrors that system perpetrated, on the one hand, with the embarrassed silence that greeted his unique ideas on what might replace it, on the other.[27]

With the advent of Mikhail Gorbachev as leader of the U.S.S.R. in 1985, Americans came to acknowledge explicitly what their own actions had long implicitly suggested: that the United States and its allies had a vested interest in the survival in some form—although not necessarily in its post-World War II configuration—of the Soviet Union. And as it became clear that Moscow would not seek to reverse the principal consequences of the 1989 revolutions in Eastern and Central Europe—the breakup of the Warsaw Pact and a reunified Germany still linked to NATO—it was even argued that the Soviet Union had accepted the functional equivalent of "unconditional surrender" in what had been the peaceful equivalent of World War III.[28] Few manifestations of gloating or self-congratulation accompanied this development, though; instead old Cold War adversaries now found themselves thinking about how they might assist in reconstructing—not eliminating—the Soviet Union, very much in the way that the the United States had done with Germany and Japan after 1945.[29] The search for a post-Cold War equivalent of the Marshall Plan was under way.

The United States government at no point committed itself wholeheartedly to the objective of overthrowing the Soviet regime. It did not, after 1933, overtly or systematically challenge that government's legitimacy. It had not, since the earliest days of the Bolshevik Revolution, regarded itself as having no interests in common with the Soviet Union; such interests existed—especially in the economic field—even during the period of non-recognition. Although the United States did, after 1945, take the lead in containing the expansion of Moscow's influence in the postwar world, it did not seek nor was it prepared for any effort to remove the Soviet government from its position of authority. Nor did official Washington ever claim that postwar global stability required the elimination of the Soviet regime; instead the intention was always to incorporate that regime in some way *within* the framework of stability. There were, however, varying opinions at varying times about how to do this, and it is to these that I now want to turn.

Confining Soviet Influence Within the Boundaries of the U.S.S.R.

A second conceivable objective of United States policy with respect to the Soviet Union could have been to limit that country's ability to wield influence in the world at large, but without challenging the authority of its government at home. This approach would have rested on the assumptions: (1) that the Soviet regime shared no interests in common with the United States; but that (2) the United States had neither the obligation nor the resources to attempt to eliminate that regime; therefore (3) Washington's objective should be to frustrate the expansion of Soviet power *beyond* the boundaries of the U.S.S.R.; with the expectation that (4) repeated foreign policy failures would in time cause Soviet leaders themselves to modify their system and to moderate their ambitions.

It was George Kennan, of course, who first put forward the original concept of "containment," implicitly in his famous "long telegram" of February, 1946, and then explicitly in the equally influential public elaboration of that dispatch, the "X" article on "The Sources of Soviet Conduct," published in *Foreign Affairs* in the summer of 1947.[30] Three years later, Paul Nitze and the other authors of NSC-68, the first major reassessment of postwar national security policy, reaffirmed Kennan's conclusion that the United States should assign first priority to the containment of Soviet expansive tendencies.[31] There were, to be sure, major differences between Kennan and Nitze over *how* to achieve containment; those disagreements would continue for decades afterwards, and through their echoes in government one can trace many of the difficulties that have arisen in implementing that strategy.[32] But when it came to the *objectives* of containment, Kennan and Nitze had similar views. Together they succeeded in making the restriction of Soviet influence within the boundaries of the U.S.S.R. the principal goal of American foreign policy during the years that immediately followed the end of World War II.

Kennan based his position on what he saw as the unique characteristics of the Soviet state under Stalin's rule. Because of its need for external enemies to justify its own domestic oppression, traditional diplomacy could never reassure the regime in Moscow about the intentions of other governments. The unimaginative bosses of the Kremlin needed excuses "for the dictatorship without which they did not know how to rule, for cruelties they did not dare not to inflict, for sacrifices they felt bound to demand." Only by picturing the outside world as hostile could Soviet leaders sustain their own precarious legitimacy; nothing that the West could do would disarm their suspicions, nor was it worthwhile even to try.[33]

But neither was the Soviet leadership irrational. If confronted by repeated foreign policy failures, Kennan insisted, it would in time learn from experience and moderate its own aggressiveness from within. "[T]he Soviet leaders are prepared to recognize *situations*, if not arguments," he wrote in 1948. "If, therefore, situations can be created in which it is clearly not to the advantage of their power to emphasize the elements of conflict in their relations with the outside world, then their actions, and even the tenor of their propaganda to their own people, *can* be modified."[34] The task of American diplomacy, Kennan concluded, should be to ensure that Moscow's attempts to widen its influence were unsuccessful, and by those indirect means to persuade Soviet leaders to moderate their unrelenting hostility toward the outside world.

Kennan sought to accomplish this goal in two ways, one that was made clear at the time, the second one obvious only in retrospect. The first was to build countervailing centers of power along the periphery of the Soviet Union. If one could have strong and self-confident societies in vulnerable areas, capable of resisting intimidation from Moscow whether in military, ideological or psychological forms, then the Soviet sphere of influence could hardly expand. That was the assumption that lay behind the Marshall Plan, together with simultaneous decisions to end punitive occupation policies and to seek the economic revival of Germany and Japan. But it is clear now that this was only the first stage of Kennan's strategy; he sought not just to contain Soviet influence within its existing sphere, but also to roll it back by encouraging the emergence of nationalism among Moscow's satellites. "[T]here is a possibility," Kennan noted in 1949, "that Russian Communism may some day be destroyed by its own children in the form of the rebellious Communist parties of other countries. I can think of no development in which there would be greater logic and justice."[35]

If these two things could be made to happen—if the Soviet Union could be prevented from expanding its influence beyond the point at which it then held sway, and if Moscow's control over its own satellites could be eroded—then, in time, Kennan thought, this succession of failures would compel Kremlin leaders to moderate their internally driven suspicion of the outside world; to recognize "that the true glory of Russian national effort can find its expression only in peaceful and friendly association with other peoples and not in attempts to subjugate and dominate those peoples."[36]

Much the same set of assumptions informed NSC-68, the sweeping revision of national security policy that took place early in 1950 under the direction of Paul Nitze. If one could succeed in "frustrating the Kremlin design," that document concluded, then "it might be possible to create a situation which will induce the Soviet Union to accommodate itself, with or without the conscious abandonment of its design, to coexistence on tolerable terms with the non-Soviet world." This would not require overthrowing the Soviet government or attempting to impose punitive conditions on its citizens; even in the event of war itself, American objectives would "not include unconditional surrender, the subjugation of the Russian peoples or a Russia shorn of its economic potential." Rather, the goal would be to bring about "Soviet acceptance of the specific and limited conditions requisite to an international environment in which free institutions can flourish, and in which the Russian peoples will have a new chance to work out their own destiny."

The authors of NSC-68 foresaw, like Kennan, the possibility of exploiting potential fissures within the international communist movement. "The Soviet monolith," they concluded, "is held together by the iron curtain around it and the iron bars within it, not by any force of natural cohesion. These artificial mechanisms of unity have never been intelligently challenged by a strong outside force." If confronted by an adversary "which effectively affirmed the constructive and hopeful instincts of men and was capable of fulfilling their fundamental aspirations, the Soviet system might prove to be fatally weak."[37]

Kennan and Nitze did differ emphatically over how to implement containment. Because Kennan viewed the international balance of power as relatively stable and American resources (including wisdom) as limited, he favored efforts to contain Soviet expansionism only in areas deemed vital to American interests, only by means consistent with American capabilities, and only to the extent that success appeared likely. Nitze, conversely, saw the balance of power as decidedly unstable and regarded American resources as virtually unlimited; as a consequence, he favored efforts to contain Soviet expansionism wherever it ventured, by whatever means necessary, at whatever the cost, and whatever the prospects for success.

But the existence of these differences, substantial though they were, ought not to obscure the *common* assumptions behind what Kennan and Nitze were trying to do: (1) that it was up to the United States to act in some way to maintain the balance of power in the face of Soviet expansionist pressures; (2) that this would not require war with the Soviet Union, and that if war with a Soviet proxy should occur—as it did in Korea—the war would be kept carefully limited; (3) that internal change within the Soviet Union itself was not a prerequisite for the success of containment, but that the success of containment might in turn bring about internal change; and (4) that, once such changes had occurred, the assimilation of the Soviet Union into the established international order might be possible.[38]

There were, admittedly, difficulties with the Kennan-Nitze approach. It left unresolved the tension between credibility and capability: how did one contain challenges to the balance of power without spreading one's resources so thinly around the world as to invite such challenges, as the Truman administration seemed to have done prior to the outbreak of the Korean War? But, alternatively, if one chose to increase the resources allocated to containment, how did one do this without sacrificing solvency, a concern much on the minds of Truman's critics once the United States had decided to intervene in Korea?[39]

It raised the dilemma of ends versus means: how did one resist Soviet "imperialism" without taking on "imperialist" characteristics one's self?[40] By what right did the United States seek widely dispersed spheres of influence of its own—as in Latin America, East and Southeast Asia, and Western Europe—when it denied to the Russians the right to do the same thing in those parts of the world adjacent to it? How did one build coalitions without dominating them, as Washington hoped to do with the Marshall Plan? How did one seek allies—as in NATO—without turning them into puppets?

It ran the risks, as well, of self-fulfilling prophecy: was not the perpetual "frustration" of Soviet designs likely to produce greater, not lesser, antagonism toward the West? How could one expect negotiations to take place when the United States had reached a "position of strength" if for the Russians this meant a "position of weakness"?[41] How did one know when containment had been achieved, and one could then safely grant the reciprocity upon which a true balance of power must be based? All of these issues would come up over the next four decades, and on most of them Kennan and Nitze themselves would take opposite positions.

Finally, the Kennan-Nitze strategy of containment promised no immediate results. It depended upon the ability of Kremlin leaders to free themselves from their own self-generated illusions and to accommodate to the realities of international life; but no one could know how long that would take.[42] Certainly this invisibility of results contributed to the urge subsequent administrations felt to experiment with other approaches to containment; that experimentation, in turn, made the process of containment less efficient than it might otherwise have been.[43]

Still the Kennan-Nitze vision of a Soviet Union that would ultimately recognize the futility of its own system and undertake itself to change it was as accurate a prediction as anyone made during the Cold War of how that conflict would eventually end. Countervailing centers of power did develop, both in Europe and Asia, to such a point that in all categories of power except military, the Soviet Union by 1980 was no longer a major competitor for global influence. The international communist movement did break up, to such an extent that, by 1990, the only true believers left were Fidel Castro in Cuba and Kim Il Sung in North Korea. Under the leadership of Mikhail Gorbachev and his chief foreign policy architect, Eduard Shervardnadze, the Soviet Union did move after 1985 to settle long-standing conflicts with the United States and its allies, whether over Eastern Europe, Germany, the arms race, Third World rivalries, or human rights. It was as if Gorbachev had taken literally one of the favorite jokes of his chief Americanologist, Georgii Arbatov, who liked to warn that the Soviet Union was out to "contain" the West through the simple expedient of depriving it of an adversary.[44]

One can argue, to be sure, that these things would have happened in any event, even if the Kennan-Nitze version of containment had never developed. Still, one test of an effective strategy is the extent to which it associates itself with what is likely to happen in any event; alignment with inevitability is not a bad way of ensuring that one's objectives are eventually met. The idea of containment, as Kennan and Nitze understood it, was a shrewd anticipation

of what was to come. It assumed that Soviet efforts to destabilize the international system would in time generate their own resistance, and that Soviet
leaders would in time see the logic of changing their own domestic system
in response to these developments; it defined the goal of American policy
largely as one of helping that historical process along.

Competitive Coexistence

A third possible objective the United States could have had in its relationship
with the Soviet Union would have been to compete for influence within a
framework of shared systemic interests. Such an approach would operate on
the assumptions: (1) that great nations can have both cooperative and competitive interests at the same time; (2) that the United States and the Soviet
Union had a common interest in avoiding mutually destructive war or any
dramatic shifts in the status quo that might lead to war; but (3) that, for both
geopolitical and ideological reasons, Moscow intended to compete with the
United States for influence in the world by means that did not risk war;
therefore (4) the task of American statesman would have to be to find ways
of countering that Soviet influence without upsetting the overall structure
of international relations that had evolved since 1945.

Until the Eisenhower administration came into office in 1953, most
Washington officials had regarded the Cold War as a transitory phenomenon.
However tense the confrontation with the Russians might be, it would not
last indefinitely; either war would bring it to an end or, more likely, the
Kremlin leaders' realization that they were not going to have their way would
push them toward more moderate policies, making continuing efforts at containment unnecessary. Kennan himself had regarded that strategy as appropriate only for Stalin and had expected new situations—and new American
policies—to emerge upon the dictator's death.[45] Nitze, less optimistic, worried that growing Soviet military strength might tempt Stalin or his successors
into irresponsible actions that could risk war. But he too expected that American rearmament, if implemented along the lines advocated in NSC-68, would
prevent that from happening and eventually open up possibilities for a negotiated resolution of differences on terms favorable to the West.[46]

Eisenhower and his advisers, in contrast, anticipated a long-term competitive relationship with the Soviet Union for two reasons. First, Moscow's
progress in developing nuclear weapons and the means to deliver them meant
that war could destroy the United States itself; with this fact in mind, Eisenhower quietly ruled out direct military confrontation as a viable option.[47]
Second, attempts to end the Cold War through containment—by building
centers of resistance to the Russians in those parts of the world threatened
by them—ran the risk, Eisenhower thought, of bankrupting the United States
and ultimately undermining its way of life.[48] The President thus neither
expected nor sought a quick end to Soviet-American competition; rather he

concentrated on finding ways to sustain that rivalry without war over an extended period of time.

His preferred strategy was the so-called "New Look," an approach that relied heavily upon the prospect of nuclear retaliation to deter Soviet expansionism while at the same time conserving limited American resources. But that strategy did not depend wholly upon the deterrent effect of nuclear weapons; an integral—if overlooked—aspect of it was the use of negotiations to establish limits within which competition would be carried on. Just because the Russians insisted on attaching the adjective "peaceful" to the noun "coexistence" did not make it "appeasement," Eisenhower told a press conference in 1955: "To my mind, coexistence is, in fact, a state of our being as long as we are not attempting to destroy the other side."[49]

Several considerations led Eisenhower to endorse negotiations as a way of reducing the danger of war while lowering the costs of confrontation. The death of Stalin in March, 1953, provided grounds for expecting greater flexibility on Moscow's part than had been present in previous years. European allies—and particularly Winston Churchill—were strongly encouraging Washington to test Soviet intentions in this regard. Eisenhower himself believed that the West would be negotiating from a position of strength, both because of the military rearmament that had taken place since Korea, but also because, like Kennan and Nitze before him, he saw signs of developing ideological fragmentation within the international communist bloc.[50] It was, as well, the President's strongly held conviction, based on his reading of Clausewitz, that strategies without objectives made no sense.[51] Since surrender was unthinkable, military victory impossible, and the cost of long-term containment unacceptable, it seemed logical to explore possibilities for incorporating Soviet-American rivalry—which was certain to continue—within a mutually acceptable framework of coexistence.

The idea that one could negotiate with the Russians without appeasing them was by no means widely accepted in the United States at the time Eisenhower took office. Even so experienced (and tough) a diplomat as Charles E. Bohlen had come close to being denied Senate confirmation as ambassador to the Soviet Union in 1953 for the simple reason that he had been present at the Yalta conference eight years earlier.[52] All that had changed, though, by the end of Eisenhower's term. Despite a decidedly mixed record of accomplishment, three summit meetings, a succession of foreign ministers conferences, and extended bilateral contacts at lower levels had, by 1961, legitimized the idea that one could talk to the Russians without at the same time being taken in by them.[53] This was an important legacy for the incoming Kennedy administration, burdened as it was by the memory of past Democratic foreign policy humiliations and by a paper-thin electoral mandate. Had Eisenhower not made negotiations with the Russians "respectable," the new President and his advisers might well have found it impossible to pursue contacts with them—as indeed happened with regard to the Chinese.[54]

In fact, Kennedy continued Eisenhower's objective of seeking competitive coexistence. As Walt Rostow put it in a 1962 internal memorandum, "we should try to work over the longer run toward tacit understandings with the USSR as to the ground rules covering our competition." If the Russians "are convinced of our capacity and will to deal with their efforts to extend power into the free community, it may become increasingly possible to make them feel that we share a common interest in the exercise of restraint."[55] Kennedy himself made much the same argument in his American University address of June, 1963: the idea, he stressed, was to convince Kremlin leaders "that it is dangerous for them to engage in direct or indirect aggression, futile for them to attempt to impose their will and their system on other unwilling people, and beneficial to them, as well as to the world, to join in the achievement of a genuine and enforceable peace."[56]

The strategy of seeking to embed competition within a framework of coexistence created several important precedents. First, it established personal contact, for the first time during the Cold War, between American and Soviet leaders. It comes as a bit of a surprise to recall that four summit conferences took place between 1955 and 1961 (one of them, that of 1960, broke up in disarray). This compares with a record of no Soviet-American summits during the preceding decade (except for Potsdam, which was really a wartime summit), and only one—Glassboro, 1967—in the decade that followed. Students of international relations are, with reason, wary of summits; they are thought to lead to exaggerated expectations, unforeseen confrontations, and unnecessary misunderstandings, a perception amply reinforced by the ill-prepared meeting at Reykjavik in 1986. But summits probably also moderate perceptions on both sides. It is difficult to view one's adversary as the embodiment of evil once one recognizes him to be human, and quite probably a grandfather as well. To the extent that personal relationships create a basis for cooperation among nations—and the extent of this is admittedly questionable—then summits are an important mechanism for bringing that about.

A second accomplishment was limited achievements in arms control. The decade preceding 1955 had seen no progress whatever toward the control of nuclear weapons. But during the next ten years, Soviet and American officials would reach several significant agreements: an informal moratorium on atmospheric nuclear testing that lasted from 1958 until 1961; the Limited Test Ban Treaty of 1963; and, later that year, a United Nations resolution banning the placement of nuclear weapons in outer space. Easily as important as these public accords was a tacit understanding that had also emerged by 1963: that neither the Russians nor the Americans would attempt to shoot down each other's recently launched and—because of their role in preventing surprise attacks—critically valuable reconnaissance satellites.[57] To be sure, these accomplishments fell well short of hopes for progress toward general and complete disarmament. But they did reflect the emergence of an avowed common interest in limited arms control, and that in itself was progress when compared with what had gone before.

A third accomplishment had to do with success in crisis management. The fact that World War III had not occurred by the time Eisenhower became president suggests that Moscow and Washington had not wholly failed in managing crises prior to that time. But the 1950s and early 1960s did see a remarkable sequence of potentially dangerous confrontations—Dienbienphu, 1954; Quemoy-Matsu, 1955; Hungary-Suez, 1956; Lebanon, 1958; Berlin, 1958–59; the U-2 incident, 1960; Cuba, 1961; Berlin, 1961; Laos, 1961–62; the Cuban Missile Crisis, 1962—*every one* of which was resolved without major military involvement by either superpower. The same could not be said of Korea in 1950, or of Vietnam and Afghanistan later on. This was, in retrospect, an impressive record of Soviet and American cooperation in restraining competition where it seemed likely to lead to war; it was consistent with a pattern of rivalry conducted within mutually understood limits.

Why, then, did the "competitive coexistence" regime not survive? In one sense, it did, at least for a time. Lyndon B. Johnson saw himself as continuing and even building upon Kennedy's strategy; Khrushchev's deposition in 1964 brought no dramatic shifts in Moscow's approach to the West. And yet, in more subtle ways, the pattern of Soviet-American relations, by the mid-1960s, was changing. Washington was becoming preoccupied to the point of obsession with the war in Vietnam, which meant that relations with the Russians attracted proportionately less attention than in the past. Simultaneously—and perhaps with this fact in mind—the new Soviet leadership was devoting its energies to the quiet but steady accumulation of strategic military hardware, thus reversing Khrushchev's old habit of ostentatiously rattling rockets he did not possess.

These events suggest a major difficulty in pursuing "competitive coexistence," which is that the point at which competition ends and cooperation begins is not always similarly perceived. The Johnson administration discovered this—belatedly—when it sought to enlist the Soviet Union's help in ending the Vietnam War. That assistance was not forthcoming, and in retrospect one is hard pressed to think of anything that could have been more to Moscow's advantage at the time than to have had the United States distracted by, and bogged down in, such a costly, indecisive, and unpopular guerilla war.[58] Nor, to the apparent surprise of the Kremlin, was Johnson prepared to cooperate on strategic arms control after the Soviet invasion of Czechoslovakia and the simultaneous proclamation of the "Brezhnev Doctrine" in 1968.[59]

No one in Washington had explicitly repudiated the goal of "competitive coexistence" by the time Johnson left office early the following year, but the conditions of competition had dramatically changed by then, and not to the advantage of the United States. The nation had severely weakened itself, both at home and in the world at large, through its unsuccessful quest for a military solution in Southeast Asia. The Soviet Union had used the resulting opportunity to strengthen significantly its own military position, and with somewhat less success—events in Czechoslovakia having done little to enhance its external image—to widen its influence in the rest of the world. The incoming Nixon administration saw the Kennedy-Johnson strategy as having produced something new and decidedly unpleasant in the history of the Cold

War: a situation of approximate military parity between the United States and the Soviet Union. The new administration's determination to reverse this trend—or, in the eyes of its critics, to accommodate itself to it—would lead it to embrace yet another objective in relations with Moscow: "cooperative coexistence."

Cooperative Coexistence

A fourth objective the United States might plausibly have identified in its relationship with the Soviet Union could have been to enlist the assistance of that country in the joint task of preserving world order. The assumptions underlying such an approach would be: (1) that geopolitical interests tend to override ideological interests; (2) that the United States and the Soviet Union, despite conflicting ideologies, shared interests that went beyond simply perpetuating the international system; (3) that these interests involved a *balancing* of power rather than its unilateral expansion; and (4) that the United States could therefore best secure its own interests by seeking the Soviet Union's cooperation at multiple levels of activity within that system.

Historical evidence for the existence of this approach exists in two very different periods and under two very different administrations whose similarities—at least with respect to the Russians—turn out to be greater than one might have suspected: those of Franklin D. Roosevelt and Richard M. Nixon.

We have already seen how Roosevelt refrained from exploiting opportunities presented by the rise of Nazi Germany to seek the elimination of the Soviet regime; nor did he make any serious effort, either before or during World War II, to change its character. What, then, did Roosevelt really want in his relationship with the Russians? With the passage of time and the gaining of perspective, it appears that the President was pursuing a consistent—if mostly unarticulated—policy throughout his term in office, and that it was aimed toward securing Moscow's assistance in the preservation of a global balance of power.

The idea appears first in Roosevelt's decision to establish diplomatic relations with the Soviet Union in 1933, an action that the President took for several reasons. There was the obvious fact that the sixteen-year policy of non-recognition, proclaimed at the end of Wilson's administration, had neither weakened nor isolated the Soviet government. Soviet-American economic contacts had flourished despite non-recognition, and could be expected to increase still further—a point of no small importance in the midst of a depression—if that policy were changed. But the strongest justification, in Roosevelt's mind, for normalizing relations with Moscow was the need to counter the rise of potentially aggressive regimes in Berlin and Tokyo. Soviet Foreign Minister Maxim Litvinov, who negotiated the recognition agreement with Roosevelt, reported back to Moscow that the President had gone so far as to suggest signing a non-aggression pact with the Russians, aimed at deterring the Germans and the Japanese.[60]

Even to have raised that possibility, given the domestic and international situation Roosevelt confronted in the mid-1930s, now seems irresponsible. American isolationism, which became more intense as the depression deepened, imposed obvious limits on the extent to which Washington could do anything more than maintain minimal diplomatic contacts with the Russians. The Western European democracies were themselves appeasing Hitler, therefore limiting any prospect of establishing common resistance to him. And the nature of the Soviet regime itself militated against the kind of cooperative relationship Roosevelt had envisaged. Moscow's refusal to honor the admittedly loosely negotiated agreement establishing diplomatic relations conveyed a strong impression of duplicity; the onset of Stalin's purges made the idea that common interests might exist with such a government so distasteful to most Americans as to preclude their even thinking about it.

What is interesting about Roosevelt's policy is the persistence with which he tried to preserve prospects for cooperation, despite these unpromising circumstances. His appointment of the egregiously pro-Soviet Joseph E. Davies as ambassador in 1936, together with his own "purge" the following year of the allegedly anti-Soviet East European Division in the Department of State, can be understood in this context;[61] so too can Roosevelt's surprising receptivity to Stalin's equally surprising idea of having the United States construct warships for the Soviet Navy.[62] Then there is also the President's handling of Soviet-American relations after the Nazi-Soviet Pact and the invasion of Finland, already discussed above. All of these actions reflected Roosevelt's conviction that Germany and Japan posed greater threats to American interests than did the Russians, and that, despite differences on other points, Moscow and Washington had a common interest in opposing those aggressors.

That assumption was critical to the success of the World War II Grand Alliance. The effectiveness with which Russians fought Germans made the joint Soviet-American interest in victory over the Third Reich obvious to all but the most obtuse observers. Certainly these considerations influenced the speed with which Roosevelt made Lend-Lease available to the U.S.S.R. in the fall of 1941; the special treatment granted the Soviet Union by attaching no political or economic conditions to the aid it received; the President's sincere—if, given the target, misguided—efforts to win Stalin's trust during the war; and Roosevelt's sensitivity to postwar Soviet security interests, even to the point of temporarily supporting the Morgenthau Plan for the destruction of German industry as a means of relieving Stalin's insecurity about his western border.[63]

One should not conclude from this, though, that Roosevelt was naive about the Russians. He did foresee the possibility that Soviet and American interests might clash after the war, particularly in connection with the question of self-determination in Eastern Europe. He quietly withheld from the Russians potential instruments of "linkage"—atomic bomb information, postwar reconstruction assistance, reparations from the American zone in occupied Germany—that could be used to exert pressure if they became difficult. But he did hope that the long-term Soviet-American interest in maintaining a mutually beneficial postwar international system would override whatever short-term differences existed; certainly he was prepared to explore, to the maximum possible extent, opportunities for integrating the Soviet Union into that system.[64]

Why did Roosevelt's effort fail? Insofar as the war was concerned, it did not. Russian assistance against Germany was forthcoming in abundance and proved to be decisive; similar help would have been available against Japan as well had the atomic bomb not so abruptly removed the necessity for it in August of 1945. But the President had expected more: he assumed that Stalin shared his interest in constructing a stable postwar order and would participate in a great-power condominium—the so-called "Four Policemen," made up of the United States, the Soviet Union, Great Britain, and Nationalist China—to maintain it.

This proved not to be the case, as Roosevelt himself was coming to realize at the time of his death.[65] In order for a condominium to succeed, each participant must define its own security requirements conservatively, taking care not to infringe upon those of the others. Stalin showed no such restraint; his paranoia was so abiding as to render him incapable of specifying where, if at all, Soviet security interests ended.[66] The effect could only be to compel the other "policemen" to expand their own security requirements beyond what they otherwise would have been, and to end any prospect that wartime cooperation against Hitler could survive without Hitler.

A similar effort to find common ground with the Russians in sustaining the status quo occurred three decades later under Richard Nixon and Henry Kissinger. Like Roosevelt before and during World War II, the Nixon administration confronted the unpleasant reality that the United States could not, acting alone, ensure its security requirements. Just as the Soviet Union's assistance had been required to defeat Nazi Germany, so now in the wake of the Vietnam War—a period that had seen American power weaken while that of the Soviet Union had grown—cooperation with the Russians appeared necessary if the international balance of power was to be maintained. It was a matter, in each instance, of accepting what could not be avoided, but at the same time attempting through innovative and frequently personal diplomacy to improve the situation.

This approach differed from the "competitive coexistence" sought by Eisenhower and Kennedy in its pessimistic assessment of American power. There had been little question during the 1950s and 1960s that the United States enjoyed military superiority over the Russians. Under those circumstances, one could confidently expect a competitive relationship to preserve American interests, so long as limits existed that would avoid escalation to nuclear war. But Nixon and Kissinger had no such confidence: the Russians' attainment of strategic parity, together with the blow to American credibility inflicted by the Vietnam War, left them worried that even competition *within* such limits could place the United States at a substantial disadvantage.[67] Existing trends were working against American interests, they believed, in a manner that would find echoes among the "declinists" of a subsequent generation.[68] Moscow's cooperation beyond the joint goal of avoiding war would be needed if the balance of power was to be preserved.

But if Nixon and Kissinger were pessimistic about American strength, they were at the same time optimistic about their own ability, through skillful diplomacy, to secure Soviet cooperation. They sought to do this in several interrelated ways:

First, they were ready explicitly to acknowledge the Soviet Union's status as one of the world's two superpowers. Nixon and Kissinger recognized, and were prepared elaborately to defer to, the Soviet government's determination to be treated with respect. They shared Roosevelt's view that personal contacts could often achieve what exchanges between foreign offices could not; moreover, they had the advantage—unlike Roosevelt—of dealing with a Soviet leadership that was prepared to respond to such treatment.

Second, they sought to create, through such direct contacts, Soviet-American "regimes"—rules and procedures defining the limits of acceptable behavior—in the important fields of arms control and crisis management. The intent here was to restrain Soviet action that might upset the status quo, whether through the additional deployment of strategic weapons or the exploitation of Third World crises, but to do it by negotiating understandings to govern each side's behavior in such matters. The resulting agreements— SALT I and the statement on "Basic Principles" of Soviet-American relations, both concluded at the 1972 Moscow summit—went well beyond the earlier "competitive coexistence" pattern, which had assumed a continuation of rivalry in these areas, limited only by the restraint necessary to avoid war.

Third, they intended to use "linkage"—carefully arranged combinations of inducements and constraints—to secure these agreements. The inducements lay primarily in the economic realm. Nixon and Kissinger offered the Russians access to the trade, technology, and investment capital they would need to modernize their economy in return for cooperation on arms control and crisis management. But there were constraints as well, not the least of which was the prospect of improved relations between the United States and the People's Republic of China.

The Nixon-Kissinger search for "cooperative coexistence" was a thoughtful and sophisticated attempt to make the best of a bad situation. To the extent that American influence in the world was higher when the Republicans left office in 1977 than it had been eight years earlier—and it probably was— they can be said to have succeeded. Certainly the "opening" to China more than compensated for the "loss" of South Vietnam. But the long-term objective of "cooperative co-existence" proved as elusive in the 1970s as it had in the 1940s and, once again, the Russians bore much of the responsibility for this outcome.

Just as Stalin had never accepted Roosevelt's view that Soviet interests would best be served by a cooperative rather than a unilateral search for security, so Brezhnev and his associates, despite the fact that they had welcomed the SALT I and "Basic Principles" agreements, could not bring themselves to refrain from exploiting opportunities as they arose, whether by stretching the vague language of SALT I to justify new strategic weapons deployments, or by taking advantage of post-Vietnam/post-Watergate passivity in Washington to intervene in a succession of otherwise unrelated crises ranging from Angola to Afghanistan. Both the Roosevelt and the Nixon administrations made the mistake of assuming that Soviet willingness to cooperate extended much farther down into the "strata" of Soviet-American relations than in fact it did.

There were, to be sure, mitigating circumstances. Even as they pushed for the "Basic Principles" agreement, the Russians made it clear that they would not cease to support "wars of national liberation" in the Third World, a reservation Washington incautiously ignored.[69] Moscow could also claim, with good reason, that the Americans had failed to deliver the economic inducements that were to have accompanied agreements on strategic arms; as will be seen, these fell prey to a sudden and ill-conceived enthusiasm on the part of Congress for promoting reform inside the Soviet Union. It is also the case that the United States itself was pursuing unilateral advantages in its efforts to destablize the Marxist government of Salvadore Allende in Chile and in its determination to deny the Russians a role in the Middle East after the 1973 Yom Kippur War.[70]

But the fact remains: there was an American administration in the early 1970s—as there had been in the early 1940s—that was prepared to accord the Soviet Union the legitimacy, the respectability, and the great power status its leaders have so persistently sought. In both instances, the temptation of short-term unilateral gains caused Moscow to squander the potential that existed for long-term cooperation. In both instances, the results were ultimately to the Russians' disadvantage. It is difficult to see how American rearmament in the late 1940s and early 1950s made the Soviet Union any more secure than did American rearmament in the late 1970s and early 1980s. Confronted twice with "windows of opportunity" for building a cooperative relationship with the United States, the Russians both times blew it.

Changing the Soviet Union's Internal Structure

Neither "competitive" nor "cooperative" coexistence sought to produce any significant alteration in the internal structure of the Soviet government. The assumption was that common external interests would override differences in internal systems to make possible a stable Soviet-American relationship. The original Kennan-Nitze strategy of containment had sought to encourage Soviet leaders ultimately to change their own system from within, but the role of the United States was to be limited to helping create the external circumstances that would cause them to do this. It was a strategy that involved waiting for a Gorbachev, however long it took him to arrive on the scene. But the United States could, in theory at least, have sought a more active role: it could have attempted to contain the threat posed by the Soviet government by seeking through its own actions to alter that regime's internal character.

The assumptions behind such an approach would be: (1) that foreign policy is ultimately a reflection of internal political structure; (2) that although the Soviet regime was legitimate by the standards normally required for diplomatic recognition, it was also an autocratic government and, because of this, a destabilizing force in world affairs; (3) that without changes in the domestic character of the Soviet regime, one could not expect changes in its external behavior; but (4) that the United States did in fact have the capability, through a judiciously applied combination of pressures and inducements, to bring about such changes.

The historical origins of this line of thought go back to the point, early in the twentieth century, at which Americans began inferring the *behavior* of governments on the basis of the *form* governments take.[71] International stability now appeared to depend upon transforming the nations of the world into democracies based on the American model. Certainly the League of Nations, Woodrow Wilson's main preoccupation after victory in World War I, involved imposing a structure derived principally from the American constitutional example upon the postwar international system. One of the President's rationales for intervention in Russia was, as has been seen, to recapture opportunities for democratic reform he thought had been lost with the overthrow of the Provisional Government. For Wilson, the boundaries between domestic reform and foreign policy were, at best, indistinct. In an impressive expansion of the American progressive tradition, he seemed to be arguing that the powers of government should be enlisted, in both realms, to produce democracy as a result.[72]

But the nation's enthusiasm for seeking stability through democratization proved sporadic, at best. Wilson himself made only half-hearted efforts along these lines in Russia, and his countrymen's ardor for the League also quickly cooled. As the domestic reform impulse waned, so too did support for reform in the world at large. Nor did it revive when economic distress brought new reforms a decade and a half later in the shape of the New Deal. It would take another war to resuscitate the view that peace required democracy and justice, and even then a fair amount of un-Wilsonian skepticism persisted, not least in the mind of Franklin D. Roosevelt himself.

It is true that Roosevelt, like Wilson, sought to justify American participation in World War II in reformist terms; the Atlantic Charter was, after all, little more than a restatement of the Fourteen Points. And, of course, Roosevelt did strongly support creation of—and American membership in—the United Nations. But the President's aspirations for international reform were more superficial than substantive. It was useful to articulate them—if for no other reason than to cloak the realism that in fact shaped his policies[73]— but those policies would not stand or fall upon prospects for a global New Deal.

For Roosevelt, cooperation in international affairs required no necessary congruence of domestic institutions and priorities; states with very different systems could have common interests. Nor did most Americans at the time question the wisdom of cooperating with one dictator to defeat another. Some even reversed the traditional equation, deducing from the effective *behavior* of the Russians in fighting the Germans the conclusion that their *form* of government had already evolved toward democratic capitalism.[74] Certainly the attraction of defeating adversaries with minimal casualties and maximum effectiveness was sufficient to override whatever qualms might have existed, as Roosevelt himself once put it, about "hold[ing] hands with the devil."[75]

One statesman who did worry deeply about the gap separating American domestic institutions from those of the Soviet Union, though, was Roosevelt's Secretary of War, Henry L. Stimson. The chief difficulty in Washington's postwar relations with Moscow, the old progressive warned President Harry S. Truman in July, 1945, was likely to be the contrast

> between a nation of free thought, free speech, free elections, in fact a really free people, [and] a nation which is not basically free but which is systematically controlled from above by secret police and in which free speech is not permitted. . . . [N]o permanently safe international relations can be established between two such fundamentally different national systems. With the best of efforts we cannot understand each other.

Stimson wrote those words with the recently tested but still secret atomic bomb very much in mind, and in the weeks that followed he toyed with one of the most remarkable ideas in the history of American reform: that the bomb might be used as an instrument with which to induce—or even to compel—Soviet leaders to abandon once and for all the totalitarian character of the system they had imposed upon the Russian people.

No sooner had he articulated this thought, though, than Stimson backed away from it; the reasons suggest something of the difficulties involved in making domestic reform a foreign policy goal. First, Stimson found that although his own close advisers—notably John McCloy—shared his concern about prospects for postwar cooperation with the Russians, they did not see domestic incompatibility as a necessary barrier to it. Second, W. Averell Harriman, a man of vastly greater experience than Stimson's in dealing directly with the Russians, insisted that Stalin would regard as a hostile act any attempt to use the bomb to extract reforms. The old dilemma of how to encourage change from outside without provoking nationalism from within remained as real as it had in Wilson's day. In the end, Stimson departed from Truman's Cabinet with the recommendation that the United States try to win Stalin's trust by offering to share information about the bomb, on the grounds that "the only way you can make a man trustworthy is to trust him."[76]

The Truman administration did not follow that recommendation, but it did put forward during the next two years two imaginative proposals that would have—if implemented—produced changes of a sort inside Russia, although not the thoroughgoing reforms Stimson had in mind. One of these was the Baruch Plan for the international control of atomic energy, which would have resulted in the transfer of American atomic weapons to the United Nations in return for Soviet willingness to allow international control over all sources of fissionable material within the U.S.S.R. The second was the Marshall Plan, which the Russians were invited to join on the condition that they reveal detailed information about their internal economic situation. Neither of these initiatives originated as attempts to alter the Soviet system; the goals rather were to control atomic energy and to revive Europe. But Washington officials did assume that Moscow's cooperation in either of those efforts would require internal changes within the Soviet Union; predictably, the Russians rejected them both.

Stimson's brief consideration of how one might seek to reform the Soviet system from the outside, together with the less sweeeping requirements for change stipulated in the Baruch and Marshall plans, were the only significant examples of such thinking in Washington for many years. Not until the 1970s would American officials return to the goal of attempting, as a conscious policy objective, to modify the internal political structure of the U.S.S.R. To be sure, it became a staple of both public and private rhetoric during the Cold War to stress the obvious differences between American democracy and Soviet totalitarianism, but few concluded from this that the coexistence of the two systems required their convergence. The Kennan-Nitze strategy of containment had anticipated evolution within the Soviet system, but never to the point of correspondence with Western democratic principles and certainly not as the result of any open American crusade to bring such a thing about. There were those within the Nixon administration who suggested that increasing economic and cultural contacts with the West would render Soviet society more "permeable," and hence more relaxed and tolerant;[77] but these changes were always seen more as a consequence of improved relations than as a prerequisite for them.

The major postwar effort to make reform in Russia an objective of policy in the United States arose, during the early 1970s, outside the Nixon administration. It took the form of attempts by Senator Henry Jackson and his Congressional colleagues to transform Kissinger's concept of "linkage" into a Stimson-like instrument with which to secure greater respect for human rights inside the Soviet state. Kissinger's intentions with regard to "linkage" had been modest. He had held out the prospect of trade, investment, and technology transfers to induce Moscow's cooperation in limiting arms and in managing crises, but he doubted whether the Russians needed economic concessions badly enough to relax internal controls in order to get them.[78] Jackson, however, wanted to use such American economic leverage as existed to make life more tolerable—and departure from the U.S.S.R. more feasible— for Soviet Jews and dissidents; he was also profoundly skeptical about detente and not at all reluctant to see it held "hostage" to the issue of human rights inside the Soviet Union, particularly if this might advance his own 1976 presidential ambitions.[79]

As it turned out, this mixture of principle with expediency did little to help Jackson, who was never a strong contender for the Democratic nomination, or Jews and dissidents in the Soviet Union, whose emigration in substantial numbers would remain restricted for another decade. But Jackson's injection of "human rights" into the campaign did provide his rival, Jimmy Carter, with a potent means by which to attack Kissinger simultaneously from the right and the left. Carter could appeal both to critics of detente and to supporters who nonetheless worried about its perceived "amorality."

This was a clever domestic political ploy, but it worked less well when the new administration attempted to apply it officially, early in 1977, to the realm of geopolitics. Determined to assert independence from his predecessors but convinced as well of the need to improve Soviet-American relations, Carter ostentatiously announced the demise of "linkage," combined an offer of "deep cuts" on strategic missiles with highly public expressions of sympathy for Andrei Sakharov and other Soviet dissidents, and then appeared surprised when the offended Russians themselves established a "linkage" and refused to budge on either point.[80]

It was Carter's unfortunate habit to think in compartmental but not integral terms. He combined Kissinger's emphasis on arms control with Jackson's emphasis on human rights, but he failed to see—as both Kissinger and Jackson had seen—the contradictions in these two approaches. Soviet leaders were unlikely to extend the trust upon which arms control had to depend to an administration they perceived as challenging their legitimacy. The fact that what Carter had in mind was reform, not revolution, made little difference from the Soviet perspective; in an inversion of the American "domino" theory, the Russians took the view that if the United States gained *any* capability to effect change within the Soviet Union, this would only encourage it to seek more. It was better, therefore, to resist such efforts from the start. As a result, Carter wound up achieving the objectives of *neither* Kissinger nor Jackson; his accomplishments—or, more precisely, the absence of them—were uniquely his own.[81]

The Reagan administration, too, gave thought to how it might change Soviet society during its first years in office, but here the emphasis was on exhaustion, not reform. Convinced that the Soviet economy was in serious trouble, the new President and his advisers talked frankly of engaging Moscow in an all-out arms race, with the expectation that this would force an increasingly hard-pressed Kremlin leadership to choose between economic collapse at home or acknowledgment of a resurgent American military superiority in the world at large.[82] The administration's enthusiasm for reviving the MX missile and B-1 bomber programs, for building a 600-ship Navy, and for upgrading conventional ground force capabilities all can be understood in this context, as can President Reagan's own imaginative contribution to this effort, the Strategic Defense Initiative.

Strangely, of all the efforts to promote internal reform in the Soviet Union through external pressure, SDI—which was never even intended for that purpose—may have been the most effective. For as the Soviet Union sank more and more deeply into the "stagnation" that characterized the final Brezhnev years, the task of keeping pace with a new American military buildup imposed heavier and heavier burdens on an already severely strained economy, especially in connection with developing the sophisticated technology required to operate new weaponry. Coming at this moment of exhaustion, SDI's challenge to yet another round of costly research and development can only have been discouraging in the extreme to the Russians. The resulting sense of desperation in Moscow made the need for new systems of economic and political organization crystal clear, even to those who had hitherto resisted the idea.[83] It clarified the price of continued backwardness, and in this way—as visions of defeat stemming from backwardness have often done in Russian history[84]—cleared the path for dramatic change. It was as if Henry Stimson's fleeting 1945 vision of technological advance within the United States serving as an instrument of reform within the Soviet Union had at last been realized.

The infrequent attempts Americans made after 1917 to "reform" the Soviet Union from the outside suffered from an exaggeration of their ability to influence events inside that country, and a corresponding underestimation of the extent to which the Russians would resist carrying out reforms they might otherwise undertake for fear of seeming to yield to external pressures. They neglected the tendency of a still highly defensive Soviet regime to confuse calls for reform with challenges to legitimacy. They failed to take into account the persisting strength of Russian nationalism, a force rarely sympathetic to outside ideas, however praiseworthy the rest of the world might find them to be. They miscalculated the capacity of the Congress—and of the American people—to sustain the consistent action necessary to effect change within the limited range in which it might be possible.

It would be wrong, though, to claim that these efforts wholly failed. Whatever the motives for it, the attention paid to victims of oppression did limit the abuses inflicted on them; and ultimately it gave the Kremlin a self-interested reason of its own—improving its abysmal public image in the eyes of the world—for releasing them. Restrictions on the import of sensitive technologies, together with the challenge posed by the Reagan military buildup, did strain the ability of Soviet economic planners to continue to function in the old way; the prospect of SDI may well have pushed them over the edge. By the end of the 1980s, Soviet officials had given up on trying to keep foreign influences out. They now took the quite opposite tack of inviting in Western advice on how to organize a democratic government and a market economy.

What was going on here was not so much skillful American diplomacy—although there was some of that—as a fundamental change in the prerequisites for technological innovation. A totalitarian state running a command economy could build an atomic bomb of its own in the late 1940s, or even a pioneering earth satellite and long-range rocket program in the late 1950s; but similar procedures would not work to produce foolproof computer programs, miniaturized electronic circuitry, or pinpoint guidance systems in the late 1980s. The means of production themselves had shifted—very much as Marx had described them as doing a century before the Cold War began[85]—and it was this, as much as anything else, that brought the Cold War to an end. Stimson had been right: technology could be the means of sparking democratic reforms. He had just been forty years ahead of his time.

Conclusion

Any essay that emphasizes points of agreement—as this one has—in the views of Franklin D. Roosevelt and Richard Nixon, George Kennan and Paul Nitze, Dwight Eisenhower and John F. Kennedy, and Jimmy Carter and Ronald Reagan is, to put it politely, taking a counter-intuitive approach. These interpretations go against the conventional wisdom that has accumulated during years of research and writing on Cold War history; they are not, I feel confident, likely to gain easy acceptance.

But Cold War historians have labored under a peculiar disability that has not afflicted historians of more distant pasts: they have tried to write the history of a great event without knowing its outcome. A history of the American Civil War written at the beginning of 1863 would hardly resemble one composed at the end of 1865; a history of World War I that stopped in March, 1918, would have a wholly different character from one that extended through November of that same year. The inability to view an event from beginning to end invariably narrows perspectives and constricts conclusions. The demise of the Cold War presents us with an important opportunity to reconsider conventional wisdom, to see things from new angles of vision, and to ask once again that most useful of historians' questions: "What was it all about?"[86]

What it was all about, with respect to containment, was both simple and complex: simple in the sense that that strategy was another in a long series of efforts by the United States to preserve its security through the maintenance of a balance of power in the world; complex in that, despite their consistent support for this strategy, American leaders so often failed to agree on the specific objectives it was supposed to accomplish. Given opportunities to redesign the Soviet Union in their own minds, they came up, over the years, with strikingly different results.

Today citizens of the Soviet Union are themselves redesigning their country, and it is by no means clear what the outcome of their efforts is going to be. A broader range of alternatives is now open than at any point since 1917; implications for the future security of the United States and the rest of the world extend across an equally broad range. Whatever their opinions on the matter, Americans are likely to have little direct influence in determining which possible future for the Soviet Union becomes the real one. But the choice that is made—whatever it is—will affect American interests, and that in turn will determine what form of containment, if any at all, will be necessary in the post-Cold War world. All the more reason, then, for being clear—even if counter-intuitively clear—about the alternatives that have existed in the minds of those Americans who have sought to make containment work in the past.

## THREE

Morality and the American Experience in the Cold War

One would have to look long and hard to find a topic more fraught with peril than the question of how morality relates to foreign policy. Morality is a difficult enough problem in the lives of individuals, where externally imposed standards of behavior, whether founded on personal belief or political commitment, generally apply. In the lives of nations, where there exist few such standards, the problem is almost insurmountable. A just war for one country may appear as aggression to another, and who is to say which is right? Actions that violate the moral standards of a particular people may be required by those of another; and in states where moral standards provide no guidance, ideology may, with equally variable results. The world may applaud actions taken in one context, but then condemn the same actions when carried out under different circumstances. In short, we stand here on the edge of an intellectual morass, and I, for one, am reluctant to wade into it.

This essay attempts no resolution of these controversial issues. Its purpose, rather, is to examine the extent to which moral standards affected the conduct of United States foreign policy during the Cold War. It concentrates, not on the ethicists who sought to define those standards, but rather on the way in which government officials themselves went about reconciling the claims of morality with the requirements of wielding power. It focuses specifically on the relationship between national security and national ideals: on the question of how the nation could defend itself against what appeared to be mortal peril without compromising those deeply rooted values that had caused the nation to exist in the first place.

"Morality [in foreign policy]," Arthur M. Schlesinger, Jr., has written, "is basically a matter of keeping faith with a nation's own best ideals.... A democracy is in bad shape when it keeps two sets of books—when it uses one scale of values for its internal policy and uses another in foreign affairs."[1] And yet, survival in a world that was not democratic raised just this problem:

To what extent was the United States obliged, in the course of ensuring its own safety, to adopt the strategies and tactics of those who threatened it? To what extent could the nation act in a manner consistent with its moral standards when the other side did not share those standards? To what extent, in short, was it necessary to sacrifice what one was attempting to defend, in the course of defending it?

The questions, of course, were hardly new ones. The competing requirements of security and morality permeate Thucydides' somber account of the Peloponnesian War, written some 2400 years ago. Nor was the dilemma unfamiliar to Americans: the Civil War, World War I, and World War II had all posed the painful question of how one reconciles moral standards with lethal technology in an environment of unrestrained violence.[2] But for all of their intensity those had been exceptional circumstances; it was only with the onset of the Cold War that the problem of having to choose between the demands of morality and security become an enduring one for the leaders of the United States. It is to the question of how they have made that choice that I want to address myself here.

Containment, the Marshall Plan, and American Ideals

"The issue of Soviet-American relations is in essence a test of the over-all worth of the United States as a nation among nations," George F. Kennan wrote in the most famous of all Cold War texts, the 1947 "X" article in *Foreign Affairs*. "To avoid destruction the United States need only measure up to its own best traditions and prove itself worthy of preservation as a great nation."[3] Kennan was rarely optimistic about the ability of Americans to conduct a coherent and responsible foreign policy, but there was in this observation an uncharacteristic optimism regarding one point: the possibility of mounting an effective defense against Soviet expansionism without compromising the fundamental principles for which the United States stood. We could, Kennan seemed to be saying, contain the Russians and still be true to ourselves.

Americans did in fact have reason to hope that they would be able to fight the Cold War that had appeared so suddenly after the conclusion of the World War without violating standards of behavior to which they, as well as those elsewhere who wished them well, liked to hold themselves. The United States had, after all, made a sincere effort during the war to build a new international order based on the principles of self-determination, open markets, and collective security. When difficulties with the Russians began to arise, it had attempted with great persistence to settle them through diplomatic means. It had demobilized its armed forces with little regard to the rapidly worsening international situation, and it had even offered to relinquish to the United Nations its monopoly over the most powerful military weapon the world had ever seen, the atomic bomb. That none of this had availed to lessen the Soviet Union's distrust of the West, or to build a firm basis for postwar cooperation, was regrettable, to be sure. But the view at the time was that, if the United States had anything to reproach itself for, it was an excess of patience and forbearance, not belligerence.[4]

Few historians today would entirely share that assessment. The passage of time and the opening of documents have long since called into question the assumption of total American innocence in the coming of the Cold War.[5] What is important for our purposes here, though, is the fact that few Americans then believed that the United States had caused that conflict, and that most foreign observers probably agreed with them. The British embassy in Washington summed up the prevailing attitude well in May, 1947: "To those critics who accuse her of taking undue advantage of her own strength and of the weakness of others, America might well reply in the words of Clive when arraigned by a committee in the House of Commons for having exploited his unrivalled power in India for purposes of personal aggrandizement: 'By God, Mr. Chairman, at this moment I stand astonished at my own moderation.' "[6]

The year 1947, then, was one of those moments when national interest and national morality seemed to coincide. One could justify the strategy of containment in cold-blooded geopolitical terms, to be sure: it was not in the interests of the United States to have Europe fall under the domination of a single hostile power in 1947, anymore than it had been in 1940, or in 1917. But, as in those earlier instances, this geopolitical reality coincided neatly with the defense of freedom. Americans of that age believed firmly that aggression was linked to autocracy, and that a stable international order would best grow out of the maximum possible diffusion of such domestic virtues as freedom of speech, freedom of belief, freedom of enterprise, and freedom of political choice. As President Truman himself put it in September, 1947 (in a speech that Kennan helped to draft): "The attainment of worldwide respect for essential human rights is synonymous with the attainment of world peace."[7]

The supreme example of this linkage between domestic and international principle was, of course, the Marshall Plan. Here was an initiative that addressed the central geopolitical problem—the extension of Soviet power into Eastern and Central Europe, and the insecurities that event had set off elsewhere on the Continent—without violating domestic standards of behavior. It appeared to be a disinterested humanitarian gesture on a grand scale, with even the Soviet Union and its Eastern European satellites invited to participate. It provided subtle inducements for its recipients to move toward European unity, while at the same time allowing them considerable latitude to decide how they would use the assistance they received. It involved no burdensome military buildup for either the United States or its allies; rather, the plan was to counter the Soviet threat by economic means, thereby building the self-confidence necessary for the Europeans eventually to handle their military problems on their own. Finally, it had the not inconsiderable advantage of potential profitability, both in terms of the immediate demand for American products the aid program would generate, and the longer-term prospects for a revival of world trade it would create.[8]

Given these multiple advantages, it is hardly surprising that those who devised and implemented the Marshall Plan looked back on it for decades afterwards with misty-eyed nostalgia. At no other point in the history of the Cold War would there be a closer correspondence between the perceived requirements of security and morality. Kennan's vision of a strategy that would work simply by manifesting the nation's own best instincts seemed, with astonishing ease, to have been realized.

Containment and Moral Compromises

In fact, though, there was already reason to believe that things were not going to be that simple. In subtle ways at first, but with increasing clarity as time went on, it became apparent that the United States would not always be able to adhere to traditional standards of behavior if containment was to be made to succeed. That this was so should hardly have come as a surprise; no nation that had just concluded a world war by dropping an atomic bomb should have found the use of extraordinary means to achieve praiseworthy ends particularly shocking. But that had been wartime, and the possibility that the morality of war might now become the morality of peace did cause concern in a nation that had always sharply distinguished war from peace. "How much evil we must do in order to do good," Reinhold Niebuhr wrote worriedly in 1946. "This, I think, is a very succinct statement of the human situation."[9] It would not be long before the some of the things that had to be done to implement containment—or that policy-makers thought it necessary to do—began to raise qualms, and not just in the exceedingly sensitive mind of Kennan, that strategy's chief architect.

One of these was the tactic of exaggerating external threat as a means of prying appropriations out of a still largely isolationist Congress. It is now generally accepted that the sweeping language President Truman used in requesting aid for Greece and Turkey in 1947—his portrayal of the world as divided between antipathetic ways of life, and his open-ended pledge "to support free peoples who are resisting attempted subjugation by armed minorities or by outside pressures"—reflected not so much conviction as a calculated assessment of what it would take to prod parsimonious legislators into acting.[10] The administration used similar expedients in subsequent years to win approval of the Marshall Plan and the North Atlantic Treaty. "For many citizens of this country," the British embassy in Washington noted early in 1948, "a grudging recognition of America's stake in the modern world can only be produced by the administration of periodic shocks, which inevitably take the form of a warning, open or implied, that 'the Russians will get you if you don't watch out.' " "The State Department has almost come to rely," the embassy added a few months later, "upon the Soviet Union to stampede Congress into acting favourably and promptly on its proposals."[11] Dean Acheson acknowledged as much with characteristic bluntness years later: "If we made our points clearer than truth, we did not differ from most other educators and could hardly do otherwise."[12]

It followed from this that, despite public protestations of willingness to negotiate with the Russians, American officials were in fact highly wary of such contacts. Negotiations, they feared, might reduce the climate of international tension that was necessary to sustain both domestic and overseas support for containment. A strategy aimed ultimately at persuading the Russians to embrace diplomacy had to forgo diplomacy in order to set itself in motion. To be sure, the opportunities for negotiations did not seem promising in the late 1940s, and the Soviet Union did nothing to help matters along by making public one well-intentioned effort to investigate the possibilities that did exist—a supposedly confidential exchange of notes between American Ambassador Walter Bedell Smith and Soviet Foreign Minister Vyacheslav Molotov in May, 1948.[13] Still, the administration was forced into a position that was, at best, insincere: calling for negotiations, while at the same time keeping fingers crossed that they would not take place.

If the principle of candor now went by the boards, so too did that of non-interference in the internal affairs of other states. Admittedly, Washington's policies had not always met this test in the past, especially in those parts of the world where the Monroe Doctrine was thought to sanction, shall we say, a special relationship. But elsewhere, for the most part, the United States had refrained from such intervention in peacetime, whether because of superior moral character or—more likely—because inducements and capabilities were absent. Inducements and capabilities existed in abundance in the late 1940s, though, as anxious West Europeans, Italians, Greeks, Turks, and even Iranians sought to enlist American power—already greatly expanded as a result of the war—to counter that of the Soviet Union. The postwar American sphere of influence, it is worth emphasizing, arose in large measure at the invitation and with the fervent approval of the governments and the peoples who became part of it, a procedure very much in contrast to that by which Soviet influence expanded.[14] Still Americans, like Russians, did have a sphere of influence, and that involved them in several painful moral choices.

Should the Truman administration, for example, allow geopolitical interests to override the traditional American inclination to support only democracies? The governments of Greece and Turkey by no stretch of the imagination met that standard, and yet, their incorporation into the Soviet sphere would hardly benefit the causes of self-determination and human rights either. "The thing that bothers me," David Lilienthal wrote in his diary four days after the Truman Doctrine speech, "[is whether we are] supporting democracy—which is our purpose—by the measures we are adopting? Or are we going to make people, here and abroad, cynical about our democratic purposes?"[15]

A related problem had to do with the extent to which the United States should involve itself surreptitiously in the internal affairs of those nations that lay within its sphere. The Russians clearly did this, within and even beyond the areas they controlled. By the spring of 1948, with large amounts of cash flowing from Moscow into the coffers of the Italian Communist Party, Washington had to decide whether to adopt similar tactics. To allow the communists to win the April elections would be to consign Italy to the Soviet sphere by default, or so it seemed. To support non-communist parties publicly would appear to be interference in the electoral processes of another sovereign state. The Truman administration's solution, it turned out, was to authorize a covert action capability for the newly created Central Intelligence Agency: it says something about the ambiguities involved in this decision that the Agency itself resisted the innovation, and that the official who most ardently pressed for it was George Kennan.[16]

There was, to be sure, a certain innocence about CIA operations in those early days. They were mostly confined to trying to influence public opinion, whether through the use of acknowledged or unacknowledged propaganda, the manipulation of cultural and scholarly organizations, or attempts quietly to swing elections—as in Italy—in directions favorable to the United States. In those instances when more extreme measures were contemplated, the perceived iniquity of the opposition, as had been the case with Office of Strategic Services operations during World War II, tended to justify them. It was perfectly possible for people with a keen sense of the relationship between morality and foreign policy to participate in such activities.[17] Still, the procedure was not always easy to reconcile with traditional principles of nonintervention and self-determination.

Yet another dilemma for the architects of containment had to do with the relationship between force and diplomacy. Few people took seriously talk of a preventive war against the Soviet Union, but the question of how much military strength would be necessary to discourage a Soviet attack against the West—of just where the line lay between deterrence and provocation— was a difficult one indeed. Convinced that the Russians had nothing to gain by starting a war, Kennan was content, as was the administration in 1947 and 1948, to concentrate on the economic rather than the military instruments of containment, accepting the calculated risk that the Russians would not attack. The Czech coup and the Berlin Blockade set off pressures from the Europeans themselves for American military guarantees, though, and the Truman administration ultimately had to respond, over Kennan's protests, by creating the North Atlantic Treaty Organization. Kennan objected to NATO because he thought it would militarize what was primarily a political-economic problem and because it would impede long-term prospects for negotiations; but by 1949 the process of containment had come to overshadow these ultimate objectives. Security seemed preferable to risk, whatever the long-term consequences, and Kennan found himself more or less alone in his concerns.[18]

An even more painful dilemma relating to deterrence developed later that year with the news that the Russians had successfully tested their first atomic bomb. Not only did this event raise, for the first time, the prospect of retaliation; it also brought to the forefront the question of whether the United States should respond by building a "super" or hydrogen bomb. There followed the most serious discussion that had yet taken place within the government regarding the moral implications of deterrence by weapons of mass destruction.

Opponents of the H-bomb, among them Lilienthal, Kennan, and J. Robert Oppenheimer, based their arguments, not simply on the question of whether the new weapon would add any measure of security not already provided by atomic bombs, or whether it would irreparably damage prospects for the eventual control of atomic weapons, or whether it would provoke the Russians into developing H-bombs of their own; they raised as well the even more fundamental question of whether the principal deterrent to Soviet aggression should rest on nuclear weapons in the first place. Such instruments of mass destruction, Kennan argued,

> reach backward beyond the frontiers of western civilization, to the concepts of warfare which were once familiar to the Asiatic hordes. They cannot really be reconciled with a political purpose directed to shaping, rather than destroying, the lives of the adversary. They fail to take account of the ultimate responsibility of men for one another, and even for each other's errors and mistakes. They imply the admission that man not only can be but is his own worse and most terrible enemy.[19]

Proponents of the H-bomb, among them Paul Nitze, Lewis Strauss, and the Joint Chiefs of Staff, argued that whatever the military value of the new weapon, it was necessary to build it because the Russians surely would.[20] "Possession of a thermonuclear weapon by the USSR without such possession by the United States would be intolerable," General Omar Bradley argued, both because of its "profoundly demoralizing effect on the American people" and the "tremendous psychological boost" it would give to Moscow. President Truman, in approving the decision to build the bomb, added an even more mundane reason. "We have got to have it," he told his staff, if "only for bargaining purposes with the Russians."[21]

All of these examples of tolerating evils in the pursuit of good—lack of candor in portraying the threat, the postponement of negotiations, intervention in the internal affairs of other countries, even the decision to build the ultimate weapon in order to avoid psychological insecurities and to have a bargaining chip—were made by men with good intentions in the interests of what they thought to be good causes. Nevertheless, these decisions could not help but raise the question of where such compromises would stop. How much evil did one have to put up with, to return to Niebuhr's terminology, in order to accomplish good?

NSC-68 and the Problem of Moral Choice

The Truman administration made an effort of sorts to answer this question early in 1950, in connection with the drafting of NSC-68. That document involved a fundamental reexamination of national strategy, authorized by President Truman at the same time that he made the decision to build the hydrogen bomb, and carried out by an ad hoc committee of State and Defense Department officials, under the chairmanship of Paul Nitze. The committee took its charge very seriously, to the point of inquiring not only into the effectiveness of current and future strategies, but of attempting to fit them as well into a framework of moral standards appropriate to the conduct of United States foreign policy in the new Cold War. The result was the most morally self-conscious state paper of the era—but one that wound up justifying, in the end, amoral policies.[22]

NSC-68 began with a ringing endorsement of what it referred to as "the fundamental purpose of the United States": this was "to assure the integrity and vitality of our free society, which is founded upon the dignity and worth of the individual." The strength of free men, it argued, grew out of their ability to tolerate diversity; the task of a free society, therefore, was "to create and maintain an environment in which every individual has the opportunity to realize his creative powers." In international relations, "the prime reliance of the free society is on the strength and appeal of its idea, and it feels no compulsion sooner or later to bring all societies into conformity with it."

It followed that "the free society is limited in its choice of means to achieve its ends." The use of force, whether internally or externally, had to be a last resort, because "compulsion is the negation of freedom, except when it is used to enforce rights common to all.... The necessity of the act must be clear and compelling; the act must commend itself to the overwhelming majority as an inescapable exception to the basic idea of freedom; or the regenerative capacity of free men after the act has been performed will be endangered."[23]

Totalitarian societies felt no such constraints. There the individual "finds and can only find the meaning of his existence in serving the ends of the system. The system becomes God, and submission to the will of God becomes submission to the will of the system." Hence, "the Kremlin is able to select whatever means are expedient in seeking to carry out its fundamental design," which was suppression of the very climate of diversity free societies needed in order to function. It could act simultaneously on political, economic, military, ideological and psychological fronts without worrying about contradictions between them, or about undermining ultimate national objectives. "The Kremlin has inextricably engaged us," the authors of NSC-68 concluded, "in the conflict between its design and our purpose."

What to do? Here the authors of NSC-68 fell back upon none other than Alexander Hamilton, who had pointed out in *The Federalist* number 28 that "the idea of governing at all times by the simple force of law ... has no place but in the reveries of those political doctors whose sagacity disdains the admonitions of experimental instruction." There would surely be cases when the national government would have to resort to force, Hamilton had insisted. When this happened, the rule should be that "the means employed must be proportioned to the extent of the mischief."[24] This doctrine of proportionality provided, for Nitze and his colleagues, an answer to the agonizing question of how a nation that had to be scrupulous about means could, without risking moral bankruptcy, defend itself and its allies against a nation possessed of no such scruples:

> Our free society, confronted by a threat to its basic values, naturally will take such action, including the use of military force, as may be required to protect those values. The integrity of our system will not be jeopardized by any measures, overt or covert, violent or non-violent, which serve the purposes of frustrating the Kremlin design, nor does the necessity for conducting ourselves so as to affirm our values in actions as well as words forbid such measures, provided only they are appropriately calculated to that end and are not so excessive or misdirected as to make us enemies of the people instead of the evil men who have enslaved them.

This paragraph expresses better than any other document I have seen the way in which American officials resolved the fundamental moral dilemmas of containment through most of the Cold War. Survival, not only of the nation but of an external environment conducive to it, came first. In order to achieve those minimum requirements, there were no holds barred; anything was fair game. Beyond that point, though, the doctrine of proportionality came into play: the means employed were to be proportioned to the extent of the mischief.

Moral Relativism

For roughly the next two decades, this doctrine—perhaps we should call it "moral relativism"—held sway. Few, if any, of the officials who espoused it were eager to depart from traditionally acceptable standards of behavior; some of those who did worried deeply about their actions.[25] But most of them, in the end, came around to the view, first worked out in NSC-68, that in periods of mortal peril those standards could not stand in the way of whatever seemed required to defend national security. President Eisenhower put it best in 1955, in one of those remarkably candid private letters one finds throughout his papers: "I have come to the conclusion that some of our traditional ideas of international sportsmanship are scarcely applicable in the morass in which the world now flounders.... Truth, honor, justice, consideration for others, liberty for all—the problem is how to preserve them, nurture them and keep the peace—if this last is possible—when we are opposed by people who scorn to give any validity whatsoever to these values. I believe we can do it, but *we must not confuse these values with mere procedures, even though these last may have at one time held almost the status of moral concepts.*"[26]

As a result of this line of reasoning—which many in addition to Eisenhower shared—moral compromises made tentatively and with some anguish during the early days of the Cold War now became "mere procedures." Take, for example, the habit of exaggerating external threat in order to maintain public and Congressional support for containment. We now know that Eisenhower and Dulles never saw the Sino-Soviet bloc as a unified monolith; that Dulles even sought to implement strategies, some of which may have been successful, for driving a wedge between the two communist giants.[27] But the public knew nothing of this. Instead official rhetoric continued, well into the Kennedy and Johnson administrations, to portray a monolithic communist threat to the "free world"—primarily, one gathers, for fear that the domestic consensus in support of containment might crumble if the threat came to seem less awesome than in fact it appeared to be.

On a related issue, the so-called "missile gap," it is to Eisenhower's credit that he did not seek to exaggerate what proved to be an almost non-existent threat. But Kennedy, who had made much of the issue during the 1960 campaign, carried out a massive missile-building program even after learning what Eisenhower had known all along: that the Soviet threat had been grossly overrated. It was as if the new administration preferred to escalate the arms race—in the process probably setting off the actual Soviet building program that would bring the Russians to the point of parity with the United States in missile launchers by the end of the decade—rather than admit that it had been mistaken during the campaign.[28]

Exaggeration continued to be employed in other areas as well, most notably during the Vietnam War, where a succession of administrations tried to convince the American people, at first successfully but then with increasing difficulty, that an indigenous communist takeover in a country 10,000 miles away would endanger their vital interests at a time when the nation had just learned to live with an outright Soviet satellite 90 miles off its coastline. That this campaign worked at all testifies to what government can accomplish when it takes advantage of public credulity to stretch the truth; it also illustrates another danger of exaggeration, though, which is that those who indulge in it tend to lose touch over time with what the truth actually is.[29]

Intervention in the internal affairs of other countries also became accepted practice during those years. The administration of military and economic aid programs had evolved, by the time of Kennedy entered the White House, into efforts to restructure the nature of whole societies.[30] Relatively modest CIA operations of the late 1940s had grown into large-scale paramilitary maneuvers, attempts to overthrow entire governments, and even assassination plots against foreign leaders.[31] Somehow the idea had developed that the United States had not only the right but also the competence to reshape the behavior of states from within as well as from without, whenever, wherever, and by whatever means it thought necessary.

All of this was done, I would like to stress again, with the best of intentions. Every one of the interventions the United States carried out in other countries could be rationalized, convincingly or not, as a defense of self-determination. The "loss" of one of those countries to the "other side," Washington officials argued time and time again, would compromise the right of free choice far more than American intervention would. Confronted by what seemed to be extreme danger, one could engage in extreme actions, as the authors of NSC-68 had suggested, and still justify the latter as the lesser of two evils.

That same rationalization also drove the arms race, as official strategists came to emphasize deterrence through the accumulation of overwhelming and instantly deliverable force. Eisenhower, for example, saw nothing immoral about reliance on nuclear weapons as a deterrent, even in limited war situations. The alternative, he thought, would be the still greater evil of a permanent "garrison state," and the perpetual inflation that would result from trying to finance it. Eisenhower's successors never abandoned nuclear deterrence, but they did try to develop alternative means of discouraging enemy action that would not involve automatic escalation to all-out war: Kennedy's "special forces" were a conspicuous example. But, as the events of the 1960s would show, these in turn increased the chances of involvement in limited wars.

The difficulty in all of this was that in order for deterrence to work, the prospect of retaliation, whether at the nuclear or non-nuclear level, had to be made credible. One had to threaten the use of weapons one did not want to use in order to avoid having to use them. At the nuclear level, this strategy in effect held the world hostage to the ability of each side, as John Foster Dulles allegedly put it, to keep from going over the brink. At the conventional level, it encouraged the actual use of troops to project determination and discourage escalation by the other side, as in Vietnam. Deterrence therefore functioned by putting at risk what one was attempting to accomplish, and that procedure raised moral questions that are still very much with us today.[32]

My point is not to condemn those who engaged in these acts of "moral relativism"—this tactic of embracing one evil in order to forestall what seemed to be a greater one. It may well be that in periods of crisis this is the only way in which one can proceed: certainly that would appear to be the implication of much of Niebuhr's writing on this subject, and no one has written about it better. I am simply suggesting that the doctrine of "moral relativism" provided men at the top with a way of resolving this Niebuhrian dilemma during the more than two decades that separated the beginning of the Korean War from the end of the Vietnam War. And I am suggesting further that, until the very end of this period, they incurred surprisingly little criticism for acting in this way. Only in the late 1960s and early 1970s did "moral relativism" come under attack, and it is to that attack that I now want to turn.

The Attack on Moral Relativism

The event that, more than anything else, brought "moral relativism" into disrepute was, of course, the Vietnam War. It is important to recognize, though, that critics of that war did not always agree among themselves. There developed, during the conflict, two very different criticisms of American foreign policy, both of them strongly opposed to the "moral relativism" that had dominated thinking about containment for the previous two decades, but from dissimilar perspectives.

One of these we might characterize, for want of a better term, as the "realist" critique. Associated most clearly with Kennan himself and with Hans Morgenthau, advocates of this viewpoint did not dispute the assertions of NSC-68 that the United States had a vital interest in maintaining the world balance of power, or that the Soviet Union posed the most significant threat to that balance. Nor did they question the claim that the United States, in order to deal with the Soviet challenge, would have to embrace certain strategies associated more with old-fashioned "power politics" than with traditional American approaches to such matters. Where the "realists" differed from the policy-making community was over the issue of proportion: were the means being employed proportionate to the extent of the mischief?

The question had first come up in connection with the Eisenhower-Dulles "massive retaliation" strategy during the 1950s, when the "realists" charged the administration with having failed to proportion responses to offenses in a credible way; as a consequence, they argued, the nation retained no options other than escalation or surrender.[33] These criticisms failed, however, to undermine the Cold War foreign policy consensus, partly because some leading members of the Eisenhower administration quietly agreed with them,[34] but more significantly because Kennedy and his advisers moved rapidly after taking office in 1961 to adopt the "flexible response" strategy "realist" critics had been calling for.

By the mid-1960s, though, "flexible response" had produced disproportions of its own in Southeast Asia, with far more serious consequences for consensus at home. The "realists" charged that the Johnson administration had mistaken a peripheral interest for a vital one in Vietnam: that in its effort to have its way there it was committing American forces in a manner wholly inappropriate to the extent of the threat that existed; and that, as a consequence, it was neglecting other more serious dangers, both external and internal. These criticisms were based not so much on the immorality of American actions in Vietnam as on their disproportionality. Called into question here was not so much the view that in situations of mortal peril all means are justified to secure desired ends, but rather the assertion that the situation in Vietnam posed such a mortal peril. Major means, in short, had been dispatched to counter minor mischief.

The other critique, which we might here label "radical," proceeded from fundamentally different assumptions. It did not accept the "realist" view that conflict was endemic in the international system. It questioned the efficacy of such strategies as "containment" and "deterrence" for dealing with such conflicts as did arise. It assigned to the United States, to a much greater extent than the "realists" did, responsibility for the origins, escalation, and perpetuation of the Cold War. And it challenged, above all else, "moral relativism," not on the grounds of disproportion, as had the "realists," but on the more fundamental basis that to tolerate behavior in the international sphere that would not be acceptable in personal or in domestic affairs was to be inconsistent, hypocritical, and ultimately immoral, regardless of the justification for such behavior. There could be, in the "radical" view, no double standard.[35]

To be sure, domestic political as well as intellectual trends contributed to the decline of "moral relativism." I refer here, of course, to the dramatic weakening of presidential authority over foreign policy that resulted from the Vietnam War and from the Watergate scandal, in itself an episode that provoked powerful indictments of "moral relativism." A bewildering array of individuals and organizations—official and otherwise—rushed in to fill the vacuum, with the consequence that the direction of foreign affairs became more diffused than it had been at any other point during the Cold War. Not surprisingly, this left more room than in the past for evaluating the policy process from divergent frames of moral reference.[36]

It is worth noting as well that the overwhelming sense of international crisis that had produced the doctrine of "moral relativism" in the first place had, by the early 1970s, begun to fade. The authors of NSC-68 themselves had suggested, at least by implication, that such "relativism" was appropriate only in periods of great peril; they would probably have accepted the notion that a relaxation of tensions on the world scene—a move toward detente, if you will—might provide a proper occasion to tighten standards distinguishing appropriate from inappropriate behavior in international affairs.

The combined effect of all of this was to bring about, by the mid-1970s, a more serious debate about the relationship of morality to foreign policy than had taken place since the earliest days of the Cold War. Basically, the argument revolved around the competing priorities of order and justice. Should the nation's geopolitical interest in building a stable international order take precedence over its moral commitment to human rights? Or should human rights come first, even if that approach jeopardized the prospects for stability?

The "realist" position on this was clear: order was the prerequisite for justice. Niebuhr had worked out the argument years before when he had pointed out that human rights could hardly flourish in conditions of war, anarchy, or revolution. "Some balance of power is the basis of whatever justice is achieved in international relations," he had written in 1942.[37] Kennan had made the same point consistently throughout his career.[38] And Henry Kissinger embraced it as well in a series of eloquent speeches as Secretary of State that have never been given the attention they deserve. "The true task of statesmanship," he argued in 1975, "is to draw from the balance of power a more positive capacity to better the human condition." Or, as he put it in his memoirs: "If history teaches anything it is that there can be no peace without equilibrium and no justice without restraint."[39]

But the opposite position, with its view of human rights as the primary American interest, in the end overwhelmed the "realist" approach; although this happened more, one suspects, for domestic political than for intellectual reasons. The issue of human rights provided the only common ground around which both liberal and conservative critics of Kissinger could rally. Liberals could protest the Nixon and Ford administrations' alignment with regimes such as those of the Shah in Iran, or of Pinochet in Chile. Conservatives could use human rights violations as excuses to berate the Soviet Union and other communist countries, with a view to undermining support for detente. Jimmy Carter responded to both appeals during the 1976 campaign, pledging to bring the conduct of American foreign policy back into line with the moral principles for which the United States was supposed to stand: "We've seen a loss of morality...and we're ashamed of what our government is as we deal with other nations around the world....What we seek is...a foreign policy that reflects the decency and generosity and common sense of our own people."[40]

The result was that human rights gained a higher priority during Carter's administration than at any other point in the history of the Cold War; ironically, the effect of this was to intensify the Cold War rather than to make it possible to move beyond it, as Carter had hoped to do. Complaints about human rights violations in the Soviet Union undermined the atmosphere of relative good will that had developed between Washington and Moscow during the Nixon and Ford administrations; the most prominent resulting casualty was progress in the strategic arms limitation talks. Whether Carter's preoccupation with human rights induced the Russians to exploit what they saw as Western weaknesses in places like Angola, Ethiopia, Mozambique, and Afghanistan is still unclear; what is clear, though, is that his cautious attempts to disassociate the United States from authoritarian regimes in Iran and Nicaragua backfired when those governments gave way to outspokenly anti-American regimes. They probably would have done so in any event, but Carter got credit for having given them the final push. By the beginning of 1980, the Russians had actually invaded Afghanistan, the SALT II treaty was dead, and Ronald Reagan was building his presidential campaign around precisely the opposite emphasis from the one Carter had employed four years earlier. The focus now would be on a return to the Cold War, and, at least by implication, the same "moral relativism" that had characterized its earlier prosecution.[41]

Reagan and the Return to Idealism

But history is full of ironies. Far from abandoning the connection between morality and foreign policy, as most people had expected it to do, the Reagan administration wound up re-establishing that connection in much the way Carter had hoped—but had ultimately failed—to do. By 1989, there was a closer correspondence between traditional American ideals and the actual conduct of American diplomacy than at any point since the Marshall Plan. The country did once again have a foreign policy it could be proud of, but it had achieved it on Ronald Reagan's watch. There were several reasons for this surprising development:

The first had to do with the strange tendency, in politics, for expediency to become conviction. The immediate impulse that had caused conservatives like Reagan to join with liberals in embracing the cause of human rights during the early 1970s—a common distrust of Henry Kissinger and his policies—gradually transformed itself into a new foreign policy consensus. Kissinger himself had deferred to it, somewhat reluctantly, by insisting upon the conclusion of agreements safegarding human rights at the thirty-four nation Conference on Security and Cooperation in Europe, held at Helsinki in 1975: these for the first time established a basis in international law upon which states could protest human rights violations inside other states.⁴² And by raising the issue so conspicuously in relations with Moscow, the Carter administration inadvertantly confirmed its value for conservatives, who—unlike liberals—were prepared to use concern over human rights to undermine detente. By the time Reagan took office in 1981, he had become a staunch supporter of the Helsinki agreeements (despite having opposed them in 1975);⁴³ his administration was ardent in its support for human rights in the Soviet Union and Eastern Europe, if not always elsewhere. Domestic politics, therefore, brought about a return to at least the appearance of idealism in foreign policy.

Second, it was becoming increasingly difficult even for supporters of detente to continue to make excuses for the gap between ideals and accomplishments in the domestic and foreign policies of the Soviet Union. After six and a half decades of Marxism-Leninism the state had not withered away, the classless society had not materialized, proletarians of all nations had not arisen, standards of living had not improved, and the personal liberty that communism had long promised looked like a cruel hoax. It had been possible for sympathetic observers to attribute these shortcomings, over the years, to the difficulties of industrializing a peasant society, or to the destruction suffered in fighting World War II, or to the pressures of Cold War competition with the United States; but only up to a point. Soviet leaders could not indefinitely postpone the objectives they had set for their society without the world—and the Soviet people themselves—taking note of the growing disparity between intentions and results.⁴⁴ If departures from ideals existed in American policies, they were nothing compared with what the Kremlin had managed to achieve.

Third, the leaders of the Soviet Union had chosen this inopportune moment to increase military and economic assistance to Marxist governments in South and Southeast Asia, southern and eastern Africa, and Central America and the Caribbean, apparently in the belief that Marxism was the wave of the future in those parts of the world. When that vision proved to be myopic, Moscow was stuck with the messy task of supporting an unpromising array of unpopular clients against increasingly critical populations; in Afghanistan that task had even involved the Soviet military in a costly, Vietnam-like, no-win war. For once, it was Russians, not Americans or their European allies, who looked like imperialists in a post-imperial age, and that too was a different pattern from the one that had existed throughout most of the Cold War.

The effect of these intersecting trends was to give Reagan's administration an opportunity not enjoyed by any since that of Truman: the chance to make containment work by standing for, rather than by compromising, American ideals. It was possible, once again, to be for human rights, for self-determination, for economic development, for nationalism, even for the minimal use of American military force in the world, and still have these positions produce the desired geopolitical outcome. The loosely defined Reagan Doctrine—which proclaimed that the United States would assist "freedom fighters" seeking to throw off the stifling constraints of externally-imposed authoritarianism—provided a way to bring aspirations and accomplishments back into line with one another. "Our mission," President Reagan told the Congress in February, 1985, "is to nourish and defend freedom and democracy and to communicate these ideas everywhere we can."[45] And he added, two years later, in words that could as easily have come from Carter—or, for that matter, from Truman: "A foreign policy that ignored the fate of millions around the world who seek freedom would be a betrayal of our national heritage."[46]

The Reagan administration also rejected, or appeared to reject, Cold War moral compromises in the realm of nuclear strategy. Like most Americans, Reagan himself had never understood, and hence had never been comfortable with, the conventional wisdom on arms control and deterrence. The SALT negotiations, he argued, had become an elaborate subterfuge that allowed the Russians—and, he might have added, the Americans as well—to continue building precisely the weapons the negotiators were seeking to control: why not simply junk the whole process and begin talking about *reducing*, not just *limiting*, nuclear arms?[47] The idea of "mutual assured destruction," he later recalled, "somehow . . . didn't seem to me to be something that would send you to bed feeling safe."[48] The Strategic Defense Initiative, Reagan's most distinctive personal policy innovation, managed brilliantly to call into question old approaches to arms control but also to accelerate that process. Not only did it condemn, by implication, the "morally relative" doctrine of MAD; it also defused a growing nuclear freeze movement by endorsing as the administration's avowed objective the ultimate abolition of *all* nuclear weapons; and, as noted in a previous chapter, it served as a major impetus to reform—and therefore to future progress on arms control—within the Soviet Union.[49] One could be for defense, deterrence, military spending, technological advance, and a nuclear-free world all at the same time, it appeared. Or, at least, Ronald Reagan could be.

There was yet another way in which the Reagan administration brought aspirations into line with accomplishments, and that had to do with the familiar problem of when to negotiate with the Soviet Union. Like most of his predecessors, Reagan endorsed the principle—dating back to the Truman and Eisenhower administrations—of "negotiation from strength." He differed from previous presidents, though, in that he took the principle literally: once one had achieved strength, one negotiated. Even while indulging in the strident Cold War rhetoric that characterized his first two and a half years in office, Reagan was careful never to rule out negotiations; the emphasis during that period, though, had been on rebuilding American military strength, and also—equally important—American self-confidence.[50] But from 1983 on, the President made it clear that he was absolutely serious about negotiations, and in 1985 he found a willing partner in Mikhail Gorbachev. It was no longer necessary to *claim* to be eager for negotiations while actually trying to avoid them; negotiations were now taking place, and producing significant results.

To be sure, the Reagan administration's record of reconciling ideals and interests in foreign policy was hardly perfect. The President's support for human rights in those parts of the Third World not under Soviet control or the threat of it was, at best, lukewarm.[51] Under the leadership of William Casey the Central Intelligence Agency shifted back to its old pattern of combining covert action with inadequate accountability, especially in connection with the mining of Nicaraguan harbors and the subsequent Iran-Contra scandal.[52] And, as this latter episode made very clear, there was always a distressing vagueness about who was actually running things during the Reagan years. The President himself seemed so remote from the details of his own policies that some scholars have begun to see his administration as a textbook example of "dispersion of the decision-making process in a pluralist democracy."[53]

The criticism is fair enough: Reagan was by no means a "hands-on" chief executive. Nor was he a sophisticated student of international affairs, or of anything else, for that matter, except the making of images. But images have always been an important aspect of political leadership, and they relate closely to the problem of morality in foreign affairs. For if that problem does in fact boil down to what Schlesinger suggests it does, which is avoiding the double bookkeeping that comes from having one set of aspirations for what government does at home and a different one to guide its activities overseas, then the linkage of ideals with policies—an exercise that requires the invocation of images—becomes crucial. Reagan's tendency to think in terms of images put him in closer touch with the thinking of most Americans than were most of the "professionals" who had run American foreign policy over the past several decades; his skill at manipulating images allowed him to succeed where several of his predecessors had failed by re-establishing a sense of direction in American diplomacy that the American people could support.[54]

The result was not necessarily a "moral" foreign policy. As I noted at the beginning of this essay, absolute standards of morality are difficult to establish in international relations, and it has not been my purpose here to try to do so. My point is simply that Ronald Reagan, as the end of the Cold War approached, had brought the practice of American foreign policy into a closer correspondence with traditional American ideals than had existed since the earliest days of the Cold War. That single accomplishment, even if it took place largely in the realm of imagery, went quite a way toward compensating for the President's many other, but mostly less significant, shortcomings.

Conclusion

"The greatest danger that can befall us in coping with this problem of Soviet Communism," George Kennan had written in the conclusion to the famous "long telegram" of February, 1946, "is that we shall allow ourselves to become like those with whom we are coping."[55] We have, for the most part, avoided that danger: the United States at the end of the Cold War no more resembles a Stalinist state than it did at the beginning of that conflict. Given the dangers of taking on an adversary's characteristics in the process of resisting that adversary, that is an important accomplishment. But even more impressive is the fact that the world at large, and even the Soviet Union itself, has gradually moved toward repudiating authoritarianism as well. The process had been under way for many years, but it took the events of 1989 to make clear just how thorough that repudiation has actually been. One early Cold War visionary, it is worth recalling, had expected the Western democracies to have arrived at their own Stalinist phase five years earlier.[56] George Orwell, a man keenly aware of the importance of keeping what one does aligned with what one is supposed to stand for, would have relished knowing how inaccurate his timetable—and his vision of ultimate destinations—has turned out to be.

FOUR

 The Unexpected
John Foster Dulles

The cartoon images, thanks to the malicious genius of Herblock, still stick in our minds: John Foster Dulles as a pudgy Superman, pushing an alarmed Uncle Sam over the brink with the reassuring comment, "Don't be afraid—I can always pull you back." Or a complacent Secretary of State following Chiang Kai-shek down into a swamp filled with rotting garbage and voracious alligators, pulling a befuddled Eisenhower and—again—a worried Uncle Sam along behind him. Or a sour-faced Dulles standing with bags packed for the summit, swathed in layers of coats, blankets, earmuffs, scarves and caps, grimly clutching a hot water bottle and an umbrella, while a smiling short-sleeved Eisenhower tells the Russians over the telephone: "Yes, we'll be there, rain *and* shine." Or Dulles as an aloof grocer, presiding over a freezer stocked with "frozen attitudes," "frozen platitudes," and "frosted fruitless policies," while a frustrated American housewife plaintively asks: "Don't you ever have anything fresh?"[1]

It has often been said of Dulles that he lent himself to caricature: the public appearance of sanctimonious stuffiness, the tendency to let self-confidence become self-congratulation, the penchant for grandiloquent phrase-making, the apparent lawyer-like rigidity in the face of change, even his obvious fondness for diplomacy by airplane—all seemed to confirm Herblock's image of the determined but narrow-minded ideological crusader, relentlessly assaulting the ramparts of monolithic communism, brandishing nuclear weapons at every opportunity, heedless of the risks this involved to the nation, and to the world.

Like most caricatures, this one did less than justice to its subject, a fact that has not escaped the attention of Dulles's biographers. Early studies by Louis Gerson and Michael Guhin suggested something of the extent to which the real Dulles only approximately resembled his public image.[2] Townsend Hoopes's 1973 biography, although basically critical of Dulles and certainly quite wrong in its underestimation of Eisenhower, was still a more balanced account than its lurid title suggested.[3] And, most recently, Ronald Pruessen has given us an impressive account of Dulles's career up to the time he became Secretary of State, one that takes fully into account his multi-dimensional character and sometimes puzzling complexities.[4]

But there still is no major reassessment of Dulles's role as Secretary of State in the light of the vast body of archival materials from the Eisenhower administration that have been opened for research during the past decade and a half.[5] Eisenhower's own reputation has soared as these documents have become available, and it is generally accepted now that it was he, not Dulles, who really ran foreign policy.[6] The Secretary of State was by no means a cipher, however; despite careful deference to the President, Dulles still influenced administration policy in important ways. The new documents suggest that the positions he took on the issues and the manner in which he dealt with them are, in some ways, as surprising as what we have now learned about Eisenhower himself.

What follows is a preliminary reconstruction of Dulles's thinking, based on these new materials, with regard to three important issues: nuclear weapons, international communism, and the possibility of ending the Cold War through negotiations with the Soviet Union. My intent, in this essay, is twofold: to suggest the need for reassessing the nature of Dulles's influence on the Eisenhower administration's foreign and national security policy; and to make the more general point that even those public figures whose outward behavior persuades us that we know them very well can in fact remain largely unknown to us. If we are to avoid oversimplifying the role of individuals in positions of leadership—and if we are to take advantage of the opportunity the end of the Cold War gives us to reconsider its major personalities—then we will need to take into account the possibility that these "hidden" or "unexpected" characteristics played a role in determining "what actually happened.'"[7]

Nuclear Weapons

Dulles's ideas on nuclear weapons had become widely known, even before his appointment as Secretary of State, through a controversial article he had published in *Life* magazine in May, 1952. Appropriately titled "A Policy of Boldness," it criticized the Truman administration's approach to containment as too costly: the expenditures necessary to sustain a policy of resisting aggression wherever it occurred, without either escalation or capitulation, were unbalancing the budget, alarming allies, and even eroding civil liberties. If a single limited war in Korea could produce these effects, Dulles seemed to be saying, where would more serious conflicts lead? "Ours are treadmill policies which, at best, might perhaps keep us in the same place until we drop exhausted."

The solution, Dulles argued, was to regain the initiative: to find ways to make containment work more efficiently at less cost. One way was to rely, to a greater extent than in the past, upon American technological superiority over the Russians—particularly as reflected in the development of nuclear weapons and the means of delivering them—to *deter* the outbreak of war. Those devices had been thought of, up to that point, as instruments with which to *fight* wars. If war occurred, though, "it will be because we have allowed these new and awesome forces to become the ordinary killing tools of the soldier when, in the hands of the statesmen, they could serve as effective political weapons in defense of the peace." The way to ensure peace was to "develop the will and organize the means to retaliate instantly against open aggression by Red armies, so that, if it occurred anywhere, we could and would strike back where it hurts, by means of our own choosing."[8]

Curiously, though, Dulles did not stress his strategy of "retaliation" during the early months of the Eisenhower administration, despite the fact that the President himself had been quick to raise the possibility of actually using nuclear weapons to end the fighting in Korea.[9] It was true that the Russians had succeeded "in setting atomic weapons apart from all other weapons," the new Secretary of State told the National Security Council in February, 1953; as a consequence, there was a "moral problem" that tended to inhibit their actual use in limited war situations like Korea. "We should try to break down this false distinction."[10] But when Dulles briefed the National Security Council the following month on prospects for global war, he did not even mention nuclear deterrence as a way to prevent it, placing his emphasis instead on solidarity with allies, the retention of outposts around the periphery of the Soviet bloc, and the possibility of "inducing the disintegration of Soviet power" by taking advantage of its overextension.[11]

Dulles did lecture the National Security Council in June, 1953, on the virtues of what would later come to be known as "brinksmanship." The United States, he suggested, should "undertake certain efforts to prevent further significant expansion of Soviet power, even at the risk of war." These would not require actually going to war, "but rather that we would take actions which the Soviets, if they chose, could consider a *casus belli*." It was unlikely, Dulles thought, that they would do so: the formation of NATO and the signing of the Japanese peace treaty had "greatly irritated" the Russians, but they had not gone to war. Washington should not refrain from acting simply out of fear that it might push the Russians into initiating hostilities.[12]

But Dulles also stressed that unilateral threats of nuclear retaliation, if they risked disrupting relations with allies, could be dangerously counterproductive. News that the Russians had tested their own thermonuclear weapon in August, 1953, caused the Secretary of State to worry about how long the United States could maintain military bases overseas, especially "if the countries containing these bases increasingly look upon them as lightning rods rather than umbrellas." Alternatively, though, if the United States were to reduce its conventional forces in Europe—as the administration's "New Look" strategy seemed to imply it might—this would appear to Europeans as "final proof of an isolationist trend and the adoption of a 'Fortress America' concept. . . . The balance of world power, military and economic, would doubtless shift rapidly to our great disadvantage."[13] The presence of American bases therefore invited allied demoralization through the threat of Soviet attack; but the prospect of withdrawing those bases was equally certain to demoralize allies by raising fears of American abandonment.

The dilemma suggests something of the importance Dulles accorded to alliances: just because one had nuclear superiority did not mean that one was free to act as one liked, without considering what allies might think. When an American thermonuclear bomb test in the Pacific accidentally irradiated the crew of a Japanese fishing boat in March, 1954, the Secretary of State reacted very strongly, warning Atomic Energy Commission Chairman Lewis Strauss of the need to be sensitive to "the tremendous repercussions these things have." The "wave of hysteria" that had resulted "is driving our Allies away from us. They think we are getting ready for a war of this kind. We could survive but some of them would be obliterated in a few minutes. It could lead to a policy of neutrality or appeasement."[14]

Several weeks later, Dulles recommended a nuclear test moratorium to the National Security Council, provided it could be demonstrated that the recent series of tests had placed the United States ahead of the Soviet Union, and if the moratorium could be policed. The basic reason the British had not been more helpful in sustaining the American position at the Geneva Conference on Indochina "was their obsession over the H-bomb and its potential effect on the British Isles." Comparisons were even being made between American "militaristic" tendencies and "Hitler's military machine." It simply was not possible to "sit here in Washington and develop bigger bombs without any regard for the impact of these developments on world opinion. In the long run it isn't only bombs that win wars, but having public opinion on your side."[15]

Dulles in the end allowed himself to be talked out of the moratorium for a variety of reasons: it might impede the enterprise of American atomic scientists by discouraging experimentation; it might be difficult to monitor; the Russians might be able to turn to their advantage any moratorium "tailored" to preserve American superiority; such a moratorium could create a "climate" of opinion in which it might be difficult to resume testing if that became necessary.[16] The decision not to seek a moratorium, Dulles told the National Security Council on June 23, illustrated "the power of reason against the power of will," since the hope had been to be able to reach a different conclusion. But as long as the United States remained opposed to the total abolition of nuclear weapons except as part of a general disarmament program, it could not accept "any position which would in effect set these weapons apart from other weapons as morally bad."[17]

The Secretary of State returned to the difficulty of dealing with allies when the National Security Council reconvened the following day. Because of what appeared to be the growing danger of atomic war, he insisted, "our 'tough policy' was becoming increasingly unpopular throughout the free world; whereas the British 'soft policy' was gaining prestige and acceptance both in Europe and Asia." The Joint Chiefs of Staff had recommended that the United States take full advantage of its nuclear superiority to exert pressure on the Soviet Union. "If we do so, however, very few of our allies will follow us." Geneva had provided confirmation that "the tide is running against us in the channel of this tough policy. If we are to continue to pursue it we shall lose many of our allies, and this in itself compels a reappraisal of our basic policy....We must recognize the fact that we can no longer run the free world, and accordingly review our basic security policy."[18]

Dulles further developed his position in a National Security Council discussion in August, 1954. NSC 5422/1, a revision of the administration's basic "New Look" strategy, had contained language providing that "if general war should occur, the United States should wage it with all available weapons and should continue to make clear its determination to do so." Dulles expressed no objection to this contemplated use of "all available weapons" in all-out war, but he did find unwise the "boast of our nuclear capabilities" which the statement implied. "Talk of atomic attack," he noted, "tended to create 'peace at any price people' and might lead to an increase of appeasement sentiment in various countries. The Russians are smarter on this question because they never talk about using atomic weapons."[19] It would be difficult to overestimate the importance of appearing before the world "as a peaceful state," he added a week later. Propaganda picturing us as warmongers on account of our atomic capabilities has done incalculable harm."[20]

All of these comments—with their clear implication that the most fundamental aspects of national strategy needed rethinking—came only months after Dulles had called, in his much-quoted January, 1954, speech to the Council on Foreign Relations, for reliance on the "deterrent of massive retaliatory power" as a way to show potential aggressors that they could not, henceforth, hope to achieve their aims.[21] They also followed the Secretary of State's careful reformulation of his public position in the April, 1954, issue of *Foreign Affairs*.[22] And they came after Dulles had told a NATO ministerial meeting that same month that "it should be our agreed policy, in case of either general or local war, to use atomic weapons as conventional weapons against the military assets of the enemy whenever and wherever it would be of advantage to do so, taking account of all relevant factors."[23] They suggest, at a minimum, that Dulles's conspicuous public statements about the virtues of "massive retaliation" were a less than complete reflection of what he actually believed.

It might well be, Dulles acknowledged in a top secret assessment of national strategy late in 1954, that "the increased destructiveness of nuclear weapons and the approach of effective atomic parity are creating a situation in which general war would threaten the destruction of Western civilization and of the Soviet regime, and in which national objectives could not be attained through a general war, even if a military victory were won. A situation of mutual deterrence to general war could result." Miscalculations could, of course, always happen. Efforts by the communists to spread their influence by means short of war would still take place. But because "total war would be an incalculable disaster," the primary aim of future American policy would have to be "to deter any Communist armed aggression and to avoid the danger that such aggression would develop into general nuclear war."

What that required was for the United States and its allies to "maintain sufficient flexible military capabilities, and firmness of policy, to convince the Communist rulers that the U. S. and its allies have the means to ensure that aggression will not pay and the will to use military force if the situation requires." The West should, however, forgo "actions which would generally be regarded as provocative," and "be prepared, if hostilities occur, to meet them, where feasible, in a manner and on a scale which will not inevitably broaden them into total nuclear war." These cautions were necessary "to assure the support of our allies against aggression and to avoid risks which do not promise commensurate strategic or political gains."[24] The distance separating the architect of "massive retaliation" from what would later come to be known as the doctrine of "flexible response" was, it seems, less than one might have thought.

The basic policy the United States had followed through the end of 1954, Dulles admitted, had been "pretty good," even if "it hasn't got us into war." Not getting into a war, after all, was no bad thing. The positions the United States had taken with regard to the German question, Indochina, and the Chinese offshore islands could hardly be described as "craven": "it would be difficult to argue that our policies are not strong, firm, and indicative of a willingness to run risks. But our policy was none the less one which fell short of actually provoking war."

That policy had assumed, though, continued American nuclear superiority. The great difficulty Dulles saw on the horizon was "the forthcoming achievement of atomic plenty and a nuclear balance of power between the U. S. and the U. S. S. R." It was not at all clear how the United States could prevent the Russians from achieving that "nuclear balance" without going to war with them. More active policies in such areas as Indochina or China, of the kind the Joint Chiefs of Staff had advocated, would not solve that problem.[25]

Dulles expanded on this argument at a National Security Council meeting later in December, 1954. He could not help but have some sympathy for the Joint Chiefs' call for "greater dynamism" in American policies toward the Russians and the Chinese Communists; he himself had campaigned on just this point in 1952. "However, experience indicated that it was not easy to go very much beyond the point that this Administration had reached in translating a dynamic policy into courses of action, and in any case we had been more dynamic than our predecessors." Preventive war was "of course" ruled out. Strong and forceful efforts to change the character of the Soviet system, or to overthrow communist regimes in Eastern Europe and China, or to detach those countries from the Soviet bloc "would involve the United States in general war." Even if the United States could somehow break up Soviet control over Eastern Europe and China, "this in itself would not actually touch the heart of the problem: Soviet atomic plenty." And although these more aggressive policies, if successful, "might result in the disintegration of the Soviet bloc, they would almost certainly cause the disintegration of the free world bloc, . . . for our allies would never go along with such courses of action as these."[26]

In the end, Dulles concluded, the only real solution for the problem of expanding Soviet nuclear capabilities might be nuclear abolition. It was true, he admitted, that if the United States should agree to eliminate nuclear weapons alone, "we would be depriving ourselves of those weapons in which the U. S. was ahead and would not be taking action in the area of Soviet superiority, the conventional armaments field." It was unlikely that the means would ever be developed to monitor conventional force disarmament. But "it could be argued that atomic weapons are the only ones by which the U. S. can be virtually destroyed through a sudden attack, and if this danger of destruction should be removed by eliminating nuclear weapons this would help the U. S. by enabling retention intact of our industrial power which has acted both as a deterrent against total war and as a principal means of winning a war."[27]

A year later, almost on the eve of the famous *Life* magazine interview with James Shepley in which he had extolled the virtues of going to the brink of war as a means of preserving peace, Dulles discussed the future of nuclear deterrence with a recuperating Eisenhower—the President had suffered his heart attack three months earlier—in the White House. As Dulles himself recorded the conversation: "I said that I had come to the conclusion that our whole international security structure was in jeopardy. The basic thesis was local defensive strength with the backing up of United States atomic striking power. However, that striking power was apt to be immobilized by moral repugnance. If this happened, the whole structure could readily collapse."

Dulles went on to say that he had come to believe "that atomic power was too vast a power to be left for the military use of any one country." Its use, he thought, should be "internationalized for security purposes." The United States might well consider calling together the forty-two nations with which it had security treaties, placing before them a proposal for an international group that would decide "when and how to use atomic weapons for defense—always reserving of course the right of the United States, in the event that it was directly attacked, to use whatever means it had." If and when the Soviet Union was prepared to forego the right of veto, the group might then transfer this responsibility to the United Nations Security Council, "so as to universalize the capacity of atomic thermonuclear weapons to deter aggression." Eisenhower's response, somewhat neutrally, was that the idea was "an interesting one."[28]

Encouraged by the President to develop his ideas, the Secretary of State prepared a long memorandum early in 1956, in which he noted that Soviet nuclear capabilities might well grow, within a few years, to the point at which they could "at a single stroke, virtually obliterate our industrial power and . . . simultaneously gravely impair our capacity to retaliate." That retaliatory capacity would then lose its deterrent effect, and "the United States might become endangered as never before." Indeed, the *psychological* loss of superiority might well precede its *actual* loss, because "it would be generally assumed that the use of *our* nuclear power is so restricted by constitutional and democratic processes and moral restraints that we would never be able to use it *first*; and conditions could be such that only the first use would have great significance.... Repugnance to the use of nuclear weapons could grow to a point which would depreciate our value as an ally, undermine confidence in our 'collective defense' concepts, and make questionable the reliability of our allies and the availability to SAC of our foreign bases."

All of this only reflected the fact that "there is throughout the world a growing, and not unreasonable, fear that nuclear weapons are expanding at such a pace as to endanger human life on this planet.... The peoples of the world cry out for statesmanship that will find a way to assure that this new force shall serve humanity, not destroy it." This responsibility very largely fell to the United States, but meeting it would require more than the "Atoms for Peace" or "Open Skies" proposals that had already been put forward. If the nation failed to meet that responsibility, "our moral leadership in the world could be stolen from us by those whose creed denies moral principles."

The ultimate solution, Dulles suggested, would be to vest a veto-less United Nations Security Council with control "of sufficient atomic weapons, and means of delivery, as to overbalance any atomic or other weapons as might be surreptitiously retained by any nation." Prior to this, the United States might seek commitments from nations possessing nuclear capabilities to use them only in accordance with recommendations from the General Assembly. Regional groups, too—NATO would be the model—could be set up "to study and plan the means whereby nuclear weapons could most effectively be used to deter armed attack and to preserve peace in each region." The critical task would be to get the United States away from its "present vulnerable position [of having] virtually the sole responsibility in the free world with respect to the use of nuclear weapons,... a responsibility which is not governed by any clearly enunciated principles reflecting 'decent respect for the opinions of mankind'."[29]

Although nothing came of Dulles's sweeping proposals, he continued throughout the rest of his term as Secretary of State to reiterate with Eisenhower the concerns he had articulated. For example, in December, 1956, in the immediate wake of the Suez and Hungarian crises, Dulles warned that in his view "a 'showdown' with Russia would not have more than one chance in three of working, and two chances out of three of making global war inevitable."[30] But the Russians too would have difficulty translating nuclear strength into political advantage. In November, 1957, in connection with a discussion of Strategic Air Command vulnerabilities, Dulles dismissed the possibility of a Soviet surprise attack as "remote" on the grounds that "such an attack without provocation involving casualties of perhaps one hundred million would be so abhorrent-to all who survived in any part of the world that [he] did not think that even the Soviet rulers would dare to accept the consequences."[31]

In April, 1958, Dulles again raised with Eisenhower "the question of our national strategic concept." The difficulty was that "this too much invoked massive nuclear attack in the event of any clash anywhere of U.S. with Soviet forces." There were, Dulles argued, "increasing possibilities of effective defense through tactical nuclear weapons and other means short of wholesale obliteration of the Soviet Union, and...these should be developed more rapidly." It was a vicious circle: "so long as the strategic concept contemplated this, our arsenal of weapons had to be adapted primarily to that purpose and so long as our arsenal of weapons was adequate only for that kind of a response, we were compelled to rely on that kind of a response." It was, of course, the case that "our deterrent power might be somewhat weakened if it were known that we contemplated anything less than 'massive retaliation' and therefore the matter had to be handled with the greatest care."[32]

What this new evidence suggests, then, is that the traditional view of Dulles as an uncritical enthusiast for strategies based solely on nuclear deterrence is profoundly wrong; that, indeed, the Secretary of State himself anticipated many of the criticisms advocates of "flexible response" would later make of such strategies; and that he even contemplated, as a long-range goal and on both geopolitical and moral grounds, the abolition of nuclear weapons altogether.

International Communism

A second area where the documents suggest we need to revise our thinking about John Foster Dulles has to do with his understanding of international communism. In his first televised address as Secretary of State only a week after the Eisenhower administration took office, Dulles had dramatically unveiled a map showing the "vast area" stretching from Central Europe to Kamchatka and including China, "which the Russian Communists completely dominate." In the few years since the end of World War II, the number of people under their rule had expanded from 200 to 800 million, "and they're hard at work to get control of other parts of the world." The strategy was one of "encirclement": "Soviet communists" would seek to avoid all-out war but would work "to get control of the different areas around them and around us, so they will keep growing in strength and we will be more and more cut off and isolated. And they have been making very great progress."[33]

At first glance, the tone and content of this speech appear to fit the widely held view of Dulles as an ideological literalist, convinced—as were many other people at the time—that adherence to the doctrines of Marx and Lenin automatically meant subservience to Moscow. Dulles himself encouraged this view: all one had to do to anticipate communist behavior, he repeatedly said, was to read Stalin's *Problems of Leninism*, "the present-day Communist bible, ... [that] gives us the same preview Hitler gave in *Mein Kampf*."[34] Associates recall him pulling the book off the shelf at the slightest provocation and citing it "with surprising accuracy" to prove his point.[35] The world confronted, Dulles liked to stress, "a vast monolithic system which, despite its power, believes that it cannot survive except as it succeeds in progressively destroying human freedom."[36]

But Dulles said something else in that initial January, 1953, television address that should have suggested a more complex view of international communism than what could be gleaned from reading Stalin on Lenin. Resorting to what what one student of the subject has called "gastronomic" imagery, Dulles reminded his audience that although the "Russian Communists ... have swallowed a great many people to date, ... there is such a thing as indigestion. People don't always get stronger by eating more." Signs of indigestion were already apparent within the Soviet bloc: "perhaps in time the indigestion will become so acute that it might be fatal." At the time, these references seemed simply to echo Dulles's calls, made during the 1952 campaign, for the "liberation" of the Soviet Union's East European satellites; the Secretary of State himself suggested as much in his speech.[37] But the documents show that a deeper and more sophisticated understanding of international communism lay behind these pronouncements.

The "great weakness in the present brand of communism," Dulles had written in a memorandum to himself in 1949, "is insistence on absolute conformity to a pattern made in Russia. That does not work in areas where the economic and social problems are different from those in Russia and where there are deep-seated national and cultural loyalties."[38] China, he thought, was such an area: "It is not necessary to reconquer China by subsidizing a vast military operation," he wrote Senator Homer Ferguson. "Communism will disintegrate in China, and the Chinese themselves will take care of that, because of its inability to solve the problems of China."[39] The outbreak of the Korean War and China's intervention in it convinced Dulles that the break with the Soviet Union would not come soon. But, as he wrote to Dean Acheson in November, 1950, in the long run "our best defense lies in exploiting potential jealousies, rivalries, and disaffections within the present area of Soviet communist control so as to divert them from external adventures to the problem of attempting to consolidate an already over-extended position."[40]

Where Dulles differed from Acheson was not on whether the Sino-Soviet alliance would break up, but on how one could best accelerate that process. Even after the Chinese had intervened in Korea, Acheson still thought it might be possible to lure Beijing from its ties with Moscow, whether by convincing Mao and his advisers that the Russians had imperial aspirations in Asia, or through surreptitious contacts with shadowy groups believed capable of overthrowing Mao.[41] Dulles disagreed. "My own feeling," he wrote Chester Bowles early in 1952, "is that the best way to get a separation between the Soviet Union and Communist China is to keep pressure on Communist China and make its way difficult so long as it is in partnership with Soviet

Russia." The Yugoslavs had not broken with Moscow "because we were nice to Tito. On the contrary, we were very rough with Tito." If China could win American favors while remaining in the Kremlin camp, "then there is little reason for her to change."[42]

The force that would ultimately defeat international communism, Dulles believed, was the same force that had defeated all empires: their internal contradictions. In his 1950 book, *War or Peace*, he had noted that: "Dictatorships usually present a formidable exterior. They seem, on the outside, to be hard, glittering, and irresistible." But in fact, "they are full of rottenness."[43] The death of Stalin was likely to reveal the "rottenness" that lay within the Soviet system. Soviet power, he told the National Security Council soon after the Eisenhower administration took office, was "already overextended and represents tyrannical rule over unwilling peoples. If we keep the pressures on, psychological and otherwise, we may either force a collapse of the Kremlin regime or else transform the Soviet orbit from a union of satellites dedicated to aggression, into a coalition for defense only." There could be "no real replacement for Stalin the demi-god."[44]

Dulles elaborated on this strategy in a remarkable briefing he gave for President Eisenhower, British Prime Minister Winston Churchill, and French Foreign Minister Georges Bidault at the Bermuda Conference in December, 1953. There was evidence of strain in Sino-Soviet relations, Dulles noted; this was only logical, because "Mao Tse-tung was himself an outstanding Communist leader in his own right." With the death of Stalin and the absence, among his successors, of anyone whose prestige exceeded Mao's, it was becoming necessary for the Russians to treat Mao "as an equal partner on the world scene." That fact was important, and "may eventually give us an opportunity for promoting division between the Soviet Union and Communist China in our own common interest."

There were two theories about how to do this. "One was that by being nice to the Communist Chinese we could wean them away from the Soviets, and the other was that pressure and strain would compel them to make more demands on the USSR which the latter would be unable to meet and the strain would consequently increase." The British, Dulles noted (and, he might have added as well, the Truman administration prior to and even during the Korean War), had followed the first approach, but with meager results. This was not surprising, because "competition with the Russians as to who would treat the China best ... put China in the best of worlds." The better approach would be to apply "pressure ... on Communist China both politically and economically and, to the extent possible without war, military pressure should likewise be maintained." It was within that context that American assistance to Chiang Kai-shek and the Chinese Nationalists should be viewed: "This was another of the measures we liked to pursue on the theory of exerting maximum strain causing the Chinese Communists to demand more from Russia and thereby placing additional stress on Russian-Chinese relations."[45]

The Eisenhower-Dulles strategy on Quemoy and Matsu has generally been seen as reflecting the assumption that the Chinese Communists were

Soviet puppets and deference to pressures from the pro-Nationalist China Lobby in the United States.[46] This new evidence suggests the need to revise that assessment. Domestic politics may indeed have played a role in shaping the American hard line on this issue, but the belief that Mao took orders from the Russians clearly did not; indeed, the strategy was intended to drive Mao *toward* Moscow, not away from it, in the expectation that this course of action would most quickly weaken the Sino-Soviet relationship.

One of Dulles's initial recommendations after the first Quemoy-Matsu crisis broke in August, 1954, was to take the issue to the United Nations Security Council, a move that "could put a serious strain on Soviet-ChiCom relations." If the Soviet Union vetoed United Nations action, it would "gravely impair" its ongoing "peace offensive" and thus cause Moscow to lose support in world opinion. If, alternatively, the Soviet Union did not veto such action, "the ChiComs could react adversely, . . . defy the UN, [and] . . . again become an international outcast."[47] The forthcoming defensive treaty between the United States and Nationalist China, Dulles told the National Security Council in November, would be a "major challenge" to the Chinese Communists.[48]

As Dulles explained in a conversation with British Ambassador Sir Roger Makins in February, 1955, the long-term objective of American policy was to bring about "sufficient independence between Peiping and Moscow as to create the beginning of a balance of power relationship." With the two communist giants embroiled with each other, and with the gradual return of Japanese power, "the U.S. would not have to be so fully involved in the Far East as it now is."[49] Both the Soviet and Chinese communist regimes were overextended, he told Chinese Nationalist Foreign Minister George Yeh a few days later; moreover, Washington regarded "the disintegrative process as inherent in the nature of a Communist dictatorship, and as inevitable." The communist regimes were "bound to crack," if for no other reason than their inability to satisfy the needs of their own people. What was required was "faith that the dissolution of this evil system is gradually taking place even when there is no surface evidence." After all, as St. Paul had said, faith "is the substance of things hoped for, the evidence of things not seen." "We must know in our hearts that Communism contains the seeds of its own destruction. External pressures hasten the destructive process."[50]

How long did Dulles think all this would take? Here his views varied. He told Yeh that the break-up could come within a year, but that no one could tell: "it might be some years away."[51] Several months earlier, he had speculated that it might take as long as twenty-five years, and had wondered whether the West could afford to wait that long.[52] By early 1956, Dulles had become even more pessimistic: "these natural rivalries might take 100 years to assert themselves," he told British Foreign Secretary Selwyn Lloyd; precisely for that reason, the West could not relax its pressure. "[I]n World War II, it was freely predicted that the Axis partners would split, should they win. But the Allies did not stop fighting on that account."[53] Certainly Dulles showed no inclination to explore feelers from Peking, extended in the aftermath of the Quemoy-Matsu crisis, that might have led to a more amicable relationship.[54]

One thing was clear, though: the West should not push so hard in seeking to fragment the international communist monolith as to provoke a violent response. Dulles warned Yeh in February, 1955, that "a totalitarian regime when near the point of break-up may lash out recklessly in order to avoid or postpone an internal crisis." World War I had resulted more from "such a lashing out by the Austro-Hungarian and the Russian autocracies, which were near the break-up point in 1914, than by Prussian militarism."[55] Several months earlier the Secretary of State had told the National Security Council that any overt attempt to overthrow the Chinese regime or to detach Eastern Europe from Soviet control would lead to general war. The preferable course was to wait for time to bring about changes within international communism, however long it took. Once it developed that the Soviet Union could no longer "decide upon and take sudden action without considering the views of its allies and associates," then the threat posed by that nation would be "greatly diminished." Nationalism was the key: indeed it was possible "to foresee the growth within the Soviet bloc of so wide a distribution of power that no single individual could decide on a course of action which would bind all the rest."[56]

By mid-1956—largely as a result of the Khrushchev "de-Stalinization" speech to the 20th Party Congress, which the Central Intelligence Agency had arranged to have distributed throughout the world[57]—Dulles had become convinced that "the process of disintegration" within international communism was well under way. "Soviet Communism is in deep trouble," he told the Senate Foreign Relations Committee in June of that year.[58] The Russians faced the dilemma, he explained to Eisenhower, "of either allowing liberal forces to grow and obtain recognition, or else revert to [a] Stalinist type of repression, in which case they would lose the ground they had been trying to gain with the free nations as having become more civilized and more liberal."[59] The administration itself, through the Voice of America and by other means, had done much "to revive the influences which are inherent in freedom, [and] have thereby contributed toward creating strains and stresses within the captive world."[60] Where countries "were physically adjacent to the Soviet Union and where Soviet troops were there to sustain a pro-Soviet government, the people had little recourse. However, that was not the case where a country was not adjacent to the Soviet Union and where Soviet military power was not available to support the government."[61]

The speed and brutality with which the Soviets suppressed the Hungarian revolution of October-November, 1956, certainly confirmed that last proposition; it also suggested that Moscow's ability to keep its satellites in line had not eroded to the extent that Dulles thought it had. Still, even that event had its positive side, as the Secretary of State pointed out to the President in mid-December: the sixty satellite divisions could "no longer be regarded as an addition to Soviet forces—in fact they may immobilize certain Soviet forces."[62] The difficulty was knowing how much further one could prudently push the Russians. "The successive setbacks of the Soviet rulers in terms of the Communist satellite parties in free countries, in satellite countries in Eastern Europe and internal unrest in Russia itself," Dulles warned, "combined to make it hard for them to accept any further setbacks."[63]

Hope might now have to lie in the gradual evolution of communist systems into something better, a theme the Secretary of State began to emphasize publicly during the last year of his life. "I am not sure that Communism as a social and economic structure will wither away," he told a British television interviewer in October, 1958. But "I do see an evolution, away from what I call international communism . . . which tries to spread its creed all over the world . . . to a system which puts more emphasis upon national welfare . . . and will give up this fantastic dream of world conquest."[64] Later that year, in a speech at San Francisco, Dulles returned to his favorite image of "materialistic despotisms [that] with their iron discipline, their mechanistic performance, their hard and shiny exterior, always seem formidable." But these dictatorships suffered from a great internal contradiction: if they were to develop into modern industrial states, they would have to educate their people. They would then find that "minds so educated also penetrate the fallacies of Marxism and increasingly resist conformity." Internal difficulties such as these "are bound to alter the character of the Communist regimes, particularly if these regimes are denied the glamor and prestige of great external successes."

Here Dulles came as close as he ever did in public to laying out the basis of his strategy toward the communist world: "To deny external successes to International Communism is not merely a negative, defensive policy. It accelerates the evolution within the Sino-Soviet bloc of governmental policies which will increasingly seek the welfare of their own peoples, rather than exploit these peoples in the interest of world conquest." If the non-communist nations could "hold fast to policies which deter armed aggression; if they prevent subversion through economic and revolutionary processes; and, above all, if they demonstrate the good fruits of freedom, then we can know that freedom will prevail."[65]

Dulles's final word on this subject came in an undated fragment of a speech draft that was probably composed around January, 1959. "The pattern of the future," he noted, "is, I think, predictable in its broad outlines." The communists had imposed their rule on some 900 million people. There was no way for the West to disrupt that rule from the outside, "for we renounce the destructive power of so-called 'preventive war'. But we can prevent that pattern from prevailing and we can confidently expect that in due course it will be altered from within."[66]

Again, a revision of traditional interpretations seems to be called for, because Dulles clearly did not see international communism as monolithic. More than that, he had a sophisticated long-term strategy for encouraging fragmentation within the communist world that certainly influenced United States policies, and that may also—although at present we have no reliable way of confirming this—have contributed to the breakup of the Sino-Soviet alliance. It was a strategy to be pursued with caution: the "pressure" by which Dulles sought to achieve fragmentation was always to be applied by means short of war. In Dulles's last years, he even came to see that internal changes within communist states might alter their external behavior more rapidly than the deliberate application of pressure from without. Whether one agrees with it or not, Dulles's understanding of the communist world—like his thinking on nuclear weapons—turns out to have been based on a good deal more than the rigid and narrow view of the world his critics have so often attributed to him.

Negotiating an End to the Cold War

A third commonly held view of Dulles, alongside his alleged affinity for nuclear brinksmanship and for treating communism as monolithic, has been that he was reluctant to acknowledge the possibility of change within the Soviet Union, or to contemplate, in any serious way, the prospect of negotiations with that country. Townsend Hoopes best summed up this line of argument when he wrote that "Stalin did Dulles a philosophical and practical disservice by dying, but Dulles retaliated by continuing to act as though the death had not occurred."[67] Dulles himself reinforced his image as an uncompromising hard-liner with repeated warnings about the Soviet capacity for deception, "for making concessions merely in order to lure others into a false sense of security, which makes them the easier victims of ultimate aggression."[68] His whole attitude toward the Soviet Union seemed to be summed up in his famous suggestion to Eisenhower, once the Geneva summit had become unavoidable, that the President avoid social functions at which he might be photographed with Bulganin and Khrushchev, and maintain "an austere countenance on occasions where photographing together is inevitable."[69]

But was the Secretary of State's view of the Russians really that rigid? Enough evidence is available to suggest, once again, a more complex—and more interesting—Dulles than one might have expected.

Early in September, 1953, the Secretary of State raised with Eisenhower the possibility of making "a spectacular effort to relax world tensions and execute such mutual withdrawals of Red Army forces and of U. S. forces abroad" as would permit the stabilization of NATO and of German forces "at a level compatible with budgetary relief," and creation of a "strategic reserve" in the United States. The result would be a "broad zone of restricted armament in Europe, with Soviets withdrawn from satellites and U. S. from Europe."[70] The basis for this extraordinary suggestion—which resembled, as nothing else, George F. Kennan's much criticized proposal for "disengagement" put forward in his Reith Lectures five years later[71]—was Dulles's concern that what would later come to be called "extended deterrence" would not, in itself, discourage Soviet aggression in Europe. American military bases there and elsewhere were becoming an "irritant," and the new Soviet "peace offensive" threatened to invite "wishful thinking, on the part of NATO partners and Japan, that the danger is past and that neutralism and military economy are permissible."

If combined with Soviet political liberalization in Eastern Europe— Dulles mentioned the example of Finland in this respect—an end to Moscow's efforts to spread "world revolution," an opening-up of East-West trade, and progress toward the international control of nuclear weapons, the kind of settlement he proposed to Eisenhower could increase American influence in the world while minimizing costs; "it would also end the present state of strain which breeds distrust and intolerance which undermine our traditional American way of life."[72]

The President, in response, expressed "emphatic agreement that renewed efforts should be made to relax world tensions on a global basis" and acknowledged that "mutual withdrawals of Red Army Forces and of United States Forces could be suggested as a step toward relaxing these tensions." But he also reminded Dulles that although it was true that overseas bases might be unpopular, "any withdrawal that seemed to imply a change in *basic* intent would cause real turmoil abroad."[73] Dulles subsequently told his Policy Planning Staff Director, Robert Bowie, that Eisenhower had been "entirely sympathetic" to the proposal, but that "if we made a fair offer and it was rejected then we had no alternative but to look upon the Soviet Union as a potential aggressor and make our own plans accordingly." The way to proceed would be a public declaration: the President "was not inclined to look with favor upon secret preliminary discussions with the U. S. S. R. or the U. K."[74]

By October, 1953, the idea of a mutual withdrawal of forces in Europe had been incorporated into the drafts, already under way, of a presidential speech on the international control of nuclear weapons.[75] But, as Bowie pointed out, there was a difficulty: "The withdrawal of U. S. troops is linked to control of nuclear weapons, because we cannot withdraw our forces at the same time the Russians do without abandoning our bases. Obviously we cannot abandon forward bases until nuclear weapons are controlled."[76] Dulles himself soon came to the view that no serious discussions with the Russians on these matters should take place until progress had been made in establishing the European Defense Community: "I think there may be a fair chance of some settlement with the Russians if we have a firm foundation in Western Europe—but not before."[77] As a result, he later recalled, Eisenhower's speech was limited to the subject of atomic energy. "The broader aspects on analysis were difficult of reduction to concrete acceptable proposals."[78]

Dulles's second thoughts did not mean, though, as has one recent biographer of Eisenhower has claimed, that the Secretary of State "had no faith whatsoever in any disarmament proposal [and] believed in dealing with the Russians only from a position of overwhelming strength."[79] It might well "be possible to reach general agreements with the Soviets . . . on reduction of armaments," Dulles told the National Security Council in October, 1953, but "we were certainly not in a position to impose such settlements on them. Such settlements would have to be mutually acceptable." If the United States was prepared to accept a *quid pro quo*, then "we are in a position to settle

Korea and possibly even East Germany." Negotiations by no means excluded "unilateral efforts by the United States to increase its relative power position vis-à-vis the USSR," or even "to push our power position forward against the USSR." But "we could not reduce tensions with the USSR if in each case we expected to gain all the advantage and the Soviets none."[80]

Nor did Dulles regard the Russians as impossible negotiating partners. They had been "rather cautious in exercising their power," he told the National Security Council in December, 1954. "They were not reckless, as Hitler was." The very fact that they relied primarily upon subversion rather than military force to achieve their objectives was an indication of that caution; it was also "natural," because the Communist Party was "in essence revolutionary and conspiratorial." Kremlin leaders had calculated that it would not be worth risking what they had achieved through subversion by indulging in aggressive acts hard to reconcile "with their world-wide propaganda line in favor of peace and co-existence." What this meant for the West was that if it could build up regimes "capable of maintaining internal security and... which can't be overthrown except by overt, brutal acts of aggression, it will be possible to withstand the present Soviet threat."

Eisenhower drew out the implications of what Dulles had said: to assume that entering into negotiations with the Russians "would cause the free world to let down its military guard" was to assume "that the State Department was incapable of distinguishing fraudulent from honest changes in the Soviet attitude." Besides, "we cannot hope to get the continued support of public opinion in the free world if we always say 'no' to any suggestions that we negotiate with the Soviet Union.... [W]e should negotiate wherever and whenever it looks profitable."[81]

By early 1955, Dulles was distinguishing in public between the "aggressive fanaticism" of the Chinese Communists and the "coldly calculated" but "deliberate" behavior of the Russians: "They have stated that their program will involve an entire historical era, and so far at least they have not taken reckless risks."[82] He was not optimistic about achieving a "significant political settlement" with Moscow, he told a press conference in April, "but I believe it is something that we have always got to keep trying for.... Sometimes the unexpected is what happens. It seems to me that in dealing with the Soviet Union it is oftentimes the unexpected which is more apt to happen than the thing that one anticipates."[83]

The Secretary of State was modest in his assessment of what the Geneva summit conference actually achieved. It had made relations between Russia and the West "less brittle"; it also meant that "for the predictable future, we can subject our differences to the patient processes of diplomacy with less fear that war will come out of them."[84] Divided countries like Germany, Korea, and Vietnam still remained, to be sure, but there were advantages in not carrying out reunifications by means of war. "By war you may then unify ...only for insects and not for human life."[85] Noting the recent agreement with the Russians on the withdrawal of occupation forces from Austria, Dulles acknowledged the difficulty of knowing "whether what is going on now marks a genuine change of purpose or whether it is merely a maneuver." It was necessary to plan for both contingencies: "We must not rebuff a change which might be that for which the whole world longs. On the other hand, we must not expose ourselves to what could be mortal danger."[86]

Dulles clearly distrusted the Soviet positions on disarmament in the wake of the Geneva summit. Fear of nuclear war and its consequences had induced uncritical attitudes in the West toward the Kremlin's proposals, he told the National Security Council early in 1956: "[W]e in the United States who take real responsibility must always explain the true meaning of proposals, and see that nothing unsound is done." Panaceas such as "ban the bomb" would not work, but there might be room for progress in cutting the amounts of fissionable material that went into weapons, "or even to agree if this can be done safely that after a certain point all future uses of fissionable material would be dedicated to peaceful purposes."[87] By mid-1957, he was publicly listing a wide range of possibilities for agreement with the Russians in the field of disarmament, while continuing to warn against superficial solutions and simple reliance on promises.[88]

Moreover, there were beginning to be encouraging signs of change within the Soviet Union. "[W]e . . . primarily are looking to the day when Russia will be something that we can be friends with and not have to treat as enemies," Dulles told a press conference in April, 1956. "And if, in fact, the Soviet Union is not as much to be feared as it was, if it has become more tolerant, if it has put aside the use of violence, if it is beginning to move in a liberal way within, then I would call that progress toward victory in the cold war."[89] In his private communications with Eisenhower, Dulles was even more encouraging: "within the last three years, Russia has done far more than we would have dared to expect in terms of doing away with the barbarisms of Stalin and seeming, at least, to become a respectable member of the society of nations." There were dangers in this, to be sure: "that kind of a Russia has more acceptability and less ostracism than the other kind. I wonder, however, who would like to go back to the conditions which we had three years ago."[90]

Even the suppression of the Hungarian uprising late in 1956 appears not to have shaken Dulles's conviction that trends toward liberalization were continuing inside the Soviet Union. He told a press conference in July, 1957, that Khrushchev's consolidation of power had confirmed the victory of those who were willing to allow more flexibility and improvement in the condition of the Russian people. It was an "irreversible trend," he added, and "I think we have done quite a bit to promote this trend."[91] Moscow's new emphasis on "political-economic offensives" was, of course, "highly dangerous," Dulles wrote Eisenhower in March, 1958, but "there has been a definite evolution within the Soviet Union toward greater personal security, increased intellectual freedom and increased decentralization. This also increases the chances of peace."[92]

It was chiefly the fear of attack that kept the arms race going, Dulles argued in a letter to German Chancellor Konrad Adenauer in June, 1958. If that fear could be done away with, "then I think there would almost auto-matically come about reduction on both sides." The Soviets would not want to carry the heavy expense of armament "if conditions preclude its being put to effective aggressive use." Nor would the United States wish to sustain comparable expenses "if they are not necessary to deter or withstand sudden attack." It ought to be possible "to find ways to minimize this awful risk of massive surprise attack and ... in the calmer atmosphere that succeeded this, other measures might be taken."[93]

The Secretary of State did remain skeptical about summitry. Very little had come out of such conferences in the past, he told the BBC late in 1957, "primarily because the Soviets cannot be relied to live up to their promises."[94] In his June, 1958, letter to Adenauer, he came out against any summit that would involve "a renunciation of our just and legitimate political positions ... merely in the *hope* of some significant disarmament agreement."[95] But by August, Dulles was telling Eisenhower that "I thought it would be useful if the President and Khrushchev could have a private talk to emphasize our firmness," so long as it did not degenerate into "a low-level 'slugging match'."[96]

Early in 1959, just months before his death, Dulles assessed long-term prospects for Soviet-American relations before a bipartisan meeting of Congressional leaders at the White House. Because of the regimented nature of their societies, he noted, communist countries had "possibilities for eco-nomic growth which we do not possess in a free society." There was no way for the West to stop this growth—or the "feeling of exuberance" that it produced—short of preventive war, "which is unthinkable." But the United States and its allies had held firm the previous year through crises in the Middle East and East Asia; there was every sign, as well, that NATO would not allow Khrushchev's recent threats to drive it out of Berlin. "[T]ime is working for us if we use this time correctly," because the economic growth that had produced communist "exuberance" could not be sustained. The economic system that the Russians were attempting to implement required educating their people, but "this education will militate against an attitude of servility." And, as Churchill had pointed out in his *History of the English-Speaking Peoples*, servility was necessary in order for despotisms to survive. "All this adds up to a dangerous period we are in; but ... eventually the current abnormal situation will change."[97]

In an unusual dictated note to himself early in 1958, Eisenhower had acknowledged that Dulles possessed "a lawyer's mind": "He consistently adheres to a very logical explanation of these difficulties in which we find ourselves with the Soviets and in doing so—with his lawyer's mind—he shows the steps and actions that are bad on their part; and we seek to show that we are doing the decent and just thing." It was necessary to do this; still, the President could not help but question "the practice of becoming a sort of international prosecuting attorney."[98] There is no question that Dulles did assume—certainly more frequently than Eisenhower did—a prosecutorial tone in his public pronouncements on the Soviet Union. But the still-incomplete documentary evidence suggests that behind this there lay a more sophisticated understanding of Soviet realities than one might have thought, together with a more optimistic assessment of prospects for eventually stabilizing the Soviet-American relationship—for making it more "normal"— than most of the Secretary of State's critics at the time would have suspected.

Conclusion

In his thoughtful study of John Foster Dulles's life up to the time he became Secretary of State, Ronald W. Pruessen comments on the extent to which his subject seemed simultaneously to elicit and to resist categorization: "Where some have described an unbalanced idealist with his head in the clouds, I have described a frequently devout pragmatist with a fundamental concern for the condition of the American economy. Where some have focused on deep religiosity, even fanaticism, I have pointed to a selective Presbyterian piety that always involved cognizance of the materialistic side of the Calvinist coin. Where some have condemned the ideologue that Dulles could be, I have cited the Dulles who knew the uses of ideology and melodramatic rhetoric." The Secretary of State, he concludes, was "a complex amalgam, many of whose characteristics . . . may seem contradictory in their complexity, but . . . they were all expressions of Dulles's ultimately human nature."[99]

The new documents suggest that the same complexity persisted throughout Dulles's career as Secretary of State. He was capable of articulating the doctrine of "massive retaliation" while at the same time harboring a deep and growing pessimism about the long-term effectiveness—indeed, even the morality—of nuclear deterrence. He could characterize international communism in public as monolithic while pursuing strategies behind the scenes designed to exploit the fissures he knew existed within it. He could warn repeatedly that changes inside the Soviet Union might be subtle snares to lure the West into complacency, while at the same time quietly welcoming such changes as evidence that the U. S. S. R. was ending its "abnormal" alienation from the established international order.

One might conclude from all of this simply that Dulles was devious: that he deliberately said things he knew not to be true. This may well have been the case in his strategy for fragmenting the Sino-Soviet bloc, for to have explained openly what he was trying to do—accomplish fission by encouraging fusion—would very likely have wrecked the entire initiative. A "hidden-hand" in this instance—very much in the Eisenhower style[100]—was probably the only way to proceed.

With regard to nuclear strategy, though, one has the impression that Dulles was undergoing a painful learning experience. It had been easy enough to design the "New Look" during the 1952 campaign, but when one had the actual responsibility for implementing it—and, at the same time, for keeping the alliance together in the face of growing Soviet nuclear capabilities— unforeseen difficulties arose. Left to himself, Dulles might well have dealt with these by moving toward some kind of "flexible response" strategy; what kept that from happening, one suspects, was Eisenhower's supreme self-confidence in his own crisis-management abilities, together with his determined opposition to increasing military spending.[101]

The gap between the public and private Dulles is least apparent—although it is still there—in his assessments of prospects for negotiations with the Russians. A careful reading of what the Secretary of State actually said in public would not sustain the view that he was unalterably opposed to substantive diplomatic contacts with Moscow, or that he viewed the Soviet Union itself as unalterably cast in a Stalinist mold for all time to come. His private observations—particularly from 1956 on—are surprisingly optimistic about the prospects for change within the Soviet system.

The question might fairly be asked, though: what good was Dulles's sophistication if conceptualization did not lead to implementation? After all, nuclear strategy was not rethought, and the number of nuclear weapons in the American arsenal was allowed to grow beyond any rational justification.[102] The communist "monolith" would almost certainly have fragmented whether or not Dulles had sought to apply his "fission through fusion" strategy; that strategy made no provision for seeking an accommodation with Peking after a split with Moscow had occurred. Despite his more charitable view of the Soviet Union, relations with that nation at the time of Dulles's death remained locked in a pattern of confrontation that may well have been more dangerous—as crises over the U-2, Berlin, and Cuba would soon show—than the one that existed at the time he took office.

But from a larger perspective, what the archives have revealed about Dulles's influence on postwar American foreign policy—and, of course, about Eisenhower's as well—is of considerable importance. Both men, we now know, differed from their predecessors by assuming that time was on the side of the West. Neither accepted the view, widely held within the Truman administration, that a period of "peak danger" existed in the near future by which the United States and its allies, if they did not begin crash rearmament efforts, would find themselves vulnerable.[103] Both had a clearer sense than their predecessors of Soviet and Chinese vulnerabilities; both saw clearly that if an approximate status quo could be sustained over time, the West more than the communist world would benefit from it; both accepted almost instinctively the possibility that continued Soviet-American competition, far from being an "abnormal" condition in international relations, could in fact become a "normal" environment within which limited agreements acceptable to both sides might eventually evolve. Both played a major role, in short, in accomplishing the transition from a ragged and unstable postwar *settlement* to a postwar international *system* that did, whatever else one might say about it, at least keep the peace.

Oversimplification in the writing of history—as in the drawing of maps—is a necessary exercise: reality is always too complex to replicate precisely. But one particular form of oversimplification, the caricature, is best left to cartoonists; the historian should always be suspicious of the tendency to describe individuals exclusively in terms of images, categories, or even first impressions. As the scholars who have discovered the "hidden" Eisenhower during the past two decades have found out, those who make history are generally a good deal more complicated—and therefore more interesting—than their public images might suggest. The end of the Cold War is an appropriate time to begin to apply this lesson, as well, to the "unexpected" John Foster Dulles.

## FIVE

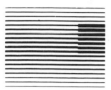 Intelligence, Espionage, and Cold War History

We have learned a great deal over the past two decades about the impact of the "intelligence revolution" on World War II strategy.[1] That knowledge has led, in turn, to a reassessment of the role of intelligence in earlier periods, and to the emergence of intelligence "studies" as a distinct sub-discipline, complete with its own newsletters, journals, organizations, scholarly meetings, and university courses.[2] But this proliferation of scholarship thins out with the conclusion of the war. It is as if the possibilities for serious research on intelligence end with September, 1945, in a manner almost as decisive as President Harry S. Truman's when in that same month he abolished with the stroke of a pen the first full-scale intelligence organization the United States had ever had, the Office of Strategic Services.[3]

The two phenomena are not, of course, unrelated: the very fact that OSS did not survive into the postwar era has made possible the declassification of most of its records. There is little reason to expect comparable openness anytime soon for the records of the Central Intelligence Group, which Truman created only four months after dismantling OSS, or for those of its more famous successor, the Central Intelligence Agency, whose official existence dates from July, 1947.[4] Nor does documentation on codebreaking activity in Great Britain and the United States—documentation that for the wartime years has largely sparked scholarly interest in intelligence matters—seem likely to be made available soon for the early postwar era.

We generally assume that the "intelligence revolution" played an important role in the coming and subsequent evolution of the Cold War, but we know relatively little, as yet, about just what that role was. The historian of postwar intelligence activities has been forced to rely upon a thread of evidence spun out in a bewildering array of mostly unverifiable writings and recollections by former officials (both disgruntled and not), defectors, journalists, parahistorians, and novelists. As the sheer volume—and marketability—of this kind of material suggests, the subject does not lack fascination. What has been missing so far, however, is the basis for solid history.

Much of the sensitivity of this topic, together with the difficulties that sensitivity posed for historians, grew out the fact that the Cold War, until recently, was still going on. Now that the Cold War is over, the climate for serious research on intelligence and espionage during it is likely, in time, to improve. That has not happened yet. But the writing of history begins with the framing of questions, even if one lacks the evidence to answer them. It is not too soon, therefore, to begin to assess what we know about the impact of the "intelligence revolution" on postwar diplomacy, and to begin to ask that most useful of the historian's interrogatories: What difference did it all make? From the answers, we may at least perceive the boundaries of our ignorance with respect to this subject, and perhaps identify an agenda for future research.

The Cold War during the World War

Let us begin with World War II. It now seems clear that the United States and Great Britain directed their intelligence activities during that conflict almost entirely against their military adversaries. Although the British and the Americans did routinely intercept Soviet communications, they made no serious attempts to decypher them, despite the impressive codebreaking capabilities both London and Washington had developed. To be sure, cryptanalysts in both countries had their hands full in dealing just with German and Japanese intercepts: the price of "listening in" is, after all, inundation.[5] Soviet codes also were known to be harder to crack than those of the Germans and the Japanese, although as postwar developments would show, they were not unbreakable.[6] But it was not simply the codebreakers' workload and the difficulty of the task they would have faced that kept them from taking on Soviet material. The documentary evidence is elusive, but it seems likely that President Roosevelt and Prime Minister Churchill actively discouraged their codebreakers—and perhaps actually forbade them—from putting their formidable cryptoanalytic skills to use against the Russians.[7]

Nor, as far as we now know, did the Western allies take advantage of their expanded wartime contacts with the U.S.S.R. to conduct espionage or to attempt to plant agents there. There were occasional amateurish efforts to gather information on Soviet military installations and other targets of interest;[8] but when opportunities for major intelligence coups arose, they do not appear to have been seized upon. For example, OSS Director William J. Donovan passed up the chance, in 1942, to exploit a Washington source close to Soviet ambassador Maxim Litvinov. When Donovan raised the possibility, early in 1943, of cooperation with British intelligence to gather information on the U.S.S.R., the State Department vetoed the idea on the grounds that "if any undercover agent were disclosed, the repercussions could be serious both from a military point of view and politically."[9] The British Special Operations Executive, too, apparently lacked the authority to conduct covert operations within, or directed against, the Soviet Union.[10]

Nor were the Western allies hesitant about sharing sensitive information with the Soviet Union. Within two days after the German attack in June, 1941, Churchill ordered that ULTRA-derived military intelligence be made available to the Russians;[11] indeed Moscow almost certainly benefited from ENIGMA decrypts before Washington did.[12] Although the Roosevelt administration did balk at a 1944 plan to exchange OSS and NKVD missions, this happened for domestic political reasons—the fear that FBI Director J. Edgar Hoover might leak the information to hostile columnists—rather than from any reluctance on the Roosevelt administration's part to provide intelligence and counterintelligence data to the Russians. Despite the absence of a formal link between the two intelligence organizations, a substantial amount of information went to Moscow: it apparently included the transfer of microdot and microfilm technology, information on German-organized anti-Soviet spy networks in Europe, and even, early in 1945, the return of some 1,500 pages of Soviet cypher material that the OSS had secretly purchased from the Finns. This sharing of information with the Russians—from both British and American sources—continued through the end of the war.[13]

The Russians were not, of course, told everything. Churchill stipulated that they were not to know the means by which the British had obtained ULTRA information; nor were the Russians officially informed, at any point prior to the Potsdam Conference, of the joint Anglo-American project to develop the atomic bomb.[14] But, beyond that, the amount of information conveyed was remarkable when one considers the long history of Western suspicions about the Soviet Union, together with the impossibility of knowing what form postwar relations with that country were likely to take.

Did the Russians reciprocate? In the area of military intelligence, only grudgingly: neither the passage of time nor the opening of documents has called into question the accuracy of General John R. Deane's 1947 memoir, *The Strange Alliance*, which chronicled with great precision the difficulties Western military representatives in Moscow had in obtaining the information necessary for even the simplest forms of joint action against the Germans and the Japanese.[15] If the Russians did manage to crack enemy codes—and there is some reason to think they might have[16]—there seems to be no evidence that they shared the information thereby gained with their allies.

When it came to espionage, the Russians did not in any way reciprocate Western restraint; indeed, the most striking disparity between Anglo-American and Soviet wartime behavior with respect to intelligence has to do with spying. It is now a matter of record that during the 1920s and 1930s the Russians launched an ambitious effort to recruit agents, chiefly in Great

Britain but also in the United States, who might over time rise to positions of influence or even authority in those countries.[17] The sheer scope of this operation is extraordinary in retrospect, as is the Russians' willingness to wait years for it to produce results. Whatever Stalin's suspicions may have been, neither the United States nor Great Britain was ever in a position to mount—or even to contemplate mounting—any remotely comparable operation against the Soviet Union.[18]

Although by all accounts the British and Americans abruptly ceased whatever covert operations they may have been running against the Russians after June, 1941, the Soviet Union, if anything, intensified its efforts to penetrate Western security. The bulk of this activity took place in Great Britain, the country in which the Russians had had their greatest success in placing agents, although it occurred in the United States as well.[19] It took two principal forms: infiltration of the secret Anglo-American project to construct an atomic bomb; and the activation of "moles" recruited during the 1930s who had now come to occupy positions of influence in London and Washington.

To be sure, the Russians did not recruit Klaus Fuchs: he recruited them. The German émigré scientist, then in Britain, offered information about bomb development as early as the fall of 1941, and the Russians immediately accepted.[20] This happened before anyone knew whether such a device could be made to work, and certainly prior to the 1944 Anglo-American agreement not to share atomic bomb information with "third parties"; indeed there is reason to think that latter decision may have been influenced by preliminary indications that the Russians had already penetrated Manhattan Project security.[21] But what is even more important here is the contrast between the restraint the United States and Great Britain showed in exploiting intelligence targets of opportunity against their Soviet ally, and the eagerness with which the Russians seized upon this one.

That same appetite for surreptitiously obtained information is apparent when one considers how, during the war, the Russians used the "moles" they had earlier recruited in Britain and the United States. There was no order to "inactivate" these individuals after the British and Americans became allies in 1941, in the same way London and Washington refrained from using their codebreaking capabilities against the Russians. There is no evidence that Stalin saw any impropriety in spying upon his allies, or that he worried about the risks the exposure of such activity might pose. Although there is at present no way to know how extensive a volume of information the American and British spy rings transmitted to Moscow, it apparently continued to flow without significant interruption through the end of the war.[22]

Why did the Russians run such risks? One possible explanation is that they had reason to think that, if their spies were detected, neither the Americans nor the British would make an issue of it. General Walter Krivitsky, the former chief of Soviet military intelligence for Western Europe, had defected to the United States in 1938, but little had been done about the information he provided. When Whittaker Chambers came forward in 1939 with what later proved to be accurate information about the American spy ring, the response was much the same.²³ The British were known to be casual about vetting procedures for Secret Service and Foreign Office appointments, even for communists and Soviet sympathizers.²⁴ Indeed, the general climate in the West during the war was one of bending over backwards to trust the Russians; far from reciprocating this treatment, though, Moscow took full advantage of it. The result was to give the Soviet Union its own equivalent of ULTRA and MAGIC, but in this case directed against its allies, not its adversaries.

This asymmetry is worth emphasizing, because it provides a new perspective on the old question of responsibility for the Cold War. Stalin's reliance, throughout World War II, on espionage directed against his most important allies suggests the kind of postwar relationship he expected to have with them. Having carried on, in effect, his own cold war during the world war, he cannot have been surprised when the real Cold War so quickly followed the achievement of victory. American and British leaders, who carefully avoided undertaking intelligence operations that might arouse their Soviet ally's suspicions, would hardly have shown such restraint if they had anticipated the sharp deterioration in relations with Moscow that was soon to happen. Expecting something, of course, need not imply responsibility for its occurrence. But to hold one side responsible for something it did *not* expect when the other side clearly did would be an even less logical way in which to proceed.

Discovering the Deception

The first evidence of Soviet espionage to be taken seriously in London and Washington came only three days after the Japanese surrender, with the defection of Soviet embassy code-clerk Igor Guzenko in Ottawa. Additional corroboration—although none of the documentary evidence Guzenko had provided—emerged from the voluntary confession of former NKVD courier Elizabeth Bentley two months later.²⁵ One can only speculate about what might have been done with this evidence had the war still been going on. It could hardly have been ignored, and yet public disclosure might have been ruled out because of its potential effect on the joint war effort.²⁶ As it happened, the Guzenko case was not announced until February, 1946; and although the Soviet agents named by Bentley were gradually eased out of the government in the months that followed, the information she provided did not become public knowledge until she appeared before the House Un-American Activities Committee more than two years later. The delay in publicizing the Guzenko-Bentley revelations was partly dictated by the need to verify the information they had provided,²⁷ but there was also very likely a reluctance within the Truman administration to accept the implications of what this information suggested about the future of Soviet-American relations.[28]

Nevertheless, the quiet "purge" that occurred in Washington was apparently effective in removing from positions of authority those officials now known to have been involved with Soviet espionage in the 1930s and early 1940s. The same was not true, of course, in London. With the exception of charges brought against atomic scientist Alan Nunn May, the Guzenko affair, for whatever reason, produced no comparable purge within the British security establishment.[29] Soviet agents Kim Philby, Donald Maclean, and Guy Burgess continued to send information of high quality to the Russians through the first six years of the Cold War.[30] The effect must have been to render largely useless efforts the Americans had made to counter Soviet espionage after the Guzenko-Bentley defections of 1945, since so much sensitive information was routinely shared with the British during this period.[31] For practical purposes, Moscow's equivalent of ULTRA/MAGIC continued in operation until Burgess and Maclean finally fled to the Soviet Union in 1951.

This raises the question, then: Did the Americans and the British have any equivalent capability that could be directed against the Russians? Apart from three instances about which we have anecdotal evidence, we know very little about postwar efforts to break Soviet codes. One involved the Army Security Agency's success, in 1949, in deciphering a KGB codebook that had been part of the material Donovan's OSS had obtained from the Finns five years earlier. (Although Roosevelt had ordered that these items be returned to the Russians, a copy had quietly been retained.) This cryptoanalytic breakthrough led directly to the identification as spies of Klaus Fuchs, Harry Gold, David Greenglass, Julius and Ethel Rosenberg, and a considerable number of lesser figures involved in Soviet espionage in the United States, although for security reasons the decyphered KGB messages could not be used in prosecuting them.[32] These decrypts were of little value in assessing current Soviet intentions, however, because the Russians, who knew that their codes had been compromised, had long since changed them.[33] There is also less precise evidence that the British managed to crack other encrypted Soviet communications that had been recorded, but not decyphered, during the war.[34] Finally, the CIA apparently achieved a successful interception of clear-text Soviet land-lines communications in Vienna in 1951: this appears to have provided some assurance that the Russians intended no military initiatives in Europe during the Korean War.[35] We also know that the United States had established listening posts around the periphery of the Soviet Union by the end of the 1940s and was regularly conducting reconnaissance flights—both by airplane and (much less usefully) balloon—over portions of its territory;[36] some of these activities would have permitted the interception of electronic information, but it is not yet clear what, if anything, it revealed.

From all that we know now, Anglo-American efforts to place agents and to conduct covert operations inside the Soviet Union and Eastern Europe in the early postwar years were thoroughly unsuccessful. Given the fact that the Central Intelligence Agency and its British counterpart, MI6, operated under the double disability of having to penetrate a closed society at a time when the latter organization's own internal security had been severely compromised, this result is not surprising. Support for anti-Soviet forces in the Baltic states and the Ukraine got nowhere; the effort to organize a Polish resistance force was monitored by the Russians from the beginning; and in the most notorious example, Philby's treason not only wrecked repeated attempts to overthrow the communist government in Albania, but resulted in the deaths of several hundred participants in those operations.[37]

Outside the Soviet bloc, things went better. The CIA was reasonably successful in its efforts to supplement the Marshall Plan by influencing the 1948 Italian elections, weaning Western European labor unions and intellectual groups from the communists, and making use of defectors and emigres to gain information on, and conduct propaganda against, the U.S.S.R.[38] Early intelligence estimates on Soviet intentions and capabilities, although bland, were generally accurate in reflecting Stalin's reluctance to risk war and the poor condition of his armed forces; after 1949 the estimates did, however, became more alarmist than seems justified in retrospect.[39] The Agency did not anticipate Tito's 1948 expulsion from the Cominform, or the North Korean attack on South Korea in 1950; but it was able to balance these failures with its success in detecting the first Soviet atomic bomb test in 1949.[40]

On the whole, though, one would have to conclude that Soviet intelligence had the edge on its Western counterparts through the first half-decade of the Cold War. This achievement resulted in part from the Russians' "built-in" advantage of having relatively open societies as their target; but it also stemmed from their remarkable success in penetrating the Manhattan Project, British intelligence, and through it, certain key activities of the CIA. Historians of postwar Soviet-American relations, this one included, have hesitated to incorporate this evidence into their scholarly writing. The reason is that the subject of espionage got so quickly caught up with the spread of McCarthyism that we refused to take it seriously; the fact that some cases were exaggerated led too easily to the assumption that all had been.[41] But within the past decade, the work of Allen Weinstein on the Hiss case and of Ronald Radosh and Joyce Milton on that of the Rosenbergs, together with revelations by former FBI agent Robert Lamphere and KGB defector Oleg Gordievsky, have shown that these were not right-wing fabrications: espionage did go on in the United States in the 1930s and 1940s, and on a remarkably extensive scale.[42] Because of more stringent secrecy rules, we lack this kind of precise corrobative evidence in studying the extent and nature of the British spy rings that operated during the same period; as a result, arguments still rage over them.[43] But no one would now question the seriousness of the penetration that took place, or the laxity of British authorities in failing to detect it.

So What?

Professor Robin Winks, in his book on Yale University and the world of intelligence, very wisely reminds us of the importance of asking "so what?" questions: "So, what difference does it make that . . . Hitler had one testicle, that Sicilians still use sixteenth-century vulgarisms, that narrow-gauge track is not the same in New South Wales as in the Sudan?"[44] As stacks of books about the history of espionage amply demonstrate, it is easy to get so caught up in the fascination of esoteric minutiae that one loses sight of what, if anything, it all meant. What difference did it make that the Russians spied on their Anglo-American allies throughout the war, that they knew much of what went on within the British and American governments during the early postwar years, and that London and Washington failed to discover this until 1951? Is the world today—was the world then—discernibly different as a result?

The first reaction, when one discovers that one has been the victim of an intelligence coup, is that all secrets have been compromised and that the other side has been operating with complete knowledge of one's own intentions and capabilities.[45] It takes time to realize that even the most perfect of spy operations is likely to operate under severe limitations. For one thing, the clandestine collection of information, whether by human or electronic means, always involves filtration: someone must decide what information to obtain or intercept, what to transmit or decypher, and finally what to incorporate within the necessarily laconic analyses that go to those few at the top who have the authority to act.[46] For these reasons alone, an intelligence breakthrough is likely to provide less accurate information than one might expect; one need only cite the ineffectiveness of MAGIC in anticipating Pearl Harbor, or of ULTRA in warning of Hitler's 1944 attack in the Ardennes, to make the point.

The difficulty is likely to be compounded when decision-makers distrust the source of such information. We know, for example, that Stalin dismissed American and British reports warning of a German attack in June, 1941, because he was convinced the West was trying to use disinformation to undermine Soviet-German relations.[47] There is little reason to think that his wariness regarding his wartime allies abated very much in the years that followed: his 1944 comment to Milovan Djilas about Churchill stealing kopecks from one's pocket but Roosevelt dipping his hand in only for "bigger coins" speaks volumes, both about Stalin's personality and about the failure of F. D. R.'s persistent efforts to overcome the Soviet leader's distrust.[48] We can get another glimpse into how Stalin's mind worked from a comment he made to Italian socialist Pietro Nenni in 1952: Cardinal Spellman, he claimed, had been present at the Yalta Conference in disguise; it had been he who, on orders from the Vatican, had turned Roosevelt against the Russians.[49]

Given that mentality, how much trust can we expect Stalin to have placed in the reports of a Burgess, Maclean, or Philby, particularly if he had any inkling of the success the British had had during the war in turning German spies back against their masters?[50] Even in retrospect it is surprising that no Soviet "moles" were turned—at least as far as we know;[51] one wonders how long it would have taken Stalin to begin to give credence, if he ever did, to the belief that what he was getting was genuine information, not skillfully contrived deception.[52] Any comprehensive assessment of the impact of Soviet espionage on postwar diplomacy will have to give attention to the particular characteristics of its primary consumer, and to the question—fundamental to an understanding of Stalin—of whether he ever overcame the fear of being fooled sufficiently to be able to act on the basis of information conveyed to him through sources he could not completely control.[53]

But let us assume, for the sake of argument, that Stalin did take seriously the reports of his spies. What would he have learned from them that he would not already have known? There might well have been a fair amount during the period prior to the 1941 German attack, when relations with London and Washington were tense and little was voluntarily shared with the Russians.[54] But the flow of information increased exponentially after that; indeed, with the exceptions of ULTRA's source and the atomic bomb project, one is hard pressed to identify any major aspects of wartime strategy or postwar planning that Roosevelt and Churchill did not, in one form or another, share with the Soviet leader. It was, after all, they—not the spies—who indicated to Stalin that the West would not contest an expansion of Russian influence into Eastern Europe; it was they who sought Soviet entry into the war against Japan and were prepared to pay for it; it was Roosevelt who raised the possibility that the United States might not even keep troops in Europe after the war.[55] None of this was disinformation: it reflected what Roosevelt and Churchill really thought at the time. It was not that the Anglo-Americans surprised the Russians by deliberately misleading them during the war; rather, Western leaders surprised themselves by what they found it necessary to do to counter the Russians after the war had ended.

At lower levels within the American and British governments, it is again difficult to see how espionage could have given the Russians much information they would not otherwise have had. That would especially have been the case inside the Roosevelt administration, where the President's chaotic organizational arrangements created an effective, if unintended, compartmentalization. If Roosevelt's own subordinates did not know what his policies were—as they did not, much of the time[56]—then it is difficult to see how the Russians could have learned very much either. Administrative structures were more coherent in Britain, of course, and the extent of Soviet penetration there was more extensive. It seems probable, therefore, that the Russians had more complete information about the inner workings of the British than of the American government, but again—and apart from information on ULTRA and the atomic bomb—it is not clear how much Stalin would have learned from these sources that he would not already have known, or could have found out by more straightforward means.

One supports "moles," though, not just to collect information; one hopes to be able to use them, as well, to influence the policies of the government within which they function. It is important to determine, then, whether the existence of Soviet "moles" in London or Washington gave Moscow the capacity to shape American or British policy at any point during the war. This is, of course, a very controversial question, dependent for its answer on the tricky business of distinguishing between things that would have happened in any event, and those that—in the absence of the critical variable—would not have. Several suggestions have been made as to how Soviet moles might have shaped Western policy; there is space here to examine them only briefly:

The British failure to support an anti-Hitler resistance movement. Anthony Glees has argued that Kim Philby's major wartime achievement was to undermine efforts to create an exile resistance force that could have worked with Hitler's opposition inside Germany to overthrow him and negotiate peace.[57] There is a surface plausibility to this assertion: as Vojtech Mastny has pointed out, Stalin does appear to have followed a general pattern of undercutting anti-Nazi resistance forces where he could not control them.[58] But, given the Anglo-American "unconditional surrender" policy, it is not at all clear what the British would have done with a successful anti-Hitler resistance movement had they been able to sustain one; nor is it apparent that there was sufficient resistance to Hitler within Germany itself to have ensured success. There is, in short, enough reason for skepticism to regard Glees's argument as, at best, unproven.

The misreading of Soviet postwar intentions. Glees has also suggested that British security failed miserably in detecting Stalin's "plan" for the postwar domination of Europe.[59] But he appears here to confuse Stalin's general determination to expand postwar Soviet influence—something Roosevelt and Churchill were surely aware of, since they gave him reason to believe they would not resist it—with the existence of a detailed blueprint for dominating Europe. Soviet specialists are much less certain than Glees that Stalin had such a plan in the first place;[60] and it is also worth noting that even if he did, the Americans were no better at detecting it either, despite the absence in Washington of spies comparable in preeminence to those in London.[61]

Harry Hopkins. The most sensational assertion in KGB defector Oleg Gordievsky's recent history of the agency, prepared in collaboration with Christopher Andrew,[62] is that Roosevelt's closest wartime adviser, Harry Hopkins, was an "unconscious" Soviet agent. Gordievsky bases this claim on having heard KGB official Iskhak Akhmerov lecture, years later, on his secret meetings with Hopkins in the United States during the war. Hopkins was known to be sympathetic to the Soviet cause, but in taking this position he was acting in a manner perfectly consistent with that of the Roosevelt administration at the time, one that would also have commanded the support of millions of Americans impressed by the scope and success of Soviet military operations against Nazi Germany. Gordievsky's allegation, based as it is on what he remembered Akhmerov saying *he* remembered, needs much more precise corroboration before it can be taken seriously.

Harry Dexter White and the Morgenthau Plan. The most plausible instance in which an American "mole" might have sought to influence Roosevelt administration policy would appear to be the 1944 Morgenthau Plan for the "pastoralization" of postwar Germany. It is now generally accepted that a key architect of that plan, Harry Dexter White, Assistant to Treasury Secretary Henry Morgenthau, Jr., had been a part of a Soviet spy ring in the 1930s.[63] But since the Russians themselves expressed opposition to the Morgenthau Plan when they learned of it, and since the strongly anti-German attitudes of both Morgenthau and Roosevelt himself provide a powerful alternative explanation for the plan, there is no reason to think that this particular American "mole"—if he was still functioning in that capacity—affected United States policy on this issue in any substantial way.[64]

Alger Hiss and the Yalta Conference. Much was made, after Hiss was charged in 1948 with having been a Soviet agent, of the fact that he had been present at the Yalta conference where, it was alleged, an enfeebled Roosevelt had "sold out" both Eastern Europe and Nationalist China. Although Hiss's involvement with the Russians is no longer questioned (except by Hiss himself), the most thorough and critical examination of his career has turned up no evidence that he significantly influenced the Roosevelt administration, whether at Yalta or with respect to any other major foreign policy issues.[65]

In short, the case has yet to be made that either an American or British "mole" succeeded in altering in any identifiable way any wartime policy of the United States or British government. This is not to say that such a case cannot at some future point, and in the light of new evidence, be made. But that has not occurred to this date.

What about the early postwar years? Because the flow of information voluntarily supplied to the Russians was almost totally cut off soon after the war, there is little reason to doubt that Soviet "moles"—by that time, almost exclusively those operating in Britain[66]—were in a position to supply valuable information the Russians would otherwise have found it difficult to obtain. In addition to access to top-secret British codes, this would have included the reassessments of Soviet intentions that were going on within the American and British governments, planning with respect to the British withdrawal from Greece and Turkey, the creation of the Marshall Plan, the discussion of options for dealing with the Berlin Blockade, the formation of the North Atlantic Treaty Organization, and, perhaps most significantly, through Maclean's position on the Combined Policy Committee, American, British and Canadian consultations on atomic energy matters.[67] Philby helped analyze American intelligence data on the first Soviet atomic bomb in 1949, and he would have known about the deciphered KGB codes that were later used to identify Fuchs, the Rosenbergs, and other Soviet agents charged with espionage in the United States, although he apparently made no effort to warn them.[68] The British spies would have been in a position, as well, to convey information about American efforts in 1949–50 to bring about a break between the Chinese Communists and the Russians,[69] and about plans—or the lack of them—for the defense of Korea. And once the Korean War began, there would have been ample opportunities to inform the Russians of evolving Anglo-American strategy for countering North Korean and Chinese military operations.[70]

But so what? What difference did all this make? Again, it is useful to try to specify how, if at all, Soviet espionage appears to have altered the history of early postwar international relations:

Compromising covert operations. The most obvious effect of the treason Philby and his compatriots committed appears to lie in the ease with which the Russians were able to detect and eliminate—or turn to their own purposes—certain clandestine Western intelligence operations. The pattern that emerged can be seen first in the so-called Volkhov affair of September, 1945, an attempted defection by a Soviet intelligence officer in Istanbul which Philby apparently frustrated by reporting the matter to the Russians, who in turn abducted the individual in question and returned him to Moscow before British agents could reach him.[71] It seems safe to assume that subsequent British and American efforts to infiltrate agents and arms into the Soviet Union, Eastern Europe, and the Balkans came to grief at least in part because Philby betrayed them in much the same way;[72] although one must also ask what the chances would have been of these operations succeeding had Philby never existed. There is, of course, no sure way to answer that question, but it is worth pointing out that the history of Western efforts to shake Soviet authority by such means was, at least until the mid-1980s in Afghanistan, unimpressive.[73]

The atomic bomb. The next clearest postwar effect of Soviet espionage is that it probably accelerated the date at which the Russians succeeded in testing their first atomic bomb. Fuchs himself estimated that the information he provided enabled Soviet scientists to speed up their atomic bomb project by "several years";[74] others have pointed out that the Russians could have obtained the most critical information they needed from what the overly generous Americans themselves revealed about their own achievement.[75] It seems safe to conclude that Fuchs—and, to a lesser extent, the Rosenbergs—saved the Russians some time by suggesting short-cuts, but that they would have developed the weapon in any event not very much later than they did. Certainly there is no evidence that Fuchs or anyone else transmitted useful information on thermonuclear weapon technology.[76]

Soviet risk-taking in Berlin and Korea. Maclean may well have known that the B-29 bombers Truman ordered to British bases at the time of the 1948 Berlin blockade carried no atomic weapons with them; he may also have been generally aware of the doubts American military planners had at that time as to whether the limited number of atomic weapons then available would be sufficient to defeat the Soviet Union if war came.[77] He was certainly in a position to inform the Russians of the critical Truman-Attlee talks that followed Chinese intervention in Korea in November, 1950, at which the limits of the United Nations military response were agreed upon.[78] But what Stalin would have made of such information is not at all clear: he could conceivably have found it either reassuring or tempting. We know that he ran risks in initiating the Berlin blockade and in authorizing the North Korean attack; we also know that, once Western resolve had become firm in each of these situations, he behaved very cautiously.[79] What we do not know is what role, if any, the reports of his spies played in shaping this behavior.

Anglo-American relations. The Russians may not have anticipated one important effect of their postwar espionage, because it resulted from the exposure of these efforts: it is the damage done to Anglo-American relations as for years afterwards recriminations flew back and forth across the Atlantic about who was to blame for what had happened. The arrest of Fuchs early in 1950 effectively ended whatever possibility there might have been for cooperation on nuclear matters;[80] and we can assume—certainly well-informed spy novelists have led us to believe—that the 1951 defection of Burgess and Maclean severely limited the willingness of American intelligence organizations to share information with their British counterparts.[81] The issue no longer figures so prominently in relations between London and Washington, but there are those who have suggested a certain satisfaction in Moscow with the highly publicized efforts of British "molehunters" that continued well into the 1980s.[82]

Negotiations with the Russians. One might have expected Soviet agents to have used their influence in London and Washington to attempt to move the British and American governments toward a more accommodating diplomatic posture regarding the Soviet Union, especially in the light of the Russians' own persistent "peace offensive" of 1948–50.[83] There is, interestingly, no evidence that they did so; indeed, if anything Philby appears to have gone out of his way to appear *suspicious* of Soviet intentions.[84] But, more important, revelations of Soviet espionage can only have reinforced the sense that was growing in the minds of Western statesmen that the Russians were not to be trusted, and that serious negotiations with them therefore were not to be risked. There is every reason to think that the Guzenko-Bentley revelations of late 1945 helped convince President Truman that he could not, as he had hoped he might, trust Stalin;[85] it is also interesting to consider the extent to which the Hiss, Fuchs, and Rosenberg cases may have contributed to the Americans' insistence, in dealing with the Russians after 1950, on "negotiation from strength," which meant for all practical purposes no negotiations at all.[86] It now seems clear that Stalin would like to have had negotiations, albeit on his terms.[87] But success in espionage can, in other areas of foreign policy, bring failure.

That point raises the more general question: Was it all worth it, from the Russians' own standpoint? There is good reason to doubt whether the benefits Stalin gained from spying on his allies during and after the war counter-balanced the problems created for him once his indulgence in espionage became known. The British diplomat Roger Makins has called attention to an important rule of statecraft: "You do not spy on your friends."[88] What is often forgotten about Stalin is that he wanted, in his way, to remain "friends" with the Americans and the British: his objective was to ensure the security of his regime and the state that it governed, not to bring about the long-awaited international proletarian revolution; he hoped to do this by means short of war, and preferably with Western cooperation.[89] The difficulty was that he defined "security" so expansively that it meant insecurity for much of the rest of Europe, Asia, and ultimately the United States as well; he also chose methods—espionage being one of them—that seemed at the time and still seem inconsistent with the objective he was trying to achieve. Seeking security by dubious means, he managed only to alarm and as a consequence to provoke the West into rearming: the effect produced cannot have been what was intended.[90]

Successes and Failures

Intelligence coups are one thing; the *uses* of intelligence are something else again.[91] If Philby, Fuchs, Hiss, and their associates were to the Russians what ULTRA and MAGIC were to the British and the Americans, then it is worth asking why Soviet foreign policy in the early postwar years was as ineffective as it was. After all, it could be argued that Stalin himself, more than any other individual, deserves the credit for the Marshall Plan, the North Atlantic Treaty Organization, a West Germany that was capitalist and firmly linked to the United States, a Japan that was also capitalist and equally firmly linked to the United States, and the massive Western (including German) rearmament that followed the outbreak of the Korean War; without the Soviet autocrat's intransigence on the German question, or his complicity in the Czech coup and the Berlin blockade, or his authorization for the North Koreans to attack South Korea,[92] most of these things would never have happened. In any minimally functional parliamentary democracy, the historian Vojtech Mastny has acidly noted, Stalin would long since have been sacked for incompetence.[93]

But the performance of Soviet diplomacy was not much better under Stalin's successors. It was Khrushchev, after all, who provoked the American defense build-up of the early 1960s and who strengthened NATO just at the time that General Charles de Gaulle was trying to weaken it; without the Kremlin leader's boastful exaggerations of Soviet strategic rocket capability, his Berlin "deadlines" of 1958 and 1961, his multi-megaton nuclear tests, and his decision to place intermediate-range missiles in Cuba, these things might never have happened. It was Brezhnev, after all, who distrusted and therefore did everything he could to discredit Jimmy Carter, the first American president who genuinely hoped to end the Cold War during his term in office;[94] what Brezhnev got for his trouble was not only Ronald Reagan but also the third major American military buildup of the Cold War, one that the Soviet Union this time was unable to match. One can only conclude from this pattern that either Soviet intelligence served its consumers badly in failing to anticipate Western reactions to Moscow's behavior, or that those consumers themselves were incapable of using the intelligence they received. Perhaps it was both.[95]

The United States had its own intelligence failures during the Cold War, to be sure. Historians may well conclude that the most persistent one was the tendency to overestimate Soviet and Warsaw Pact military and economic capabilities, as well as the political cohesion of U.S.S.R. itself. During the first decade and a half after World War II, American officials assumed—or found it convenient to assume—that the Soviet Union and its allies had the capability on short notice to overrun Western Europe; only in 1961 was it acknowledged that intelligence estimates had been counting as full divisions units that were only one-third the size of their NATO counterparts.[96] The Central Intelligence Agency was accurate in estimating Soviet missile-building capabilities during the late 1950s, and may even have underestimated them during the 1960s and early 1970s; but it probably overestimated the size and productivity of the Soviet economy, and it certainly failed to give sufficient attention to the survival of ethnic rivalries inside the U.S.S.R. and among its European satellites.[97] The fact that Soviet authority in East Central Europe collapsed as easily as it did in 1989—and that it was no longer possible to assume the continued existence of the Soviet Union itself after that date—suggests that processes of disintegration had been at work within the Soviet "empire" long before Western observers became aware of them. That, too, was an intelligence failure of major proportions.

All of which suggests a relationship between forms of government, on the one hand, and intelligence failures, on the other. Autocracies may be adept at penetrating other societies while resisting penetration themselves, but when it comes to the uses of intelligence, hierarchical organization is probably a liability. Dictators tend to be told what it is thought they want to hear, and that invariably limits the value of even the most subtle and well-placed spy; it also restricts a dictatorship's ability to calculate the consequences of its own actions.[98] Democracies may be gullible, lax about security, and ham-handed in conducting covert operations, but their relative absence of hierarchy makes more likely the critical scrutiny of intelligence and the decisions that are based upon it. Precisely because democracies are as self-conscious as they are about their own shortcomings, though, they tend to err on the side of "worst-case" analysis, and that in turn leads to the artificial inflation of adversary capabilities.[99] The playing field in the "great game" of intelligence may be more level than is often realized; that in turn may help to account for the fact that the game has gone on for as long as it has.

What about intelligence successes? Traditionally, of course, they are supposed to remain hidden: to reveal a success is often to compromise it, while with failures the damage is already done. But the end of the Cold War may render obsolete at least some of the reasons for concealing past intelligence successes; if so, a clearer picture of their significance will emerge, and of the context in which we should seek to place it. As that happens, we may also begin to alter our understanding of what an "intelligence success" really is. The old view defined success in terms of *withholding* information from an adversary: whether the activity in question involved codebreaking, espionage, disinformation, or even scholarly research and analysis, the important thing was to keep the enemy from knowing what was going on. It is already apparent, though, that the greatest intelligence success of the Cold War, for both sides, was the development of the reconnaissance satellite, the effect of which was so greatly to diminish the fear of surprise attack.[100] That breakthrough worked not because it withheld information, but because it *provided* it. Transparency became a mutual benefit, and by the end of the Cold War its two major protagonists were regularly exchanging information on how to make critical weapons systems *visible*—for the purpose of verifying arms control agreements—to the new kind of spies each of them regularly dispatched to observe the other. Distinguishing intelligence "failures" from "successes," therefore, may turn out to be more difficult than one might expect.

Intelligence and History: The Future Agenda

What should be the agenda for future research in this admittedly difficult field? What follows are nothing more than personal observations, based on my own sporadic and mostly ineffective efforts to come to grips with this subject.

First, and most important, we need documents. Although a substantial quantity of end-product *analyses* from the CIA and other American intelligence organizations period have been declassified for the post-1945 period, these only scratch the surface of what we need to know about the impact of intelligence on postwar diplomacy. We have no knowledge, at present, of the sources on which these analyses were based; nor are we in a position to track the process by which they were put together. Even worse, virtually no documents have been released on covert operations, despite the fact that we probably now have information—at least in general terms—on most of what occurred in this area during the early Cold War years. We are left in the position of having to write the history of postwar intelligence from a position roughly comparable to where historians of the OSS were a decade ago: of trying to derive solely from research and analysis reports the full scope of an intelligence organization's activity. It could not be done adequately for OSS; nor can we expect to treat the early CIA with anything approaching scholarly responsibility until this situation is remedied.[101]

The Agency's own response has been that it cannot officially acknowledge covert operations for fear of compromising "sources and methods," but that argument carries less and less plausibility as time passes. Given what the Russians knew four decades ago about Anglo-American intelligence activities—not to mention what has been unofficially revealed since—it is difficult to accept the argument that there could be much in the Agency's early postwar archives that would, if declassified, significantly jeopardize current "sources and methods." Another less frequently voiced justification for keeping these documents secret is that the Agency has never formally acknowledged covert activities of any kind. As one Agency official explained to me several years ago: "We have never admitted even to having agents stationed overseas, except in Saigon between 1965 and 1975." But in addition to being silly this claim is simply not true: if there were innocent souls in this country or abroad who believed that the CIA refrained from covert operations, that innocence was surely lost when the Agency itself put its most secret "family jewels" on display before the Senate Select Committee on Intelligence in 1975.[102] If this did not constitute an official acknowledgment of covert activities, one wonders what would have.

It is also the case that the withholding of documents, although bureaucratically an easy thing to do, exacts a price: one generally appears to have been more sinister—and often less bright—than one actually was. It is difficult to think of an instance in which the systematic declassification of documents, as opposed to sensational selective revelations, actually harmed a nation's interests; the more frequent pattern is that opening the archives either makes no difference at all or, as in the 1955 release of the State Department's Yalta papers, actually enhances official reputations. Things imagined are usually worse than things really are. One need only look at the long search, in Great Britain, for the "fifth" man—it might be more accurate to say for the "nth" man[103]—to see how official silence feeds, more than it restrains, conspiracy theories.

Second, we need to begin systematically to interview, and to cross-check interviews, with retired intelligence officials.[104] Perhaps because of their frustration over the slow progress of declassification, a number of these individuals are now willing to talk about their activities. But memories of events long passed are notoriously unreliable; and when the events in question were shrouded in secrecy, the possibility for error is very much compounded. The only corrective to this, apart from the actual release of documents, is careful cross-checking of what these people say, perhaps even by bringing them together—as has been done successfully in the field of nuclear history—for "memory jogging" conferences.[105] Historians and participants in historical events are always trying to set each other straight. Why not use this creative tension more systematically to illuminate those areas where documents are not yet available to us?

Third, we would do well to incorporate more of what we already know about psychology into the study of intelligence. We all know that intelligence is no better than the degree of receptivity its primary consumers bring to it. But we know very little about what determines a policy-maker's receptivity to certain kinds of information and not to others. It is not that we lack the means of finding out: the field of cognitive psychology does exist, and its insights have been fruitfully applied in other areas.[106] Why not to the world of intelligence? A closely related area of considerable importance—and one almost totally ignored by students of the subject—has to do with comparative morality. How does a policy-maker decide what kind of behavior is appropriate in conditions of crisis? To what extent does the promise of concealment encourage latitude in choosing means? Is there such a thing as "national style" in intelligence that causes some nations to worry more about this sort of thing than others do, and, if so, from what does it stem?

Fourth, we probably do not need a great many more studies of how intelligence is organized. Precisely because it does not require access to classified materials, a good deal of work has already been done in the United States on the relation of the intelligence agencies to one another, to the Congress, and to the Executive. Much of it, while solid, begins with organizational charts, and ends with conclusions drawn therefrom. But anyone who has worked with historical materials would surely know that organizational structure is only part of the story. It can be important in certain instances,[107] but it is also worth noting Ernest May's observation, in his study of pre-World War I and II intelligence assessment, that the "type of organization appears to have had little effect on the quality of assessment."[108] It may well be that in this field, as in most others, what particular individuals do to, within, and apart from bureaucracies is generally more important than the structure of the bureaucracies themselves.

Finally, and most important, we need to try to begin to make the linkage between intelligence and the policy it is supposed to inform. The field of intelligence studies, like the history of the American Civil War, lends itself too easily to "buffism," which is to say, to a preoccupation with details and a neglect of context. This is not at all surprising, since the subject carries with it the fascination of dealing with what was once surreptitious, sneaky, and sly. But just as good military history is more than the sum total of available "war stories," so good intelligence history will have to be more than an accumulation of "spy stories": it will have to try to answer Robin Winks's "so what" question; it will have to show how what governments actually did relates to what they knew, or did not know. It is, admittedly, a tall order, but it is not too soon to begin to think about how we might fill it.

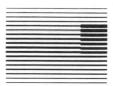

SIX

The Essential Relevance
of Nuclear Weapons

It is not given to many generations to witness a completely unprecedented event. The collapse of empires, the overthrow of dynasties, the outbreak of plagues, the onset of revolutions, and even the improvement of the human condition itself—all of these are *categories* of events, which means that they have happened before and will almost certainly happen again. There are very few occurrences of which it can be said that nothing like them has ever taken place; there are not very many true points of departure in human affairs, after which nothing can be even remotely similar again.

But what took place in the New Mexico desert on July 16, 1945, surely qualifies as such an occurrence. The first test explosion of an atomic bomb—together with the actual use of that weapon three weeks later against the Japanese cities of Hiroshima and Nagasaki—was as sharp a break from the past as any in all of history. Theory had intersected reality to produce a weapon that was regarded at the time as unlike any other that had ever been invented, and that is still so regarded today, almost half a century later. The result, it now appears, has been a fundamental—and possibly permanent—change in human behavior.

Two and a half millennia before the test at Alamogordo, Thucydides had predicted that cataclysms might come and go, but that human nature would remain much the same.[1] The events that caused atomic bombs to be developed appeared to confirm this gloomy prophecy, for mankind's predisposition toward self-destructive war seemed as great in the first half of the twentieth century as it had been when Athens confronted Sparta in the last half of the fifth century B. C. "The unleashed power of the atom has changed everything save our modes of thinking," Albert Einstein wrote in 1946, "and thus we drift toward unparalleled catastrophe."[2]

But the last half of the twentieth century has not, so far, borne out that prophecy, and the "catastrophe" is now long overdue. Einstein would have been as surprised as anyone else who lived through the early Cold War years to learn that Nagasaki would be the last occasion upon which atomic weapons would be used in anger for at least the next four and a half decades, despite the fact that the great geopolitical rivalry between the United States and the Soviet Union would drag on throughout that length of time. History is full of unexpected developments, but few have been as completely unexpected as that the great powers would produce tens of thousands of nuclear weapons between the end of World War II and the present day, without a single one of them having been used for the gruesome purpose for which they were designed. Perfecting the ultimate instrument of war has made the ancient institution of war, for the first time in history, obsolete. Or so it would appear.

Correlations and Causes

But roosters crow every morning, and shortly thereafter, with unfailing regularity, the sun rises; that does not mean that the first event made the second one take place. It is important, in matters like these, not to confuse correlations with causes. Because the atomic bomb preceded the onset of the Cold War, it has been too easy for us simply to assume that nuclear weapons are what transformed that conflict into a long peace, thereby deflecting it from the violent course most other great-power rivalries in the past have followed. There has been no serious attempt to test that proposition, though, and as a result the end of the Cold War finds us with little greater understanding of the role nuclear weapons have played in the post-1945 international system than we had at the time that conflict began.

This ignorance poses dangers as we move beyond the Cold War. For if it should turn out that nuclear weapons did prevent World War III, then we would have good reason to want to keep them around as insurance against the outbreak of future wars. But if nuclear weapons had nothing to do with preserving the peace—if Cold War history would have been much the same if they had never been developed—then we are wasting money and running unnecessary risks in continuing to build them. It is difficult to think of an area in which the judgment of historians could have greater importance for future policy; and yet until recently few historians—or political scientists, or even nuclear scientists, for that matter—had given this question very much thought.

All of that began to change with the publication, early in 1989, of John Mueller's engagingly written but controversial *Retreat from Doomsday: The Obsolescence of Major War*,[3] a book that challenges conventional wisdom on this subject in a careful and surprisingly persuasive way. Mueller argues that the escalating costs of war in advanced industrial societies, revealed so painfully in World War I, had made military conflict between great powers impractical in the eyes of most statesmen long before World War II broke out. It took the evil genius of Hitler, the bumbling belligerence of Mussolini, and the romantic risk-taking of a few Japanese militarists to produce that conflict;[4] the experience of fighting it confirmed the catastrophic results of modern warfare for anyone who might have doubted that point; and, as a consequence, a long postwar peace would have ensued after 1945, even if nuclear weapons had never existed. The fear of another conventional war on the scale of the disasters of 1914–18 and 1939–45 would, in itself, have deterred the great powers from ever again using force against each other. It follows, then, that nuclear weapons have been, in Mueller's words, "essentially irrelevant" in bringing about the remarkable durability—and therefore stability—of the international system that emerged during the Cold War.

The reaction of most of us, upon hearing this argument, is that it has to be wrong. We somehow *know* that nuclear weapons have been critically "relevant" to the postwar long peace. But when one asks just *how* we know this, an embarrassing silence sets in. For although most people believe that nuclear weapons did in fact prevent World War III, most of them base that belief on little more than faith; few have ever bothered to try to *prove* that nuclear weapons play the role that almost everyone assumes they do. The great value of Mueller's book is that it forces us to confront that issue squarely for the first time.

If we are to test Mueller's hypothesis—if we are to determine how, or whether, nuclear weapons have influenced the postwar international system—we will have to draw upon a variety of investigative techniques, and we will have to do so in an ecumenical manner. Archival research can suggest what statesmen actually believed about nuclear weapons as opposed to what they or their advisers said for public consumption: the distinction has at times been an important one.[5] Counterfactual analysis can provide the intellectual equivalent of a "laboratory" in which to "rerun" history under circumstances that can be controlled, and even shifted, at will. Theory gives us ways to "model" the workings of international systems, both real and imagined, in various configurations and under varying conditions.[6]

The difficulty with these methods, though, is that they provide no universally-accepted standard of verification. History is not like chemistry, where the combination of known elements in known quantities produces known compounds, no matter who does the experiment, no matter how many times it is repeated. The historian's "proof" can never be as conclusive—or as rigorously replicable—as the "proofs" laboratory science routinely provides.

But of course chemistry laboratories are not like the real world, where elements rarely exist in a pure state, where compounds interact in uncontrolled ways, and where the very act of setting up an experiment is to isolate the substances one is dealing with from their natural environment. From this perspective, historians and scientists have more in common than one might think, because both simplify reality in order to generalize about it. The historian does this by selecting—from the infinite variety that is the past—what to research and write about. The scientist does this by isolating—from the infinite variety that is the external world—what to simulate, or model, in the laboratory. Each of them operates by advancing hypotheses; both of them assume, if hypotheses hold up, that they have attained at least an approximation of the truth, if not truth itself.[7]

This common procedure suggests a way to test the proposition that nuclear weapons were "essentially irrelevant" to the long postwar peace. The remainder of this essay will advance four hypotheses relating to the role nuclear weapons have played in the post-World War II international system, any one of which, if shown to be plausible, would falsify Mueller's argument. These hypotheses by no means exhaust the range of possible ways in which nuclear weapons may have influenced world politics since 1945: so broad a subject would require its own very big book.[8] But they are intended to suggest how what we think happened did in fact happen. I will conclude with some thoughts about what these hypotheses might imply for the post-Cold War world.

Hypothesis I: Nuclear weapons reinforced an already declining propensity on the part of great powers to fight one another.

There is no necessary inconsistency in Mueller's argument, on the one hand, that the willingness of great powers to use force against each other has been declining since World War I, and, on the other hand, the argument Mueller seeks to refute, which is that the existence of nuclear weapons has made force more difficult to use. The pattern here could as plausibly be one of "reinforcement" as the "irrelevancy" Mueller emphasizes; the development of nuclear weapons could well have reinforced—powerfully—a trend toward the obsolescence of war that was already under way. As Carl Kaysen has put it: "These new technologies of war have amplified the message of this century's war experiences by many decibels, and set it firmly in the minds of the wide public as well as those of political and military leaders."[9]

Mueller's argument for "irrelevancy" depends on showing that World War II grew out of the isolated actions of Hitler, Mussolini, and the Japanese militarists. But world wars, if they are to take place, require collective action: the populations of Germany, Italy, and Japan had to agree to fight, and so too did their adversaries. A state that had come to regard war as truly obsolete would have surrendered rather than fight; but the British, the French, and even the doomed Poles thought they would gain something by resorting to arms in 1939, and so did the nations Japan attacked in 1941. Many states were reluctant to enter World War II, and admittedly that is a striking difference from the enthusiasm that greeted the outbreak of World War I. But those nations nonetheless preferred war to capitulation: World War I was not so catastrophic as to make World War II unthinkable.

There was little tendency at the time to see World War II, as so many had seen World War I, as a "war to end all wars." Planning for new conflicts was going on even as the war against Germany and Japan was being fought;[10] certainly the avidity with which both American and Soviet intelligence organizations sought to capture German scientists and to obtain German military technology does not suggest that future wars—at least before the advent of nuclear weapons—had been ruled out.[11] It is one thing to say that everyone was tired of war by 1945; no doubt everyone was. But mutual exhaustion is not enough to keep mutual suspicion from arising, and suspicion can lead to the fear of war, even if its actual prospects are remote. The fear of war, in turn, can lead to warlike behavior, because measures taken for defensive reasons can often appear offensive in character. Given the suspicion and fear that existed in Soviet-American relations during the early Cold War years, Mueller's assertion that the memory of World War II alone would have prevented all future wars remains, at best, unproven.

There is yet another difficulty with Mueller's argument that nuclear weapons were irrelevant to the long postwar peace. It fails to take into account a peculiar characteristic of those weapons that made them unique: the fact that, because of Hiroshima, the full consequences of using the atomic bomb became apparent at the moment the world became aware of its existence. The invention of nuclear weapons did not resemble such other breakthroughs in military technology as the development of machine guns, poison gas, or aerial bombardment, in which the effects of use had not been immediately apparent. Visions of the Somme, if they had been available in 1914, or of Dresden, if they had been available in 1939, might well have deterred the wars that followed; indeed it is precisely Mueller's argument that the experiences of World Wars I and II provided a glimpse into the future (by way of the past) that was enough to deter anyone contemplating World War III.

The vision of future war that Hiroshima burned into everyone's mind was vastly more frightening than any that had existed before.[12] For although the bomb's devastation may not have been greater than that inflicted by conventional means on other Japanese targets, the fact that a single weapon had vaporized most of a city in a single instant was something new. Destruction elsewhere in Japan had required months of bombing, and even though Dresden was largely destroyed in a single night, it had certainly taken more than a single bomb to do it. The atomic bomb's quantum jump in destructive power, when coupled with the realization that progress in long- range bomber and missile technology might soon make it possible to deliver this new weapon anywhere on the face of the earth, created a psychological impression that went well beyond anything conventional operations during the war had produced.[13]

Students of history too often assume that change in human affairs takes place gradually and at a regular rate. But students of evolutionary biology know that conditions of "punctuated equilibrium" can exist: sudden shifts in environment can kill off old species and create favorable conditions for the emergence of new ones; the new status quo can then stabilize for long periods in between.[14] The abrupt psychological effect of nuclear weapons was a moment of historical "punctuation," in that it represented a sharp acceleration in the trend toward the obsolescence of war that Mueller describes, and that was indeed already under way. The stability that followed[15]—that is, the perpetuation, for over four and a half decades, of a world order dominated by two nations preeminent in nuclear capability—resulted, in large part, from that initial shock.

None of this is to say, and Mueller does not claim, that nuclear weapons have made all war impossible. One need only look at conflicts in Korea, Vietnam, Afghanistan, and the Persian Gulf, as well as a long series of smaller-scale military interventions in the Third World, to see that even under conditions of Cold War great powers continued to use force when they did not directly confront other great powers. Middle-level powers also used force against one another: witness a succession of Arab-Israeli wars, India-Pakistan wars, the Iran-Iraq War, the Falklands War, and the Iraqi invasion of Kuwait. Two of these cases—Egypt's attack on Israel in 1973 and Argentina's on the Falkland Islands (a British possession) in 1982—even involved non-nuclear powers attacking nuclear powers, which suggests that simply possessing a nuclear capability does not guarantee deterrence.[16] The nuclear revolution, therefore, has hardly made the world as a whole a more peaceful place.

But the fact that no great power has gone to war with another great power since 1945 is, nevertheless, a remarkable record, unparalleled in modern history. Consider how many citizens of great powers died in wars in the forty-five years that separated 1900 from 1945, as compared with the number who died in such wars in the forty-five years that followed.[17] Consider how many crises have been managed without resorting to war since 1945, as compared with how few were prior to that date.[18] One can lock up roosters inside dark barns and still reasonably expect the sun to rise each morning. It is much less plausible to assume that, in the absence of nuclear weapons, these abrupt changes in patterns of international behavior would have taken place.

Hypothesis II: The possession of nuclear weapons diminishes, more than it encourages, the tendency of nations to take risks.

A key aspect of Mueller's argument is that Japanese cultural isolation made that nation prone to risk war long after Europeans and Americans had become aware—from their common experience in World War I—of the counterproductive consequences of doing so. The implication is that cultural diversity impedes learning of the kind that, Mueller thinks, is making war obsolete. No one would question that World War II "educated" Japan in the most emphatic possible way; since that time that country has been among the states least inclined even to consider the use of military force. But what about the some hundred or so states—many of which experienced neither World War I or II—that have become independent since 1945? Why should the cultural isolation that Mueller tells us induced Japan to risk war in 1941 not have caused any number of wars, given the proliferation of culturally diverse states since that time?

There have, of course, been some such wars, and some of them have even involved proclaimed (or assumed) nuclear powers. But nuclear weapons have never been used in any of them, and that is easily as remarkable a development as has been the pattern of non-use among the superpowers, where the possibilities of retaliation encouraged restraint. No such possibility could have deterred Israel from using nuclear weapons against Egypt in 1973, for example, or China against Vietnam in 1979, or Great Britain against Argentina in 1982. Nor would there even have been any immediate danger of retaliation if the United States had used nuclear weapons during the Vietnam War, or if the Soviet Union had employed them in Afghanistan.

But one need only state these possibilities to be struck by their improbability. The reason for this—the reason a pattern of nuclear non-use seems solidly to have established itself even where retaliatory capabilities do not exist—is that there are severe limits to what one can accomplish by actually using a nuclear weapon. The problem is obviously one of proportion: the means employed are almost always disproportionate to the extent of the mischief. One causes greater difficulties by using nuclear weapons than the difficulties that cause one to consider their use in the first place.[19]

Indeed, nuclear weapons have become an effective instrument of cross-cultural education, in that they have made the limitations of military force apparent, in similar ways, to very dissimilar societies. Nations as diverse as the United States, the Soviet Union, Great Britain, France, China, India, and a number of as yet unannounced nuclear powers all have developed these weapons without finding occasions upon which to use them.[20] A kind of international "taboo" has evolved that forbids the use of nuclear weapons except in the direst of circumstances—circumstances so dire that they have yet to manifest themselves anywhere since the end of World War II.[21]

Nuclear weapons also appear to have restrained risk-taking in connection with the initiation of crises, at least among the superpowers. The historical record suggests that qualitative and quantitative superiority in nuclear weaponry has not made the side possessing it confident that it can take greater risks than a less well-equipped adversary; indeed, the process appears to have worked in just the opposite way. For it was states with a qualitative or quantitative *disadvantage* in nuclear weaponry that initiated the most severe Cold War crises: witness Stalin's risk-taking in authorizing the Berlin blockade of 1948 and the North Korean attack of 1950; or Mao's with regard to Quemoy and Matsu in 1954–55 and 1958; or Khrushchev's in connection with Berlin in 1958–59 and Cuba in 1962. There was no comparable pattern of American adventurism, despite the fact that these were the years in which the United States enjoyed nuclear superiority.[22]

The history of international relations would show few examples in which military plenty imposed constraints upon freedom of action, and military poverty induced attempts to upset the status quo. To the extent that there is a pattern here—and the total absence of great power war since 1945 suggests that there is one—it appears to be that the possession of large numbers of nuclear weapons induces a sense of responsibility and diminishes the temptation to take risks, whatever one's own culture, history, or circumstances happen to be.

One is left, then, with strong indications that the advent of nuclear weapons has not only made great power war much less likely than it was in the pre-nuclear era, but that possessing nuclear weapons in large quantities turns states into defenders of the status quo. Both of these propositions undercut Mueller's argument that nuclear weapons have been "irrelevant" to the workings of the postwar international system, for even if they have only reinforced trends that were already under way, the strengthening—and stabilization—of a system is as "relevant" to its functioning as are the original circumstances that gave rise to it. And nuclear weapons appear to have been a very powerful stabilizer indeed.

Hypothesis III: Although nuclear weapons did not create the bipolar character of international relations during the Cold War, they did prolong its life.

Bipolarity—the evolution of an international system that was worldwide in scope but dominated by only two major powers—was something new when it appeared at the end of World War II. International relations for the past several centuries had taken place within systems that normally contained four or five great powers: hence the logically impossible but still-convenient term "multipolarity" with which we label such systems.[23] Multipolarity was already eroding, though, before nuclear weapons were developed.

It was the two great conventional wars of this century that exhausted the Europeans, thus allowing the United States and the Soviet Union (itself only partly a European power) to dominate the postwar international order. In this sense, Adolf Hitler—not the atomic bomb—created bipolarity, for by declaring war on the Soviet Union *and* the United States in 1941, he brought both powers into a European arena at a time when the Europeans themselves were creating a power vacuum there.

Post-World War II bipolarity had several components. The immense geographical size, population base, and natural resource endowment of the United States and the Soviet Union would have made them actors of consequence on the world scene in any event. But these were also nations with global ideological aspirations: Marxism-Leninism, with its self-proclaimed ambition to undermine capitalism throughout the world, had been in place since 1917; it is often forgotten, though, that Woodrow Wilson had put forward a rival ideology that same year when he justified American entry into World War I as a fight "to make the world safe for democracy."[24] The concept of self-determination, subsequently enshrined in Wilson's Fourteen Points, would in time prove to be just as potent an ideology—and certainly a more durable one—than the one Lenin and Trotsky were embracing at exactly the same time.

Neither their physical resources nor their ideologies were enough to transform the United States and the Soviet Union into superpowers, though; it took their wartime military performance in defeating Nazi Germany and Japan to do that, together with the massive economic and industrial infrastructures needed to accomplish that task. Soviet and American power at the end of the war existed, therefore, in several different forms—geographical, demographic, economic, ideological, and military. The diversified character of this power, and the hegemonies that resulted from it, are what gave rise to the new bipolar system of international relations that appeared after 1945.

Over the subsequent four and a half decades, however, the diversified character of Soviet and American hegemony has gradually disappeared. That condition had always been somewhat artificial, in the sense that recovery from the war was sure to allow competitors to arise who would gradually undermine the two superpowers' positions of pre-eminence. Decolonization produced a "third" world determined to carve out its independence from the "first" and "second" worlds. The rehabilitation of Germany and Japan re-established old centers of power that would create future economic rivals for the United States; meanwhile, political repression and economic failures in communist countries were discrediting the once potent appeal of Marxism outside of the Soviet Union. Because of its economic backwardness, that country's status as a superpower had always been more problematic than that of the United States, and by the mid-1980s Moscow's ability to influence world events had dramatically declined. But "decline" was a major concern as well for Americans, who saw their country neglecting its internal infrastructure, piling up massive deficits, and losing its competitive edge in the world economy.[25]

And yet, one category of power continued to set off the United States and the Soviet Union from all other states: each still possessed much larger quantities of nuclear weapons than anyone else. Nuclear pre-eminence maintained a facade of Soviet-American bipolarity long after the reality of it had begun to disappear. It did so, it now seems clear, not because the possession of nuclear weapons conferred specific benefits upon the nations that controlled them; as we have already seen, those nations found themselves constrained more often than liberated by having "gone nuclear." Rather, it appears that the possession of nuclear weapons had become the principal symbolic indicator of what it was to be a great power in the post-World War II era.[26]

Theorists tell us that hegemony in international politics depends as much on acquiescence as on imposition: other nations accord hegemonic power a certain legitimacy, even as hegemonic power asserts itself. The diversified character of Soviet and American power during the early Cold War did elicit deference on the part of other powers; hence the division of Europe—and portions of the rest of the world as well—into spheres of influence owing allegiance either to Moscow or Washington. What is interesting, though, is that this habit of deference survived, for so long, the contraction of Moscow's and Washington's power base. There is no way to "prove" that continued nuclear hegemony preserved the façade of hegemony in other areas; still we know that hegemony, once established, tends to persist after the original conditions that gave rise to it have passed from the scene.[27] And the fact that nuclear weapons, once built, do not easily disappear—even as other forms of power do—suggests that they contributed to that persistence.

Nuclear weapons provided a power "gradient" that distinguished the United States and the Soviet Union from the rest of the world, even if the power that constituted that gradient was not usable in any practical way. It was by perpetuating the impression that the United States and the Soviet

Union still counted as superpowers—indeed by providing the most succinct definition of what a "superpower" is in the first place—that nuclear weapons prolonged, even if they did not create, bipolarity.

How, in turn, did bipolarity enhance the stability of the postwar international system? Here international relations theory provides at least partial answers. Kenneth Waltz has pointed out that bipolar systems are easier to manage than their multipolar counterparts, because the means of communication are simpler, and the dangers of misperception are correspondingly less.[28] Robert Axelrod has suggested yet another reason for the stability of bipolarity: game theory shows that cooperative behavior tends to emerge among antagonists with the passage of time, provided the "players" have reason to believe that the "game" they are playing will continue into the future.[29]

It is difficult, from a counterfactual perspective, to see what else besides nuclear weapons could have sustained bipolarity beyond the point at which it otherwise would have eroded, thus buying the time that was necessary for patterns of cooperation among former superpower adversaries to emerge. The passage of time has had just this effect, though, to such an extent that it requires a major effort now—even for former participants in the events of that era—to recall what the Cold War was all about in the first place. The inducement of a benign form of collective amnesia, therefore, may be another way in which nuclear weapons enhanced the stability of the postwar international system.

Hypothesis IV: Nuclear weapons perpetuated the Cold War by making its costs bearable on both sides.

Strategy is largely a matter of balancing costs against risks. The things one does to minimize risks in seeking to safeguard national security tend to drive up costs: defenses are always expensive, and the more elaborate one's defenses are—the more one has sought insurance against a wide spectrum of potential threats—the more one can expect to have to pay for them. Conversely, the things one does to minimize costs tend to drive up risks: budget cuts render defenses less formidable and hence less capable of covering the range of possible dangers. The dilemma is an ancient one, and every nation that has had to exist in an insecure environment for any length of time has had to face it.[30]

At first glance, it would appear that the development of nuclear weapons did little to resolve this dilemma. For during those periods in which the United States relied primarily upon nuclear deterrence for its security—for example, 1945–50, 1953–61, and (less overtly) 1969–80—critics were able to show how ineffective this strategy was in countering such threats as the overthrow of American clients, or the rise of "national liberation" movements, or even—as Korea and Vietnam clearly demonstrated—limited war. And the consequences of actually using any nuclear weapon under any circumstance were so unpredictable that the weapons themselves came to be regarded as major sources of risk.

During those periods in which the United States sought more "balanced" defenses that did not rely primarily upon nuclear deterrence—the late Truman administration, the Kennedy and Johnson administrations, and the early Reagan administration—the nation developed capabilities to attempt to meet threats at whatever level they occurred, but only by raising defense budgets to levels that threatened to overwhelm the national economy.[31] In each of these instances, it quickly became apparent that taxpayers were not prepared to sustain expenditures at such levels for long periods of time; bankruptcy, it seemed, could pose as much of a danger as did the nation's external adversaries.

The American people have never been willing to support costly "risk-minimizing" strategies over the long haul, and yet, they have sustained the American commitment to containment with remarkable steadiness and durability throughout the Cold War.[32] The most plausible explanation for this apparent contradiction is that nuclear weapons made the costs of bearing global responsibilities tolerable.

Without nuclear weapons, the defense establishment and the military-industrial complex that supported it might well have been larger than it was.[33] But so massive a defense establishment might also have produced a reversion to isolationism, and that would have meant an abandonment by the United States, once again, of its global responsibilities: the 1950s could have been a replay of the 1920s. Had that happened, the international system as a whole would surely have been less stable than in fact it turned out to be.

If the United States was unwilling, on a permanent basis, to defend itself without relying on nuclear weapons, the same was also true of its major allies. The history of the North Atlantic Treaty Organization can largely be written in terms of a persistent effort, over the years, to find ways of deterring an attack from the Soviet Union and the Warsaw Pact without placing an unacceptable strain on the economies—and the taxpayers—of the nations that benefited from that protection. NATO's doctrine of nuclear "first use" made that compromise possible, as did the decision of the United States—now over four decades old—to station its own troops in Europe on an indefinite basis. But that commitment of troops, too, could hardly have been sustained in the absence of the assurance that nuclear weapons would be used, if war came, to protect them.[34]

Western European attitudes toward this strategy have been, to be sure, ambivalent: this is hardly surprising since its implementation might well have left what was to have been defended in ruins. Anti-nuclear movements have waxed and waned since the late 1950s depending on the intensity of Cold War tensions. But it is significant that at no point have those movements, or those tensions, become sufficiently strong to force NATO to revise its basic nuclear strategy. The cost-minimizing role of nuclear weapons has, on the whole, made the risks of relying on them acceptable to Europeans; in their absence, the history of the NATO alliance, like the history of the American role in the world at large, would have been quite different.

The same pattern can be seen with respect to Japan. It is interesting that

that nation—the only one ever to have had the direct experience of nuclear war—should have been willing to rely for its defense, to the extent that it has, on an American nuclear "umbrella." Even more clearly than has been the case with NATO, successive Japanese governments have apparently concluded that the ability to shift most of the burden of defense to others while transforming their own nation into the world's most successful "trading" state is no bad bargain.[35]

Whether this pattern of relying on nuclear deterrence to minimize the costs of containment would have held up if the risks of war with the Soviet Union had been greater is difficult to say. We do now know that during the Cuban missile crisis the United States, which possessed both overall nuclear and regional conventional force superiority, was prepared to make substantial concessions to avoid having to use either of those capabilities.[36] But the prospect of nuclear war was never strong enough, most of the time, to overcome the attractions of relying on nuclear weapons to make the costs of defense acceptable to both domestic and allied constituencies, and that had implications for the perpetuation of the Cold War.

For without nuclear weapons and the relatively cheap means of defense they provided, the West might either have exhausted itself in the effort to contain the threats to its security that appeared to exist during the early years of the Cold War, or have been forced to compromise its differences with the Soviet Union, or both. Nuclear weapons provided a way to "extend" deterrence not only geographically but also in time. Without those "extensions," the Cold War as we know it would almost certainly have ended at an earlier stage, and possibly with a different result, than it actually did.

The Soviet Union and the People's Republic of China also relied upon nuclear weapons as cost-minimizing—if risk-maximizing—instruments, but for different reasons. Neither the Russians nor the Chinese ever came close to challenging the United States and its Western allies in overall economic and industrial strength. But their possession of nuclear weapons was an "equalizer" of sorts, in that it gave those countries the ability to compete with the West at least in military terms; without such weapons, these Marxist economies would have been hard-pressed to maintain that rivalry for as long as they did. If that is in fact the case—and if nuclear weapons also reduced the West's costs of providing for security in what was perceived to be an insecure world—then it seems likely that they perpetuated the Cold War itself, and thus, the very sources of the insecurity they were relied upon, by both sides, to guard against.

Prospects for the Future

Was it a good thing that nuclear weapons perpetuated the Cold War, even as they stabilized the behavior of those nations that were caught up in it? We will have no very good way to answer that question until we know more about what the post-Cold War world is going to look like, and how it will compare with what preceded it. But the end of the Cold War is certain to raise questions about the role of nuclear weapons in the future international system, and it is not too early to begin to think about what some of these might be. For example:

1. Assuming that significant reductions in nuclear arsenals take place over the next decade, what are the lowest numbers the great powers can agree on without removing the inhibitions nuclear weapons provide against the use of force by the great powers? Are non-nuclear inhibitions sufficiently powerful to deter that prospect in a world in which only a few or even no operational nuclear weapons continue to exist?

2. How far can reductions in nuclear weapons be negotiated without bringing the United States and the Soviet Union down to the level of the other nuclear powers and thus reviving multipolarity, with all the dangers that both theory and history suggest it brings? What is likely to be the stability of an international system that reverts to multipolarity, but in which nuclear weapons continue to exist?

3. Is nuclear bipolarity sustainable (or even meaningful) in a situation where—quite independently of what is negotiated with respect to arms control—one super-power's internal legitimacy is collapsing? What happens to bipolarity—even if the Soviet Union does not collapse—if there is no longer an antagonistic relationship between Washington and Moscow?

4. Is there not the paradoxical possibility that a diminishing sense of threat could force *greater* reliance on nuclear weapons for deterrence in the future, because only they would remain in place ready for use, while more costly conventional forces and weapons might not? But if nuclear weapons themselves are to be reduced in number, then it is not clear how reliance upon such weapons in a resource-constrained budgetary environment would work.[37] At a minimum, there will exist the old problem of a mis-match between the weapons themselves and the kinds of threats they are expected to counter. And one wonders how long the concept of "extended deterrence" can remain viable, as old Cold War threats diminish and as local opposition to the stationing of nuclear weapons on foreign territory mounts.

5. If the possession of nuclear weapons does in fact cause great powers to behave more responsibly, should we not welcome nuclear proliferation?[38] At what point does the risk of irrational action—which presumably increases as the number of nuclear-capable states increases—outweigh the benefits of the "sobering effect" nuclear capability apparently brings?

6. History suggests that asymmetries in the kinds and numbers of nuclear weapons the great powers have possessed meant relatively little in terms of the actual security of those states. But history also suggests that domestic constituencies—whether military, industrial, scientific, or political—have rarely been prepared to accept that conclusion. Will they be more likely to do so in a post-Cold War world?

This is hardly the place even to attempt to answer this set of questions, any one of which would be sufficient to keep the experts busy for a long time to come. They do suggest, though, the difficulty of foreseeing the shape of a post-Cold War world in which nuclear weapons continue to exist. That lack of clarity makes it all the more important that we enter this world with a clearer view than we now have of what the past relationship between nuclear weapons and international systemic stability has actually been.

Conclusion: The Relevance of Redundancy

It is often claimed that, by developing nuclear weapons, mankind made a "Faustian" bargain—a pact with the devil, so to speak—that was certain sooner or later to exact a terrible price. It would be both foolish and complacent to argue that we have escaped that prospect, for even if the danger of nuclear war appears to have receded into the background, surprises as well as accidents can still happen. And no one should claim that nuclear armaments are particularly "forgiving" of unexpected developments, for no one has any clear idea of what the result might be if they should ever be used, nor is there any safe way to find out.

But an international system in which nuclear weapons exist and are *not* used—if the post-World War II system is any guide—can be very "forgiving" indeed: what is striking about this system is the number of miscalculations, challenges, and even outright insults it has tolerated while preserving its fundamental character intact. Nuclear weapons are by no means the only explanation for this; there are others, not the least of which is good luck.[39]

If one could replay the history of the past forty-five years without nuclear weapons, though, would one be willing to do so on the assumption that things would come out in the same way? John Mueller may well be right; at a minimum his book has forced a clarification of our thinking on this subject. But it is worth remembering that people purchase insurance all the time against contingencies that never arise. Redundancy in the mechanisms that insure the security of one's family, one's property, and one's life is considered to be a good thing to have, even if one is never called upon to use it: redundancy is "relevant" in providing reassurance. Nuclear weapons have been, and are likely to continue to be, "relevant" to the stability of the international system in much the same redundant way.[40]

## SEVEN

# The Unexpected
Ronald Reagan

The task of the historian is, very largely, one of explaining how we got from where we were to where we are today. To say that the Reagan administration's policy toward the Soviet Union is going to pose special challenges to historians is to understate the matter: rarely has there been a greater gap between the expectations held for an administration at the beginning of its term and the results it actually produced. The last thing one would have anticipated at the time Ronald Reagan took office in 1981 was that he would use his eight years in the White House to bring about the most significant improvement in Soviet-American relations since the end of World War II. I am not at all sure that President Reagan himself foresaw this result. And yet, that is precisely what happened, with—admittedly—a good deal of help from Mikhail Gorbachev.

The question of how this happened and to what extent it was the product of accident or of conscious design is going to preoccupy scholars for years to come. The observations that follow are a rough first attempt to grapple with that question. Because we lack access to the archives or even to very much memoir material as yet, what I will have to say is of necessity preliminary, incomplete, and almost certainly in several places dead wrong. Those are the hazards of working with contemporary history, though; if historians are not willing to run these risks, political scientists and journalists surely will. That prospect in itself provides ample justification for plunging ahead.

The Hard-liner

It is difficult, now, to recall how far Soviet-American relations had deteriorated at the time Ronald Reagan entered the White House. Some of the responsibility for this rested with Jimmy Carter: at a time when defeat in Vietnam had severely shaken American self-confidence, when the energy crisis appeared to be demonstrating American impotence, when the military balance seemed to be shifting in the Russians' favor, and when the domestic consensus in favor of detente was rapidly dissolving, he had chosen to launch an unprecedented effort to shift the entire basis of foreign policy from power to principle.[1] Carter's timing was terrible; his implementation was haphazard and inconsistent; only his intentions were praiseworthy, and in the climate of the late 1970s, that was not enough.

But the primary responsibility for the decline of detente must rest with the Soviet Union itself, and its increasingly senescent leader, Leonid Brezhnev. Given the long-term economic and social problems that confronted it, the Kremlin needed detente even more than Washington did. And yet, Brezhnev failed to see that he had, in Carter, an American counterpart who sincerely shared that objective; instead he chose to view the administration's fumbling earnestness as a sinister plot directed against Soviet interests. As if to compound this error, Brezhnev also allowed Soviet foreign policy to get caught up in a pattern of imperial overextension like the one that had afflicted the United States in the 1950s and 1960s. For just as the Americans had felt obliged, during those years, to prevent the coming to power of Third World Marxist governments, so the Russians now believed it necessary to sustain such governments, whatever the effect on the Soviet economy, on relations with the West, or on Moscow's overall reputation in world affairs. By equating expansionism with defense, the Soviet leader made the same mistake Stalin had made in the late 1940s: he brought about what he must have most feared. Brezhnev cannot have found it reassuring to know, as he approached the end of his life, that the invasion of Afghanistan had tarnished the Soviet image in the Third World; that a new American military buildup was under way with widespread domestic support; that an unusually determined NATO alliance had decided to deploy a new generation of missiles capable of striking Moscow itself; that detente was dead; and, most unsettling of all, that Ronald Reagan had become president of the United States.

Soviet behavior was by no means the only reason for Reagan's victory in 1980. Carter and his advisers had provoked the ire of voters on a score of issues quite apart from their handling of the Russians. But these inadequacies, taken together, had conveyed an unmistakable impression of weakness and irresolution; the effect could only be to place Carter at a greater disadvantage than Gerald Ford had been four years earlier as voters assessed his record in dealing with Moscow. Reagan had come close to denying Ford the 1976 Republican nomination by charging that detente had failed to prevent Soviet expansionism. Carter's failures made him an even easier target, and Reagan quite decisively defeated him by running on a platform calling for rejection of the SALT II treaty, a rapid increase in defense spending that would produce military superiority over the Soviet Union, and a return to containment in its most militant form. There was little visible evidence, at the time he took office, that the new president expected anything other than a renewed Cold

War: indeed he went out of his way in his first White House press conference to assert that the Soviet Union had used detente as "a one-way street ... to pursue its own aims," that those included "the promotion of world revolution and a one-world Socialist or Communist state," and that "they reserve unto themselves the right to commit any crime, to lie, to cheat, in order to attain that."[2]

Key foreign policy appointments reflected this hard line. Reagan named, as Secretary of State, the hyperbolic former general Alexander M. Haig, Jr. Contemptuous of what he would later characterize as "the Carter experiment in obsequiousness," Haig warned that the Soviet Union's "tremendous accumulation of armed might has produced perhaps the most complete reversal of global power relationships ever seen in a period of relative peace."[3] Leadership of the Defense Department went to Caspar Weinberger, who took an equally jaundiced view of detente. Pointing out that Soviet military spending had grown "more rapidly and more steadily" during that period than in "the so-called 'cold war'," Weinberger quickly raised Carter's projected increases in defense expenditures, authorized significant improvements in ground combat readiness, reinstituted the B-1 bomber program that Carter had cancelled, and approved construction of a 600-ship Navy which would now have the task, if war came, not simply of protecting sea lanes but of actually attacking the Soviet Navy in its own home ports.[4]

Arms control did not appear to be among the new administration's highest priorities; indeed the President seemed to have entrusted that responsibility to some of its most fervent critics. Eugene V. Rostow, one of the founders of the Committee on the Present Danger, became head of the Arms Control and Disarmament Agency. Paul Nitze, another pillar of the Committee on the Present Danger and a vociferous opponent of the SALT II treaty, took on the task of negotiating reductions in intermediate-range nuclear forces (INF) in Europe, a condition the NATO allies had insisted on before agreeing to deploy American Pershing II and cruise missiles on their territory. Equally striking were the appointments of Harvard historian Richard Pipes as chief Soviet specialist on the National Security Councill—Pipes had headed the 1976 "Team B" exercise that had criticized the Central Intelligence Agency for underestimating Soviet strategic capabilities—and, as Assistant Secretary of Defense for International Security Policy, of Richard Perle, a long-time staff aide to Senator Henry Jackson and an ardent foe of arms control in all its forms: characteristically, Perle is said to have worried that Nitze might be too *soft* in dealing with the Russians and actually agree to something.[5]

The administration's proposals on arms control seemed designed to subvert rather than to advance that process. Perle himself proposed the elimination of *all* Soviet SS-20 missiles—whether in Europe or Asia—in return for NATO's agreement not to deploy Pershing II and cruise missiles. Despite complaints that the Russians would never agree to trade actual missiles for non-existent ones (the NATO deployment was not to take place until 1983), President Reagan endorsed this "zero option" late in 1981, thereby confirming his critics' suspicion that he was not really interested in reaching an INF agreement.[6] At the same time, Rostow and other advisers had recommended shifting the focus of strategic arms talks from "limitation" to "reduction"— the new acronym would be START instead of SALT—and in May, 1982, Reagan accepted this proposal as well, calling publicly for deep cuts in land-based ballistic missile warheads on each side.[7] But because START would have required the Soviet Union to make disproportionate cuts—seven out of every ten of its ICBMs were land-based, as opposed to two out of ten for the United States—most observers regarded it, along with the "zero option," as an effort to stalemate arms control rather than as a sincere attempt to achieve the real reductions the two proposals professed to seek.[8]

Meanwhile, President Reagan and his advisers had gained a reputation for irresponsibility, even recklessness, on nuclear issues. The administration's obvious preference for rearmament over arms control contributed to this; so too had a series of injudicious remarks by key officials about the development of nuclear "war-fighting strategies," the firing of nuclear "warning shots," and, in one case, the possibility of surviving a nuclear attack provided everyone had "enough shovels" to build backyard bomb shelters.[9] By the end of 1982 there had developed, as a consequence, the strongest upsurge in public concern over the danger of nuclear war since the Cuban missile crisis: in Europe this took the form of demonstrations against the planned 1983 deployment of Pershing II and cruise missiles; in the United States it produced a widespread movement calling for an immediate "freeze" on the production, testing, and deployment of both Soviet and American nuclear weapons—a proposal popular enough to win in eight out of nine states where it was placed on the ballot in the November elections.[10]

It was with advocates of the "freeze" very much in mind that President Reagan in March, 1983, made his most memorable pronouncement on the Soviet Union: condemning the tendency of his critics to hold both sides responsible for the nuclear arms race, he denounced the U.S.S.R. as an "evil empire" and as "the focus of evil in the modern world."[11] Two weeks later, the President surprised even his closest associates by calling for a long-term research and development program to create defenses against attacks by strategic missiles, with a view, ultimately, to "rendering these nuclear weapons impotent and obsolete."[12] The Strategic Defense Initiative was the most fundamental challenge to existing orthodoxies on arms control since negotiations on that subject had begun with the Russians almost three decades earlier. Once again it called into question the President's seriousness in seeking an end to—or even a significant moderation of—the strategic arms race.

Anyone who listened to the "evil empire" speech or who considered the implications of "Star Wars" might well have concluded that Reagan saw the Soviet-American relationship as an elemental confrontation between virtue and wickedness that would allow neither negotiation nor conciliation in any form; his tone seemed more appropriate to a medieval crusade than to a revival of containment. Certainly there were those within his administration who held such views, and their influence, for a time, was considerable. But to see the President's policies solely in terms of his rhetoric, it is now clear, would have been quite wrong.

For President Reagan appears to have understood—or to have quickly learned—the dangers of basing foreign policy solely on ideology: he combined militancy with a surprising degree of operational pragmatism and a shrewd sense of timing. To the astonishment of his own hard-line supporters, what appeared to be an enthusiastic return to the Cold War in fact turned out to be a more solidly based approach to detente than anything the Nixon, Ford, or Carter administrations had been able to accomplish.

The Negotiator

There had always been a certain ambivalence in the Reagan administration's image of the Soviet Union. On the one hand, dire warnings about Moscow's growing military strength suggested an almost Spenglerian gloom about the future: time, it appeared, was on the Russians' side. But mixed with this pessimism was a strong sense of self-confidence, growing out of the ascendancy of conservatism within the United States and an increasing enthusiasm for capitalism overseas, that assumed the unworkability of Marxism as a form of political, social, and economic organization: "The West won't contain communism, it will transcend communism," the President predicted in May, 1981. "It won't bother to...denounce it, it will dismiss it as some bizarre chapter in human history whose last pages are even now being written."[13] By this logic, the Soviet Union had already reached the apex of its strength as a world power, and time in fact was on the side of the West.

Events proved the optimism to have been more justified than the pessimism, for over the next four years the Soviet Union would undergo one of the most rapid erosions both of internal self-confidence and external influence in modern history; that this happened just as Moscow's long and costly military buildup should have begun to pay political dividends made the situation all the more frustrating for the Russians. It may have been luck for President Reagan to have come into office at a peak in the fortunes of the Soviet Union and at a trough in those of the United States: things would almost certainly have improved regardless of who entered the White House in 1981. But it took more than luck to recognize what was happening, and to capitalize on it to the extent that the Reagan administration did.

Indications of Soviet decline took several forms. The occupation of Afghanistan had produced only a bloody Vietnam-like stalemate, with Soviet troops unable to suppress the rebellion, or to protect themselves and their clients, or to withdraw. In Poland a long history of economic mismanagement had produced, in the form of the Solidarity trade union, a rare phenomenon within the Soviet bloc: a true workers' movement. Soviet ineffectiveness became apparent in the Middle East in 1982 when the Russians were unable to provide any significant help to the Palestinian Liberation Organization during the Israeli invasion of Lebanon; even more embarrassing, Israeli pilots using American-built fighters shot down over eighty Soviet-supplied Syrian jets without a single loss of their own.[14] Meanwhile, the Soviet domestic economy, which Khrushchev had once predicted would overtake that of the United States, had in fact stagnated: during the early 1980s, Japan by some indices actually overtook the U.S.S.R. as the world's second largest producer of goods and services, and even China, a nation with four times the population of the Soviet Union, now became an agricultural exporter at a time when Moscow still required food imports from the West to feed its own people.[15]

What all of this meant was that the Soviet Union's appeal as a model for Third World political and economic development—once formidable—had virtually disappeared; indeed as Moscow's military presence in those regions grew during the late 1970s, the Russians increasingly came to be seen, not as liberators, but as latter-day imperialists themselves.[16] The Reagan administration moved swiftly to take advantage of this situation by funneling military assistance—sometimes openly, sometimes covertly—to rebel groups (or "freedom fighters," as the President insisted on calling them) seeking to overthrow Soviet-backed regimes in Afghanistan, Angola, Ethiopia, Cambodia, and Nicaragua; in October, 1983, to huge domestic acclaim but with dubious legality, Reagan even ordered the direct use of American military forces to overthrow an unpopular Marxist government on the tiny Caribbean island of Grenada. The Reagan Doctrine, as this strategy became known, sought to exploit vulnerabilities the Russians had created for themselves in the Third World: this latter-day effort to "roll back" Soviet influence would, in time, produce impressive results at minimum cost and risk to the United States.[17]

Compounding the Soviet Union's external difficulties was a long vacuum in internal leadership occasioned by Brezhnev's slow enfeeblement and eventual death in November, 1982; by the installation as his successor of an already-ill Yuri Andropov, who himself died in February, 1984; and by the installation of his equally geriatric successor, Konstantin Chernenko. At a time when a group of strong Western leaders had emerged—including not just President Reagan but also Prime Minister Margaret Thatcher in Great Britain, President François Mitterand in France, and Chancellor Helmut Kohl in West Germany—this apparent inability to entrust leadership to anyone other than party stalwarts on their deathbeds was a severe commentary on what the sclerotic Soviet system had become. "We could go no further without hitting the end," one Russian later recalled of Chernenko's brief reign. "Here was the General Secretary of the party, who is also the Chairman of the Presidium of the Supreme Soviet, the embodiment of our country, the personification of the party, and he could barely stand up."[18]

There was no disagreement within the Reagan administration about the desirability, under these circumstances, of pressing the Russians hard. Unlike several of their predecessors, the President and his advisers did not see containment as requiring the application of sticks and carrots in equal proportion; wielders of sticks definitely predominated among them. But there were important differences over what the purpose of wielding the sticks was to be.

Some advisers, like Weinberger, Perle, and Pipes, saw the situation as a historic opportunity to exhaust the Soviet system. Noting that the Soviet economy was already stretched to the limit, they advocated taking advantage of American technological superiority to engage the Russians in an arms race of indefinite duration and indeterminate cost. Others, including Nitze, the Joint Chiefs of Staff, career Foreign Service officer Jack Matlock, who succeeded Pipes as chief Soviet expert at the NSC, and—most important—Haig's replacement after June, 1982, the unflamboyant but steady George Shultz, endorsed the principle of "negotiation from strength": the purpose of accumulating military hardware was not to debilitate the other side, but to convince it to negotiate.[19]

The key question, of course, was what President Reagan's position would be. Despite his rhetoric, he had been careful not to rule out talks with the Russians once the proper conditions had been met: even while complaining, in his first press conference, about the Soviet propensity to lie, cheat, and steal, he had also noted that "when we can,...we should start negotiations on the basis of trying to effect an actual reduction in the numbers of nuclear weapons. That would be real arms reduction."[20] But most observers—and probably many of his own advisers—assumed that when the President endorsed negotiations leading toward the "reduction," as opposed to the "limitation," of strategic arms, or the "zero option" in the INF talks, or the Strategic Defense Initiative, he was really seeking to avoid negotiations by setting minimal demands above the maximum concessions the Russians could afford to make. He was looking for a way, they believed, to gain credit for cooperativeness with both domestic and allied constituencies without actually having to give up anything.

That would turn out to be a gross misjudgment of President Reagan, who may have had cynical advisers but was not cynical himself. It would become apparent with the passage of time that when the Chief Executive talked about "reducing" strategic missiles he meant precisely that; the appeal of the "zero option" was that it really would get rid of intermediate-range nuclear forces; the Strategic Defense Initiative might in fact, just as the President had said, make nuclear weapons "impotent and obsolete." A simple and straight-forward man, Reagan took the principle of "negotiation from strength" literally: once one had built strength, one negotiated.[21]

The first indications that the President might be interested in something other than an indefinite arms race began to appear in the spring and summer of 1983. Widespread criticism of his "evil empire" speech apparently shook him: although his view of the Soviet system itself did not change, Reagan was careful, after that point, to use more restrained language in characterizing it.[22] Clear evidence of the President's new moderation came with the Korean airliner incident of September, 1983. Despite his outrage, Reagan did not respond—as one might have expected him to—by reviving his "evil empire" rhetoric; instead he insisted that arms control negotiations would continue,

and in a remarkably conciliatory television address early in 1984 he announced that the United States was "in its strongest position in years to
establish a constructive and realistic working relationship with the Soviet
Union." The President concluded this address by speculating on how a typical
Soviet couple—Ivan and Anya—might find that they had much in common
with a typical American couple—Jim and Sally: "They might even have decided that they were all going to get together for dinner some evening soon."[23]

It was possible to construct self-serving motives for this startling shift
in tone. With a presidential campaign under way, the White House was sensitive to Democratic charges that Reagan was the only postwar president not
to have met with a Soviet leader while in office. Certainly it was to the
advantage of the United States in its relations with Western Europe to look
as reasonable as possible in the face of Soviet intransigence. But events would
show that the President's interest in an improved relationship was based on
more than just electoral politics or the needs of the alliance: it was only the
unfortunate tendency of Soviet leaders to die upon taking office that was
depriving the American Chief Executive—himself a spry septuagenarian—of
a partner with whom to negotiate.[24]

By the end of September, 1984—and to the dismay of Democratic
partisans who saw Republicans snatching the "peace" issue from them—a
contrite Soviet Foreign Minister Andrei Gromyko had made the pilgrimage
to Washington to re-establish contacts with the Reagan administration.
Shortly after Reagan's landslide re-election over Walter Mondale in November, the United States and the Soviet Union announced that a new set
of arms control negotiations would begin early the following year, linking
together discussions on START, INF, and weapons in space.[25] And in December, a hitherto obscure member of the Soviet Politburo, Mikhail Gorbachev, announced while visiting Great Britain that the U.S.S.R. was
prepared to seek "radical solutions" looking toward a ban on nuclear missiles
altogether.[26] Three months later, Konstantin Chernenko, the last in a series
of feeble and unimaginative Soviet leaders, expired, and Gorbachev—a man
who was in no way feeble and unimaginative—became the General Secretary
of the Communist Party of the Soviet Union. Nothing would ever be quite
the same again.

Reagan and Gorbachev

Several years after Gorbachev had come to power, George F. Kennan was
asked in a television interview how so unconventional a Soviet leader could
have risen to the top in a system that placed such a premium on conformity.
Kennan's reply reflected the perplexity American experts on Soviet affairs
have felt in seeking to account for the Gorbachev phenomenon: "I really
cannot explain it."[27] It seemed most improbable that a regime so lacking in
the capacity for innovation, self-evaluation, or even minimally effective public relations should suddenly produce a leader who excelled in all of these

qualities; even more remarkable was the fact that Gorbachev saw himself as a revolutionary—a breed not seen in Russia for decades—determined, as he put it, "to get out of the quagmire of conservatism, and to break the inertia of stagnation."[28]

Whatever the circumstances that led to it, the accession of Gorbachev reversed almost overnight the pattern of the preceding four years: after March, 1985, it was the Soviet Union that seized the initiative in relations with the West. It did so in a way that was both reassuring and unnerving at the same time: by becoming so determinedly cooperative as to convince some supporters of containment in the United States and Western Europe—uneasy in the absence of the intransigence to which they had become accustomed—that the Russians were now seeking to defeat that strategy by depriving it, with sinister cleverness, of an object to be contained.[29]

President Reagan, in contrast, welcomed the fresh breezes emanating from Moscow and moved quickly to establish a personal relationship with the new Soviet leader. Within four days of Gorbachev's taking power, the President was characterizing the Russians as "in a different frame of mind than they've been in the past.... [T]hey, I believe, are really going to try and, with us, negotiate a reduction in armaments." And within four months, the White House was announcing that Reagan would meet Gorbachev at Geneva in November for the first Soviet-American summit since 1979.[30]

The Geneva summit, like so many before it, was long on symbolism and short on substance. The two leaders appeared to get along well with one another: they behaved, as one Reagan adviser later put it, "like a couple of fellows who had run into each other at the club and discovered that they had a lot in common."[31] The President agreed to discuss deep cuts in strategic weapons and improved verification, but he made it clear that he was not prepared to forgo development of the Strategic Defense Initiative in order to get them. His reason—which Gorbachev may not have taken seriously until this point—had to do with his determination to retain SDI as a means ultimately of rendering nuclear weapons obsolete. The President's stubbornness on this point precluded progress, at least for the moment, on what was coming to be called the "grand compromise": Paul Nitze's idea of accepting limits on SDI in return for sweeping reductions in strategic missiles.[32] But it did leave the way open for an alert Gorbachev, detecting the President's personal enthusiasm for nuclear abolition, to surprise the world in January, 1986, with his own plan for accomplishing that objective: a Soviet-American agreement to rid the world of nuclear weapons altogether by the year 2000.[33]

It was easy to question Gorbachev's motives in making so radical a proposal in so public a manner with no advance warning. Certainly any discussion of even reducing—much less abolishing—nuclear arsenals would raise difficult questions for American allies, where an abhorrence of nuclear weapons continued to coexist uneasily alongside the conviction that only their presence could deter superior Soviet conventional forces. Nor was the Gorbachev proposal clear on how Russians and Americans could ever impose abolition, even if they themselves agreed to it, on other nuclear and non-nuclear powers. Still, the line between rhetoric and conviction is a thin one: the first Reagan-Gorbachev summit may not only have created a personal bond between the two leaders; it may also have sharpened a vague but growing sense in the minds of both men that, despite all the difficulties in constructing an alternative, an indefinite continuation of life under nuclear threat was not a tolerable condition for either of their countries, and that their own energies might very well be directed toward overcoming that situation.

That both Reagan and Gorbachev were thinking along these lines became clear at their second meeting, the most extraordinary Soviet-American summit of the postwar era, held on very short notice at Reykjavik, Iceland, in October, 1986. The months that preceded Reykjavik had seen little tangible progress toward arms control; there had also developed, in August, an unpleasant skirmish between intelligence agencies on both sides as the KGB, in apparent retaliation for the FBI's highly publicized arrest of a Soviet United Nations official in New York on espionage charges, set up, seized, and held *USNews* correspondent Nicholas Daniloff on trumped-up accusations for just under a month.[34] It was a sobering reminder that the Soviet-American relationship existed at several different levels, and that cordiality in one did not rule out the possibility of confrontation in others. The Daniloff affair also brought opportunity, though, for in the course of negotiations to settle it Gorbachev proposed a quick "preliminary" summit, to be held within two weeks, to try to break the stalemate in negotiations over intermediate-range nuclear forces in Europe, the aspect of arms control where progress at a more formal summit seemed likely. Reagan immediately agreed.[35]

But when the President and his advisers arrived at Reykjavik, they found that Gorbachev had much more grandiose proposals in mind. These included not only an endorsement of 50 percent cuts in Soviet and American strategic weapons across the board, but also agreement not to demand the inclusion of British and French nuclear weapons in these calculations—a concession that removed a major stumbling block to START—and acceptance in principle of Reagan's 1981 "zero option" for intermediate-range nuclear forces, all in return for an American commitment not to undermine SALT I's ban on strategic defenses for the next ten years. Impressed by the scope of these concessions, the American side quickly put together a compromise that would have cut ballistic missiles to zero within a decade in return for the right, after that time, to deploy strategic defenses against the bomber and cruise missile forces that would be left. Gorbachev immediately countered by proposing the aboliton of *all* nuclear weapons within ten years, thus moving his original deadline from the year 2000 to 1996. President Reagan is said to have replied: "*All* nuclear weapons? Well, Mikhail, that's exactly what I've been talking about all along.... That's always been my goal."[36]

A series of events set in motion by a Soviet diplomat's arrest on a New York subway platform and by the reciprocal framing of an American journalist in Moscow had wound up with the two most powerful men in the world agreeing—for the moment, and to the astonishment of their aides—on the abolition of all nuclear weapons within ten years. But the moment did not last. Gorbachev went on to insist, as a condition for nuclear abolition, upon a ban on the laboratory testing of SDI, which Reagan immediately interpreted as an effort to kill strategic defenses altogether. Because the ABM treaty does allow for some laboratory testing, the differences between the two positions were not all that great. But in the hothouse atmosphere of this cold-climate summit no one explored such details, and the meeting broke up in disarray, acrimony, and mutual disappointment.[37]

It was probably just as well. The sweeping agreements contemplated at Reykjavik grew out of hasty improvisation and high-level posturing, not careful thought. They suffered from all the deficiencies of Gorbachev's unilateral proposal for nuclear abolition earlier in the year; they also revealed how susceptible the leaders of the United States and the Soviet Union had become to each other's amplitudinous rhetoric. It was as if Reagan and Gorbachev had been trying desperately to outbid the other in a gigantic but surrealistic auction, with the diaphanous prospect of a nuclear-free world somehow on the block. As an illustration of what can happen when a summit conference gets out of control, Reykjavik resembled as nothing else the 1905 meeting between Tsar Nicholas II and Kaiser William II in which, in a single memorable evening, they personally negotiated and signed a treaty settling long-standing Russo-German differences, only to have their horrified governments—and allies—immediately repudiate it. "One should never forget," one of the Kaiser's advisers later commented, "that a discussion between two princes is propitious only when it confines itself to the weather."[38]

Negotiations on arms control continued in the year that followed Reykjavik, however, with both sides edging toward the long-awaited "grand compromise" that would defer SDI in return for progress toward a START agreement. Reagan and Gorbachev did sign an intermediate-range nuclear forces treaty in Washington in December, 1987, which for the first time provided that Russians and Americans would actually dismantle and destroy— literally before each other's eyes—an entire category of nuclear missiles.[39] There followed a triumphal Reagan visit to Moscow in May, 1988, featuring the unusual sight of a Soviet general secretary and an American president strolling amiably through Red Square, greeting tourists and bouncing babies in front of Lenin's tomb, while their respective military aides—each carrying the codes needed to launch nuclear missiles at each other's territory—stood discreetly in the background. Gorbachev made an equally triumphal visit to New York in December, 1988, to address the United Nations General Assembly: there he announced a *unilateral* Soviet cut of some 500,000 ground troops, a major step toward moving arms control into the realm of conventional forces.[40]

When, on the same day Gorbachev spoke in New York, a disastrous earthquake killed some 25,000 Soviet Armenians, the outpouring of aid from the United States and other Western countries was unprecedented since the days of Lend Lease. One had the eerie feeling, watching anguished television reports from the rubble that had been the cities of Leninakan and Stipak— the breakdown of emergency services, the coffins stacked like logs in city parks, the mass burials—that one had glimpsed, on a small scale, something of what a nuclear war might actually be like. The images suggested just how vulnerable both super-powers remained after almost a half-century of trying to minimize vulnerabilities. They thereby reinforced what had become almost a ritual incantation pronounced by both Reagan and Gorbachev at each of their now-frequent summits: "A nuclear war cannot be won and must never be fought."[41]

But as the Reagan administration prepared to leave office the following month, in an elegiac mood very different from the grim militancy with which it had assumed its responsibilities eight years earlier, the actual prospect of a nuclear holocaust seemed more remote than at any point since the Soviet-American nuclear rivalry had begun. Accidents, to be sure, could always happen. Irrationality, though blessedly rare since 1945, could never be ruled out. There was reason for optimism, though, in the fact that as George Bush entered the White House early in 1989, the point at issue no longer seemed to be "how to fight the Cold War" at all, but rather "is the Cold War over?"

Ronald Reagan and the End of the Cold War

The record of the Reagan years suggests the need to avoid the common error of trying to predict outcomes from attributes.[42] There is no question that the President and his advisers came into office with an ideological view of the world that appeared to allow for no compromise with the Russians; but ideology has a way of evolving to accommodate reality, especially in the hands of skillful political leadership. Indeed a good working definition of leadership might be just this—the ability to accommodate ideology to practical reality—and by that standard, Reagan's achievements in relations with the Soviet Union will certainly compare favorably with, and perhaps even surpass, those of Richard Nixon and Henry Kissinger.

Did President Reagan intend for things to come out this way? That question is, of course, more difficult to determine, given our lack of access to the archives. But a careful reading of the public record would, I think, show that the President was expressing hopes for an improvement in Soviet-American relations from the moment he entered the White House, and that he began shifting American policy in that direction as early as the first months of 1983, almost two years before Mikhail Gorbachev came to power.[43] Gorbachev's extraordinary receptiveness to such initiatives—as distinct from the literally moribund responses of his predecessors—greatly accelerated the improvement in relations, but it would be a mistake to credit him solely with the responsibility for what happened: Ronald Reagan deserves a great deal of the credit as well.

Critics have raised the question, though, of whether President Reagan was responsible for, or even aware of, the direction administration policy was taking.[44] This argument is, I think, both incorrect and unfair. Reagan's opponents have been quick enough to hold him personally responsible for the failures of his administration; they should be equally prepared to acknowledge his successes. And there are points, even with the limited sources now available, where we can see that the President himself had a decisive impact upon the course of events. They include, among others: the Strategic Defense Initiative, which may have had its problems as a missile shield but which certainly worked in unsettling the Russians; endorsement of the "zero option" in the INF talks and real reductions in START; the rapidity with which the President entered into, and thereby legitimized, serious negotiations with Gorbachev once he came into office; and, most remarkably of all, his eagerness to contemplate alternatives to the nuclear arms race in a way no previous president had been willing to do.[45]

Now, it may be objected that these were simple, unsophisticated, and, as people are given to saying these days, imperfectly "nuanced" ideas. I would not argue with that proposition. But it is important to remember that while complexity, sophistication, and nuance may be prerequisites for intellectual leadership, they are not necessarily so for political leadership, and can at times actually get in the way. President Reagan generally meant precisely what he said: when he came out in favor of negotiations from strength, or for strategic arms reductions as opposed to limitations, or even for making nuclear weapons ultimately irrelevant and obsolete, he did not do so in the "killer amendment" spirit favored by geopolitical sophisticates on the right; the President may have been conservative but he was never devious. The lesson here ought to be to beware of excessive convolution and subtlety in strategy, for sometimes simple-mindedness wins out, especially if it occurs in high places.

Finally, President Reagan also understood something that many geopolitical sophisticates on the left have not understood: that although toughness may or may not be a prerequisite for successful negotiations with the Russians—there are arguments for both propositions—it is absolutely essential if the American people are to lend their support, over time, to what has been negotiated. Others may have seen in the doctrine of "negotiation from strength" a way of avoiding negotiations altogether, but it now seems clear that the President saw in that approach the means of constructing a domestic political base without which agreements with the Russians would almost certainly have foundered, as indeed many of them did in the 1970s. For unless one can sustain domestic support—and one does not do that by appearing weak—then it is hardly likely that whatever one has arranged with any adversary will actually come to anything.

There is one last irony to all of this: it is that it fell to Ronald Reagan to preside over the belated but decisive success of the strategy of containment George F. Kennan had first proposed more than four decades earlier. For what were Gorbachev's reforms if not the long-delayed "mellowing" of Soviet society that Kennan had said would take place with the passage of time? The Stalinist system that had required outside adversaries to justify its own existence now seemed at last to have passed from the scene; Gorbachev appeared to have concluded that the Soviet Union could continue to be a great power in world affairs only through the introduction of something approximating a market economy, democratic political institutions, official accountability, and respect for the rule of law at home.[46] And that, in turn, suggested an even more remarkable conclusion: that the very survival of the ideology Lenin had imposed on Russia in 1917 now required infiltration—perhaps even subversion—by precisely the ideology the great revolutionary had sworn to overthrow.

I have some reason to suspect that Professor Kennan is not entirely comfortable with the suggestion that Ronald Reagan successfully completed the execution of the strategy he originated. But as Kennan the historian would be the first to acknowledge, history is full of ironies, and this one, surely, will not rank among the least of them.

## EIGHT

How the Cold War Might End: An Exercise in Faulty Prediction

Most historians, most of the time, wisely avoid making predictions. But in those rare instances when they do succumb to that temptation, they ought to keep track—their colleagues in economics and political science too often do not—of how well those predictions turned out. Certainly anyone who was foolish enough to try to predict how the Cold War might end owes his readers such an accounting. I wrote the following essay in the summer of 1987, and it appeared in The Atlantic *in November of that year, exactly two years before the Berlin Wall came down.[1] I have included it here in its original form, with only slight changes in wording and the addition of a few footnotes. But I have inserted a retrospective critical commentary along the way—a literary post-mortem, if you will—that seeks to explain why this exercise in prediction, like so many similar efforts, turned out to be so wrong.*

In his splendid book, *Arctic Dreams: Imagination and Desire in a Northern Landscape*, Barry Lopez describes the most striking of Arctic mirages—the *fata morgana*, in which sharply delineated mountain ranges appear suddenly from a featureless sea, creating the illusion of land where none exists and tempting unwary explorers to set off in search of constantly receding and, in the end, unattainable objectives. Bleak horizons combined with cold climates, he suggests, can alter consciousness and redirect ambitions in wholly unpredictable ways.[2]

What President Ronald Reagan and General Secretary Mikhail Gorbachev saw on the sub-arctic horizon that lay outside Hofdi House when they met in Reykjavik, Iceland, has not been recorded. But the austere surroundings do appear to have tempted them—briefly, at least—into contemplation of what many would regard as a political *fata morgana*: the possibility one might rid the world of nuclear weapons and the missiles that carry them. Only at the last minute did astonished advisers manage to pull their bosses back from the abyss that yawned before them: it was, James Schlesinger has written, quoting the Duke of Wellington, "the nearest-run thing you ever saw."[3]

But the view from Reykjavik may yet turn out to have been more than a mirage. The geopolitical ice is shifting beneath our feet these days in unexpected ways. For the first time since World War II ended, the superpowers are about to eliminate from their arsenals, by mutual consent, an entire category of nuclear weapons—those carried by intermediate-range missiles. Former opponents of arms control like Richard Perle support this accord, while former supporters like Henry Kissinger oppose it. In a striking reversal of past practice, Moscow appears more willing than Washington to allow intrusive on-site inspection to verify compliance. And all of this is happening under an American administration that only five years ago was characterizing the Soviet Union as "the focus of evil in the modern world." Familiar verities, it seems, no longer apply; it is difficult to know where one stands.

It would be unwise, therefore, to dismiss the Reagan-Gorbachev discussions at Reykjavik as the aberrant consequences of leaving heads of government alone in the same room, with only their interpreters present. Certainly this attempt to cut through current differences by defining a vision of future harmony will merit more than the puzzled footnote that historians normally accord the summit's only modern analogue: the treaty settling Russo-German differences which Kaiser Wilhelm II and Tsar Nicholas II personally negotiated and signed in a single memorable meeting on a German warship in the Baltic in 1905, only to have their horrified governments—and allies—immediately repudiate it.

At least I was right about that. And I liked the analogy to the abortive 1905 Treaty of Björkö so much that I wound up using it twice, as readers of the preceding chapter will have noticed.

But the Reykjavik vision of a nuclear-free world implied something larger still: the possibility that the Cold War itself—the occasion for deploying such vast quantities of nuclear armaments in the first place—might one day end, and that some of us might actually live to see the emergence of a new international system capable of moving beyond the condition of perpetual confrontation that has overshadowed our lives for the past four decades. Mirage or not, the view on the horizon was impressive, however fleeting.

Correct again, but a safe enough prediction. This paragraph certainly did not anticipate an end to the Cold War within two years.

But just what would constitute an end to the Cold War, and how might the elimination of nuclear weapons relate to that objective? The question did not come up at Reykjavik, nor has it received very much attention anywhere else. We have so preoccupied ourselves with the bomb and its associated technical, intellectual, and bureaucratic appurtenances that we neglect the larger geopolitical context in which these exist. Would nuclear abolition in fact end the Cold War or simply make it more dangerous? Could the Cold War end with nuclear weapons still in place? And, for that matter, would we even *recognize* an end to the Cold War, should that event someday come to pass?

Precisely because they sound naïve, questions like these tend to escape the attention of geopolitical sophisticates. But there are precedents for thinking about how one would like conflicts to end even as one engages in them: in both world wars elaborate postwar planning exercises were under way in Washington just weeks after the fighting had begun. War, for those who lived through the upheavals of 1917–18 and 1941–45, was an exceptional event, to be ended as quickly as possible, but not without careful thought about what victory was supposed to accomplish.

Our generation has had the undeniable advantage of not having to fight a "hot" war on the tremendous scale and at the tragic price that our parents and grandparents had to. But a consequence may be that for us the Cold War has become a way of life: it has been around for so long that it is a thoroughly familiar, if unwelcome, presence. Few of us can remember with very much precision how it started; fewer still take the time to consider what the world might look like without the Cold War. We have become so accustomed to this phenomenon—by now the dominant event in the lives of more than one generation of statesmen—that is simply does not occur to us to think about how it might end or, more to the point, how we would like it to end.

The resulting intellectual vacuum violates not only logic and good sense but also a basic Clausewitzian principle, which is that strategy has no rational basis unless it is informed by some awareness of the objective it is intended to achieve; this is what the great Prussian strategist really meant when he described war as the continuation of politics by other means. In our own time, thank goodness, the equation has been reversed: politics has become a way of conducting war by other means, and that is a considerable improvement. But the fact of the reversal hardly lessens the importance of linking the efforts we make to the objectives we seek. It is all very well to think about how one is going to make a trip—in what style, at what speed, and at what cost—but unless one has some idea of what the ultimate destination is to be, then the journey is apt to be long, circuitous, and ultimately unrewarding.

Thinking about destinations requires linking one's direction of travel to the intended point of arrival, a task made trickier in geopolitics than in geography by the fact that such points are often indistinct to begin with, and—like the Arctic ice pack—given to shifting their location in unanticipated ways. Still, the future of the Cold War is not wholly concealed. There are a few broad predictions one can make about it that may help us begin to think about how we would like it to come out.

One, quite simply, is that the Cold War will in fact end someday, and in some form. Nothing lasts forever in history: even the Hundred Years War had a conclusion, although it took a while to get there. The Cold War may end with a bang or a whimper or—more likely—with something in between, but it will end, as all historical episodes sooner or later do. Whether we, as contemporaries, would recognize that event if it should occur in our lifetimes is, of course, another matter; contemporaries are rarely the best judges of the history through which they live. The great Spanish monarch Philip II, were he able to return four centuries after his reign to read what historians are writing about his era, would be surprised—and not a little annoyed—to see them concentrating on things like sheep herding, the prevalence of malaria, and the Portuguese pepper trade. Historians four hundred years hence, if there are any left by then, will surely view our era from angles of vision quite different from our own; from their perspective, indeed, the Cold War could already have ended, without our even noticing.

As it turned out, we had no difficulty at all in recognizing the end of the Cold War when it finally came. What we failed to recognize were the forces that were bringing that event about, together with the possibility that they might manifest themselves all at once, and in such a decisive manner. I will have more to say about these forces and their interactions in Chapter Nine, below.

It also seems safe to say that when the Cold War does end, it will not do so with the total victory of one side and the unconditional surrender of the other; it will not be a replay of World War II. The principal reason for this is obvious: today's Great Powers possess nuclear weapons that preclude, in a manner quite unprecedented in modern history, the absolute imposition of one's will upon the other. But even if nuclear weapons had never been invented, there would still be reason to question the prospects for total domination, because the world these days is less hospitable to hegemonial aspirations than ever before. The day when a single imperial power could, with minimal expenditure of effort, control vast territories—the Mongols in Russia, or the Spanish in Central and South America, or the British in India—has now most assuredly passed. If Americans and Russians have such difficulties managing inconvenient next-door neighbors—Cubans and Nicaraguans, for example, or Afghans and Poles—then what could ever lead either of us to believe that we could successfully dominate the other? Empires are just not what they used to be.

Right about empires, perhaps, but badly wrong about victory. The Soviet Union's withdrawal from Eastern Europe, together with its acceptance of a reunified Germany linked to NATO, did amount to an unconditional surrender of positions held since the beginning of the Cold War. The possession of nuclear weapons in vast quantities proved quite useless in preserving the Soviet Union's authority beyond its borders, and by accepting economic assistance, including even food, from the West during the winter of 1990–91, Gorbachev placed old Cold War adversaries in a position to influence the future of his government, and perhaps his country as well. The West did not have to impose *its will on the Soviet Union; rather, an increasingly desperate Kremlin leadership in effect* invited *it to do so.*

A third prediction that can be made with confidence [*sic!*] is that the end of the Cold War will not bring an end to all international rivalries, or even to all aspects of the rivalry that now exists between the United States and the Soviet Union. Barring an improbable and necessarily simultaneous change in the mass consciousness of more than 160 nations, conflict in one form or another will remain a prominent feature of the international landscape, much as it was for millennia before the Cold War began.

This prediction looks a good deal more solid than the one that preceded it, what with the Persian Gulf crisis and the chill in Soviet-American relations occasioned by Gorbachev's shift back toward authoritarianism in late 1990 and early 1991. There will continue to be Soviet-American differences in the post-Cold War world, but they seem likely to take the form of those that normally exist between normal states, not competing superpowers.

The "Martian Scenario"

From here on, though, things get murkier. Consider the question of *what* might end the Cold War. One obvious possibility, of course, is a nuclear war, but there is not a great deal one can say about that, because we have so little basis for anticipating what the results of such a conflict might be. What one can say, though, is that the widespread sense of *inevitability* about a nuclear holocaust that existed during the 1950s and 1960s appears, at least among "experts" on the subject, to be waning. Although public concern about the possibility of a nuclear war remains high, specialists point to the obvious irrationality of starting such a conflict on purpose, to the remarkably low frequency of "accidental" wars in history, to the increasingly effective safe-guards against unauthorized use of nuclear weapons that exist on both sides, and to the marked decline in the incidence of both overt and implied nuclear threats that has occurred in recent years, quite independently of shifts in the Soviet-American political relationship from detente to confrontation and back again. There can be, of course, no guarantees. Irrationality in high places will always be a risk, and because Murphy's Law operates in capitalist and socialist societies alike—as the *Challenger* and Chernobyl disasters have re-cently reminded us—accidents can hardly be ruled out. Still, the record of four decades having passed without *any* nuclear weapons having been used for *any* military purpose whatever is an impressive one. One need only con-sider how improbable such an outcome would have seemed in the immediate aftermath of Hiroshima and Nagasaki to get a sense of what a remarkable development this has been.

So far, an accurate prediction. But it had not occurred to me, when I wrote this, that we might soon be worrying about the possibility that the Soviet

*Union itself might break up, and that the nuclear weapons it has amassed might fall into the hands of competing successor states, factions, or ethnic groups.*⁴ *Should that happen, the likelihood that someone someday might actually* use *a nuclear weapon would increase dramatically. And then there remains the possibility of nuclear proliferation to other states, the dangers of which are now much clearer in the wake of Saddam Hussein's success in using the international arms market to obtain sophisticated and lethal military technology for Iraq.*

So let us assume—because otherwise there is not much point in discussing the matter—that we will not require the services of the Apocalypse to end the Cold War. History provides more examples than one might think of Great Power rivalries that evolved unspectacularly into something else, without vast conflagrations or annihilations. It is worth looking at some of these to see what they might suggest about our own prospects for undramatic survival.

Great power rivalries have most often ended peacefully because of the rise of some third power, equally dangerous to both sides. This possibility is known in certain circles as the "Martian scenario": Reagan is said to have suggested to Gorbachev at the 1985 Geneva summit that if Martians were suddenly to land, Russians and Americans would settle their differences very quickly.⁵

There are, in fact, a good many historical instances of the Martian scenario. One conspicuous example is the long cold war between Great Britain and tsarist Russia that went on for most of the nineteenth century, erupting into actual combat only briefly, during the Crimean War, in 1853–56. The rise of Germany finally compelled London and St. Petersburg to settle their differences in the decade before World War I broke out. The same thing was happening at about the same time, and for much the same reason, to an even more ancient antagonism that had produced multiple wars in the past: that between Britain and France. Third power threats also produced brief but decisive military cooperation between the Soviet Union and its Western allies against Nazi Germany during World War II; they have led as well, but this time with the Soviet Union as the perceived danger, to more recent and more durable reconciliations between such bitter former enemies as France and Germany, Japan and China, and Germany, Japan, and the United States.

Is there a third power on the horizon that could compel a resolution of Soviet-American differences? What seems most likely is not that some new rival will emerge, capable of challenging the superpowers militarily, but rather that the standards by which we measure power will shift, with forms other than military—economic, technological, cultural, even religious—becoming more important. To some extent, this is already happening: one superpower, the Soviet Union, will soon be eclipsed by a third power, Japan, in gross national product; another third power, China, has already demonstrated what the Soviet Union has not, which is how a socialist economy can become agriculturally self-sufficient. Nor should Americans be so complacent as to consider themselves exempt from such trends, particularly if we persist in transforming our economy from its traditional industrial and agricultural base into one geared chiefly toward the provision and consumption of "services," the role of which, in the broad calculus of world power, is not at all clear.

The important question, therefore, may be whether the United States and the Soviet Union will continue to divert vast resources into military spending at a time when military strength is beginning to count for less than it has in the past as a determinant of world power. The answer is by no means apparent, but to the extent that both nations face at least a figurative Martian threat (by which I mean a situation in which old rules may not apply, one that might force us into new forms of cooperation), this quiet shift in the criteria by which we determine who can do what to whom would appear to be the most likely possibility.

Here I was partially right. I did foresee, if only dimly, the growing discon-nection between economic and military forms of power that has been de-veloping since the end of World War II, together with the possibility that this might begin to render old Cold War antagonisms between the United States and the Soviet Union irrelevant. For more on this, see Chapter Nine.

A second way in which great power rivalries have traditionally ended has been through the exhaustion of one of the major competitors, while the other remains vigorous. History is not normally so obliging as to arrange for the simultaneous and symmetrical enfeeblement of great powers. Consider Spain's long decline in the face of first French and then English hegemony, or the slow erosion of China's strength in the nineteenth century while that of Japan was increasing, or what was by historical standards the remarkably rapid withdrawal of the European colonial powers from Asia and Africa after World War II.

But rivalries that end through unilateral decline do not always do so peacefully: Britain's graceful withdrawal from empire after 1945 was the rare exception. More often the fact of decline—or even the appearance of it—has induced desperate actions to reverse the trend. Historians today would hardly describe imperial Germany prior to World War I as a declining power, but its leaders' perception of waning strength, together with the bumptious way in which their diplomacy and strategy sought to compensate for it, made Ger-man fear of decline a major contributor to the outbreak of that great conflict. Japan's attack on Pearl Harbor now appears to have been an act of desperation set off by anxiety over a naval balance of power in the Pacific that seemed to be shifting in favor of the United States. And it is worth recalling that a recurring justification for our own disastrous military involvement in South-east Asia was the concern that if we did not demonstrate the capacity to act we would become, in President Richard Nixon's evocative phrase, a "pitiful, helpless giant."[6]

What this suggests is that some of the most dangerous moments in world politics come when a great power perceives itself as beginning to decline—

as standing at the top of a slippery slope—and is tempted into irresponsible action against its rival to redress the balance while it still has the strength left to do so.

It is too early to say whether the United States or the Soviet Union will be the first to confront that prospect, although there is reason to suspect that Gorbachev, for one, has not been wholly oblivious to the possibility. But decline on one side or the other will eventually take place; despite the fact that the two superpowers' rivalry—and the geopolitical status that results from it—has lasted for a remarkably long time, nothing in history ensures that it is permanent. Exhaustion, inflexibility, and lack of imagination will eventually take their toll in one or the other of these countries, much as they do among individuals. The problem each country will then confront (and it will be a delicate one, because both are likely still to be sitting atop huge piles of armaments) will be that of managing asymmetrical decline without provoking the violence that desperation—or, in the case of the unaffected superpower, temptation—so often brings.

Correct, insofar as this passage anticipated the national debate over "decline" set off by the publication of Paul Kennedy's book, The Rise and Fall of the Great Powers, *late in 1987; quite incorrect, though, in arguing that asymmetric decline would be a dangerous way for the Cold War to end. I certainly did not foresee the possibility that the Soviet Union would give up its position as a superpower without even the slightest hint of either nuclear or conventional military action. I was, however, in good company.[7]*

But there is a third and more hopeful way in which the Cold War might end: a change in the outlook of its participants. Shifts in attitudes do occur from time to time; after all, Russia and the United States abolished their ancient institutions of serfdom and slavery within a decade of each other, in the middle of the nineteenth century. Is it beyond possibility that comparable changes might occur that could bring an end to the Cold War?

Liberals have long wanted to believe that the more democratic states are at home, the less prone they are to initiate the use of force in the world at large: autocracy and aggression, by this logic, go hand in hand. The proposition is questionable on the face of it if one considers how easily a number of scrupulously democratic states—our own included—were able to justify to themselves the virtues of imperialism in the nineteenth century or the necessity for interventionism in the twentieth. But, as the political scientist Michael Doyle has recently pointed out, there is a historical basis for arguing that liberal democracies tend not to go to war with one another.[8] This raises the question: could the extension of democracy—especially within the superpower that has not, until now, had much of it—bring an end to the Cold War?

Stranger things have happened. Both Germany and Japan were, within living memory, autocratic militaristic societies, much given to glorifying the uses of force. The experience of defeat and occupation after the World War

II changed them profoundly, in ways that at times exasperated even former adversaries, who would like them now to become a bit more militant than they are. But war in a nuclear age seems an improbable instrument of social and political reform, nor is there likely to be much call in the future for the services of draconian "reformers" like Generals Lucius Clay and Douglas MacArthur. What if the existence of nuclear weapons should serve, though, as the moral equivalent of a Clay or a MacArthur in reshaping Soviet and American attitudes toward military force? Might such a development help to compensate for the absence in the Soviet American relationship of compatible domestic institutions and ideologies?

There may be something in this. History prior to 1945 provides little support for the proposition that as military strength increases, the willingness to use it correspondingly decreases. But the United States and the Soviet Union since 1945 have amassed the largest and most powerful military arsenals the world has ever known, without ever having used their weapons directly against each other and, with one or two exceptions, without even having come close to doing so. Where each has sought to challenge the other's position militarily, it has done so through proxies: North Koreans, North Vietnamese, and Cubans in the case of the Russians; Nicaraguan contras, Angolan guerillas, and Afghan rebels in the case of the Americans. Where each superpower has actually used its military force—as the Americans did in Korea and Indochina and as the Russians have done in Afghanistan— it has consistently been against a third party.

Precisely because they possess nuclear weapons in such quantity and out of fear that any military confrontation between them might escalate, the United States and the Soviet Union have evolved a new kind of Great Power rivalry: one in which disputes are resolved not through direct combat but, as in certain animal species, through impressive but (so far) non-lethal displays of posturing, threat, and bluff. Such displays may be unnerving. They are hardly a behavior one would like to think characteristic of enlightened nations. But they do reflect a growing pessimism on both sides about what military force can accomplish, and that in itself is a considerable improvement over the old days, when periodic wars between Great Powers were routine events.

Right and wrong. If I had stopped with the prediction that democratization inside the Soviet Union would play a powerful role in ending the Cold War, my record as a prognosticator would have been pretty good. But that possibility seemed so improbable at the time I was writing this that I shifted instead to a rather convoluted argument about how the existence of nuclear weapons might be changing attitudes toward the use of force in both the Soviet Union and the United States. This was much too timid. Russians and Americans long ago learned the limits of using force against one another; indeed much of the history of the nuclear arms race could be written in terms of the posturings, threats, and bluffs mentioned above. But the Cold War continued long after this lesson had been learned. What brought it to an end was what I was on the verge of predicting, but did not: the realization, by one of its major competitors, that its own system of government—indeed its own view of human nature—was defunct.

The Virtues of Bipolarity

Ending the Cold War, then, could bring both rewards and risks. If the event occurred because of an emerging third-power threat or as a consequence of changing attitudes toward the uses of military force, then the result might be a relationship between Washington and Moscow not too different from the one that exists today between former adversaries like France and Germany, or the United States and Japan. But if the Cold War should seem to be ending as the result of asymmetrical decline, then the danger of a hot war might actually increase. The key to ensuring that the Cold War ends peacefully, therefore, appears to lie in what one might at first glance regard as highly improbable: the emergence of a vested interest among Russians and Americans in the survival and even the prosperity of each other's admittedly very different institutions.

I will stand by this prediction. Despite the fact that the Cold War did end as the result of asymmetrical decline, and despite the surprise that this happened peacefully, I am still prepared to argue that the stability of post-Cold War international relations requires the continued survival in some form—not necessarily its present form—of the Soviet Union. The reasoning behind this assertion is explained at greater length in Chapter Eleven. It also seems safe enough to predict that the domestic institutions of that country, whatever its eventual configuration, will not soon resemble those of the United States.[9]

How, though, could such a thing happen in the anarchic, ideologically polarized, and highly competitive international system the two of us have been stuck with since the end of World War II? Theorists have long described this system as a zero-sum game, in which gains for one side automatically mean losses for the other. It has never been easy to see how concern for an adversary's interests could arise in such a setting: each state, one assumes, seeks to increase its own power at the expense of the other, thus producing the geopolitical equivalent of a seesaw. Even when one introduces into such a game the possibility that a failure to cooperate might destroy both players, simulations have shown little tendency on either side to sacrifice immediate advantages in the interest of long-term common survival, if only because one can never be sure that one's adversary will do the same.

But curious things have been happening to game theorists lately: their characteristic gloom has quietly been giving way to a measured degree of optimism. Professor Robert Axelrod, of the University of Michigan, has demonstrated that if players are allowed to repeat a game several times, they begin to perceive the advantages to themselves of ensuring the other's survival, even in a competitive environment. Perpetuating the game itself becomes a shared interest.[10] The behavior of large corporations tends to confirm Axelrod's findings: they often limit competition where it might endanger the overall market within which they operate. Much the same pattern appears to hold for international banks and even for nations engaged in international trade rivalries.[11] As a result, the possibility of "cooperation under anarchy," together with what such a pattern might imply for Soviet-American relations, is now attracting considerable attention.

International relations theorists are also rethinking old ideas about bipolarity. For years they assumed that a multipolar world order—a system with three or more Great Powers—had to be more stable than a bipolar one: three or more points of support appeared to provide a greater likelihood of remaining upright than did only two. But why should the rules of geopolitics correspond with those of geometry? International systems are not, after all, pieces of furniture. And, indeed, sophisticated theorists such as Kenneth Waltz, at the University of California, Berkeley, and Robert Gilpin, at Princeton University, have begun to argue that under certain circumstances bipolar international systems can be more stable than their multipolar counterparts.[12]

Bipolarity tends not to require the acrobatics of a Metternich or a Bismarck to sustain itself, which is fortunate, since although acrobats may be plentiful, consistently successful ones are not. By reducing the number of key actors involved, bipolarity also simplifies problems of communication in crises: this helps to explain why the European crisis of July, 1914, involving five roughly equal powers, led to war, whereas the Cuban missile crisis of October, 1962, which involved only two, did not. Finally, bipolarity tolerates defections from coalitions with less damage to the overall balance of power than do more complex and hence more delicately balanced systems. Quarrels over who was to control Morocco could bring Europe to the brink of war in 1905 and 1911; but China could abandon both its American and Soviet allies in the years that followed 1945 without the superpowers approaching anything like a direct military confrontation as a result.

So, in theory, cooperation in competitive situations—even in the absence of a referee—is not so implausible as it might seem. Given time, a mutual interest in sustaining the system within which they compete can cause even vociferous rivals to develop a stake in each other's survival. But what about the real world of international relations since the end of the World War II? Four decades of superpower competition have provided more than enough time for the advantages of cooperation to have dawned on both Washington and Moscow. And if one looks at the actual behavior of Soviets and Americans during this period—as distinct from their frequently deceptive rhetoric—such a pattern does begin to emerge, at times in unexpected ways.

Cooperation in avoiding nuclear war is the most obvious example. Despite attempts to impress each other by suggesting the opposite, the United States and the Soviet Union have in fact reserved the employment of nuclear weapons for the ultimate extremity of all-out war. They have accepted painful military reverses in limited conflicts—Korea, Vietnam, Afghanistan—rather than resort to such use. They have even shared some nuclear technology: the United States in the early 1960s deliberately leaked to the Russians information on newly developed "permissive action links," control devices intended to prevent the inadvertent or unauthorized detonation of nuclear weapons.[13] Since that time exchanges on how to monitor nuclear tests have become commonplace, even to the point at which the two sides can now seriously discuss proposals for each to explode one of its own warheads at the other's test site.

Cooperation has extended to spheres of influence as well. Despite frequent condemnations of it, the United States has made no sustained effort to "roll back" Soviet control in Eastern Europe. Similarly, the Soviets, with two exceptions, have refrained from directly challenging the much larger, though less restrictive, American sphere of influence in Western Europe, the Mediterranean, the Near East, Latin America, and East Asia. The exceptions were the North Korean attack on South Korea in 1950 (which Stalin presumably authorized) and Khrushchev's decision to place missiles in Cuba in 1962. But both of those adventures followed inadvertent signals from Washington— the withdrawal of American troops from South Korea in 1949, and the failure to overthrow Fidel Castro after the Bay of Pigs landings in 1961—suggesting that it lacked the resolve to defend its interests in those parts of the world. Both probes were conducted cautiously, and the Russians abandoned them soon after the Americans had clarified their determination to resist.

Moscow and Washington have also cooperated, at times through their very competition, to impose order on third parties whose ambitions or rivalries might otherwise have produced war. The superpowers' success in avoiding escalation during a long series of Middle East conflicts provides the most visible example of how such crisis management has been made to work, but there are even more significant—if unacknowledged—instances of Soviet-American cooperation to maintain international order. Would Europe have enjoyed an unprecedented four decades without war had the superpowers— through their mutual suspicions, to be sure—not reversed the 1871 settlement that had imposed upon that continent, with such disastrous results, a unified German state? Would Eastern Europe today be an orderly place if the Soviets should suddenly leave? Or would the Korean peninsula, if the Americans should abruptly withdraw? Even to raise such questions is to induce high states of anxiety on both sides of the superpower relationship, which is why they are so rarely discussed in public. But the very existence of these anxieties suggests how important a stabilizing mechanism the Soviet-American rivalry has turned out to be in those parts of the world.

A bad prediction in that it implied the improbability of German reunification and a Soviet withdrawal from Eastern Europe. Curiously, though, it was fairly accurate in anticipating the effects of these developments. For despite the ease with which it took place, German reunification did cause—and continues to cause—a good deal of nervousness, not least among the Ger-

mans themselves. *And although much freer, Eastern Europe certainly is not as orderly a place these days as it was when Soviet influence was present. No one in Washington has seriously argued that the end of the Cold War makes it possible to withdraw American troops from South Korea; indeed, given the unpredictability of the North Korean regime, it is doubtful that any other government with interests in the region—including the Soviet Union and the People's Republic of China—would want the United States to do that.*

The United States and the Soviet Union have even cooperated, within limits, to facilitate espionage. Spying, after all, is what reconnaissance satellites do, even if both governments prefer to cloak their functions behind the euphemism "national technical means of verification." These devices have taken over the role assigned Francis Gary Powers when he flew his U-2 (not very successfully) over the Soviet Union in 1960; today both sides have learned—as the Russians manifestly had not in 1960—the benefits of transparency. These add up to a greatly reduced capability on the part of either for surprise attack, and it is universally acknowledged now that both superpowers feel safer for not having impeded this particular version of an "open skies" inspection plan. Indeed, the principle of remotely conducted espionage had become so thoroughly incorporated into Soviet-American relations by 1979 that the SALT II treaty could provide, with remarkably little public comment, for the configuration of certain weapons systems on each side to ensure that they *would* be visible to the prying—if electronic—eyes of the adversary.

Moscow and Washington have exploited defections from each other's sphere of influence only when it was clear that the rival either could not or would not regain control. Hence the United States took advantage of Yugoslavia's break with the Kremlin in 1948 and, after a long delay, that of the People's Republic of China as well; it was not prepared to challenge reassertions of Soviet authority in Hungary in 1956, or in Czechoslovakia in 1968, or even in Poland in 1981, with the crackdown on Solidarity. The Soviet Union exploited Cuba's break with the United States after 1959, but it made no attempt to contest successful CIA intervention in Iran in 1953 and Guatemala in 1954, or our more overt moves to re-establish control in the Dominican Republic in 1965, or in Grenada in 1983. And although the Russians have provided military assistance to the Sandinistas in Nicaragua, just as the Americans have done for the Afghan rebels, there is little reason to expect that either superpower would go out of its way to save those distant clients, should their defeat appear imminent.

True enough, as it turned out.

Finally, Russians and Americans have refrained from obvious attempts to undermine leadership on either side. Both countries have suffered disarray at the top since 1945: in the case of the Soviet Union, the instability that followed Stalin's death in 1953, the erosion of Khrushchev's authority after the Cuban missile crisis, and the illness and death of three Kremlin leaders within as many years during the early 1980s; in the case of the United States, the Johnson Administration's obsessive preoccupation with the Vietnam War, Nixon's self-inflicted Watergate wounds, and, most recently, White House involvement in the Iran-Contra scandal. What is striking about these episodes is how rarely the temptation appears to have arisen in the unaffected capital to take advantage of them. There have even been expressions of regret and sympathy—how sincere these were is difficult to say—over the difficulties rival leaders were undergoing. Game theorists, to be sure, would find nothing surprising in such a tacit acknowledgment of legitimacy on both sides; otherwise the game might not continue. But students of history will recognize just how unusual such mutual forbearance among leaders of competing great powers really is.

I will stand by the above paean to bipolarity as an interpretation of history: bipolarity did help bring about the "long peace"[4] *But with the collapse of one end of the bipolar balance, this discussion now seems quaintly out of date. It therefore offers little guidance for how the great powers can or should conduct their affairs in the post-Cold War world.*

An Agenda for Ending the Cold War

Not one of these examples of Soviet-American cooperation originated as the result of formal diplomatic negotiations. They arose instead from patterns of behavior both nations quietly found it in their interests to perpetuate. These patterns have survived shifts of leadership; they have proceeded more or less independently of oscillations between detente and confrontation; they appear now to be so firmly embedded in custom and tradition that it is difficult to conceive of circumstances that might lead either side to depart substantially from them. But there are limits to tacit cooperation. One is never quite sure precisely what has been agreed to, or how long agreements will last. Nor do all points at issue between the United States and the Soviet Union lend themselves to such informal solutions. It is worth taking a look, then, at just what objects of contention remain, and at what an explicitly negotiated settlement of them might actually require.

First, it would appear, we would have to get around once and for all to ending World War II. We would have to resolve certain leftover issues from that conflict, the lifetime of which has been prolonged far beyond what anyone in 1945 would have thought possible. This would hardly be a minor undertaking: it would include finding ways to end the artificial division of Germany and Korea, to withdraw Soviet and American forces from the advanced—and therefore also artificial—positions they still occupy in Central Europe, and quite possibly to dismantle NATO, the Warsaw Pact, and the other multilateral and bilateral alliance structures established during the first tense decade of postwar Soviet-American confrontation.

In fact, what happened was the reverse of this. The Soviet Union acknowledged defeat in the Cold War, and then settled remaining issues left over from World War II—with the exception of a divided Korea and the occupation of the Kurile Islands—almost as an afterthought. It allowed the Warsaw Pact to collapse without a fight.[15] *NATO survives, and even (for the moment) prospers; but one wonders how long it can continue to do so in the absence of the adversary that brought it into existence in the first place.*

Second, we would need specific agreements between the United States and the Soviet Union to refrain from projecting their influence—cultural, ideological, and economic, as well as military—elsewhere in the world in order to gain unilateral advantage at the expense of each other. Such accords would have to distinguish between deliberate and inadvertent projections of influence; they would have to be capable as well of differentiating indigenous shifts in the status quo from those set in motion for their own immediate benefit by Washington, Moscow, or their respective clients.

The Soviet Union has taken care of this problem in two ways: first by recognizing the counterproductive effects, for itself, of seeking unilateral advantage at the expense of the United States; and second by presenting such an unattractive model to the rest of the world as to render such efforts ineffective in the first place. As the Persian Gulf War suggests, things will be less simple for the United States, which continues to provide a model that much of the rest of the world finds attractive, but which lacks the means unilaterally to defend the interests—real and imagined—that grow out of that situation.

Third, we would require a clear understanding of what each side considers necessary for its own security. This would of course include mutually verifiable agreements on the control of both nuclear and conventional armaments, but would have to extend as well to such delicate issues as levels of defense spending, the right to maintain military bases on foreign soil, access to critical raw materials, the export and import of sensitive technology, the conduct of ground-based espionage, the question of human rights, and, not least, the extent to which each side's citizens would be free to have contacts with those of the other.

The military and economic issues raised here have more or less resolved themselves as a result of the Soviet Union's abdication of superpower status. Human rights, however, will continue to be a major concern as the United States balances its commitment to the principle of self-determination against its interest in avoiding the complete disintegration of the U.S.S.R., and the chaos that would result from such a development.

Finally, we would need mechanisms of some sort to counteract the effects, on the perceptions we and the Russians have of each other, of the profound differences between our ideologies, institutions, and cultures. Contrasts between communism and capitalism have had seven decades now to develop. But even if the Bolshevik Revolution had never taken place, there would still be deep institutional and cultural gaps between our ways of life, arising out of centuries of dissimilar historical experience whose impact—even at the most inconvenient moments, as the Daniloff affair demonstrated last year—continues to make itself felt.

A valid concern when I wrote this piece, and one that remains valid today, even with the progress that has been made toward democratization in the Soviet Union.

One need only run down this list to realize two things, one of them obvious, the other less so. The obvious point is that there is enough here to keep us at the negotiating table for at least the next century, so we should probably not bring out the champagne—or relax restrictions on the consumption of vodka before midafternoon—just yet. The less obvious point is that it is not at all clear, in the event we could ever get agreement on all these issues and thus relegate the Cold War to the history books, that the world would be a safer place as a result.

Shortly after this article appeared, President Gorbachev did in fact relax restrictions on the consumption of vodka and other alcoholic beverages. I am not sure, though, that there was a direct cause and effect relationship. The events of 1990 and 1991 certainly do bear out the prediction in the last sentence.

Consider the difficulties of resolving issues left over from World War II. Germans and Koreans on both sides of the lines that divide them pay lip service to reunification, but neither they nor anyone else has given much thought to the actual political basis upon which such a thing might happen. How, for example, does one "reunite" an entire generation that has never experienced unity? Nor is it apparent what the implications would be of withdrawing Soviet and American forces from Europe. Most Eastern Europeans would welcome such a move, to be sure, but how Soviet security interests could be reconciled with it is as much a question now as it was in 1945. Nor would an Eastern Europe free of Soviet domination necessarily be an orderly place: it certainly was not prior to the World War II, and long suppressed irredentist grievances still persist in that part of the world. Would Western Europe welcome the dismantling of NATO? European members of the alliance chafe under its demands and resist meeting its obligations, but when opportunities arise for them to become even slightly more self-reliant—as with the prospect this year of a Soviet-American agreement on withdrawing intermediate-range missiles—second thoughts (along with cold feet) abruptly proliferate. There is no way to know, of course, how long the present awkward arrangements in Europe and on the Korean peninsula can last. But awkward though they may be, they have proved to be remarkably durable. No one knows what these areas left to their own devices would be like and, to be perfectly honest about it, there has been no great eagerness in either Washington or Moscow to find out.

Most of the "awkward arrangements" described in this paragraph are now history, and obviously I did not anticipate that they would so quickly become so. We do not know, and will not know for some time, though, just what the consequences of removing them are going to be.

What about agreements pledging the United States and the Soviet Union not to seek unilateral advantage at the expense of the other? Here again we have some historical basis for speculation, this time in the form of the ill-fated statement on "Basic Principles" of U.S.-Soviet relations, signed at Moscow in 1972, which promised something very much like that. The accord broke down almost at once because of disputes over how to apply its vague generalities to specific situations: Did the agreement require the Russians to warn Washington of Egypt's impending attack on Israel in 1973? Was Henry Kissinger justified in freezing Moscow out of the Middle East peace negotiations that soon followed? Which side initiated covert intervention in Angola following the Portuguese withdrawal from that country? Did Moscow do all it could—or, indeed, anything at all—to prevent the final North Vietnamese offensive against Saigon in 1975? The "Basic Principles" promoted more bickering than harmony, and the reason, in retrospect, is not hard to see: when one asks Great Powers to give up the search for unilateral advantage in international relations, what one is really asking them to do is to refrain from pursuing their own perceived interests. That is hardly a realistic thing to expect, and to hold out the prospect of accomplishing it is to invite disillusionment.

Wrong, wrong, wrong! A great power did give up the search for unilateral advantage in international relations in 1989 and 1990, and it did so precisely because it considered that course of action to be not just consistent with, but also required by, its perceived interests. This certainly says something about my own distinctly limited powers of prediction, but it is also an interesting commentary on a fundamental proposition of realist political theory, which is that those nations that have great power will always want more of it.

Would a world in which each side undertook to respect the other's security requirements be a more orderly place? Perhaps. Certainly it would appear more feasible to attempt to bring divergent superpower interests into approximate congruence with each other than to try to persuade each side of the merits of self-denial. And substantial areas of overlapping interest, as we have seen, already exist. But it is necessary to be realistic here, too, about what more could be achieved: Mutually verifiable arms-control agreements might well fall within such a zone of congruence, but up to what point? Would they continue to do so if the effect of bilateral deep cuts in nuclear arsenals was to diminish the *joint* military pre-eminence of the United States and the Soviet Union, and to increase correspondingly the importance of other actors on the international scene? Are we sure that a shift toward multipolarity would enhance stability more than the bipolarity to which we have become accustomed? How would one handle the problem of asymmetrical threats—the fact that what one nation sees as threatening, another may not? And, perhaps most daunting, how would one take into account the vastly dissimilar domestic systems we and the Soviets have, and the conflicting security requirements these might pose?

This paragraph correctly assumed the difficulty of one great power persuading its rival of the merits of "self-denial," but it failed utterly to foresee that the Russians would come to see those merits on their own. I will stand by the rest of what it says as a reasonably accurate anticipation of some of the problems we are likely to confront in the post-Cold War world.

That last point suggests, as well, the difficulty of overcoming ideological, institutional, and cultural differences. Well-intentioned efforts to do so date back to the earliest days of the Cold War; today they take a remarkable number of forms, and proceed at a multiplicity of levels. But there remains a lurking uneasiness about "people-to-people" exchanges, "sister-city" contacts, "citizen diplomacy," and the like: are we really certain, if Russians and Americans had vastly expanded opportunities for contact, that we would actually like each other all that much? Virtually every major war fought during the past century and a half has taken place between nations whose people knew each other from just such intensive contacts all too well, and who came to hate each other vigorously as a result. Even today virulent "people-to-people" animosities survive among Greeks and Turks, Arabs and Israelis, Sunni and Shiite Moslems, Irish Catholics and Protestants, Cambodians and Vietnamese. In contrast, Russians and Americans, who because we inhabit opposite sides of the earth have had so few contacts, almost alone among major nations of the world have never fought a war: the closest we have come are a few confused skirmishes during Allied intervention in Siberia and North Russia after the Bolshevik Revolution.

I see no reason to change the rather gloomy conclusions of this paragraph.

Peace

Arguments like these tempt one to invoke what history will record as the Bert Lance Principle: "If it ain't broke, don't fix it." There is, in fact, something to be said for that point of view. Results are difficult to argue with, and it can hardly be denied that the four decades we think of as the Cold War, years that have seen as high and as protracted a level of international tension without war as any in modern history, have also been four decades of great power peace, a period that compares favorably with the longest such periods of coexistence without war in modern history.

But is it not Orwellian to call such a situation "peace," knowing that a nuclear holocaust could break out at any moment? By traditional definitions of the term, it clearly is. We normally think of peace as something that has emerged from a formal process of negotiation around a conference table, and that exists within some clearly worked out and commonly agreed upon international structure, equally binding upon all who have adhered to it; something, in other words, like the system established at Versailles in 1919. But that system lasted only half as long as the present one has, despite the fact that the latter evolved as the result of no peace conference at all and with only a minimum of formal structure to perpetuate it. What has sustained the peace since 1945, many would argue, is precisely the prospect of what might ensue if it should ever come apart—a prospect insufficiently arresting to have impressed itself upon the minds of statesmen in the days before nuclear weapons existed.

We now face a situation in which the structure that sustained peace for so long has indeed come apart, but peace itself—at least at the level of the great powers—nonetheless survives. Only time will tell whether this is because the great powers are now wise enough even in the absence of a bipolar structure to avoid going to war with one another, or, alternatively, whether they have not yet been sufficiently tempted. For more on this question, see Chapter Ten.

We also think of peace as consistent with justice. But history is full of wars that have been fought with devastating effects in the interests of justice. The term *just war* itself captures the contradiction neatly. It was indeed largely a preoccupation with justice—and a corresponding neglect of the realities of power— that produced the phenomenon of appeasement in the 1930s, which in turn led so directly and so blindly to the last great war. We might do better not to equate peace and justice so precisely, given the difficulty of defining that latter quality, let alone achieving it. The more feasible approach might be to think of peace, in the way Reinhold Niebuhr suggested, as the condition of order that *precedes* justice, as the compromise with power that has to take place before one can begin to address—as one still ultimately has to—questions of right and wrong.[16]

Amen.

Finally, we tend to think of peace as something that grows out of harmony between nations, not out of the rivalries that exist among them. But why should that necessarily be so? After all, this nation has long extolled—to the point of having our principles quoted back at us more often than we would like these days—the virtues of competition as the path to economic prosperity and social justice. Is it not at least conceivable that a competitive superpower relationship, if carried on with the requisite degree of caution and restraint, might contribute to the maintenance of order—if not immediately justice—in international relations? The difficulty with traditional schemes for world order is their lack of realism regarding the problem of conflict in international life: they tend to take on the appearance of blurry utopias, more appropriate to some other world than to the one in which we are obliged to live. There has been nothing utopian about the order the superpowers have imposed since 1945; it has been firmly grounded in the world as it is. Perhaps that is why it has lasted as long as it has.

"Blurry utopia" it was not, but the old superpower order is nonetheless now dead, and something will have to arise to take its place. Ironically, in the absence of Soviet-American rivalry, the old "utopia" of collective security through the United Nations looks a good deal less "blurry" than it once did.

It has been characteristic of revolutionaries, from the Americans and the French down through the Russians, the Chinese, and even the Vietnamese, that they have sought to confirm the victory of new orders over old ones through the simple expedient of changing names. "Change a name," the historian Crane Brinton observed many years ago, "and you change the thing."[17] It may be that both we and the Russians, heirs of revolution as we are, can learn something from this. What would happen if we were to begin to think of the Soviet-American relationship not as a "cold war" but rather as a "long peace"—as the most workable, if still imperfect, set of arrangements for maintaining international order that the world has devised in this century? Might we gain new perspectives that could make the relationship a safer one, without compromising our vital interests and without losing touch with our principles? Might this be a way to combine the conservative's concern not to sacrifice what has worked in the past with the liberal's insistence upon progress toward a more equitable future? It is difficult to say.

And irrelevant as well, since whatever it was—"cold war" or "long peace"— we are clearly into a different era now. Thinking about the "cold war" as a "long peace" might, however, suggest ways to preserve some of the institutions and experiences that have worked in maintaining international stability since the end of World War II. It is always a mistake to throw out babies with bathwater.

But those who see images on distant horizons are rarely called upon to describe their details with cartographic precision. What is important is whether they are really there or not. The miscalculation that Ronald Reagan and Mikhail Gorbachev made at Reykjavik was not that they looked too far ahead with too little attention to how they might get there: who else, if not the leaders of superpowers, ought to be focusing on long-term objectives? The difficulty was that they did not look far enough. They concentrated on how one might eliminate the Cold War's most conspicuous instruments—nuclear weapons and the missiles that carry them—but not on how one might end the Cold War itself. Had they taken that wider view, they might have discovered another curious way in which light can deceive the eye in Arctic landscapes: that what appear to be distant objects can, at times, be close at hand.

At least that final prediction was right: the end of the Cold War was closer at hand than anyone—Reagan, Gorbachev, or the author of this rather myopic essay—would have suspected at the time. But that fact raises questions about why we don't do a better job at prediction. Re-reading this 1987 exercise suggests several answers:

1. The assumption that the future will resemble the past. We tend to think about the future by projecting past patterns forward; these patterns, in turn, are the means by which we try to make sense out of present and past realities. We too often fail, though, to allow for the effects of change on the patterns we create in our minds. Despite the obvious fact that change—sometimes dramatic and sudden change—is what history is all about, when we use history to think about the future we generally resort to a static version of it. We find it hard enough to agree what patterns we ought to use in thinking about the past. Extending these into the future, while at the same time allowing for the effects of change on them, is formidably difficult.

2. The temptation to turn nations into abstractions. No doubt because we find it so convenient to do so, we tend to treat great power relationships like those that exist among billiard balls, where the behavior of each affects the other, but where internal developments play no role at all. Despite the fact that the most rudimentary knowledge of history would expose the weaknesses of this assumption, we continue nonetheless to use it in thinking about the future. We assume that great powers will continue to be great powers, and that they will respond to one another in reasonably predictable ways. In fact, we would be better off to think of international relationships in terms of proverbially incommensurate apples and oranges, and perhaps also other fruit. Not only would this allow for differences in external characteristics; it might force us to take into account the possibility of internal rot as well.

3. Neglecting points of intersection between short-term and long-term phenomena. The distinction between domestic and foreign policy is only one aspect of a larger levels-of-analysis problem, which has to do with the relationship of long-term to short-term trends. We all know that both kinds of phenomena exist in history, and that they interrelate. But we give very little attention to their specific points of interrelationship, or to the question of how we might see these coming.

4. *The role of personalities. If the experience of the 1980s teaches us anything at all, it ought to be that individual leaders do still make a difference. The decade was one in which personal leadership shaped events in very important ways: any attempt to write the history of recent international relations without giving full weight to the influence of Mikhail Gorbachev, Ronald Reagan, Margaret Thatcher, Helmut Kohl, François Mitterand, Pope John Paul II, Deng Xiaoping, George Bush, and, alas, Saddam Hussein, is doomed to failure. And yet, prediction is most difficult at times when distinctive personalities are most dominant.*

5. *Chance. Unpredictable events, by definition, defy prediction. The sequence of developments that brings an individual leader to the top will always include some randomness: Would Reagan have abandoned the movies for politics if he had been a better actor? Would Gorbachev have risen beyond being a regional party functionary had not Stavropol been on the rail line Kremlin bigwigs regularly used in traveling to their Caucasus vacations? And even in the unlikely event that someone had predicted these improbabilities, would they then also have anticipated that leaders as dissimilar as Reagan and Gorbachev would get along as well as they did? There are some things that prediction, however well it is done, will never be able to foresee.*[18]

And how would I grade my own modest effort along these lines? No better than a C+, I fear. The following chapters suggest some ways in which I might have improved upon this performance.

## NINE

Tectonics, History, and the End of the Cold War

Change in the physical world, we have come to understand, does not always take place gradually: there can be abrupt and at times unexpected jumps from one condition to another. Electrons shift orbits instantly as they spin around atomic nuclei. Animal species evolve at irregular rates, and with periodic extinctions. Metal fatigue reveals its effects all at once: bridges do not collapse gradually, nor do airplanes decompress unhurriedly. Faults in earthquake zones lock themselves into place for decades at a time, releasing accumulated strains rarely but, when they do release them, very dramatically.

Events like these are not accidents; they can be understood, accounted for, and at times even predicted. But they often *appear* to us to be random or capricious occurrences, because explanations for them have to be sought in processes that lie outside our normal range of perception. These processes may operate on a different time scale from the one to which we are accustomed, so that their effects occur too rapidly, or too slowly, for us to notice them. They may take place too far above our heads (like the forces that determine the movements of weather systems) or too far beneath our feet (like those that produce continental drift). The temporal and spatial limits within which we normally operate are inadequate to account for all that affects our lives; hence, the frequency with which—in the physical world at least—we are surprised.

Surprises also happen in history; indeed one might go so far as to define that discipline as the intersection of what was expected with what was not. Change occurs constantly in human affairs, but not always at the same rate, and certainly not with consistent or easily predictable results. Conditions can persist for years with so little alteration that people come to accept them as permanent, only to have them disappear—to the astonishment of almost everyone—almost overnight.

That is what happened in Europe in the revolutionary year 1989. The

Cold War between the United States and the Soviet Union had lasted so long that it had come to be accepted as a permanent feature of international landscape; and yet within a matter of months its entire structure came apart. Soviet leaders suddenly found themselves being harangued on national television by members of a democratically elected parliament. General Wojciech Jaruzelski invited the Solidarity trade union—which he had once declared illegal—to take over the government of Poland. Hungarians dismantled their barbed wire border fences and voted their communist party out of existence. Alexander Dubcek returned in triumph to Prague and Vaclav Havel made the abrupt transition from prisoner to president of Czechoslovakia. Germans knocked holes in the Berlin Wall and began strolling amiably through the Brandenburg Gate. Once docile Romanians hooted down the "Genius of the Carpathians," Nicolai Ceaucescu, and Madame Genius, on the balcony of their own palace, and forced them, literally, up against the wall. By the end of the year, the Warsaw Pact—that fearsome (but frequently convenient) nightmare for NATO strategists—had become a hollow shell, and its Soviet sponsors, perhaps surprising themselves, had done nothing to save it.

But these developments, however unexpected, were only the surface manifestations of underlying trends that had been present for years without our noticing them, rather like the strains that build up along geologic fault lines. Just as it takes an occasional earthquake to remind us that such pressures exist beneath the surface of the earth, so it required the shocks of 1989—a shift of geopolitical fault lines, if you will—to bring certain long-term historical forces to our attention. Like the tectonic forces that move continents around on the surface of the earth, historical tectonics lie beyond our normal range of perception. No single nation or individual sets them in motion; they result, rather, from the interaction of events, conditions, policies, beliefs, and even accidents. They operate over long periods of time, and across the boundaries we use to define place. Once set in motion, they are not easily reversible: they therefore give us one of the few reasonably reliable means of predicting, in very broad terms at least, what is to come.[1]

One reason my own predictions about how the Cold War might end turned out to be mostly wrong[2] is that I failed to pay sufficient attention to historical tectonics, and particularly to three trends that would converge to produce the shocks of 1989: the emergence of new criteria for defining great powers; the collapse of authoritarian alternatives to liberalism; and the decline of brutality in both internal and international affairs. This essay seeks, belatedly, to describe these forces, and to speculate—for one can hardly do more than that at this stage—about their probable consequences.

New Criteria of Power

The history of the past 500 years has been one of Europe expanding its influence over most of the rest of the world by combining economic with military power. As the historian William McNeill has put it, Europe at the end of the fifteenth century launched itself "on a self-reinforcing cycle in which its military organization sustained, and was sustained by, economic and political expansion at the expense of other peoples and polities of the earth."[3] Paul Kennedy has argued that the ability simultaneously to maintain economic vitality and military capability—the skill with which statesmen balanced each against the other—has been the single most important determinant of influence in world politics: "The history of the rise and later fall of the leading countries in the Great Power system . . . shows a very significant correlation *over the longer term* between productive and revenue-raising capacities on the one hand and military strength on the other."[4]

This process of building economic upon military strength, and vice versa, extended into the middle of the twentieth century, with World War II providing as clear a demonstration as one could wish of how those two kinds of power could combine to shape the behavior of nations everywhere on the planet. The very term "superpower," as it emerged from that conflict and as it characterized some forty-five years of Soviet-American Cold War competition, implied the interconnection of military with economic capability in a struggle that appeared to have the potential, if it should ever get out of hand, of ending life itself on earth.[5]

But from our post-1989 vantage point, we can look back on the Cold War years and see them as something else again: as the point at which the 500-year-old linkage between military and economic strength as the path to predominance in world politics began to come apart. Underlying tectonic forces have shifted; the conditions that for so long favored a marriage of military and economic capability now seem to be bringing about a divorce.

The reasons for this involve a juxtaposition of technology with ecology. Wars throughout most of the past five centuries had been thought of, at least by those who began them, as something like sporting matches: one could compete, but generally without destroying the playing field, or the arena in which the competition was taking place, or the home to which one would return after the contest was over. The use of military force could be, as Clausewitz said it should be, a rational act of statecraft, producing rational results.[6] To be sure, anyone who had actually witnessed the physical damage wrought by World War I—or by the American Civil War, or even by the Thirty Years' War, for that matter—might well have questioned whether war could ever be a rational act, in the sense of yielding results that bore any apparent relationship to those that had been sought.[7] Certainly there was a growing sense, even before the war of 1914–18 powerfully reinforced it, that the risks and costs of conflict among highly industrialized great powers had come to outweigh whatever the benefits might be.[8] But the memory of past great wars was not sufficiently widespread, or sufficiently intense, to prevent another great war from breaking out in the middle of this century; that war in turn produced nuclear weapons, the most striking result of combining economic with military power, but also—paradoxically—the instrument that caused that combination to begin to come apart.

This happened for the simple reason that once one got the bomb it was difficult to know just what to do with it. The new weapon made possible a quantum leap in the level of violence nations could command, but the arena within which they competed did not expand proportionately. That fact discouraged actual use of the bomb because such use would have undercut the purpose of having weapons in the first place, which is to inflict damage upon one's enemy without doing the same to one's self. Once the Soviet Union had gained a nuclear capability, together with a credible means of delivery, neither the United States nor anyone else could seriously contemplate using the bomb without having to face the daunting prospect of nuclear retaliation. And as early as the 1950s, American officials, at least, were beginning to worry about another danger: the large-scale environmental consequences that would result from an all-out nuclear war, even if the United States were to "win" it decisively.[9]

The scale of violence had outstripped—exponentially—the scale of the arena in which the violence was to be employed; this made it difficult for any nation that had accumulated such military power to see how it might use it against any comparably equipped nation without risking escalation that could lead to the destruction of both of them. The great powers were therefore reduced to *threatening* each other with the bomb, but as the years passed and no one made good on those threats, they became progressively less convincing, and therefore less frequent.

In time, it began to appear as though the nuclear "superpowers" had managed to replicate the evolutionary history of the giant moose. The United States and the Soviet Union had developed an elaborate and intimidating set of "antlers" to make each secure against the other, but each of them soon found that, once deployed, its defenses were constantly getting tangled up in the undergrowth, and that the burden of carrying them around all day left little energy for anything else. The exhausted behemoths eventually came to realize that if they were ever to try to use the weapons they had evolved to protect themselves, they would probably break their own necks. Meanwhile, blissfully unarmed rabbits and mice were quietly invading their pastures, eating up the grass, exhausting the water supply, and reproducing like crazy. One had to wonder just what security amounted to in such an environment, and which of the animals was best equipped to achieve it.

Fables like this one became unsettlingly real in Moscow and Washington during the 1980s, as Soviet and American leaders contemplated the fact that their exhausting quest for military advantage had bought them so little protection against the dangers of economic decline and the social consequences that flow from it. Both sides had emphasized security over solvency, and were now paying the price that comes from such an imbalance.[10] The real "victors" in World War II, it was beginning to appear, had been the Germans and the Japanese, precisely because their defeat in that conflict had liberated them from the task of having to provide for their own security. They had been free to exploit the divorce between military and economic capability that the invention of nuclear weapons had made possible; as a consequence—and despite their substantial military inferiority when compared with the Americans and the Russians—these states were universally regarded by the end of the decade as among the probable superpowers of the twenty-first century. How successfully the old Cold War superpowers would be able to compete with them was not at all clear.

All previous great powers since 1500 had attained that status by combining military with economic strength, and by reaping the fruits of the resulting complementarity. But Germany and Japan were emerging as post-Cold War super-powers by a very different route, one that relied far more heavily upon economic rather than military capability; other states like Singapore, South Korea, Taiwan, and even Hong Kong had established a significant presence in world politics solely by economic means. These developments suggest that a fundamental tectonic shift has taken place in what is required to gain influence in the world: that the old path of using economic capacity to build military strength no longer produces the results it once did; and that it may indeed have reduced, rather than adding to, the influence of those nations that have persisted in following it since the end of World War II.

This by no means implies that military capability will have nothing to do with determining influence in the post-Cold War world. As long as nuclear weapons remain in existence, the task of deterring their use by holding out a credible prospect of retaliation will remain. Defense against attack by non-nuclear means may take on increasing importance as the technology to launch such attacks filters down to smaller and smaller political entities—and no-nentities—who nurse larger and larger grievances. Certainly the United States and its coalition partners in the Persian Gulf demonstrated one important role for military strength after the Cold War, which is to prevent predatory states from obtaining, and using for their own purposes, military technology left over from the Cold War. It is highly significant, though, that the Bush administration did not even try to pay for the Persian Gulf war on its own: for the first time in its history as a great power, the United States requested financial assistance in fighting a war, not least from its old World War II adversaries, Germany and Japan.

The question of who the post-Cold War great powers are going to be, therefore, is by no means as easy to answer as it was when the *combination* of economic with military strength was what qualified one for geopolitical pre-eminence. Geopolitical fault lines have indeed shifted: joining these two kinds of power no longer produces the results it did throughout the preceding five centuries. Advances in technology—and, in particular, the advent of nuclear weapons[11]—appear to have altered permanently the environment in which great powers live by ruling out war against each other as a viable option; as a result, those great powers who continue to prepare for such wars as if nothing had happened risk following the evolutionary path of the giant moose. Old Cold War antagonisms have become largely irrelevant under these circumstances, and that is part—but only part—of the explanation for 1989.

The Collapse of Authoritarianism

The divorce of military from economic capability as the path to influence in world politics has affected the United States and the Soviet Union more or less impartially; hence, it alone would not explain the widespread sense that not only is the Cold War over, but that the West has decisively "won" it. Everyone expects the United States to be one of several great powers in the post-Cold War world; it is not at all clear, though, that the Soviet Union will be. If we are to understand this outcome—how it was that the Cold War ended with the authority of one of its major antagonists intact but the other in disarray—we will have to take into account a second tectonic force that has been at work for many years but that has hardly been impartial in its effects: it is the collapse of authoritarian alternatives to liberalism.

Despite being at opposite ends of the ideological spectrum, fascism and communism always had a lot in common. Both glorified the state at the expense of the individual; both accepted the proposition that there was such a thing as a "science" of politics which, if imposed from the top, could make governments work with greater efficiency than if they relied on the messy and interminable procedures of democratic politics. And both ideologies, we can now see, were responses to the perceived failures of liberalism as it had developed in the nineteenth century: to problems growing out of the uneven distribution of wealth the market system had produced, and the strong sense of social and intellectual alienation that flowed from them.[12]

Fascism, of course, disappeared as the result of World War II, a cataclysm advocates of that ideology had foolishly provoked. Communism survived and for a time even prospered during the postwar era; its decline came about more gradually and (thank goodness) more peacefully, with 1989 marking the completion of that process.

Given what we now know about the inadequacies of Marxist systems, one wonders why it took so long for this to happen. Several reasons suggest themselves: that command economies work reasonably well during the initial stages of industrialization, and that it was not until the Soviet Union and Eastern Europe began to move beyond those stages that the deficiencies of Marxism-Leninism became apparent; that the coincidence of decolonization with the onset of the Cold War gave the Soviet model an appeal in newly independent Third World countries that it would not otherwise have had; that the energy crisis in the West during the 1970s may have magnified the weaknesses of market economies and concealed—for a time at least—those of command economies; and that neither the Soviet Union nor its satellites possessed effective mechanisms for replacing aging leaders and the discredited policies they perpetuated. Only death could do that, and it keeps its own schedule.

As a result, it was not until the 1980s that a consensus as to the superiority of market economics—and with it a sense of the triumph of democratic politics—began to develop. Underlying tectonic forces had been pointing in that direction for some time, but it took time for the blinders that had obscured those processes to drop away. That finally happened in 1989: suddenly it became obvious to everyone (with the exception of a few isolated holdouts like Fidel Castro and Kim Il-sung) that economic progress and centralized authority simply do not mesh.

A fundamental assumption of Marxism-Leninism had always been that hierarchy in politics would produce abundance in economics. Industrialization, Marx believed, required central planning; Lenin in turn specified the state as the provider of this service. The pre-industrial world of divided political authority and individual economic autonomy had no future, both men claimed, because the inexorable advance of technology—shifts in the means of production, to use Marx's term—left no alternative.

Curiously, however, those who advance hypotheses about inexorable forces in history often conclude that history will stop with them.[13] The founders of Marxism-Leninism were no exception, for having identified a powerful engine of historical change, they failed to allow for the possibility that it might lack a shut-off switch. Shifts in the means of production have indeed shaped economic, political, and social conditions, but with the passage of time it has become clear that the forces Marx identified and that Lenin sought to harness have turned both men's conclusions about politics upside down. Far from promoting centralization, the technology required to advance standards of living these days seems—inexorably—to discourage this tendency.

It used to be possible to modernize an economy by forcing one's citizens to produce goods and services according to a central plan: that is how the Soviet Union created the industrial base that allowed it to defeat the Germans in World War II and to compete with the United States in the Cold War that followed. But as the U.S.S.R. moved into a new phase of economic development in the 1960s and 1970s—one that should have begun to benefit consumers—it became clear that central planners could not respond fast enough to shifts in supply and demand where not just a few but thousands of producers and commodities were involved. Only old-fashioned self-regulating markets could do that, and only by means that were the antithesis of centralization, and therefore of planning. The situation became even worse in the 1980s as the computer revolution took hold: that technology thrives on individual initiative and an unconstrained flow of information, neither of which the hierarchical Soviet system was equipped to encourage.[14]

Marx, it turned out, was right. Shifts in the means of production do shape society in important ways, and they are irreversible in their effects. The difficulty is that they have continued into an age Marx never envisaged, and as they have done so they have rewarded lateral rather than hierarchical forms of organization. The effect has been to put unprecedented pressures on those who run command economies either to make them work or to abolish them altogether. And since no one has discovered how to accomplish the first alternative, the second appears increasingly to be the only viable possibility.

But to dismantle a command economy is to allow individual autonomy: the price of prosperity is ultimately democracy. And because the trend away

from centralization is so firmly based upon shifts in the means of production—
a particular irony is the extent to which Marxist countries urbanized and
educated peasant masses as a means of increasing industrial and agricultural
output, only to discover that they had created a middle class filled with
dissatisfied consumers eager to take control of their own lives[15]—even Marxist logic would suggest that it cannot now be reversed. By a kind of perverse
logic, the engine of history Marx described now appears to be propelling those
nations that have embraced his ideology into their next historically determined phase, which turns out to be liberal bourgeois democratic free-market
capitalism, or something very close to it. Irreversible historical forces, it
seems, can go around in circles, no doubt causing dead revolutionaries to
execute similar patterns of movement in their graves.

The Decline of Brutality

A third tectonic force that shaped the events of 1989 has to do with the way
in which nations treat their own citizens, and those of other nations. Historians of Europe in the eighteenth century have often looked back upon that
age as one in which there existed something approximating an international
standard of behavior for great powers. Each state acknowledged the internal
legitimacy of the others; international law had begun to emerge, for the first
time, as a significant force in world affairs.[16] Wars, it is true, were frequent,
and often fought over issues that would seem to us petty. But these were, for
the most part, conflicts conducted with limited losses of life and of resources;
they did not result, as wars of our own time have, in the annihilation of
whole states or the destruction of entire peoples. Indeed some of these wars
were fought in such a genteel way that civilian populations were hardly aware
of the fact that they were going on.

   All of this changed with the wars of the French Revolution and Na-
poleon. War became an enterprise of the masses, not just the professional
military elite; and with the democratization of politics that followed the
collapse of the Old Regime, there arose as well the irresistible impulse of
nationalism. Military operations were not only larger in scale and longer
in duration; they also became more brutal. Atrocities were committed that
would have been unthinkable in an earlier age, sometimes against entire
populations. The cause of victory took on such importance that few constraints survived on what states did to bring it about.[17]

   Developments in technology during the nineteenth century only reinforced this trend. The advent of steam-propelled vessels, of railroads, and of
armaments whose killing power far exceeded that of their eighteenth-century
counterparts—all of this combined with the intensifying forces of nationalism
to bring about the unprecedented levels of violence in war that first became
evident (lest we forget) in the United States between 1861 and 1865, but
which were reflected also in the "new" European imperialism of the late

nineteenth century, and then in turn, even more vividly, in the carnage of World War I.[18]

The rise of totalitarian political systems after that conflict—especially in Nazi Germany, the Soviet Union, and, in its own distinctive way, Japan[19]—intensified still further the trend toward brutality but linked it with a new kind of amorality that explicitly justified means in terms of ends. It was no accident that the first two regimes not only cooperated to start World War II, but also presided over the two greatest episodes of mass murder in all of history: Stalin's efforts to collectivize agriculture and to purge his opponents, and Hitler's campaign to kill all the Jews. The depths of cynicism reached in those years is very well summarized in Stalin's alleged sneer: "The Pope! How many divisions has *he* got?"[20]

The victory for human rights that occurred in 1945 was an exceedingly narrow one: it was brought about only by the militarily effective but morally questionable tactic of enlisting the aid of one tyrant to kill another; it often required the use of means that seemed indistinguishable in the brutality of their effects from those employed by the adversary;[21] and the peace that followed—because it involved the imposition of Soviet authority over unwilling Central and Eastern Europeans—was morally flawed as well.

But from our current vantage point, we can now see that World War II marked a bottoming-out in this long and depressing descent from eighteenth century standards of international behavior. The war itself was so horrible in its consequences that it shocked the international community into supporting—at least on paper—the United Nations Universal Declaration on Human Rights. In the years that have followed, whether because of this document or in spite of it, a determination to minimize brutality has increasingly come to influence the behavior of the great powers.

Consider, for example, the precedent the United States set by not using atomic weapons in the Korean War. The decision was based in part, to be sure, upon the absence of any very good targets, but the documents also show that a desire to avoid the unnecessary destruction of civilian populations—a concern rooted in considerations of both morality and expediency—played a role in it.[22] Consider the rapidity with which the great European colonial empires disappeared after World War II: this happened not so much because the victims of imperialism gained new military or economic power, but rather because of the moral strength that accrued to them as world opinion shifted against the whole idea of empire. Consider the process of de-Stalinization inside the Soviet Union, which constituted nothing short of the dismantling, from within, of a police state, not so much because autocracy had yet proven all that inefficient—this was still the late 1950s and early 1960s—as because it was judged to have been too brutal. Consider the growth of the civil rights movement inside the United States, as well as the other minority rights movements that have followed it. Consider the anti-apartheid movement in South Africa, or the relative success of the Carter administration's human rights campaign in Latin America. And, finally, consider the most sweeping victory of all for human rights: the events of 1989 in the Soviet Union and Eastern Europe.

To be sure, the process has not been consistent: witness the increasingly oppressive Israeli treatment of the Palestinians, or the very different path—compared with what was happening elsewhere in the world—that events in China took in 1989. Certainly Saddam Hussein was not minimizing brutality when he attacked Iran, gassed the Kurds, swallowed Kuwait, and waged ecological warfare in the Persian Gulf. Still, as the international coalition that rallied against Iraq suggests, the progress toward collective action against brutality that has been achieved since Stalin made his crack about the Pope is impressive. One measure of it is the fact that the current leader of the Soviet Union felt obliged, in 1989, to pay his respects at the Vatican to Pope John Paul II—who is in himself, and in the role he has played in Eastern Europe over the past decade, as convincing a demonstration as anyone might need of why popes do not need divisions in the first place.[23]

What appears to have happened here is another of these shifts in historical tectonics that have been going on for a long time, but that have only now become visible: it is that repression no longer represses. Several developments appear to have produced this trend, none of them easily reversible. One has to do with the shifts in the means of production mentioned earlier. Half a century ago, a Stalin could simply order workers to run a tractor, or a steam shovel, or a blast furnace; they might not do it efficiently, but they would do it, and the job would eventually get done. But a Gorbachev cannot order anyone to write an imaginative computer program, or to invent a more efficient silicon chip: people have to *want* to do these things, or they will not get done. The means of production today are based as much on what the "working class" does with its brains as with its muscles, and no one has yet discovered how to command thought. Coercion therefore ensures obsolescence, not advance.

A second and related explanation has to do with education. The efforts the Soviet Union and other Marxist governments undertook to educate their people have not only made them more aware than in the past of superior living standards in the West; they have also become more difficult to intimidate. They have realized that the authorities cannot lock up an entire nation: when, after initial efforts to suppress them, the size of demonstrations in East Berlin, Leipzig, Prague and Bucharest in the fall of 1989 swelled by factors of ten, twenty, or thirty, the governments in charge simply gave up. As Timothy Garton Ash describes the process:

> A few kids went on the streets and threw a few words. The police beat them. The kids said: You have no right to beat us! And the rulers, the high and mighty, replied, in effect: Yes, we have no right to beat you. We have no right to preserve our rule by force. The end no longer justifies the means![24]

Even where that did not happen, as in Beijing, the existence of an educated core of young people makes eventual revolution as certain as the forecasts drawn from an actuarial table. It takes little imagination to guess what is going through the minds of an extraordinarily sophisticated generation of Chinese students as they endure month after month of stifling "political re-education" classes. As any parent of a rebellious teenager would know, there could be no better way to guarantee the overthrow, sooner or later, of an old order that has hung on well past its time.

There is yet a third irreversible development that makes a return to brutality difficult: it is the increasing permeability of borders. Repression always worked best when one could prevent all contact between those to be repressed and everyone else. But the means of communication have shifted, like the means of production; increasingly efficient and decreasingly expensive information technology makes it almost impossible to wall a nation off from what is happening in the rest of the world. As the experiences of China, East Germany, Czechoslovakia and Romania all demonstrated in 1989, closed political borders have become open to ideas in ways even police states cannot prevent. The result has been to create a new kind of "domino" effect, in which the achievement of liberty in one country can cause repressive "dominos" to topple, or at least to wobble, elsewhere. The sheer impact of example, in an information age, has itself become an engine of history.

The instruments of brutality, therefore, have become about as unusable for the great powers in the post-Cold War era as the instruments of war were for them during the Cold War itself. Any effort to reverse that trend—as the geriatrics who still lead China are discovering, and as those who attempted to undo the effects of *glasnost* and *perestroika* inside the Soviet Union in August, 1991, did discover—is likely to be an uphill battle indeed.

Juxtapositions

But the three tectonic forces mentioned above—the emergence of new criteria for defining great powers, the collapse of authoritarian alternatives to liberalism, and the decline of brutality—still will not explain what happened in 1989 unless we consider how they interacted with one another. It was not just their existence that was important; after all, these trends had been present for years prior to the *annus mirablis*. It was the juxtaposition of these forces at that particular time that produced such remarkable consequences.

The emergence of new criteria of power in world politics, for example, would seem to have implied the *symmetrical* decline of the United States and the Soviet Union, since both of them had become great powers by the old method of combining economic with military strength. This tectonic force would explain the exhaustion both superpowers felt after more than four decades of Cold War; it would not account for the fact, though, that one side simply gave up and the other did not. The U.S.S.R. in the 1980s faced not only external exhaustion but also a simultaneous internal crisis occasioned by a second tectonic force: the inability of command economies to cope with the growing demands of post-industrial societies. Even then, Soviet authorities might have tried to deal with these crises, as they had with others in the past, by using coercion to attempt to reverse historical processes. But this time, a third tectonic force—the declining effectiveness of brutality—ruled that option out. There was little choice, therefore, but to accept "defeat."[25]

This is by no means to deny the roles key individuals played in the events of 1989. Mikhail Gorbachev's was obviously decisive, and a diverse array of other distinctive individuals—among them Lech Walesa, Vaclav Havel, Margaret Thatcher, Ronald Reagan, Helmut Kohl, Andrei Sakharov, Alexander Solzhenitsyn, and, not least, Pope John Paul II, to name only a few—shaped the outcome as well. But creative statecraft, like the creative process in literature that so strongly influenced several of these individuals, is often a matter of recognizing the direction in which tectonic forces are moving and adapting one's own purposes to them. Leadership that tries to resist tectonic forces is certain sooner or later to be swept away, leaving few traces behind. Leadership that accommodates itself to these forces may have no better record of survival—indeed because of the risks involved, it could actually be worse—but such leaders do have a much better chance of imposing their particular visions of the future upon that which is to come. Whatever ultimately happens to him, historians a hundred years from now will have much to say of—and probably considerable respect for—Gorbachev. They are likely to accord Brezhnev little more than a footnote.

Conclusion

Being aware of tectonic forces in history does not imply the ability to control them, anymore than an understanding of plate tectonics gives geologists the capacity to direct continental drift. We live in a world that imposes many conditions about which we can do nothing; the extent to which human behavior can alter the course of events in both science and history is quite limited. But no geologist would conclude from this that the study of plate tectonics serves no useful purpose, for in addition to giving us the means—in a very general way—of predicting the location and frequency of earthquakes, this theory provides the most convincing explanation we have of how the terrain upon which we live came to be the way that it is.

That is a useful kind of thing for statesmen, as well as geologists, to know. For if history is indeed the conjunction of the expected with the unexpected, then it is only by enhancing our understanding of long-term trends—of the tectonic forces that shape our political, economic, social and moral worlds, as well as our physical world—that we can prepare ourselves, with any success at all, for the surprises that are certain to come. Predictions based on past experience are at least plausible; predictions based on amnesia or ignorance are just random guessing.

But understanding such trends requires extending our temporal and spatial horizons, because historical tectonics, like those in geology, operate beyond our normal range of analytical vision. We need to try to decide which of these forces are reversible and which are not. We need to think about how they reinforce, or undercut, one another. And we need, most importantly, to get some sense of the extent to which—if at all—human intervention can deflect, redirect, or otherwise alter these forces. Only by doing so can we begin to comprehend, and perhaps even in limited ways begin to shape, the forces that have, so surprisingly but so decisively, brought an end to the Cold War and thereby confronted us with the quite urgent task of thinking about what is to come next.

## TEN

Great Illusions, the Long Peace, and the Future of the International System

"How do you know that you're not going to wind up like Norman Angell?" The question—polite but pointed—came from a graduate student in a seminar I taught at Princeton in the fall of 1987. *The Long Peace* had just come out and I had inflicted it on my students without waiting for the paperback edition, so I had probably asked for something like this. My answer, at the time, was a historian's cop-out: I had written that book as history, not prophecy; even if the post-World War II great power system were to break up tomorrow, its record of more than four decades without great power war would more than justify use of the term "long peace" to characterize it.

But having said that, I was not wholly satisfied with it. A "long peace" on the verge of collapse would hardly be as robust an explanation of past events as a "long peace" whose perpetuation seemed likely. By implication my thesis would stand as good history only to the extent that it anticipated at least the immediate future. I had, it appeared, backed into the business of prophecy without having really intended to.

So I thought I should take my student's question more seriously. What assurance did I have that my treatment of the Soviet-American "cold war" as a "long peace" would not repeat the unfortunate fate of Angell's book, *The Great Illusion*, which had demonstrated so eloquently in 1910 that there could never be a protracted great power war, only to have its argument proven, after 1914, to have been a great mistake? One easy answer was that Angell had based his assertion on a single generalization about the international system: that as industrialization progresses, nations become less able to afford the risks and costs of all-out war.[1] Clearly other forces were shaping world affairs at that time; had Angell been more sensitive to these—and to the possibility that they might cancel out the one he had relied on—then his record as a prophet might have been better, if gloomier.

Because I had intended the "long peace" thesis as a historical and not a theoretical explanation of the postwar international system, I had not explicitly specified the assumptions that lay behind it; indeed, in a manner quite characteristic of historians, I had not really attempted to sort them out in my own mind. But if the issue of "robustness" was to be addressed—which is to say, if I was going to establish why the "long peace" was not going to turn out to be a "great illusion"—then it seemed worth reconsidering the argument in terms of international relations theory with a view to identifying the conceptual foundations upon which it might rest. Solid foundations, after all, imply durability; shaky ones suggest the need to rebuild or, at a minimum, to rethink.

The end of the Cold War has made this task all the more urgent. The "long peace," after all, grew out of that conflict; if Soviet-American rivalry is no longer to dominate world politics, then one cannot help but wonder what will. It would be ironic if the Cold War should turn out to have been a safer and more stable era than one in which the relationship between Washington and Moscow has become "normal." But the fading of Cold War antagonisms has already altered the pattern of relations between nations in fundamental ways: we have little basis, therefore, for simply assuming a perpetuation of the "long peace," now that the conditions that gave rise to it are disappearing.

International relations theory, however, suggests surprisingly little about the post-Cold War world. Much of it is based upon generalizations drawn from the Cold War itself; some theorists appear to have assumed (like some policy-makers) that the contest between Washington and Moscow would last forever, and therefore could be made to yield universally-applicable propositions. Theorists also expend so much of their energy debating methodology—what with neo-realists clashing with neo-Marxists, empiricists with deductivists, quantifiers with non-quantifiers, and behaviorists with particularists—that one wonders at times if they will ever get around to substance at all. Nor is there even a consensus among theorists as to what the function of theory ought be: is it to describe, prescribe, or proscribe?[2] It is all very bewildering for simple historians, who tend not to attach very much importance to theoretical refinement in the first place; and yet one of the few ways a historian can say anything meaningful about the future is to project past patterns forward. That requires generalization—which is to say, theory—in some form.

I have decided to resolve this problem by regarding myself as a consumer, not a producer, of theories.[3] Consumers select merchandise from a wide variety of sources according to their own utilitarian standards; producers specialize by turning out only commodities for which they believe markets exist. No producer, however ambitious, can hope to satisfy all consumer needs; no consumer would feel obliged to purchase only what a single producer makes. Why, therefore, should a historian not take the view that a single international system exists in reality, and that the theorists' conflicting conceptions of it are simply efforts at characterization from varying perspectives and for different purposes? To "buy into" any single theory would restrict one's ability to explain the wide range of events with which any historian must deal; but to accept each of them uncritically would leave one unable to explain anything at all, since this field so obviously lacks the synthesis that would show how its theories complement or are even consistent with one another. My approach in this essay then, like that of the consumer in the marketplace, has been to take from the shelf those theories that help me to understand the foundations of the "long peace," to reject those that do not, but to try to do all of this without producing the unfortunate side-effects that come when incompatible ideas—or indigestible commodities—are mixed together.[4]

This "consumerist" approach, I hope, will provide a way to assess the likelihood that the "long peace" will survive the end of the Cold War. For if I can show that certain theoretical explanations complement or reinforce each other in accounting for the international system that evolved after World War II, that would seem to suggest what the theorists like to call "overdetermination," which is to say, redundancy in those mechanisms that support and sustain the system in question. Foundations that combine concrete, steel, and brick are likely to be more durable than those consisting exclusively of any one of those materials. But if theories contradict, negate, or otherwise undermine each other, that may be an indicator of potential, if not actual, instability: the analogy would be living in a flimsy house on a slippery slope with poor drainage in an earthquake zone.

In the essay that follows, I have attempted to apply "consumerist" criteria to see what theory might suggest about the future of the "long peace." In doing so, I have sought to ask the following questions:

(1) Does the "long peace" thesis depend upon an exclusionary or ecumenical theoretical base? "Paradigm pluralism," I acknowledge, is not always a virtue.[5] But any generalization that bases itself upon a single pattern of events and on the exclusion of others risks an opposite deficiency, which is "underdetermination": that, it would seem, is what happened to Norman Angell. It is often said that redundancy enhances deterrence—witness the strategic weapons "triad." Why should it not also fortify arguments?

(2) If the "long peace" thesis does meet this test of "paradigm redundancy," does it then avoid yet another danger with an analogue in realm of strategic weaponry, which is the possibility that intersecting theories, when applied to support specific generalizations, might cancel each other out? There could be, after all, such a thing as "paradigm fratricide":[6] theories derived from different disciplines or from disparate phenomena might well undercut, and even invalidate, the conclusions each might suggest by itself.

This entire exercise rests, I hasten to add, upon the assumption that theories do in one way or another describe reality. If they do not—if our most sophisticated assumptions about international relations are only imaginary castles floating around on wispy clouds—then my tests of paradigm "redundancy" and "fratricide" would be equally insubstantial, and quite irrelevant to the task at hand.[7] But I prefer to believe that the field of international relations theory is based on more than vapor. This essay will test that assumption—as well as prospects for the "long peace"—by considering five theories that have been advanced to explain the absence of great power war since 1945 : nuclear peace; bipolarity; hegemonic stability; "triumphant" liberalism; and long cycles. I will conclude by considering what these theories suggest about our chances for sustaining the "long peace" into the post-Cold War era.

Nuclear Peace

The most widely-accepted explanation for why the Cold War became a "long peace" is, of course, that nuclear weapons deterred those who might have sought a different outcome. Once this quantum leap in destructive capabilities became available to both the United States and the Soviet Union, the argument runs, neither was willing to risk the use of force to achieve its objectives in the way that nations had routinely done prior to the end of World War II. Nuclear weapons provided a kind of "crystal ball" into which statesmen could look to see the consequences of war before acting to initiate war: as a result prudence, even wisdom, shaped the conduct of postwar great power relations to an unprecedented degree.[8] The record of "atomic diplomacy"—the use of nuclear threats to achieve political objectives—may have been unimpressive; the number of nuclear weapons actually built may have exceeded by far what would have been necessary to achieve the "crystal ball" effect. But, as the most thoughtful historian of the Soviet-American nuclear relationship has concluded: "The imperative of avoiding nuclear war imposes great caution on both governments. . . . What each can do to the other, whoever goes first, is more than enough to stay every hand that does not belong to a madman."[9]

A few theorists find the concept of "nuclear peace" so convincing that they have even called for proliferating nuclear weapons to states that do not now have them. Kenneth Waltz suggested in 1981 that "the slow spread of nuclear weapons will promote peace and reinforce international stability,"[10] and a decade later John Mearsheimer insisted that the United States could best stabilize post-Cold War Europe by encouraging "the limited and carefully managed proliferation of nuclear weapons."[11] To say that these arguments have not elicited widespread support would be putting it charitably; the harsher criticism is that they show what happens when theory is pursued beyond common sense. The assumption upon which these propositions rest, though, is an entirely plausible one: it is that optimism encourages war, while pessimism promotes peace.[12] Nations do not normally use military force when they expect their own destruction to be the result. The prospect of even a few retaliatory nuclear strikes succeeding, Waltz and Mearsheimer believe, is quite enough to turn optimists into pessimists, whatever the differences in culture, circumstances, and overall military capability that might divide them. Nuclear weapons, from this perspective, make real the Clausewitzian abstraction of absolute war; and that fact transforms the once real possibility of war among nations that possess nuclear weapons into an abstraction.[13]

But these arguments only *suggest* that nuclear deterrence caused the "long peace"; they do not *confirm* that role.[14] Leaders do not always behave as logically as theorists assume they do: that makes the application of theoretical principles to practical statecraft a risky business. And even if the concept of "nuclear peace" is convincing, it need not have been the only foundation upon which the "long peace" was built; it is easy to suggest other stabilizing mechanisms that might have complemented nuclear weapons in sustaining postwar international stability.[15] Nor—as the end of the Cold War is showing—can the presence of nuclear arsenals indefinitely perpetuate the superpower relationship that emerged from World War II.[16] It is even possible, as John Mueller has argued, that nuclear weapons had little or nothing to do with the fact that the Cold War never become hot: that believers in "nuclear peace" have confused the short-term effects of a new weapons technology with a long-term trend toward the obsolescence of great power war, and have therefore, by concentrating on trees, missed a forest.[17] It would be unwise to conclude, therefore, that nuclear weapons alone transformed the Cold War into a "long peace," or that by themselves they can guarantee its survival. We must broaden our theoretical perspectives if we are to avoid great illusions.

Bipolarity

Another explanation frequently offered for the "long peace" has to do with the historic shift in the structure of the international system that is said to have occurred at the end of World War II: the replacement of a "multipolar" with a "bipolar" configuration of power. Conventional wisdom had long held multipolarity to be necessary for systemic stability, but as Waltz pointed out in 1979, "international conditions have not conformed to the theorists' stipulations." A balance of power, he maintained, required only two things: "that the [international] order be anarchic and that it be populated by units wishing to survive." Not only could a bipolar balance exist; it would even have certain advantages over a multipolar balance, in that responsibility for maintaining the system would be concentrated, not dispersed; defections from alliances would be tolerable, not catastrophic; and the existence of high stakes would encourage responsibility, not risk-taking. Thus, Waltz noted of the United States and the Soviet Union, "two states, isolationist by tradition, untutored in the ways of international politics, and famed for impulsive behavior, soon showed themselves—not always and everywhere, but always in crucial cases—to be wary, alert, cautious, flexible, and forbearing."[18]

But since the world's experience with bipolarity is limited to the years since 1945,[19] and since those years coincide precisely with the existence of nuclear weapons, it is difficult to determine whether bipolarity itself created stability, or whether that condition merely reflected the effects of a nuclear standoff. Waltz himself has been less than clear on this point: "the perennial forces of politics are more important than the new military technology," he argued in 1979, but he also acknowledged that "states armed with nuclear weapons may have stronger incentives to avoid war than states armed conventionally."[20] Certainly his subsequent position in favor of nuclear proliferation seemed to imply at least as stabilizing a role for deterrence as for structural bipolarity.

One thing at least is apparent: nuclear weapons had nothing to do with the *emergence* of bipolarity. That condition grew out of the collapse of multipolarity, a development brought about by the Europeans' general imprudence in disregarding Norman Angell in 1914, and by Adolf Hitler's particular imprudence in declaring war on *both* the Soviet Union and the United States in 1941. Even if nuclear weapons had never been invented, a bipolar structure of international relations would have emerged in 1945, and would very likely have lasted for quite a while.

But would it have lasted for four and a half decades? Recent studies of great power "decline"[21] suggest that it has become more and more difficult to maintain large spheres of influence for long periods of time: authority tends to erode either because of the external resistance it provokes or the internal exhaustion it produces. By this logic, the postwar pre-eminence of the United States and the Soviet Union should have ended as old adversaries recovered, new rivals arose, and the phenomenon of "overstretch," to use Paul Kennedy's term, began to set in.[22] That of course did happen in certain areas. The conventional military power that Washington and Moscow accumulated proved usable only against third parties, as in Korea, Vietnam, Afghanistan, and the Persian Gulf; even there its use was not always successful. Allies and clients became more assertive—at times even rebellious—as the years passed.[23] Bipolarity never existed in the economic realm: there power shifted from a unipolar to a largely tripolar configuration dominated by the United States, the European Community and Japan, with the Soviet Union an isolated bystander.[24] And although bipolarity did once take the form of a worldwide ideological competition, communism has long since lost the contest with capitalism when people have the right to choose between them.[25]

Nevertheless, the *image* of a bipolar as opposed to a multipolar structure of international relations persisted well into the 1980s, long after the reality had ceased to exist. It is difficult to account for this except by citing the tens of thousands of nuclear weapons that filled Soviet and American arsenals: nothing else, I think, could have sustained such an *appearance* of bipolarity for so long beyond the time the actual condition had begun to pass from the scene.[26]

Nuclear weapons created a symbolic form of strength; they became, as McGeorge Bundy has suggested, the chief psychological indicator of what it was to be—or to continue as—a great power.[27] They served, in this way, much the same function that overseas colonies and expensive battleships once did,[28] or that subsidized national airlines still do. No one knows with any precision how a colony or a battleship or an airline will enhance a nation's power; indeed, when subjected to strict cost-benefit analysis, such symbols often produce greater losses than profits. But the rules of accounting rarely discourage nations from seeking the prestige the possession of symbols brings, and it has largely been the prestige of having nuclear weapons that has led statesmen—at least in states that aspire to great power status—to insist on obtaining them.[29] That prestige, more than anything else, maintained a façade of Soviet and American bipolarity, and that façade, in turn, helped to shape structural stability in the postwar international system.

One might raise an objection here, though: if nuclear weapons were so important in enhancing prestige, why did more nations not build them, thus bringing us closer than we now are to a Waltzian proliferated world? Some nations did, of course, but without announcing it, a fact that is in itself significant: What is it that has made nuclear capability, for the last several nations to have attained it, a condition they are unwilling to acknowledge? Why has there been no public confirmation of a new nuclear arsenal since the Indians' somewhat embarrassed disclosure in 1974? One answer may be that prestige wears thin once one gets to the point of having six or seven nuclear or near-nuclear powers; another could be the stigma attached, in the eyes of many countries, to possessing such weapons in the first place. That stigma has arisen from various sources, but one of them may be that the very structure of postwar bipolarity, sustained as it was by nuclear deterrence, created a presumption against anyone who might do anything to destabilize it. The additional proliferation of nuclear weapons—Waltz's optimism to the contrary notwithstanding—was seen as something that would have such an effect, and that prospect in itself may have deterred some potential nuclear powers from becoming actual ones.[30]

A curious complementarity—even circularity—exists, therefore, between "bipolarity" and "nuclear peace" theories as explanations of Cold War history: bipolarity could not have lasted as long as it did in the absence of nuclear weapons; but nuclear weapons did not spread more widely because of the desire to preserve bipolarity. To the extent that the "long peace" depended upon both the structural prerequisite of bipolarity and the behavioral prerequisite of nuclear deterrence, "paradigm redundancy" would appear to exist; the case for either theory in accounting for postwar international stability would be much weaker without the other.

But what does this suggest about the future? Will their possession of vastly greater quantities of nuclear weapons than anyone else continue to qualify the United States and the Soviet Union as superpowers, or will the world revert in image as well as fact to what is, historically, the more normal pattern, which is multipolarity? What about Waltz's claim that multipolar structures are less stable, and therefore more dangerous, than their bipolar counterparts?

It is only by maintaining its nuclear arsenal that today's Soviet Union keeps up a semblance of its old bipolar relationship with the United States, and even this pattern from the past is beginning to wear thin. Strategic arms negotiations no longer command the urgency or the interest they once did. The possibility that Moscow might use its nuclear strength to intimidate its neighbors seems improbable at a time when several of them have successfully expelled—or are expelling—the Red Army from their territories, and when the Kremlin is relying upon the generosity of the West to help feed its own people. Given the internal disarray that afflicts the Soviet Union these days, there is reason to wonder how much longer that state itself can continue to exist in the form that we have known it for the past seven decades. Nuclear-based bipolarity has suddenly become an anachronism: what worries people now is not so much *how* the Soviet Union might use its nuclear weapons, but rather *who* might control whatever nuclear stockpiles may survive the disintegration of the country that created them.[31]

"Bipolarity" theory, therefore, can help us to understand Cold War history, but it is unlikely to yield post-Cold War prophecy. There are still other theoretical approaches that explain how the "long peace" developed in the first place, though, and that may shed light on its future. It is to them that I now want to turn.

Hegemonic Stability

"Hegemonic stability" is a third theory that has been cited to account for the durability of the postwar international system, but it is one, at first glance, that seems to have little to do with Soviet-American relations. It evolved from efforts to account for the relative prosperity the world has enjoyed since 1945; Cold War history has seemed almost irrelevant to it. Nevertheless, "hegemonic stability," "nuclear peace," and "bipolarity" theories reinforce each other in interesting ways; there are potentially fruitful, if mostly unexplored, possibilities for integrating them.

The theory of hegemonic stability presupposes a single dominant power committed to maintain—and capable of maintaining—the rules necessary to the functioning of a "liberal" economic order, that is, one based on minimizing barriers to trade and investment throughout the world. It assumes a receptive international environment: if the hegemon is not to become "illiberal," it must achieve legitimacy through consensus, not intimidation. International economies can operate in the absence of such a hegemon, but they will not be "liberal" in character; and the history of autocracy shows that hegemons can survive without being "liberal." But if one is to have the kind of world economy that has existed since 1945—one characterized by unprecedented flows of commodities and capital across international boundaries—then according to the theory there must have been a "hegemon" to make that possible: "hegemony" is a prerequisite for this particular form of systemic stability.[32]

The United States is said to have played the role of hegemon after World War II by working through the International Monetary Fund and the General Agreement on Tariffs and Trade to stabilize currencies and reduce trade barriers on a global scale. In doing so, it approximated the achievement of Great Britain after the Napoleonic wars; it had been the failure to sustain such a system after World War I—because neither Britain nor the United States would assume the necessary responsibilities at the time—that hastened the cataclysm of 1939–45.[33] An important question for the future is whether the international economic system can continue to function on a "liberal" basis as the authority of the United States to impose and enforce "rules" gradually erodes—in part, as a consequence of its very success in having created an environment in which prosperous rivals can flourish.[34]

But "hegemonic stability" theorists have had little to say about the Soviet Union, or even about the Cold War.[35] It is as if our thinking about the post-World War II international system has proceeded along separate but parallel tracks, never intersecting, and yet aimed toward the same objective, which is accounting for the fact that World War III has not occurred. Does it make sense to keep "hegemonic stability" theory in a separate intellectual compartment from "nuclear peace" and "bipolarity"? What happens if the compartmental barriers are removed, and cross-fertilization is allowed to occur?

Much depends, obviously, on whether one is prepared to accept the possibility of dual hegemons. The concept may be difficult to conceive of in the world economy,[36] but it would be hard to think of world politics in terms of anything other than multiple hegemons: there has not been, at least in modern times, a truly "unipolar" system. Certainly Waltz's concept of "bipolar" stability assumes the existence of dual hegemons; indeed functionally it depends upon them. But do geopolitical hegemons perform the same "stabilizing" roles that economic hegemons do? And can they do this at the same time that they compete with one another, as balance of power theory suggests they must?

An economic hegemon stabilizes by providing "collective goods" from which all are eager to benefit but for which few—apart from the hegemon—are willing to pay: the examples of tariff non-discrimination, fixed currencies, and even international security come to mind. But what "collective goods" could dual geopolitical hegemons provide?[37] An obvious possibility is the joint "management" of world affairs in such a way as to avoid global war, a service from which all nations would benefit but which only super-powers would be in a position to furnish. And it is precisely "management" that Waltz cites as the most important operational reflection of postwar Soviet-American bipolarity: despite recurring crises in their own relations, the two superpowers so ordered their affairs during the "long peace" that they neither stumbled into another war nor allowed others to upset the international system within which they coexisted.[38]

This pattern of dual hegemonic "management" functioned at several levels. Even as they piled up huge quantities of nuclear weapons, Russians and Americans cooperated—through arms control agreements, the discouragement of proliferation, the exchange of technical information, and a general pattern of cautious behavior in moments of crisis—to lower the risk that any one of those weapons, or those of any other nation, might actually be used. Even as they condemned each other's spheres of influence in Europe, the Middle East, Latin America, and East Asia, Moscow and Washington made only half-hearted efforts to "roll back" that influence and at times worked together quietly to sustain it. Rhetoric to the contrary notwithstanding, it is not at all clear that either side was eager to dismantle the Berlin Wall, or to end the division of Germany, or to seek the reunification of Korea. Certainly the United States and the Soviet Union acted jointly to keep crises initiated by third parties from getting out of hand. The history of Arab-Israeli wars since 1948 cannot be written without taking into account what both super-powers have done to limit them, and that record of cooperative crisis-management is by no means restricted to that part of the world. Consider Europe itself, where the effect of Soviet and American hegemonic "management" was to suppress long-standing national rivalries on both sides of what used to be the "iron curtain"—rivalries that have, more than once in the past two centuries, sparked hegemonic wars.[39]

Such dual hegemonic stability by no means stifled change: one need only compare today's membership in the United Nations General Assembly with that of 1945 to see just how much change occurred under Soviet-American "management."[40] But the "managers" did maintain a certain structural integrity, much as a dam in a flood-control project would: a great deal of water was allowed to flow through, but only in carefully-regulated amounts. The system accommodated change at one level, even as it resisted it at another.

What this implies, then, is a cooperative interest in maintaining the system despite the fact that competition proceeds within it. Here, too, hegemonic stability theory would appear to reinforce its "nuclear peace" and "bipolar" counterparts in accounting for the long postwar peace. Political economists have shown that cooperation and competition can co-exist in the field of international trade: rivalries can be intense, and yet still take place according to hegemonically imposed—but subsequently widely agreed upon—rules. Indeed, such cooperation may survive the decline of the hegemon that established it: regimes can come to serve in the place of a rule-maker, even in what might appear at first glance to be an anarchic international environment.[41]

Regime theorists are not entirely comfortable with attempts to apply their model to the field of international security,[42] but if regimes can function in the absence of a single hegemon, then it is difficult to see why they cannot operate in the presence of two. Recent developments in game theory show how cooperation can evolve among antagonists, even in anarchic situations; historical case studies have confirmed that such patterns are possible, although by no means inevitable.[43] Even more recently, analysts of postwar Soviet-American relations have begun to draw on regime theory, with promising results.[44] To the extent that these developments grow out of the "hegemonic stability" concept, they confirm the relevance of that approach as yet another way of explaining the "long peace."

It would be inaccurate, though, to imply that the Soviet and American hegemons had equal influence in shaping world politics since 1945: they did not. The idea of "legitimacy" as a prerequisite for hegemonic stabilization can help us to understand why this asymmetry has existed. Historians now understand that potential clients *encouraged* the United States to become a hegemon at the end of World War II: the term "empire by invitation" has come to characterize what happened.[45] The Soviet bid for postwar influence lacked any comparable quality of legitimacy, and so quickly came up against a condition that creates major difficulties for hegemons, which is lack of consent. The problem may be more serious in economic than in political/military affairs, but even in the latter field statesmen eventually learn that influence spread by acquiescence tends to cost less than the other variety, a not insignificant consideration.[46]

Why, though, did the American form of hegemony—political and economic—command such widespread support? Here the tendency of hegemonic stability theorists to neglect politics may have caused them to miss something important, for it is difficult to see what could have legitimized an American hegemonic role so quickly and so thoroughly, both in the world at large and, equally important, within a recently isolationist United States, if not the widely perceived Soviet threat to the postwar balance of power in Europe and Northeast Asia. Could the United States have even become a hegemon without a good deal of inadvertent help from the Russians? The experience of 1919–39, when Americans had the power to play such a role but lacked the motive, suggests how important a clear and present danger can be in persuading a nation to take on global responsibilities. Nor is it likely that those responsibilities could have been handled as successfully in the absence of explicit guarantees against Soviet aggression: these are precisely what the European architects of a well-known instrument of American hegemony, the North Atlantic Treaty Organization, had in mind when they first proposed it.[47]

What all of this implies is not only that hegemonic stability theory has something to offer the historian of Soviet-American relations; it also suggests an artificiality in efforts to describe the American hegemonic role—even in international economic matters—without considering what the Russians did to bring it about, and how they unintentionally helped to sustain it. And that, in turn, points to a more controversial conclusion: that if Russians and Americans in fact came to function as co-hegemons in "managing" the postwar international system,[48] then perhaps we should recast hegemonic stability theory to take that dual role into account, broadening its purview from political economy to politics in general. Certainly if one makes this modification, there is nothing in hegemonic stability theory that undercuts—and much that reinforces—theories of nuclear peace and bipolarity; their integration might well bring us closer than we are now to a comprehensive explanation for postwar international stability.

That integration might also allow us to draw certain conclusions about the future. For if dual hegemonic "management" reinforced nuclear peace and bipolarity in ensuring stability during the Cold War, then the absence of any one of those phenomena might suggest instability in the post-Cold War world. The Soviet Union has had great difficulty playing its traditional management role in the Third World during the past several years. And the United States too, in the wake of the "revolutions" of 1989, so preoccupied itself with their consequences in Europe that it neglected management responsibilities elsewhere. Under these circumstances, one might well have expected a disruption like the one that took place on August 2, 1990, when Iraq invaded Kuwait: this was exactly the kind of crisis that tends to occur when hegemons cease to behave in a hegemonic manner.[49] The already evident erosion of stability in the post-Cold War world is as clear a confirmation as one might wish of just how stabilizing joint Soviet-American management was while the Cold War was still going on.

"Triumphant" Liberalism

One difficulty with using structural theories like bipolarity and hegemonic stability to account for the long postwar peace, though, is that there is a static quality to them. They give little attention to the forces that made stability possible in the first place, and even less to those that might sooner or later undermine it. They help us to understand configurations of power across space, but not across time. A Waltzian systemic analysis would see significant change as having occurred once—in 1945—and would regard the progression of events prior to that time and after it as relatively unimportant. A "hegemonic stability" theorist, by definition, would be more concerned with what holds a system together than with how it came into being or how it might come apart. But international systems are not immortal: they exist in time as well as in space, and that fact suggests the need to be as sensitive to their evolution and prospects as to their structure.[50]

The adaptation of structure to environment is, of course, a fundamental characteristic of living organisms; as continents drift and climates change, new species arise among plants and animals, which is to say, structures evolve. Why should the same not be true of international systems when confronted with long-term alterations—tectonic shifts, if you will—in the political, economic, technological, intellectual, or even moral environment? Like the effects of natural selection, these changes might not be apparent overnight; but they could be detectable over decades, and certainly would be over centuries. And they might well be dramatic in character: if white moths could become black in response to a specific historical event—the advent of the industrial revolution in England and its effect in darkening tree-trunks— why should not comparably significant but gradual changes in the social and cultural environment affect international systems?[51]

Consider the shift from religious to secular authority that took place in Europe in the fifteenth and sixteenth centuries: the modern state system grew out of that environmental change, but structural theorists pay little attention to how that happened, or to the possibility that future transformations might change the system into something else.[52] Or look at what happened to slavery in the nineteenth century: the institution had been present since the beginning of recorded time, and yet the climate of legitimacy that sustained it eroded so rapidly as to bring about almost universal abolition within a single lifetime.[53] Or contemplate the implications, for statecraft, of the communications revolution of the late nineteenth and early twentieth centuries: suddenly it became possible to know simultaneously what was going on all over the world; one could no longer deal with distant events—precisely because they were distant—in a leisurely and disconnected manner.[54]

Neither the individual behavior of nations nor the structure of international systems is sufficient to account for phenomena like these: they show, rather, that moral, economic, and technological conditions evolve quite independently of behavior and structure, but in such a way as to affect both. Even the words "power" and "influence"—so basic to the realist view of international relations—do not necessarily mean the same things in all cultures, at all times. Russians and Americans might well develop a common interest in sustaining the long postwar peace, so that behavior would reinforce structure,[55] but tectonic shifts and the environmental changes associated with them could still then alter behavior and structure in ways neither level of analysis would predict by itself.

Are such forces reshaping the international system today? The sudden convergence of historical tectonics that ended the Cold War so abruptly in 1989 suggests this: the new importance of economic over military forms of power, the growing advantages of lateral over hierarchical organization, and the declining utility of repression[56] all point, many people argue, to nothing less than the emergence of a democratic political order throughout much of the world. "Something very fundamental has happened," Francis Fukuyama claimed, in the most influential article of 1989: it is "the total exhaustion of viable systemic alternatives to Western liberalism."[57]

This "triumph of liberalism" consensus (it is too early to call it a theory) appears to rest upon three related propositions: that war among the great powers has become unthinkable, that international boundaries are increasingly permeable, and that authoritarian regimes based on command economies are no longer viable.[58] Assuming, for the sake of argument, that these trends are indeed under way, I should like to discuss how each of them might affect the theoretical underpinnings, and therefore the probable future, of the "long peace."

The obsolescence of great power war. John Mueller bases his argument for the "essential irrelevance" of nuclear weapons to postwar systemic stability on the assertion that war itself, at least among the great powers, has long been on the way to becoming obsolete. Norman Angell was right all along, Mueller suggests, just ahead of his time. World War I convinced those who participated in it that the costs of war had now far exceeded whatever conceivable benefits it could bring. World War II occurred only because of the irrational actions of a single evil genius—Adolf Hitler—and because a largely isolated Japan had not directly suffered from the 1914–18 experience. After 1945, no great power could contemplate war without the most painful awareness of its consequences: that fact in itself would have ensured a "long peace," Mueller believes, even if nuclear weapons had never been invented.[59]

This last conclusion is more categorical than many, myself included, would be prepared to accept.[60] But allowing for the deterrent effect of nuclear weapons does not invalidate Mueller's argument that great power war is becoming obsolete; indeed, the two propositions powerfully reinforce one another. And surely Mueller is on to something important when he argues that we should not assume the indefinite perpetuation of social institutions, however long their previous history.[61] "Structural realism" is not well equipped to account for the possibility that as technology makes war more devastating, economics and even morality might combine to make it less likely.[62] Nor would it easily explain the rise of something we might call, for want of a more precise term, "world opinion," a constraint that has inhibited the use of nuclear weapons in situations where no realistic prospect of retaliation existed,[63] that has undermined colonial empires more effectively than the most militant revolutionary ever could have, and that has even changed the way in which great powers go about collecting their debts: nobody, these days, sends a gunboat to shell a village.[64]

None of this is to say that war itself is passing from the scene. The eight-year Iran-Iraq war, after all, came as close to replicating the experience of World War I trench warfare as anything that has occurred since that time; and the United Nations itself approved the use of force against the victor in that conflict after Iraq forcibly annexed Kuwait in 1990. What seems to be happening, rather, is that the world's most powerful nations are increasingly reluctant to get into wars themselves. Four and a half decades have passed since the last all-out great power war; Korea was the last conflict in which one great power engaged a quasi-great power; and the corrosive experiences of fighting third parties in Vietnam and Afghanistan created powerful presumptions against anyone in either Washington or Moscow who would propose repeating even those "limited war" experiences.[65] Those presumptions, to be sure, were not enough to prevent the United States and its allies from going to war to liberate Kuwait early in 1991, but they did powerfully shape the way in which that war was fought, as well as the unprecedentedly protracted public debate over whether—and how—to fight it.

Great powers no longer look upon war, in the way they did for centuries, as just another instrument of statecraft. Today they see it as an exceptional event, to be entered into only upon extreme provocation and (where possible) after careful deliberation. And the possibility of war *between* great powers is so remote that, in this area at least, the old liberal dream of "perpetual peace" seems much more plausible than it did when Angell prematurely announced its arrival eight decades ago.

What might the "obsolescence of war" imply for the "long peace"? To claim anything other than "paradigm redundancy" here would be silly; it normally takes wars to bring an end to peace, and if wars are not to occur among great powers, then peace among them should endure. Certainly the assumption that war between the United States and the Soviet Union was ruled out facilitated their joint "management" of crises elsewhere in the world during the Cold War. One does wonder, though, how well crisis-management will continue work if Soviet decline leaves the United States as the only international "manager." The Iraqi invasion of Kuwait required Washington to assume a disproportionate share of the responsibility for restoring order in the Persian Gulf, and even in the light of this successful experience it is not at all clear that Americans will be prepared to bear such burdens in the future. But neither is it evident who else would be.

All of this suggests, then, that we would do well to welcome the obsolescence of great power war but not necessarily the erosion of great power authority: the trick will be to find ways to sustain that authority—and therefore to allow "management" to continue—without reversing the trend away from war. And that, in turn, will require greater insight than we now have into the nature of great power authority itself, and the legitimacy that sustains it.

The permeability of borders. Classical "realism" came under criticism during the 1970s for neglecting the emergence of transnational phenomena— chiefly economic in character—that were said to be making the world more "interdependent." The argument here was that balance of power theory could not account for regional integration; not only had cooperation emerged under conditions of anarchy, but a whole network of relations had developed, quite apart from traditional military alliances and ideological alignments, that was undermining state authority as it had once been understood.[66]

The difficulty with this theory—as with earlier Marxist predictions about states withering away under communism—was that one never quite seemed to arrive at the anticipated destination. Interdependence grew apace, but with little evidence of a declining role for states in the world at large. Nor are there any imminent indications—even in a Europe poised to establish a true common market—that regional institutions are about to make the domestic functions of states obsolete. "The development of regional integration theory," Joseph S. Nye, Jr., has acknowledged, "outstripped the development of regional communities."[67] One wonders, therefore, whether we have not got our terms wrong: transnational phenomena are real enough, but "interdependence"—with its implied diminution of state sovereignty—may not be the best way to characterize them.

If there is a tectonic force at work here, it is probably not so much interdependence as permeability: the declining ability of states—even as they retain their sovereignty—to keep external influences from crossing their borders, or, for that matter, to keep state secrets from flowing the other way. It used to be possible for nations to wall themselves off from alien cultures, technologies, ideologies, and commerce. But no government today can keep its citizens totally isolated from outside influences, and few even try very hard to do so. Nor is it easy, these days, for governments to keep secrets: the transparency that comes from satellite reconnaissance has made it difficult to conceal, not only deployments of military forces, but even such setbacks as nuclear accidents, forest fires, and mediocre harvests. Nations may not be that much more dependent upon one another than in the past[68] but their borders—whatever the direction of the flow of information and commodities across them—are surely more permeable than ever before, and they are likely to become more so with the passage of time.

It is not just ideas and objects that penetrate, though, for as improbable as this may seem in an age of sophisticated surveillance, it appears to be more and not less difficult than in the past to keep people from crossing borders against the will of governments. Influxes of undocumented aliens have already altered demographic profiles in Western Europe and in the United States; and the international drug traffic provides powerful evidence that modern technology may favor violators of boundaries more than it does those who patrol them. Nor, as the examples of Vietnam and East Germany suggest, is coercion very effective any longer in keeping populations from fleeing political repression and economic stagnation. An ironic but quite serious consequence of the West's "victory" in the Cold War is now the fear, in those portions of Europe that "won," of being swamped by refugees from those portions that "lost."[69]

What does all of this imply for international systemic stability? There is a striking disconnection here between what people believe and what history suggests. It has been and remains almost an article of faith among liberals that the more contact that takes place between states and the people who inhabit them, the less the danger of war.[70] But the historical record suggests precisely the opposite: those nations that have most frequently gone to war with one another have been those that had the most contact with one another.[71] Since permeability clearly exists and is probably increasing, the possibility of "paradigm fratricide"—and therefore of potential systemic instability—would appear to be present: one would want to know at a minimum what basis we have for believing that this historical pattern of familiarity breeding contempt will not sooner or later repeat itself.

Is there evidence that permeability has worked either to perpetuate or to undermine the long postwar peace? To the extent that one is talking about transparency, the effect is almost certainly stabilizing: with very little public notice, the advent of satellite reconnaissance has almost ruled out the possibility of surprise attack, a prospect that had accompanied, and contributed to the instability of, all previous arms races.[72] Traditional concepts of military secrecy have eroded so far that the United States and the Soviet Union now regularly discuss how to make each side's weapons *visible* to the other; and with no evident sense of irony our own Air Force even introduces supposedly *invisible* weapons like the "stealth" bomber to the world with, quite literally, accompanying fanfares.[73]

Satellite reconnaissance succeeds, though, because it is unobtrusive. Other forms of permeability are more noticeable, and potentially less stabilizing. Iran's openness to Western influences under the Shah played a major role in his overthrow; more recently the Ayatollah Khomeini demonstrated how permeable other borders—our own not excepted—are to the influences of Islamic fundamentalism.[74] Terrorism, of course, presents even more threatening possibilities for exploiting permeability. The rapid Westernization of

China that took place within the past decade almost certainly helped bring about the massacre in Tienanmen Square.[75] Nor does it necessarily follow that a Soviet Union open to American cultural, economic, and intellectual influences would enjoy, as a result, a more cordial relationship with the United States: for with permeability comes the capacity to influence internal developments, or to attempt to; the historical record suggests that if temptation follows, relations are almost certain to suffer.[76]

The phenomenon of permeability will remain with us, because to reverse it one would have to abolish the technology that has made it possible. Like the obsolescence of war, permeability provides evidence of evolution in the international environment from whose effects the international system is unlikely to remain immune. Such evolution represents progress in the direction of a more liberal world, to be sure; but it by no means accounts for the "long peace." And indeed if one flips the question around to ask what has been undermining the historic prerequisites for that condition—especially bipolarity and the dual hegemonic crisis-management it made possible— environmental influences of this type, even some that appear at first glance to be benign, tend to stand out. Those who seek signs of systemic instability might do well to begin here.

The failure of command economies. World Wars I and II demonstrated, among many other things, that the liberal world order the British had attempted to build through hegemonic stability in the nineteenth century was not up to the authoritarian rigors of the twentieth. American efforts to resurrect that order after the defeat of Germany and Japan ran into another form of authoritarian resistance, directed this time from Moscow and Beijing. Today, though, barriers to the spread of liberalism that fascism and communism once imposed appear to have fallen;[77] democratic reform may now be close to a universal prerequisite for economic survival in a postindustrial age.

Autocracy was no impediment to industrialization itself; indeed, the existence of command economies in the Soviet Union and China made it possible to force modernization at rapid rates, albeit at great cost. But the extensive utilization of resources under central direction can only carry an economy so far; sooner or later, it must shift to a more efficient but less centralized form of intensive exploitation if it is to remain competitive in a world market from whose effects not even autarchic regimes can wholly insulate themselves. Here arbitrary rule is likely to impede rather than to encourage progress, for without a free flow of information among those responsible for innovation—and without payoffs in the form of an enhanced quality of life—the process of modernization is almost certain to stagnate. Competitiveness requires openness: in an inversion of the classical Marxian dialectic, bourgeois liberal democracy appears to be the path to the next stage of world economic development.[78]

One of the most eloquent spokesmen for that argument was, until recently, Mikhail Gorbachev, who during his first five years as head of the Soviet government repeatedly and explicitly made clear the linkage between democratization and economic revival.[79] The record of China under Deng Xiaoping prior to June, 1989, demonstrated with even greater clarity how political liberalization can spur economic development;[80] events since that time have only confirmed the difficulty of trying to continue modernization while reintroducing repression. And the failures of command economies in Eastern Europe produced nothing short of a revolution there during the last half of 1989, with the entire structure of communist rule in Poland, Hungary, East Germany, Bulgaria, Czechoslovakia, and Romania having collapsed in dramatic succession by the end of that year.[81]

The relationship between democratization and economic growth is by no means exact: prosperity in South Korea, Taiwan, and Singapore did not evolve under the most scrupulous democratic procedures, and states like South Africa, Chile, and Panama under Noriega were able to keep their economies functioning for some time in the face of sanctions provoked by the absence of democracy. The United States itself, where democracy flourishes, has hardly been in the vanguard of economic efficiency or technological advance in recent years. Still—and even taking into account recent events in China—we appear to be witnessing a historic shift away from command economies and repressive politics in states that once proudly invoked Marxism-Leninism to justify those practices. The end of that particular ideology as we have known it is upon us, and that development in itself could have important implications for the future of the long postwar peace.

Unfortunately, it is not at all clear what those implications might be. Michael Doyle has shown, on the basis of convincing historical evidence, that liberal democracies tend not to fight one another,[82] a view that would appear to reinforce Mueller's "obsolescence of war" thesis. But Doyle's argument by no means excludes the possibility of war between liberal and nonliberal states; nor can we expect the Soviet Union, China, or the other formerly Marxist countries now experimenting with the relaxation of economic controls to reach Western standards of democratization anytime soon. And if liberalization should continue to open the way for unrest in Eastern Europe or the Soviet Union, as it appears to be doing, the need to reassert internal control could quickly impair cooperation at the international level between Moscow and Washington. One "rule" by which Soviet-American "management" functioned during the "long peace" was the mutual toleration of spheres of influence;[83] the relative silence of both the United States and the Soviet Union on the issue of Tibet suggests that a similar principle has been at work in their relations with China as well. But tolerating spheres of influence has meant tolerating the denial of liberties: the price of great power stability has often been repression.

We would appear to have here considerable potential for "paradigm fratricide." For if one accepts the thesis that further economic progress requires democratization, one risks challenging the geopolitical status quo upon which the "long peace" has rested. But without economic reform, the Soviet Union is likely to have only the most tenuous claim to the super-power status "bipolarity" requires: that claim will rest upon the hollow shell of nuclear deterrence, a frail and potentially dangerous structure no one would want to see leaned on too heavily. The crackdown on dissent in China has already undermined what had been, over the past decade, a cordial Sino-American relationship; just how this latest version of a "new" China is to fit into the international configuration of power is as yet unclear. Nor is it evident that a post-Cold War Europe will easily accommodate a reunified Germany—or vice versa—now that that once improbable event has come about.

The expansion of democracy, therefore, seems at least as likely to destabilize as to stabilize the post-Cold War international system, and that prospect should cause Americans to think carefully about where their own nation's interests really lie. For in an irony that a great master of irony, Reinhold Niebuhr, would surely have appreciated, the world probably is becoming more like the United States; but it is not at all clear that the United States will like—or indeed ought to like—the results.

Long Cycles

The impending "triumph" of liberalism, Fukuyama has suggested, raises the prospect that "centuries of boredom" lie before us: "daring, courage, imagination, and idealism . . . will be replaced by economic calculation, the endless solving of technical problems, environmental concerns, and the satisfaction of sophisticated consumer demands."[84] "Endism" has its charms, not the least of which is its ability, while keeping tongue firmly in cheek, to elicit grave and ponderous responses. But if the preceding argument has any merit, we historians need not worry quite yet about the "end of history," for even in the most "liberal" of worlds there is likely to be quite enough of that commodity to go around.

That, indeed, is just the point: history does go around; it is not simply linear in character, with precise beginnings and triumphantly proclaimed "ends." Regression as well as advance occurs: Hitlers happen, even in supposedly enlightened centuries. What if the long postwar peace should turn out to be just one phase of a long historical cycle, one destined, sooner or later, bring us back to the circumstances of global depression and war out of which the current international system emerged? Then all of our speculation about nuclear deterrence, bipolarity, hegemonic stability, liberalism, and even "endism" would be quite irrelevant: we would be like penguins stuck on an ice floe slowly circling the Antarctic, huffing and puffing at each other, occasionally agreeing with one another, while all the time sub-surface currents of which we know nothing are determining whether we drift south and risk cracking up on the rocks, or drift north and risk melting, or whether we remain in a condition of precarious homeothermal equilibrium.[85]

There is, of course, nothing new about cyclical views of history,[86] although their periodic rediscovery does continue to upset those who too easily assume the capacity of individuals and nations to learn from, and therefore to avoid repeating, the past.[87] Such theories present special problems of verification, given the absence of any clear consensus among long cyclists on just what it is that does repeat, and how we might measure it. When one adds the difficulty of dealing with unreliable sources extending over several centuries, together with the temptation of "massaging" data to fit predetermined conclusions, together with the problem of specifying a convincing causal mechanism for such patterns as do emerge, thereby separating them from statistical quirks and haphazard anomalies[88]—when one considers all of this, it is a wonder that analysts of international relations concern themselves with long cycles at all.

They do so, almost certainly, because the very act of generalizing about phenomena implies cyclicity of a sort: if nothing that happened ever resembled anything else that had happened, history would become a random series of events—an unalphabetized telephone book, if you will—devoid of meaning. The very act of interpretation assumes repetition.[89] Once one grants this point, though, it is difficult to know where to draw the line: cycles exist for periods as brief as the milliseconds required by a single nerve impulse and as long as the 600 million years or so that it takes for supercontinents to form and then break up.[90] The test for the social scientist (who is obliged to operate somewhere in between these extremes) should be the familiar one of utility: do cyclical explanations tell us anything that we do not already know?

Not surprisingly, the most arduous efforts to find out have focused on the question of war and peace; it is here that long cycle theory—at least as applied to the study of international relations[91]—is most fully developed. Although there is disagreement about specific details, the theory sees war on a global scale as taking place roughly every 100 to 150 years. These wars result in the emergence of a single hegemon which, although not necessarily the most powerful nation, is the one best positioned to create and to dominate a worldwide system of international relations. The outcome, at first, tends to be a "long peace"; in time, though, the rise of other states that have chosen to follow the hegemon's example—together with the hegemon's own exhaustion, bureaucratization, and consequent loss of imagination—creates instabilities that lead to global war and to the emergence of a new hegemon, thereby starting the cycle all over again.[92]

What drives the cycles? Here cycle theorists are in close agreement: all of them single out uneven rates of economic and technological development as the engine propelling the process. It is, Robert Gilpin writes, "the differential or uneven growth of power among states in a system that encourages efforts...to change the system."[93] Paul Kennedy adds that "the rule seems common to *all* national units, whatever their favored political economy, that uneven rates of economic growth [will], sooner or later, lead to shifts in the world's political and military balances."[94] Joshua Goldstein makes the linkage between economic growth and hegemonic war explicit:

> Countries rebuilding from war incorporate a new generation of technology, eventually allowing competition with the hegemonic country. For these reasons, each period of hegemony gradually erodes. Recurring wars,

on several long wave upswings, eventually culminate in a new hegemonic war, bringing another restructuring of the core and a new period of hegemony.

Or, to put it more succinctly, "economic growth generates war and is disrupted by it. Great power war . . . depends on but undermines prosperity."[95]

What are we to make of long cycles from the standpoint of the "long peace?" To what extent is such an explanation consistent with, or antipathetic to, the others that underlie that phenomenon? Since long cycle theory projects no new hegemonic war until, at a minimum, the middle of the twenty-first century, one is tempted to take refuge in a famous Keynesian proposition about being dead in the long run and simply leave the matter there. For if there really is an unbreakable cycle that runs regularly from peace through prosperity to depression and war, then all that may be left for us is to chronicle its progress, nodding our heads gloomily at each point along the way.

But what if the cycle itself is not immutable? What if the penguins on the ice-floe can hoist a sail, or rig a rudder? Most long cycle theorists see the process they describe as having originated with the formation of the European state system around 1500;[96] if that is so, then the cycle has not always existed, and need not always in the future. Even Gilpin, who sees cycles as reflections of "a recurring struggle for wealth and power" present since the beginning of recorded history, does not regard them as inevitable for all time to come: the advent of nuclear weapons, he writes, has had "a profound effect on the conduct of statecraft." Although it is obviously too early to say that the nuclear revolution has made future hegemonic wars impossible, it is significant that this most pessimistic of long cyclists is not prepared to rule out such a development.[97]

If in fact nuclear deterrence can reverse long cycles, or at least bring them to a halt, then its "relevance" to the preservation of peace and stability would be confirmed in the most striking manner. Unfortunately long cycle theory provides no conclusive way to test such a proposition short of waiting for the current cycle to complete itself. Similar difficulties arise in trying to establish whether long cycles are consistent with bipolarity, hegemonic stability, and the "triumph of liberalism." The standard of verification in all of these instances will be simple enough: the absence of hegemonic war for two or more centuries. But it is going to take a while to get the necessary evidence on that point.

That assumes, though, that cycles do not vary in frequency or amplitude. They do all the time, of course, in the physical world, and it is worth considering what the implications of such variations might be in the realm of international politics. Paul Kennedy has pointed out, for example, that during the postwar decades "global productive balances have been altering faster than ever before."[98] If hegemonic cycles grow out of uneven rates of economic and technological development, and if that development itself is accelerating,[99] then we should expect to see hegemons being hegemons for shorter and shorter periods of time; the next hegemonic war might be nearer than we think.

But cycles can also vary in amplitude: their effects can increase or diminish over time. Shifting environmental conditions like the obsolescence of great power war or the liberalization of autocracies could conceivably dampen hegemonic cycles, gradually minimizing their effects. If such a development really is taking place, then it, like the phenomenon of acceleration, ought to be detectable within periods we ourselves can manage. We may not have to depend upon great-grandchildren to confirm the validity of long cycle theory.

The difficulty would come in deciding just what one would measure in seeking to detect changes in the frequency or the amplitude of long cycles. Statistics can document with precision the economic decline of the United States relative to Japan and Western Europe; the Soviet Union—never an economic superpower to begin with—would be revealed as declining even more rapidly.[100] But other statistics would demonstrate how dependent the Japanese, the Western Europeans and certain Middle Eastern states are on the United States for their military security; there are also, as Joseph S. Nye, Jr., has pointed out, "soft" forms of power—examples include the persistence of nationalism, or the influence of rock culture, or the idea of democracy itself— that do not lend themselves to statistical measurement at all.[101] Until we have specified what kind of evidence it would take to confirm shifts in long cycle frequency and amplitude, quantitative approaches alone are not likely to get us very far.

We are left, then, to fall back upon impressionistic judgments, which may be the best one can hope to accomplish in this field in any event; certainly there is little in long-cycle theory that would provide any reliable basis for prediction on a day-by-day, or even a decade-by-decade, basis. "No two hegemonic conflicts are alike," Gilpin reminds us. "Thus, although a theory of political change can help explain historical developments, . . . it is no substitute for an examination of both the static and dynamic elements responsible for a particular political change."[102] But this is only to acknowledge the limits of theory itself, for as Waltz has noted: "Theory explains regularities of behavior and leads one to expect that the outcomes produced by interacting units will fall within specified ranges. The behavior of states and of statesmen, however, is indeterminate."[103]

Long cycle theory provides only a framework, then, within which to think about the long postwar peace. It does not confirm robustness, anymore than it predicts imminent disaster. But it is a useful way of reminding statesmen that the relevant past extends well beyond what they personally have experienced: cyclicity tends to get people's attention in a way that linearity does not. It suggests our relative insignificance against the sweep of time, and is therefore a good antidote to hubris. If one views cycles as subject to modification, they can provide an incentive to focus on long-term as opposed to short-term considerations, on duties as opposed to diversions. And, taken together with evidence of environmental and even behavioral evolution, long cycles can help us to see that history can be two different things at once: just as physicists view light as having the properties of both particles and waves, just as geologists allow for both pattern and particularity, so historians—and social scientists as well—should see that linearity and cyclicity are not fratricidal at all, but rather rewardingly complementary.[104]

Chaos, Complexity, and the Future

The inability to see that point has had a good deal to do with the long-standing (and much complained about) impoverishment of international security studies. The search for predictable regularities—which is to say, for cyclicity we can count on—has had disappointing results: it is as if events have conspired to frustrate those who have sought anything approaching scientific rigor in this field. But an antithetical focus on linearity, for which my own field of diplomatic history is well known, renders generalization anemic, and so removes most possibilities for learning from history in the first place.

If there is ever to be a "grand unification theory" of international relations—and we are nowhere close to that now—it will have to accommodate both cyclicity and linearity. It will need to recognize that some phenomena recur and some do not; but, even more important, it will have to provide ways of distinguishing between them. To paraphrase the famous "serenity prayer" that Reinhold Niebuhr may have originated,[105] we will require the vision to generalize where prediction is possible, the humility to refrain from generalization where it is not, and the wisdom to know the difference. But I see little evidence that either the historians or the theorists have thought very much about how to get to that point: the historians, lacking vision, resist linking their work to theory in the first place, while the theorists, lacking humility, claim such sweeping applicability for their generalizations as to make virtually unrecognizable the history upon which they are based.

As a consequence, it has been left to other disciplines, notably the physical, biological, and mathematical sciences, to do the most interesting thinking on how to distinguish recurring from non-recurring phenomena. These so-called "hard" sciences, once supremely confident about their ability to describe and predict, are today moving in the opposite direction: under the influence of "chaos" theory they are learning to allow for randomness, unpredictability, and what the mathematicians call "non-linearity." The implications for the fields of history and international relations theory—neither of them exactly strangers to chaos—could be quite important.

What this new "science of complexity" shows is that although we can predict some things with precision—the motion of the planets around the sun, for example, or the reaction of certain elements when mixed together under the same conditions—there is another large class of phenomena for which prediction will never be possible, for the simple reason that to build a model capable of simulating subjects of this sort, one would have to replicate the subject itself. We can know with great precision how many thousand years it will take the Voyager II spacecraft to reach the nearest star because, despite the immense size of the system in question, the number of critical variables at work in it lies well within our computational capabilities. But the most sophisticated weather forecaster has only about a 50 percent chance of being right about whether it is going to rain in the next county next week: weather systems may be microscopic by galactic standards, but the number of variables that drives them approaches infinity.[106]

Simulation is for the scientist what prediction is—or ought to be—for the social scientist; to know what one can simulate is to know what one can reasonably hope to predict. But knowing that means making judgments about what is a manageable number of variables, and it is here that the field of international security studies requires work. We need clearer standards for deciding when that number is low enough to allow simulation, and hence prediction; but we also need to know when to back off, recognizing that we are dealing with so many variables that prediction exceeds our capabilities. The concepts of paradigm "redundancy" and "fratricide" can help in making that choice.

For in a field in which no dominant paradigm exists and in which we lack the capability for controlled experiments to develop one, theories are never going to be more than approximations at simulation, and theorists are rarely going to agree about how to do them. That leaves anyone who is interested in prediction little choice but to become a "consumer" in the "marketplace" of theories, taking what seems to work in simulating reality and discarding what does not. And surely we are more likely to be right in assuming continuity for the reality we seek to simulate when different theories predict similar outcomes than we are when a single theory is the sole basis for prediction, or when different theories predict dissimilar outcomes. "Overdetermination" is a safer basis for anticipating the future than "underdetermination"; "redundancy," for this purpose, is very much preferable to "fratricide."

No theory or combination of theories is ever going to provide us with the paradigmatic equivalent of a "crystal ball," in which we can perceive the future with the same clarity we take for granted when we view the past. But theories that successfully explain a system's past do not normally lose their validity as they approach, and even proceed beyond, the present. And because—whether with regard to the past or the future—we are dealing with imperfect approximations of reality in any event, the more diversified the origins and character of the theories that provide our approximations, the more robust the resulting explanations—and predictions—are likely to be.[107]

My own examination of theoretical foundations for the "long peace" reveals, on the whole, greater "redundancy" than "fratricide." It therefore provides some basis for confidence that the freedom from great power war that has characterized our era, and that has already outlasted all comparable eras in modern history, is reasonably robust, and hence likely to continue.

It also suggests, at a much less cosmic level, my own exemption from the unfortunate fate of Norman Angell.

But there is one potentially "fratricidal" force at work in the current international system; paradoxically, it is the trend most closely associated with what the historic objectives of United States foreign policy are supposed to have been. The impending "triumph" of liberalism, however gratifying that development may be for Americans and however beneficial its immediate consequences for other parts of the world, appears more likely to upset systemic stability than any other tendency now discernible on the horizon. For it is in this area, more than anywhere else, that intersecting theoretical explanations for the "long peace" seem inconsistent with one another.

This is by no means to suggest that liberalism is going to start World War III: some redundant safeguards growing out of nuclear deterrence, bipolarity, and hegemonic management will probably remain in place, and if the long cyclists are correct, we have a while to wait yet before we are due for another great hegemonic conflict.[108] But it is to say that a world of "triumphant" liberalism is not easy to simulate, and that in turn suggests unpredictability, a condition that has not been conducive to stable superpower relations in the past. One reason the Cold War evolved into a "long peace" is that Russians and Americans gradually became predictable to each other: the familiarity of adversaries, over time, began to breed not contempt but common interests. A world of unfamiliar adversaries—or even the unlikely possibility of a world in which no evident adversaries exist—would represent a wholly new environment, and that could take some getting used to.

It is here that the behavior of statesmen and not systems will make the critical difference. For in coping with unsimulatable situations, theory—which is only past experience projected forward—is, and should be, of little help: variables overwhelm the capacity for generalization; generalizations, if attempted, are almost certain to mislead. One has little choice under such circumstances but to fall back upon those elusively non-theoretical qualities that we associate with statesmanship—patience, courage, common sense, vision, and humility—qualities whose very resistance to precise definition suggests their adaptability in dealing with the unpredictable.

Human mismanagement retains the capacity to wreck even the most overdetermined of international systems; we are ourselves, through our capacity for blunder, the ultimate fratricidal force. But that is only another way of saying that old-fashioned standards of statecraft, even under the most reassuring conditions of paradigm redundancy and systemic stability, are not likely soon to become obsolete: sustaining the "long peace" into the twenty-first century is going to require not only good history and good theory, but good sense (and good luck) as well.

ELEVEN

 Toward the
Post-Cold War
World

For the first time in over half a century, no single great power, or coalition of powers, poses a "clear and present danger" to the national security of the United States. The end of the Cold War has left Americans in the fortunate position of being without an obvious major adversary, and that—given the costs of confronting adversaries who have been all too obvious since the beginning of World War II—is a condition worthy of greater appreciation than it has so far received.

It would be foolish to claim, though, that the United States after 1991 can return to the role it played in world affairs before 1941. For as the history of the 1930s suggests, the absence of imminent threat is no guarantee that threats do not exist. Nor will the isolationism of that era be possible in the 1990s: advances in military technology and the progress of economic integration have long since removed the insulation from the rest of the world that geographical distance used to provide. The passing of the Cold War world by no means implies an end to American involvement in whatever world is to follow. It only means that the nature and the extent of that involvement are not yet clear.

Whatever else one might say about them, wars—hot or cold—do have the advantage of concentrating the mind. The existence of an adversary forces one to think about strategy in the way it should be thought about: as the calculated adaptation of desired ends to available means. We can now see that containment, as a strategy, met that standard: it proved remarkably successful in maintaining the post-World War II balance of power without war and without appeasement until the Soviet Union, confronting the illogic of its own system and its own position in the world, simply gave up.

But victories in wars—hot or cold—tend to unfocus the mind. They encourage pride, complacency, and the abandonment of calculation; the result is likely to be disproportion in the balance that always has to exist in strategy, between what one sets out to do, and what one can feasibly expect to accomplish. It can be a dangerous thing to have achieved one's objectives, because one then has to decide what to do next. Past successes provide no guarantee against future failures.

Interests

"We have no eternal allies, and we have no perpetual enemies," Lord Palmerston once memorably proclaimed. "Our interests are eternal, and those interests it is our duty to follow."[1] After a period in which old adversaries have become allies and old allies have become adversaries—for that is what the end of the Cold War and the outbreak of a hot war in the Persian Gulf have brought about—we would do well to keep Palmerston's familiar maxim in mind. Conceptions of interest, if they are to be of any value, ought at least to be durable: the national interest is not something that shifts back and forth from crisis to crisis, or from adversary to adversary, or from administration to administration.

Definitions of interest, however, tend toward the bland, the abstract, and often the perfectly obvious. The proposition that all nations have an interest in survival, security, and the maintenance of a congenial international environment is universally valid, but it is also so skeletal as to be analytically useless; these bones require meat if we are to make anything of them. One way to provide it is to specify the conditions nations have historically found necessary to safeguard such fundamental interests.[2]

For the United States, these have most consistently involved the balancing of power. One need not look far to find the roots of this tradition: they are evident in the practice of eighteenth century British politics and diplomacy from which the American system of government emerged,[3] and they are firmly enshrined in the federal constitution of 1787, based as it is on the premise that individual liberty survives only when the powers of the state are separated, and held in careful equilibrium.[4] The Founding Fathers were themselves adept balancers of power: witness the relative ease with which they shifted from allegiance to Britain before 1776 to alliance with France after 1778, and then back to alignment with Britain in the wake of the French Revolution. Nor did Americans abandon their concern with balancing power during the "long peace" that followed the Congress of Vienna after 1815;[5] isolationism existed, but only because the European balance maintained itself for the next century. When challenges to that balance did materialize, in 1917, 1940–41, and again in 1945–47, the United States took decisive action to resist them, twice by military intervention and the third time through economic and military assistance as instruments of containment.

Other fundamental American interests follow from this concern with international equilibrium. This country's sympathy—and sometimes support—for democratic forms of government abroad traces back, at least in part, to the conviction that such governments are less likely than their authoritarian counterparts to upset balances of power. American efforts to open the world to trade and investment derive not just from the search for profits but also from the conviction that the prosperity capitalism generates prevents war and revolution.[6] Even the Wilsonian principle of collective security reduces, in the end, to the task of balancing the power of the rest of the world against those few who would commit aggression.

The American commitment to democracy, capitalism, and collective security has never been absolute. The nation has, at one time or another, compromised all of these principles. But these compromises, too, maintained a balance: an absolutist crusade to make the world democratic, or to make market economies universal, or to impose a collective security system everywhere, would have brought about another form of disequilibrium, the one between ends and means. Interests are—potentially at least—infinitely expandable; means never are. It can serve the interests of no state to allow ends to outstrip means.

Palmerston's dictum about eternal interests ought not to be read as precluding the emergence of new ones. Advancing technology—as well as advancing morality—can change the nature of power over time, and these shifts can affect interests in significant ways. It would not have occurred to Palmerston to make the abolition of great power war itself a national objective; but to anyone living in a nuclear age, such an interest has become, tacitly at least, widely shared.[7] Nor would that statesman have foreseen the need to end racial and sexual discrimination, or to defend the biosphere against greenhouse warming, ozone depletion, and diminishing biodiversity. "Progress," if we can call it that, does occur, and the interests of states do enlarge to accommodate it.

Even so, the traditional American conception of a national interest rooted in the balancing of power—whatever form that "power" takes—is likely to persist into the post-Cold War world, it having served us well in the world in which the United States has functioned as an independent state for more than two centuries. Just what the post-Cold War world will look like, however, is not yet clear.

Cartography

Finding one's way through an unfamiliar environment generally requires a map of some sort. But that is only to point out that we need to simplify complexity, for what is a map if not a vast simplification of the environment in which we find ourselves? Nobody would claim that a map replicates reality: if one were to have a map that accurately represented, say, the Persian Gulf, it would have to be the same size and have all of the same characteristics as the Persian Gulf, which would defeat the purpose of having the map in the first place.[8] Cartography, like cognition itself, is a necessary simplification that allows us to see where we are, and where we may be going.

If we are to identify American interests in a post-Cold War world, the first thing we will need is a geopolitical map. We have had such maps in the past. The assertion that the world was divided between the forces of democracy and those of totalitarianism—to use the precise distinction made in President Harry S. Truman's announcement of the Truman Doctrine—was of course a vast simplification of what was actually happening in 1947.[9] But it was probably a necessary one: it was a starting point, an exercise in geopolitical cartography, if you will, that depicted the international landscape in terms everyone could understand, and thereby prepared the way for the more sophisticated strategy of containment that was soon to follow.

The Cold War ended with too sweeping a defeat for totalitarianism—and too sweeping a victory for democracy—for this old geopolitical map to be of much use any longer. But another form of competition has been emerging that could be just as stark, and just as pervasive, as was the rivalry between democracy and totalitarianism at the height of the Cold War: it is the contest between forces of integration and fragmentation in the contemporary international environment.[10]

Integration. I use this term in its most general sense, which is the act of bringing things together to constitute something that is whole. It involves breaking down barriers that have historically separated nations and peoples in such diverse areas as politics, economics, religion, technology, and culture. It means, quite literally, the approach to what we might call—echoing some of the most visionary language of World War II—one world.[11]

Integration is happening in a variety of ways. Consider, first, the communications revolution, which began over a hundred years ago when it first became possible to transmit information instantly from one part of the globe to the other, but which has taken on a vastly greater impetus from the more recent development of such things as photocopiers, television satellites, fax machines, and computer linkages, together with the tendency of this technology, once developed, to come down dramatically in price. We have become one world as far as communications are concerned: it is no longer possible for any nation to deny its citizens knowledge of what is going on elsewhere, and that is a new condition in international politics, the importance of which became clear as revolution swept rapidly through Central and Eastern Europe in the fall of 1989. Integration through communications has largely brought that about.[12]

Consider, next, economics. International commercial and financial contacts have been going on for centuries, but it was not until after World War II that a true global market began to develop. Americans bear much of the responsibility for this: convinced that the war had come because the international economy broke down in the 1930s, the United States used its postwar hegemony to create the basis for a worldwide integrated trade and financial network whose importance has continued to grow since that time. The incorporation into that network of two former adversaries—Germany and Japan—was, in particular, an American decision; whatever we think of it today, the current prominence of those states in the global economy comes very close to what the strategists of containment after World War II hoped would happen.[13]

The result of this movement toward economic integration is that, these days, no nation—not even the Soviet Union, or China, or South Africa, or Iraq—can for very long maintain itself apart from the rest of the world; that is because individual nations depend, for their own prosperity, upon the prosperity of others to a far greater extent than in the past. Integration also means that multinational corporations, commodity cartels, and even humanitarian organizations like Amnesty International—through the transnational pressures they bring to bear—can have a powerful impact on what happens to national states. And in Europe at least, integration has led to the creation of a potential new superpower in the form of the European Community. Europe as a whole, not just Britain, or France, or Germany, is already a major player in the world economy, and it may soon become one in world politics as well.

Consider, as a third manifestation of integration, security. Nations used to rely primarily on their own strength to provide for their security, and many of them still practice that kind of unilateralism even today. But Woodrow Wilson began the modern movement toward *collective* security with his proposal for a League of Nations after World War I. Although that organization proved ineffective—in part because of the Americans' refusal to join it—the League did give rise to the United Nations, which after many years of ineffectiveness has suddenly become a major force in international diplomacy. During the last half of the 1980s the world organization helped in rapid succession to resolve a series of long-standing conflicts in southern Africa, Central America, the Middle East, and South and Southeast Asia. Significantly, the United States waited to gain United Nations approval before going to war in the Persian Gulf; Washington has not always been as solicitous in the past, and the fact that the Bush administration proceeded in this way suggests that it has come to see important advantages in the collective as opposed to the unilateral approach—which is to say, the integrative approach—in such matters.

Another form of cooperative action to achieve security has existed for years alongside the United Nations: it is the North Atlantic Treaty Organization, itself an example of seeking security through integration that managed to keep the peace in Europe for over four decades. Many people forget that it was NATO—together with the movement toward economic integration mentioned earlier—that ended a long and bitter rivalry between France and Germany.[14] On those grounds alone NATO would have to be considered a success for integration, quite apart from whatever it did or did not achieve in deterring the Soviet Union.

Then consider the integration of ideas. The combination of easy communications, unprecedented prosperity, and freedom from war—which is, after all, the combination the Cold War gave us—made possible yet another integrationist phenomenon, which is that ideas now flow more freely throughout the world than at any other time in the past. The United States has particularly benefited from this process, for even as its military and economic power has gone into relative decline, its influence as a source of ideas and as a shaper of culture is as great, if not greater, than it has ever been. This "soft" form of power ought not to be underestimated:[15] we may deplore the fact that much of the rest of the world gets its image of this country from watching reruns of "Dallas" or from listening to rock music, but that does not prevent much of the rest of the world from aspiring to emulate—or even to emigrate to—this country. That simple fact continues to be of major significance in the international power balance.

One particular aspect of the integration of ideas is the fact that people are better educated than at any time in the past. This trend has had a revolutionary effect in certain authoritarian countries, where governments found that they had to educate their populations in order to continue to compete in a global economy, only to find that the act of educating them opened their minds to new ideas and ultimately worked to undermine the legitimacy of authoritarianism itself.[16] The consequences can be seen in Chinese students who prefer statues of liberty to statues of Mao, in Soviet citizens who taunt their own leaders in front of Lenin's tomb, and in the truly impressive sight of a president of Czechoslovakia—himself a living symbol of the power of ideas—lecturing the Congress of the United States on the virtues of Jeffersonian democracy.[17]

Finally, consider peace. It has long been a central assumption of liberal political philosophers that if only one could maximize the flow of ideas, commodities, capital, and people themselves across international boundaries, then the causes of war would drop away. It was an idea based more on faith than on reality: the outbreaks of World Wars I and II severely called it into question, since those wars arose among precisely the nations that had had just those kinds of extensive contacts with one another. But a by-product of integration since 1945 may well have been peace, at least peace among the great powers. The prosperity that is associated with market economies tends to encourage the growth of liberal democracies; and one of the few patterns that holds up throughout modern history is that liberal democracies do not go to war with one another.[18] From this perspective, then, the old nineteenth-century liberal vision of a peaceful, integrated, interdependent, and capitalist world may, at last, be coming true.

Fragmentation. Would that it were so. Unfortunately, however, the forces of integration are not the only ones active in the world: there are also forces of fragmentation at work that are resurrecting old barriers between nations and peoples—and creating new ones—even as others are tumbling. Some of these forces have begun to show unexpected strength, just when it looked as though integration was about to prevail. The most important of them is nationalism.

There is, to be sure, nothing new about nationalism: given the fact that the past half-century has seen the number of sovereign states more than triple, it can hardly be said that nationalism was in a state of suspended animation during the Cold War. Still, many of us did have the sense that, among the great powers at least, nationalism after World War II had been on the wane.

The very existence of two rival superpowers—which is really to say, two *supranational* powers—created this impression. We rarely thought of the Cold War as a conflict between competing Soviet and American nationalism; we saw it, rather, as a contest between two great international ideologies, or between two antagonistic military blocs, or between two geographical regions imprecisely labeled "East" and "West." One could even argue that the Cold War discouraged nationalism, particularly in Western Europe and the Mediterranean, where the mutual need to contain the Soviet Union moderated old animosities like those between the French and the Germans, or the Greeks and the Turks, or the British and everybody else. Much the same thing happened, although by different and more brutal means, in Eastern Europe, where the Soviet Union used the Warsaw Pact to suppress long-standing feuds between Hungarians and Romanians, Czechs and Poles, and the (East) Germans and everybody else. Nationalism might still exist in other parts of the world, we used to tell each other, but it had become a historical curiosity in Europe. There were even those who argued, until quite recently, that the Germans had become such good Europeans that they were now virtually immune to nationalist appeals and so had lost whatever interest they might once have had in reunification.[19]

Today, in the absence of the Cold War, the situation looks very different. Germany has reunified, and no one—particularly no one living alongside that new state—is quite sure what the consequences are going to be. Romanians and Hungarians threaten each other regularly now that the Warsaw Pact is defunct, and nationalist sentiments are manifesting themselves elsewhere in Eastern and Southeastern Europe, particularly in Yugoslavia, which appears on the verge of breaking up.[20] The same thing could even happen to the Soviet Union itself: nationalist pressures the regime thought it had smothered as far back as seven decades ago are coming to the forefront once again, to such an extent that we can no longer take for granted the continued existence of that country in the form that we have known it.

Nor should we assume that the "West" is immune from the fragmenting effects of nationalism. The Irish question ought to be a perpetual reminder of their durability; there is also the Basque problem in Spain, and the rivalry between Flemings and Walloons in Belgium. Growing nationalism is undermining the American position in the Philippines, and similar pressures are building in South Korea. Nationalism is even becoming an issue in Japan, what with recent controversies over the treatment of World War II in Japanese history textbooks and the Shinto ceremonies that officially began the reign of the Emperor Akihito. It is worth recalling, as well, how close the Canadian confederation has come to breaking up—as it may yet do—over the separatist aspirations of Quebec. We are even at the point now where the Mohawk Indians have been demanding—from Quebec, no less—recognition of their own rights as a sovereign state.[21]

But the forces of fragmentation do not just take the form of pressures for self-determination, formidable though those may be. They also show up in the field of economics, where they manifest themselves as protectionism: the effort, by various means, to insulate one's economy from the workings of world market forces. They show up in the racial tension that can develop, both among states and within them: the recent killings of blacks by blacks in South Africa, *after* the release of Nelson Mandela, illustrate the problem clearly. They certainly show up in the area of religion: the resurgence of Islam might be seen by some as an integrationist force in the Middle East, but it is surely fragmentationist to the extent that it seeks to set that particular region off from most of the rest of the world by reviving ancient and not-so-ancient grievances against the West, both real and imagined.[22] They can show up with respect to language: speakers of French, both in France and in Quebec, have become increasingly determined to maintain the purity of that tongue against alien Anglo-Saxon intrusions. They can even show up as a simple drive for power, which is the only way I can make sense out of the fiendishly complex events that have torn Lebanon apart since the civil war began there in 1975.[23] Indeed one can look at Beirut as it has been for the past decade and a half and get a good sense of what the world would look like if the forces of fragmentation should ultimately have their way.

Fragmenting tendencies are also on the rise—they have never been wholly absent—within American society itself. Expressions of alarm about the self-centering seductiveness of popular culture are probably exaggerated.[24] But it would be difficult to overestimate the disintegrationist effects of a worsening drug crisis in this country, or of the breakdown of our system for elementary and secondary education, or of the emergence of what appears to be a permanent social and economic "underclass."[25] Well-intentioned efforts to decrease racial and sexual discrimination have increased racial and sexual—as well as constitutional—tensions.[26] Linguistic anxieties lurk just beneath the surface, as the movement to make English the official language of the United States suggests. Immigration may well be increasing at a faster rate than cultural assimilation, which has, in itself, been a less than perfect process. Regional rivalries are developing over such issues as energy costs, pollution control, and the bailout of the savings and loan industry. And the rise of special interest groups, together with their ability to apply instant pressure through instant communications, has thrown American politics into such disarray that elections are reduced to the unleashing of attack videos, and budget negotiations between the Congress and the White House have come to resemble the endless haggling of rug-merchants in some Oriental bazaar. When the leading light of American conservatism has to call for a return to a sense of *collective* interest,[27] then disintegrationist forces have proceeded very far indeed.

Explanation? The emerging tension between forces of integration and fragmentation in the post Cold War era is not a new phenomenon, but rather the recurrence of an old dilemma: it is that although integration tends to satisfy material needs, fragmentation is often required to gratify intangible desires. One can find no better illustration of this historical pattern than to recall the two most important events of the year 1776.

That year saw Adam Smith publish *The Wealth of Nations*, an act of intellectual revolution showing conclusively that the path to prosperity lay in breaking down barriers to trade, investment, the exchange of technology, labor flows, and the transmission of innovative ideas throughout the world. The reason for this was—and remains—that the instruments of material progress tend to work in much the same way everywhere. Whether one is talking about tractors, tea-kettles, or television sets, the procedures employed to produce them and to benefit from them do not vary substantially. To use a word much favored by economists, these products are "fungible," which is to say that they can be used, without significant modification, in a great variety of circumstances, states, and cultures. Indeed, according to Smith's theory, the more these products and procedures are exchanged—or, to put it another way, the more integration that exists—the better off everyone is.[28]

But the year 1776 also saw the Americans, in an act of political revolution, claim that intangibles such as "life, liberty, and the pursuit of happiness" could be secured only by separating themselves from the British Empire. The satisfaction of material needs is not the only thing people care about; there are also intangible desires to be gratified, and these manifest themselves most dramatically, as the Founding Fathers demonstrated, in the idea of freedom. But freedoms—unlike tractors—do not work the same way throughout the world. They may well mean political democracy in most places; but people have also been known to seek "freedom" through nationalism, terrorism, racism, authoritarianism, and religious fundamentalism.[29] One person's idea of freedom may be another's idea of slavery; freedom is not always a transferable or a fungible commodity. People tend to construct it in their own ways: is not self-determination what freedom is all about?

The search for freedom, then, tends toward fragmentation in the political realm, while the search for prosperity tends toward integration in the economic realm, and therein lies a historical pattern of considerable importance for the post-Cold War world. The Cold War itself, it now appears, was a departure from that pattern, in that it fostered integration in politics as well as economics: I have in mind here the persistence of super-power bipolarity and the integrative institutions—NATO, the Warsaw Pact, the European Community—that grew out of it. We would be foolish to expect, though, that just because the Cold War has ended this old historical fault line reflecting the tension between integrative and disintegrative forces in world politics has also disappeared; indeed the evidence already suggests the opposite. It might even be argued that the Cold War stabilized that fault line, or perhaps covered it up, and that with the end of the Cold War, we can expect more frequent, not less frequent, upheavals along it.

All of this suggests, then, that the problems we will confront in the post-Cold War world are more likely to arise from competing processes—integrationist versus fragmentationist—than from the kinds of competing ideological visions that dominated the Cold War. But unlike the rivalry between democracy and totalitarianism, the new geopolitical cartography—and the historical tectonics that underlie it—provides no immediately obvious answer to the question of which of these processes might most threaten the future security interests of the United States.

Threats

It would appear, at first glance, that the forces of integration would be the more benign. Those forces brought the Cold War to an end. They provided the basis for the relative prosperity we and most of the rest of the "developed" world enjoyed during that era, and they offer the most plausible method of extending that prosperity into the era that will follow. They combine materialism and idealism in a way that seems natural to Americans, who tend to combine these traits in their own national character. And they hold out the promise of an international order in which collective, not unilateral, security becomes the norm. But is the trend toward integration consistent with the old American interest in *balancing* power? Has that interest itself become obsolete in the new world that we now confront?

Our long-standing commitment to the balance of power was based on the assumption that the United States would exist in a world of diversity, not uniformity: in a homogeneous world, presumably, one would not need to balance power at all. No one would claim that the progress of integration has brought us anywhere close to such a world; still there is a contradiction between the acts of balancing and integrating power that ought to make us think carefully about ultimate destinations. Jumping to conclusions—in favor of either integrationist or fragmentationist alternatives—could be a mistake.

The United States is not likely, for the foreseeable future, to see threats to the balance of power arising from the actions of a single hostile state, as it did from the Soviet Union during the Cold War or from Germany during World Wars I and II. But balances of power could still be imperiled by three more general categories of threat that are sure to manifest themselves in the post-Cold War world: ecological, regional, and internal. All of them, in one way or another, reflect the tension between the processes of integration and fragmentation that characterize the new geopolitical cartography.

Ecological threats. These are dangers that could imperil the international system as a whole, but that do not arise from the actions of any single state. An asteroid or comet hitting the earth and wiping out whole species—as some scientists think actually happened some 65 million years ago—would be an extreme example of an ecological threat. So too would be Ronald Reagan's "Martian" scenario: the idea that if the Martians or some other all-powerful extraterrestrial force should land, Soviet-American differences would evaporate overnight.[30]

The possibility of all-out nuclear war, of course, served as something like a "Martian" threat during much of the Cold War, causing the United States and the Soviet Union to find common cause in a surprising number of areas. The development of permissive action links on nuclear weapons, of secure second-strike capabilities, of tacitly tolerated satellite reconnaissance, of intrusive verification, and ultimately the mutually agreed-upon destruction of nuclear-armed missiles themselves all grew out of concern that an uncontrollable nuclear war might someday take place, thereby threatening the continued existence of both Cold War competitors as well as everyone else. Weapons developed for, quite literally, disintegrative purposes came to have strongly integrative effects.[31]

Similarly, the specter of global depression and the fear that war might erupt from it led the United States and its allies after World War II to construct an integrative system of economic structures, including the World Bank, the International Monetary Fund, and the General Agreement on Tariffs and Trade, all of which were designed to preserve the international economic system against the forces that had led to its fragmentation, with such devastating results, in the 1930s.[32] Within that framework—whether because of it is a more controversial matter[33]—much though by no means all of the postwar world has enjoyed unprecedented levels of prosperity and productivity for an unprecedented length of time.

The twin ecological threats of global war and global depression will not disappear with the end of the Cold War. The first danger now appears considerably diminished, to be sure, but as long as nuclear weapons exist—and there is no reason to think they will not continue to exist for some time—the possibility of their use in some form will still remain.[34] The second danger, a worldwide economic collapse, is more difficult to make judgments about. On the one hand, our understanding of how modern economies work is better than it was at the time of the last great depression. But, on the other hand, integration has linked the world economy together more closely than it was in the 1930s, so that even small disintegrative perturbations—the Iraqi seizure of Kuwait, for example—can produce widescale ripple effects. The need for a collective consciousness of these dangers, and for collective safeguards against them, has, therefore, by no means gone away.

Nor is it difficult to conceive of other ecological threats that might require collective action. The possibility of global warming looms as a long-term constraint upon future economic development conducted in traditional—which is to say, polluting—ways: integration here, in the form of expanding industrialization and increasing agricultural productivity, may have created a new kind of danger. The worldwide AIDS epidemic illustrates how one integrative force—the increasing flow of people across international boundaries—can undermine the effects of another, which is the progress that has been made toward the conquest of disease. Population pressure, the product itself of progress in agricultural productivity and in conquering disease, is in turn exacerbating differences in standards of living that already exist in certain parts of the world, with potentially disintegrative results.[35]

The forces of integration, therefore, provide no automatic protection against ecological threats: indeed, they are a large part of the problem. Despite classical liberal assumptions, we would be unwise in assuming that an ever-increasing flow of people, commodities, and technology across international borders will necessarily—at least from the ecological standpoint—make the world a safer place.

Regional threats. The sources of regional violence in the world remain as various as they have always been: they include the divisive forces of nationalism, ethnicity, religion, as well as economic and social inequality, together with the always-present possibility of incompetent leadership. But superpower crisis management provided an integrative framework within which to contain these forces during the Cold War. It is striking how many regional crises there were after 1945, and yet not one of them escalated into a direct military conflict between the United States and the Soviet Union.[36]

This system of accommodating regional crises within a structure of global stability—which is one of the things the "long peace" was all about[37]—depended, however, upon the existence of two functioning super-powers. Now that the Soviet Union no longer qualifies in this regard—and now that some are questioning the continued capacity of the United States to play this role as well[38]—regional conflicts could become more difficult to contain than they were during the Cold War. The failure to contain them, in turn, could produce dangerous consequences for the international balance of power in the post-Cold War era.

One such consequence could be a return to violence in a part of the world that has, for years, been remarkably free of it: Europe from the Atlantic to the Urals.[39] The reunification of Germany, together with the enfeeblement and possible breakup of the Soviet Union, is one of the most abrupt realignments of political, military, and economic power in modern history. It has come about as a result of those integrative forces that ended the Cold War: the much-celebrated triumph of democratic politics and market economics.[40] And yet, this victory for liberalism in Europe is producing both integrationist and fragmentationist consequences.

In Germany, demands for self-determination have led to political integration, to be sure, but the economic effects could be disintegrative: there are concerns, now, over whether the progress the European Community has made toward removing trade and immigration barriers by 1992 is going to be sufficient to tie the newly unified Germany firmly to the West; or whether the new Germany will build its own center of power further to the East, with the risk that this might undo the benefits of 1992. What happens, for example, if Germany invests heavily in Eastern Europe—as seems likely—and then some of the economies of that part of the world collapse as a result of their exposure to market forces—as also seems likely: will the new Germany be prepared to tolerate disorder and financial losses in the countries that border it to the east, or will it attempt to reimpose order and profitability there? If it does the latter, what will the Soviet Union—and indeed the rest of the world—think of that? The future of Europe, in short, is not at all clear, and it is the increasing tension between the forces of integration and fragmentation that has suddenly made the picture there such a cloudy one.

In the Soviet Union, the "triumph of liberalism" has had profoundly disintegrative consequences: we are witnessing nothing less than the dismantling of that once-mighty super-power. Here we face a painful dilemma, for while our hearts tell us that we ought to be supporting the aspirations for self-determination of groups like the Georgians, or the Moldavians, or even the Russians themselves, our heads should be asking how far are we prepared to see this process go. The Abkazians and the South Ossetians, after all, seek their independence from Georgia, as do the Gagauz from Moldavia. The Bashkirs and the Yakuts have proclaimed their independence—as could dozens of other nationality groups—from the Russian Republic, just as it in turn has been moving toward independence from the U.S.S.R. The central Soviet government is sinking into irrelevance as power diffuses down to the level of the republics, and even below;[41] no one knows what the future political configuration—to say nothing of ideological orientation—of the potential successor states is going to be. Civil war, and even international war growing out of civil war, are by no means unrealistic prospects; and such disruptions would be all the more dangerous because the Soviet Union's massive arsenal of nuclear and conventional weapons will not disappear, even if the Soviet Union itself does.[42] The wholly admirable principle of self-determination, which has drawn strength from the commendably integrative forces of education and communication, is having disturbingly disintegrative practical results.

There is yet another danger to be kept in mind in connection with these European developments. The combination of German reunification with Soviet collapse, if it occurs, will involve the most dramatic changes in international boundaries since the end of World War II. It is not at all clear what precedents this may set for other parts of the world, notably the Middle East and Africa, where boundaries inherited from the colonial era do not come close to coinciding with the patterns of ethnicity, nationality, or religion that exist there. If the Lithuanians are going to get their own state, it will not be easy to explain why the Palestinians or the Kurds or the Eritreans should not have theirs also. If the boundaries of the dying Soviet empire are to be revised, then why should boundaries established by empires long since dead be preserved?

This brings up the problem of conflict in the Third World. When regional violence has arisen there in the past—whether in the long and bitter Arab-Israeli dispute over Palestine, or in clashes between India and Pakistan over Kashmir and what is now Bangladesh, or in the protracted and costly Iran-Iraq war of 1980–88—the super-powers used their influence to prevent it from spreading more widely, with the result that these conflicts remained limited in their scope, and also (with the exception of the 1971 war that produced the independence of Bangladesh) in their consequences.

The Iraqi invasion of Kuwait, however, produced a different pattern of regional violence with disturbing implications for the post-Cold War era.

First, Saddam Hussein did not wait to exhaust diplomatic alternatives before attacking: in what seemed a throwback to pre-Cold War behavior, he simply seized a small, rich, and defenseless neighboring country without bothering to conceal the fact that an old-fashioned act of aggression had taken place. Second, it was Iraq's integration into the international market in sophisticated military technology that made it possible for him to do this. Saddam's arsenal of chemical and biological weapons, to say nothing of his SAMs, Scuds, Mirages, the nuclear weapons he probably would have had if the Israelis had not bombed his reactor in 1981, and the long-range artillery he certainly would have had if the British had not become suspicious of his orders for very thick "oil pipes" early in 1990—all of this hardware was not forged by ingenious and self-reliant Iraqi craftsmen working tirelessly along the banks of the Euphrates. He obtained it, rather, by exploiting an important consequence of integration, which is the inability or unwillingness of highly-industrialized states to control what their own entrepreneurs—even those involved in the sale of lethal commodities—do to turn a profit. Third, the global energy market—another integrationist phenomenon—created the riches that made Kuwait such a tempting target in the first place; it also brought about the dependence on Middle Eastern oil that caused so rapid a military response on the part of the United States, its allies, and even some of their former adversaries. The eagerness of this improbable coalition to defend the principle of collective security would hardly have been as great if Benin had attacked Burkina Faso, or vice versa.

There is, of course, no assurance that Saddam Hussein would have refrained from invading Kuwait if the Cold War had been at its height, but there is a fair chance that under those circumstances either the United States or the Soviet Union—depending upon which super-power Iraq was aligned with at the time—would have sought to exert a restraining influence, if only to keep its principal rival from exploiting the situation to its own advantage.[43] Certainly it is sobering to consider that the first post-Cold War year saw, in addition to the occupation of Kuwait, the near-outbreak of war between India and Pakistan, an intensification of tension between Israel and its Arab neighbors, a renewed Syrian drive to impose its control on Lebanon, and a violent civil war in Liberia. Conflict in the Third World, it appears, is not going to go away just because the Cold War is over; it may well intensify.

There is yet another form of regional conflict that is likely to affect the post-Cold War era: it is what we might call the "post-Marxist revolution" crisis. A central assumption of American foreign policy during much of the Cold War was that the processes of decolonization and modernization made Third World countries vulnerable to Marxist upheavals. Communism, Walt Rostow used to argue, was a "disease which can befall a transitional society if it fails to organize effectively those elements within it which are prepared to get on with the job of modernization."[44] Few people worry about this kind of thing today, because there are so few parts of the world left in which revolutionaries would voluntarily align themselves with a Marxist movement to overthrow an old order. Revolution itself, in the collectivist form we have most often witnessed in the twentieth century, appears to be passing from the scene.[45]

The new "revolutionary" force in the Third World may well be democracy. Certainly the current trend in Latin America is noticeably in that direction, and one can even make the argument that there is a long-term historical tendency for the number of democratic governments worldwide roughly to double with each half-century.[46] But it is no clearer in the Third World than it is in Europe that the emergence of democracy—the supposedly integrative "triumph of liberalism"—will necessarily promote peace. For just as the United States used to justify its intervention in "less developed" countries as a means of "inoculating" them against the "bacillus" of communism, so the post-Cold War era could see military interventions by democracies for the purpose of confirming in power—or restoring to power—other democracies.[47]

As democracy spreads more widely in the third world, observers from the old "first" and "second" worlds as well as from the United Nations will be invited to monitor elections and thereby legitimize the governments that emerge victorious from them: the pattern has already manifested itself in Namibia, Nicaragua, Panama, Pakistan, and Haiti. But as the outcome of the 1989 Panamanian elections shows, undemocratic elements may still succeed in subverting democratic processes. In such situations, pressures for international condemnation, for the application of sanctions, and even for the use of military force in support of democracy may become irresistible. The violent—but overwhelmingly popular—American military operation to apprehend General Manuel Noriega in December, 1989, could well be a portent of things to come.

Internal threats. Threats can arise, though, not only from external sources, for the way in which a nation chooses to respond to threats can, under certain circumstances, pose as much of a danger to its long-term interests as does what is happening beyond its borders. The United States did not *have* to involve itself, to the extent that it did, in the Vietnam War. It did not *have* to become as dependent as it has on foreign oil. It did not *have* to accumulate such massive budget deficits that the government will have no choice but to allocate a significant percentage of its revenues, well into the twenty-first century, to paying off the accumulated debt. All of these were decisions we ourselves made, not our adversaries; and yet their consequences have constrained, and in the case of energy dependency and the national debt, will continue to constrain, American freedom of action in the world for years to come.

These problems evolved from a curious unevenness that exists, within the United States these days, in the willingness to bear pain. Americans have readily accepted pain in connection with their country's integrative role as a global peacekeeper. We have repeatedly sent troops and resources overseas for the purpose of resisting aggression, even in situations where the probability of an attack was remote and where the states we were defending did not always see fit to contribute proportionately to their own defense. To the extent that such interventions were necessary to redress imperiled balances of power, they can be justified in terms of the national interest. But American interventionism has too often become an instinctive, not a considered, response: the United States has tended to jump into situations where the balance of power was not really threatened, and it has tended to do this unilaterally. We have found it difficult to distinguish, in short, between being a global policeman and a global nanny.

Americans have been unwilling to accept even moderate pain, though, when it comes either to raising the taxes necessary to support the government expenditures we demand, or to cutting back on those expenditures to bring them into line with the taxes we are willing to pay. The United States is generous, even profligate, with its military manpower and hardware, but it is selfish to the point of irresponsibility when it comes to issues of lifestyle and pocketbook.[48] As a result, a kind of division of labor has developed within the international community, in which Americans contribute the troops and the weaponry needed to sustain the balance of power, while American allies finance the budgetary, energy, and trade deficits we incur through our unwillingness to make even minimal sacrifices in living standards.[49]

Whatever the causes of this situation—certainly they include the disintegration of our domestic political process into special-interest constituencies that lack any sense of collective interest—the long-term effects cannot be healthy ones. Americans will not indefinitely serve as "mercenaries" overseas, especially when the troops recruited in that capacity come, as they disproportionately do, from the less fortunate social, economic, and educational classes.[50] Resentment over this pattern, when it develops, is certain to fragment whatever foreign policy "consensus" may remain; pressures will eventually build for *all* Americans to bear their fair share of *all* the burdens that are involved in being a world power, and that may considerably diminish the attractions of continuing to be one.

The end of the Cold War, therefore, brings not an end to threats, but rather a diffusion of them: one can no longer plausibly point to a single source of danger, as one could throughout most of that conflict, but dangers there still will be. The architects of containment, when they confronted the struggle between democracy and totalitarianism in 1947, knew which side they were on; the post-Cold War geopolitical cartography, however, provides no comparable clarity. In one sense, this represents progress: the very absence of clear and present danger testifies to our success in so balancing power during the past four and a half decades that totalitarianism—at least in the forms we have considered threatening throughout most of this century—is now defunct. But, in another sense, the new competition between the forces of integration and fragmentation presents us with difficult choices, precisely because it is by no means as clear as it was during the Cold War which tendency we should want to see prevail.

Choices

Consider, for a moment, the most extreme alternatives. A fully integrated world would be one in which individual countries would lose control of their borders and would be dependent upon others for critical resources, capital, and markets. It would mean, therefore, a progressive loss of national sovereignty, and ultimately the loss of whatever remained of national identity. A fully fragmented world would closely approximate the Hobbesian state of anarchy that theorists of international relations assume exists but that, in practice, never has. The world would be reduced to a gaggle of quarreling principalities, with war or the threat of war as the only means of settling disputes among them. Both of these extremes—for these are obviously caricatures—would undermine the international state system as we now know it: the first by submerging the autonomy of states within a supranational economic order; the second by so shattering state authority as to render it impotent.

Now, no one seriously claims that, with the end of the Cold War, we can abandon the international state system or relinquish national sovereignty: not even our most visionary visionaries are prepared to go that far. The United States therefore retains the interest it has always had in the balancing of power, but this time the power to be balanced may be less that of states or ideologies than that of processes—transcending states and ideologies—that are tending toward integrationist and fragmentationist extremes. Instead of balancing the forces of democracy against those of totalitarianism, the new task could well be to balance the forces of integration and fragmentation against each other.

What would this mean in practical terms? How can one translate this abstraction into policy recommendations? In the best of all possible worlds, one would need to take no action at all, because integrationist and fragmentationist forces would balance themselves. Unfortunately, though, things rarely work out this neatly in the imperfect world in which we live. Gaps generally exist between what one wants to have happen and what seems likely to happen; it is here that the choices of states—and of the leaders who govern them—make a difference.

These choices, in the post-Cold War world, are likely to center on those areas where integrationist and fragmentationist forces are not now balancing themselves; where the triumph of one over the other could imperil the conditions of international stability upon which rest the security interests of the United States, its allies, and other like-minded states, and where action is therefore needed to restore equilibrium. They are likely to include the following:

Reconstructing the Soviet Union and Eastern Europe. Over the next decade, the most serious source of instability in world politics will probably be the political, economic, and social fragmentation that is already developing where communism has collapsed. It is true that integrationist forces—the idea of

self-determination, the appeal of market economics, the rise of mass education—brought about that collapse; but integrative causes can produce disintegrative consequences, and that is what is happening in this case.

Marxism-Leninism could hardly have suffered a more resounding defeat
if World War III had been fought to the point of total victory for the West;
fortunately victory, this time, did not require a war. The trouble with victory,
though, is that it tends to produce power imbalances: it was precisely to avoid
this danger that the peacemakers of 1815 and 1945—who designed the two
most durable peace settlements of modern times—moved quickly after their
respective triumphs to rehabilitate defeated adversaries and to invite them
back into the international state system. Perhaps because the communist
regimes of the Soviet Union and Eastern Europe have not actually suffered a
military defeat, we in the West are not focusing as carefully as we should on
the problems of reconstruction and reintegration in that part of the world.[51]
But if fragmentationist forces should prevail there, the resulting anarchy—
and mass emigration away from anarchy[52]—could destabilize any number of
power balances. The situation then would certainly have our attention, even
if it does not now.

The peoples of the Soviet Union and Eastern Europe will of course have
to bear the principal burdens of reconstruction; but they will not be able to
accomplish this task alone, and already discouragement and demoralization
have set in among them. It is in dealing with this kind of despair that aid
from the "West"—including Japan—can have its greatest impact. A multinational Marshall Plan for former communist states sounds impractical given
the extent of the problem and the existence of competing priorities at home,
but the "highly leveraged" character of that earlier and highly successful
enterprise ought not to be forgotten. The Marshall Plan worked by employing
small amounts of economic assistance to produce large psychological effects:
it restored self-confidence in Europe just at the point—some two to three
years after the end of the war—at which it was sagging. What was critical
was not so much the extent of the aid provided as its timing, its targeting,
and its publicity; its purpose was to shift the expectations of its recipients
from the belief that things could only get worse to the conviction that they
would eventually get better.[53]

It will serve no one's interests in the West now, anymore than it would
have served the interests of the victorious allies after World War II, to allow
despair, demoralization, and disintegration to prevail in the territories of our
defeated Cold War adversaries. What happened in Germany after World War
I ought to provide a sufficiently clear example of the consequences that can
follow when victors neglect the interests of those they have vanquished, and
thereby, in the long run, neglect their own.

Creating new security and economic structures for Europe. Glaciers, when
they invade a continent, not only obscure its topography but, through the
weight of the accumulated ice, literally press its surface down into the earth's
mantle. Retreats of glaciers cause old features of the landscape slowly to rise

up again, sometimes altered, sometimes not. The expansion of Soviet and American influence over Europe at the end of World War II had something of the effect of such a glacier: it froze things into place, thereby obscuring old rivalries and bringing peace—even if a "cold" peace—to a continent that had known little of it throughout its history.

But now that the Cold War is over, geopolitical glaciers are retreating, the situation is becoming fluid once again, and certain familiar features of the European landscape—a single strong German state, together with ethnic and religious rivalries among Germany's neighbors to the east—are once more coming into view. The critical question for the future stability of Europe is the extent to which the Cold War glacier permanently altered the terrain it covered for so long. Integrationist structures like the European Community and NATO suggest such alteration; but they could also have been artifacts of the glaciation itself. If so, these organizations are likely to become increasingly vulnerable as the forces of fragmentation revive.

No economic or security structure for Europe can hope to be viable over the long term unless it incorporates—and provides benefits to—all of the major states on that continent: the classic lesson is the Versailles Treaty of 1919, which sought to build a peace that treated Germany as a pariah and excluded Soviet Russia altogether. But neither the European Community nor NATO has given sufficient attention to how each might restructure itself to accommodate the interests of the former Warsaw Pact states, including whatever is left of the Soviet Union itself. Few efforts have been made to think through how these integrative organizations might expand the scope of their activities to counter the fragmentationist challenges—coming from the reunification of Germany, the liberation of Eastern Europe, and the possible collapse of the U.S.S.R.—that are already evident.[54]

The United States has used its influence, over the years, to favor integration over fragmentation in Europe; indeed without that influence, it is difficult to see how integration could have proceeded as far as it has. But Americans cannot expect to maintain the authority the Cold War gave them on the continent for very much longer, especially now that the Soviet "glacier" is so obviously retreating. We would do well, then, to consider what new or modified integrative structures might replace the role that we—and, by very different means, our former adversaries—played in "freezing" disintegrative forces in Europe during the Cold War. Otherwise, serious imbalances could develop in that part of the world, as well.

Deterring aggression. One thing the "long peace" did was to make the use of force by the great powers against one another virtually unthinkable. It created inducements that caused states to seek to resolve peacefully—or even to learn to live with—accumulated grievances that could easily, prior to 1945, have provoked major wars.[55] It did this by appealing more to fear than to logic, but patterns of behavior that arise out of fear can, in time, come to seem quite logical. Few today would question the desirability of perpetuating, and if necessary reinforcing, the inhibitions that arose, during the Cold War, against once violent patterns of great power behavior.

The unprecedented multinational response to Saddam Hussein's aggression in Kuwait suggests that an opportunity now exists to extend disincentives to war beyond the realm of the great powers. The need to do this is urgent, not just because of the crisis in the Persian Gulf but also because the end of the Cold War is likely to end the informal crisis-management regime the United States and the Soviet Union have relied on in the past to keep such regional conflicts limited.

Woodrow Wilson's vision of collective international action to resist aggression failed to materialize in 1919–20 because of European appeasement and American isolationism, and again after 1945 because of the great power rivalries that produced the Cold War. Neither of these difficulties exists today. The world has a third chance to give Wilson's plan the fair test it has never received, and one could hardly have found a more appropriate occasion than by acting through a reinvigorated United Nations—*not* through the unilateral action of the United States—to restore the independence of Kuwait and to hold accountable the aggressor who temporarily extinguished it. The example thereby set could advance us some distance toward placing the conduct of international relations within the framework of international law that has long existed alongside it, but too often apart from it.[56]

Can such a legalistic vision sustain the realistic security interests of the United States? Whether rightly or wrongly, the answer was negative after World Wars I and II; but we may have reasons, this time, for giving a more positive reply. The "long peace," after all, has already created in the *practice* of the great powers mechanisms for deterring aggression that have worked remarkably well; these did not exist prior to the Cold War. There could be real advantages now—before the foundations of the "long peace" erode completely—in codifying and extending these practices as widely as possible. The evolution of a new world order designed to deter aggression could ensure that the most important benefits of the "long peace" survive the demise of the Cold War. It could also counteract the dangerous conviction—which American leaders still at times appear to feel—that only the United States has the will and the capacity to take the lead in policing (or nannying) the world.

Finding the appropriate limits of interdependence. The Iraqi invasion of Kuwait raises another issue, though, that will involve more difficult choices: it has to do with just how far we want economic integration to proceed. The purpose of having global markets is to ensure prosperity, not to compromise national sovereignty. And yet, it was the international market in oil and armaments that made it possible for Saddam Hussein to violate Kuwaiti sovereignty. Economic integration, in this instance, produced literal political fragmentation. This unexpected and dangerous juxtaposition suggests strongly the need to think, more seriously than we have to this point, about how the economic and political forces that are shaping our world intersect with one another, and about where our own security interests with respect to these lie.

Certainly there is much to be said, from a strictly economic perspective, in favor of reducing barriers to trade, investment, and even labor flows across international boundaries if the result is to maximize production, minimize prices, and ensure that consumer needs are satisfied. But what if the result is also to allow despots easy access to sophisticated military technology, or to increase the West's reliance on energy resources it does not control? If integration is really a good thing, then should we not applaud Iraq's enterprise in exploiting the international arms trade as well as our own craftiness in relying on cheap foreign oil? Such behavior is consistent, after all, with the principles of free markets and comparative advantage, the benefits of which Adam Smith and David Ricardo illustrated so graphically as the industrial revolution was getting under way. But do market principles also require that we welcome, on a continuing basis, the dispatch of American troops to safeguard critical supplies halfway around the world? There are political costs to be paid for economic integration, and we are only now beginning to realize what they are.

These issues are, in turn, only part of the much larger problem of how one balances the advantages of economic integration against its political and social disadvantages. Are we really sure, for example, that we want to integrate our own economy into the world market if the result of doing that is to shut down industries we have historically relied upon for both jobs and national defense? When the most visible effects of integration are to transform once-diversified industrial complexes into strings of fast-food outlets and shopping malls, with the reduction in wages that kind of employment normally brings, one can hardly expect people to be out in the streets cheering for these developments, however ingeniously economists attempt to rationalize them. What about the foreign ownership of American facilities? Japanese manufacturers have made valiant efforts to integrate themselves discreetly into the national economy, but when their presence becomes critical to the survival of particular local economies, as is the case with Japanese automobile plants throughout much of the Midwest, or when Japanese companies begin raiding universities to hire scarce computer designers, as is happening on the east and west coasts,[57] it is not at all difficult to see how a backlash against this kind of integration could arise.

Increasing labor mobility, together with the liberalized immigration policies that facilitate it, provides yet another example of how economic integration could produce political fragmentation. There are undeniable advantages to allowing immigration, not just because it provides cheap labor but also because in some instances the host nation can gain a diverse array of sophisticated skills as a result. But immigration also risks altering national identity, and the forces of integration have by no means advanced to the point at which one can dismiss concerns over that issue as anachronistic.[58] Certainly the Japanese have not done so: they long ago devised ways to be integrationist in international trade and investment, but rigidly protectionist (which is to say, fragmentationist) when it comes to matters of national culture. The difficulties confronting Turks in Germany, Arabs in France, and Pakistanis and West Indians in Britain suggest that the problem has by no means been solved in Europe; indeed, it could get much worse if the final removal of restrictions on the movement of labor within the European Community coincides with the mass emigration from the Soviet Union and Eastern Europe that the collapse of communism may bring.[59] As a nation of immigrants, the United States handles problems of cultural assimilation more easily than most.[60] Still, they are real problems, and attempts to write them off as reflections of an antiquated "nationalism," or even "racism," are not likely to make them go away.

What all of this suggests, therefore, is that we need better mechanisms for balancing integrative and disintegrative processes at the points at which economic forces intersect those of politics and culture. The increasing permeability of boundaries is going to be an important characteristic of the post-Cold War world,[61] and it would be a great mistake to assume—as market principles encourage us to assume—that in such an environment an "invisible hand" will always produce the greatest benefits for the greatest number. As in most other areas, an equilibrium will be necessary: if imbalances of power are not to develop, then a certain amount of protectionism, within prudent limits, may be required.

Regaining solvency. The principle of balancing power also requires that ends be balanced against means. National security, even in the most auspicious of circumstances, rarely comes cheap. This country's reluctance to bring the costs of providing for its security into line with what it is willing to pay— that is, its unwillingness to regain solvency[62]—suggests that integrative and disintegrative mechanisms are imperfectly balanced within the United States as well as beyond its borders.

The last American president to preoccupy himself with solvency, Dwight D. Eisenhower, regularly insisted that the National Security Council specify, as "the basic objective of our national security policies: maintaining the security of the United States *and* the vitality of its fundamental values and institutions." To achieve the former without securing the latter, he warned, would be to "destroy what we are attempting to defend."[63]

Too often during the years that have followed Eisenhower's presidency the quest for security has overwhelmed concern for the vitality of fundamental values and institutions. The military-industrial complex has, as he warned that it might,[64] taken on a life of its own, producing weapons in search of functions, bases in search of missions, strategies in search of objectives, and organizations—both military and civilian—in search of their own perpetuation. We fought the Vietnam War, which came close to tearing this country apart, for geopolitical reasons that remain obscure to this day. The Watergate and Iran-Contra scandals revealed how excesses committed in the name of national security can subvert constitutional processes. And no one would be more appalled than Eisenhower himself to see the extent to which we now finance the costs of defense—as well as everything else—

on credit extended by the unborn (who cannot object to the process) and by foreigners (who someday may).

Again, integrationist phenomena—in this case, the attempt to hold on to our Cold War role as global policeman while relying on our ability to borrow to stabilize the economy at home—have produced fragmentationist effects; only what appears to be fragmenting now is nothing short of the national consensus that used to exist on what role the United States should play in the world of which it is a part.[65]

A return to solvency in its broadest sense—by which I mean not just balanced budgets but bearing the full pain of what one is doing at the time one is doing it—might discipline our thinking about national security in the way that it should be disciplined: through the constantly annoying—but also intellectually bracing—demands of stringency. For the concept of security is, as interests are, infinitely expandable: the more widely one projects one's interests in the world, the more threats there will sooner or later be to them. One winds up, figuratively at least, chasing one's own tail. But the pursuit of security along with solvency is a much more manageable enterprise. By requiring specifications of interests in terms of available (and not future, or even imaginary) means, it guards against the principal occupational hazard of being a great power, which is paranoia and the exhaustion it ultimately produces. The result is likely to be less grandiose visions, but more sustainable policies.

Strategy

Which is going to win—integration or fragmentation? At first glance, it would seem that the forces of integration will almost certainly prevail: one cannot run a modern post-industrial economy without such forces, and that, many people would say, is the most important thing in the world. But that is also a parochial view: running a post-industrial economy may not be the most important thing to the peasant in the Sudan, or to the young urban black in the United States, or to the Palestinian who has spent his entire life in a refugee camp. For those people, forces that might appear to us to be fragmentationist can be profoundly integrationist, in that they can give meaning to otherwise meaningless lives. One person's fragmentation may be another's integration, and we need to be keenly aware of that fact.

We should also recognize that the forces of integration may not be as deeply rooted as we like to think. It comes as something of a shock to remember that the most important of them—the global market, collective security, the "long peace" itself—were products of the Cold War. Their survival is by no means guaranteed into the post-Cold War era. Fragmentationist forces have been around much longer than integrationist forces have been, and now that the Cold War is over, they may grow stronger than they have been at any point in the last half-century.

We should not necessarily conclude from this, though, that it will always be in our interest to try to ensure that the forces of integration come out on top. Surely, in the light of the Persian Gulf war, we will want to restrict future sales of arms across international boundaries, and it would not be a bad idea to develop alternatives to the worldwide marketing of oil as well. The increasing permeability of borders—the very thing we welcome when it comes to the free flow of ideas—will by no means be as welcome when commodities, capital, and labor begin flowing with equal freedom. And we are already, in this country, beginning to move away from the view that we can leave everything—international trade, energy resources, and especially the regulation of the savings and loan industry—to the "invisible hand" of market forces that the integrationist model in principle recommends.

But swinging to the other extreme—toward autarchy, nationalism, or isolationism—will not do either. The forces of fragmentation lurk just beneath the surface, and it would take little encouragement for them to reassert themselves, with all the dangers historical experience suggests would accompany such a development. We need to maintain a healthy skepticism about integration: there is no reason to turn it into some kind of sacred cow. But we also need to balance that skepticism with a keen sense of how unhealthy fragmentationist forces can be if allowed free rein.

So we are left, as usual, groping for the middle ground, for that rejection of extremes, that judicious balancing of pluses and minuses on both sides, that is typical of how essays like this are supposed to end. This one will be no exception to that rule. I would point out, though, that practical statecraft boils down, most of the time, to just this task of attempting to navigate the middle course, while avoiding the rocks and shoals that lie on either side. Certainly Americans, of all peoples, should find this a familiar procedure. For what is our own Constitution, if not the most elegant political text ever composed on how to balance the forces of integration against those of disintegration? It had been necessary, Madison wrote in *The Federalist* number 51, so to contrive "the interior structure of the government as that its several constituent parts may, by their mutual relations, be the means of keeping each other in their proper places."[66] That would not be a bad strategy to follow with regard to the external world as we think about how we might come to grips—as the Founding Fathers had to—with the combination of centripetal and centrifugal forces that is already shaping our lives.

Notes and Acknowledgments

ONE

The American Foreign Policy Style in the Twentieth Century

This essay originally appeared in a quite different form in Michael P. Hamilton, ed., *American Character and Foreign Policy* (Grand Rapids: William B. Eerdmans, 1986), pp. 23–40, and is included in this collection with the permission of the William B. Eerdmans Publishing Company. I should like to acknowledge helpful comments from Michael Hamilton, Charles M. Lichenstein, and Michael Gaddis.

1. Harry M. Geduld, ed., *The Definitive Time Machine: A Critical Edition of H. G. Wells' Scientific Romance* (Bloomington: Indiana University Press, 1987), p. 32.

2. Some of the best books about the English have been written by the French, and vice versa. An American, Gordon Craig, has produced several of the finest studies of the tortured history and psychology of Germany. We would know much less about China and Japan if we had had to rely upon the Chinese and Japanese to inform us instead of John Fairbank, Jonathan Spence, Ruth Benedict, and Edwin Reischauer. A young British historian, Timothy Garton Ash, has already taught participants in the revolutions of 1989 in East Central Europe a great deal about themselves. And of course Russian studies have always relied upon the work of distinguished outsiders, from the days of the Marquis de Custine and the first George Kennan down through Bernard Pares, E. H. Carr, Louis Fischer, Merle Fainsod, Robert Conquest, Richard Pipes, Robert Tucker, and the second George Kennan; today these authorities are acknowledged as authoritative even within the Soviet Union itself, now that that government has admitted the inadequacies of its own officially sponsored scholarship. For the United States, the classic works of Alexis de Tocqueville, Lord Bryce, and Gunnar Myrdal come to mind, but one should also perhaps add to the list Paul Kennedy's more recent and best-selling *The Rise and Fall of the Great Powers: Economic Change and Military Conflict from 1500 to 2000* (New York: Random House, 1987), a book that came closer than any in years to holding up a mirror in which Americans could see their country from a distance—both in time and space—and debate the implications of what they found there. And then, of course, the editors of *The Econ-*

omist seem to achieve these kinds of insights, in their coverage of the United States, almost every week.

3. Henry Luce's famous editorial asserting that the 20th century would be the "American Century" appeared in *Life* on February 17, 1941.

4. Which is, by definition, an amorphous topic, subject to highly impressionistic judgments. For some other recent efforts, see Robert Dallek, *The American Style of Foreign Policy: Cultural Politics and Foreign Affairs* (New York, Knopf, 1983); Knud Krakau, "American Foreign Relations: A National Style?" *Diplomatic History*, VIII(Summer, 1984), 253–72; Michael H. Hunt, *Ideology and U.S. Foreign Policy* (New Haven: Yale University Press, 1987); and Colin S. Gray, *The Geopolitics of Super Power* (Lexington: University Press of Kentucky, 1988), especially pp. 53–65.

5. Louis J. Halle provides a good discussion in his perceptive book, *The Cold War as History* (New York: Harper and Row, 1967), especially pp. 10–29.

6. It is interesting to consider why geopolitical influence did not migrate, in the wake of the two world wars, to other parts of the world that were relatively well-endowed in terms of environmental circumstances. For some possible explanations, see Donald W. White, "The Nature of World Power in American History: An Evaluation at the End of World War II," *Diplomatic History*, XI(Summer, 1987), especially pp. 187–92.

7. See, on this point, Joseph S. Nye, Jr., *Bound to Lead: The Changing Nature of American Power* (New York: Basic Books, 1990), pp. 108–12, 116–25.

8. See Kennedy, *The Rise and Fall of the Great Powers*, pp. 178–82,195. One of the best treatments of the Civil War in an international context is D. P. Crook, *The North, the South, and the Powers, 1861–1865* (New York: John Wiley, 1974).

9. For two excellent overviews, see Charles S. Campbell, *The Transformation of American Foreign Relations, 1865–1900* (New York: Harper and Row, 1976); and Robert L. Beisner, *From the Old Diplomacy to the New, 1865–1900*, 2nd ed. (Arlington Heights, Ill.: Harlan-Davidson, 1986).

10. Daniel M. Smith, *The Great Departure: The United States and World War I, 1914–1918* (New York: John Wiley, 1965).

11. See especially Michael J. Hogan, *Informal Entente: The Private Structure of Cooperation in Anglo-American Economic Diplomacy, 1918–1928* (Columbia: University of Missouri Press, 1977); and Melvyn P. Leffler, *The Elusive Quest: America's Pursuit of European Stability and French Security, 1919–1933* (Chapel Hill: University of North Carolina Press, 1979).

12. Charles P. Kindleberger, *The World in Depression, 1929–1939* (Berkeley: University of California Press, 1973), especially pp. 291–308.

13. See Donald Cameron Watt, *How War Came: The Immediate Origins of the Second World War, 1938–1939* (New York: Pantheon, 1989), especially pp. 612–13.

14. Robert Dallek, *Franklin D. Roosevelt and American Foreign Policy, 1932–1945* (New York: Oxford University Press, 1979), pp. 227, 286–87.

15. John Lewis Gaddis, *Strategies of Containment: A Critical Appraisal of Postwar American National Security Policy* (New York: Columbia University Press, 1982), pp. 6–7.

16. See Hugh Thomas, *Armed Truce: The Beginnings of the Cold War, 1945–46* (London: Hamish Hamilton, 1986), p. 176.

17. Quoted in Warren F. Kimball, ed., *Churchill and Roosevelt: The Complete Correspondence* (Princeton: Princeton University Press, 1984), III, v.

18. David Callahan, *Dangerous Capabilities: Paul Nitze and the Cold War* (New York: HarperCollins, 1990), pp. 92–138.

19. See Frank Ninkovich, *Germany and the United States: The Transformation of the German Question Since 1945* (Boston: Twayne, 1988), pp. 26–28; also D. Clayton James, *The Years of MacArthur: Triumph and Disaster, 1945–1964* (Boston: Houghton Mifflin, 1985), p. 196.

20. Loch K. Johnson, *A Season of Inquiry: The Senate Intelligence Investigation* (Lexington: University Press of Kentucky, 1985). Congress's investigation of Reagan administration involvement in the Iran-Contra scandal a decade later was, admittedly, somewhat less ardent, probably for fear of what really rigorous scrutiny would reveal.

21. John Lewis Gaddis, *The Long Peace: Inquiries into the History of the Cold War* (New York: Oxford University Press, 1987), pp. 123–46.

22. The best discussion is N. Gordon Levin, *Woodrow Wilson and World Politics: America's Response to War and Revolution* (New York: Oxford University Press, 1968); but see also the pioneering work on this subject, William Appleman Williams, *The Tragedy of American Diplomacy* (New York: Norton, 1988 [first published in 1959]).

23. Most recently by Thomas J. McCormick, *America's Half Century: United States Foreign Policy in the Cold War* (Baltimore: Johns Hopkins University Press, 1989), p. 5.

24. Levin, *Woodrow Wilson and World Politics,* pp. 236–51.

25. Frederick W. Marks III, *Wind over Sand: The Diplomacy of Franklin D. Roosevelt* (Athens: University of Georgia Press, 1988), pp. 169–79.

26. One of the best discussions is Patrick Devlin, *Too Proud to Fight: Woodrow Wilson's Neutrality* (New York: Oxford University Press, 1975).

27. Wilson's German policy is skillfully treated in Levin, *Woodrow Wilson and World Politics;* also in Klaus Schwabe, *Woodrow Wilson, Revolutionary Germany, and Peacemaking, 1918–1919: Missionary Diplomacy and the Realities of Power,* translated by Robert and Rita Kimber (Chapel Hill: University of North Carolina Press, 1985).

28. John Lewis Gaddis, *Russia, the Soviet Union, and the United States: An Interpretive History,* 2nd ed. (New York: McGraw-Hill, 1990), pp. 84–85.

29. See Jonathan G. Utley, *Going to War with Japan, 1937–1941* (Knoxville: University of Tennessee Press, 1985), especially pp. 176–82; also Waldo Heinrichs, *Threshold of War: Franklin D. Roosevelt and American Entry into World War II* (New York: Oxford University Press, 1988), pp. 8–9, 98, 154, 214.

30. Gaddis, *The Long Peace,* pp. 147–94; also David Allan Mayers, *Cracking the Monolith: U.S. Policy Against the Sino-Soviet Alliance, 1949–1955* (Baton Rouge: Louisiana State University Press, 1986); Gordon H. Chang, *Friends and Enemies: The United States, China, and the Soviet Union, 1948–1972* (Stanford: Stanford University Press, 1990). See also, on Dulles, Chapter Four of this book.

31. The distinction originated with Jeane J. Kirkpatrick, "Dictatorships and Double Standards," *Commentary,* LXVIII(November, 1979), 34–45.

32. A recent example—there are many earlier ones—is Noam Chomsky, *Towards a New Cold War: Essays on the Current Crisis and How We Got There* (New York: Pantheon, 1982).

33. See John Mueller, *Retreat from Doomsday: The Obsolescence of Major War* (New York: Basic Books, 1989).

34. Gaddis, *The Long Peace,* pp. 215–45. See also, for critical evaluations of the "long peace" thesis, Charles W. Kegley, Jr., ed., *The Long Postwar Peace: Contending Explanations and Projections* (New York: HarperCollins, 1990).

35. For further thoughts on this matter, see Chapter Three of this book.

36. Dallek, *The American Style in Foreign Policy*, pp. 146–50, argues that U.S. occupation policies in Germany and Japan grew out of American domestic attitudes and institutions. Maybe this is why they succeeded.

37. See George F. Kennan, "Communism in Russian History," *Foreign Affairs*, LXIX(Winter, 1990/91), especially pp. 170–73.

38. The best assessments of the damage are Zbigniew Brzezinski, *The Grand Failure: The Birth and Death of Communism in the Twentieth Century* (New York: Scribners,1989); and Theodore S. Hamerow, *From the Finland Station: The Graying of Revolution in the Twentieth Century* (New York: Basic Books, 1990).

39. The closest Americans came to such a "scientific" approach was probably the application of political development theory in the 1950s and 1960s. The theory is nicely skewered in D. Michael Shafer, *Deadly Paradigms: The Failure of U.S. Counterinsurgency Policy* (Princeton: Princeton University Press, 1988).

TWO
The Objectives of Containment

This essay was originally prepared for the Bronfman Foundation East-West Forum. It appears in a different form in Seweryn Bialer and Michael Mandelbaum, eds., *Gorbachev's Russia and American Foreign Policy* (Boulder: Westview Press, 1988), pp. 303–46, and is included in this collection with the permission of Westview Press.

1. Having written one book on this subject and co-edited two others, I must admit to having committed more than my own share of ecological damage.

2. See, on these points, George F. Kennan, *Soviet-American Relations, 1917–1920: The Decision to Intervene* (Princeton: Princeton University Press, 1958), pp. 379–80, 403–4; and, on the lessons of intervention in Mexico, W. B. Fowler, *British-American Relations, 1917–1918: The Role of Sir William Wiseman* (Princeton: Princeton University Press, 1969), pp. 185, 196; also John Milton Cooper, Jr., *The Warrior and the Priest: Woodrow Wilson and Theodore Roosevelt* (Cambridge: Harvard University Press, 1983), pp. 268.

3. Arthur S. Link, *Woodrow Wilson: Revolution, War, and Peace* (Arlington Heights, Ill.: Harlan-Davidson, 1979), pp. 96–97.

4. Richard Pipes, *The Russian Revolution* (New York: Knopf, 1990), pp. 545–58.

5. See Cooper, *The Warrior and the Priest*, pp. 319–23.

6. For the Colby note, see U. S. Department of State, *Foreign Relations of the United States* [hereafter *FRUS*]: *1920* (Washington: Government Printing Office, 1936), III, 463–68.

7. Non-recognition had been applied previously in Mexico, after Huerta overthrew Madero in 1913, and in China as Washington's response to Japan's "twenty-one demands" in 1915.

8. See, on this point, John Lewis Gaddis, *Russia, the Soviet Union, and the United States: An Interpretive History* 2nd ed. (New York: McGraw Hill, 1990), pp. 98–104.

9. Thomas R. Maddux, *Years of Estrangement: American Relations with the Soviet Union, 1933–1941*. (Tallahassee: University Presses of Florida, 1980), pp. 27–101; also Edward M. Bennett, *Franklin D. Roosevelt and the Search for Security:*

American-Soviet Relations, 1933–1939 (Wilmington, Del.: Scholarly Resources, 1985), pp. 69–187.

10. William L. Langer and S. Everett Gleason, *The Challenge to Isolation: The World Crisis of 1937–1940 and American Foreign Policy* (New York: Harper and Row, 1952), pp. 122–23; William W. Kaufmann, "Two American Ambassadors: Bullitt and Kennedy," in Gordon A. Craig and Felix Gilbert, eds., *The Diplomats: 1919–1939* (Princeton: Princeton University Press, 1953), p. 666. Both of these accounts exaggerate the cynicism of Chamberlain's and Kennedy's actual positions.

11. Maddux, *Years of Estrangement*, pp. 102–62.

12. See Nikolai V. Sivachev and Nikolai N. Yakovlev, *Russia and the United States*, translated by Olga Adler Titelbaum (Chicago: University of Chicago Press, 1979), p. 163; and, for a more moderate formulation, Vilnis Sipols, *The Road to Great Victory: Soviet Diplomacy, 1941–1945*, translated by Lev Bobrov (Moscow: Progress Publishers, 1985), pp. 41–42.

13. It is important to recall, in this connection, Roosevelt's comment to Stalin at Yalta that the public opinion would not allow American troops to remain in Europe for "much more than two years" after the war. [Bohlen minutes, Roosevelt-Churchill-Stalin meeting, February 5, 1945, U. S. Department of State, *FRUS: The Conferences at Malta and Yalta, 1945* (Washington: Government Printing Office, 1955), p. 617].

14. See Russell D. Buhite and Wm. Christopher Hamel, "War for Peace: The Question of an American Preventive War Against the Soviet Union, 1945–1955," *Diplomatic History*, XIV(Summer, 1990), 367–84.

15. Total U. S. military personnel on active duty as of mid–1948 were 1.4 million, down from 12.1 million in mid–1945. [U. S. Bureau of the Census, *Statistical History of the United States from Colonial Times to the Present* (Washington: Government Printing Office, 1960), Series Y 763, p. 736]. The best comparable Soviet figure for 1948 is now believed to be that given by Khrushchev in 1960: 2.9 million, down from 11.3 million in 1945. [Matthew A. Evangelista, "Stalin's Postwar Army Reappraised," *International Security*, VII(Winter, 1982/83), 115.] These statistics in no way invalidate the major point of Evangelista's article—that the Soviet Union was not capable of invading Western Europe during the years immediately following World War II. But they do suggest strongly that the United States was in no position to launch a preventive war against the Soviet Union either.

16. See the conclusions of the 1949 Harmon Committee report, in Thomas H. Etzold and John Lewis Gaddis, eds., *Containment: Documents on American Policy and Strategy, 1945–1950* (New York: Columbia University Press, 1978), pp. 360–64.

17. Warner R. Schilling, "The Politics of National Defense: Fiscal 1950," in Warner R. Schilling, Paul Y. Hammond, and Glenn H. Snyder, *Strategy, Politics, and Defense Budgets* (New York: Columbia University Press, 1962), pp. 1–266.

18. Buhite and Hamel, "War for Peace," p. 382. See also, on the historic durability but possible current erosion of this tradition, Arthur M. Schlesinger, Jr., *The Cycles of American History* (Boston: Houghton Mifflin, 1986), pp. 84–85.

19. For the objections of George F. Kennan and Dwight D. Eisenhower on this point, see John Lewis Gaddis, *Strategies of Containment: A Critical Appraisal of Postwar American National Security Policy* (New York: Oxford University Press, 1982), pp. 49n, 174n.

20. See Colin S. Gray, *The Geopolitics of Super Power* (Lexington: University Press of Kentucky, 1990), p. 70.

21. NSC 20/1, "U. S. Objectives with Respect to Russia," August 18, 1948, in

Etzold and Gaddis, eds., *Containment*, p. 193. President Truman approved the conclusions of this document as NSC 20/4 in November, 1948.

22. Nikita S. Khrushchev, *Khrushchev Remembers: The Last Testament*, translated and edited by Strobe Talbott (Boston: Little, Brown, 1974), p. 375.

23. See George F. Kennan, *American Diplomacy: 1900–1950* (Chicago: University
of Chicago Press, 1951), pp. 82–83.

24. See, on this point, Seweryn Bialer, *The Soviet Paradox: External Expansion,
Internal Decline* (New York: Knopf, 1986), p. 322.

25. *Ibid.*, p. 239. There was, to be sure, a tendency on the part of certain early
Reagan advisers—notably Richard Pipes—to picture the Soviet Union as being on the
verge of collapse, and to suggest that slight pushes in the right direction might cause
it to. But this position did not command wide support in the Reagan administration;
it also suffered from the difficulty that too much emphasis on it could paradoxically
lull the West into a sense of complacency and undermine efforts at rearmament. See,
on this point, Michel Tatu, "U.S.-Soviet Relations: A Turning Point?" *Foreign Affairs*
LXI(America and the World, 1982), 594–95.

26. The tactic was not unknown in the Soviet Union as well. Indeed, there was
a curious asymmetry in the Russians' tendency to regard anti-Soviet rhetoric in the
United States as an expression of official intent, but to express astonishment and
dismay in the relatively rare instances in which Americans reciprocated.

27. See Schlesinger, *The Cycles of American History*, pp. 111–17.

28. I am indebted, for this insight, to Robert Jervis and John Mueller.

29. R. W. Apple, Jr., "The New Embrace: U. S. Moves to Help Cold War
Rival Much as It Aided World War II Foes," *New York Times*, December 13,
1990.

30. The "long telegram," dated February 22, 1946, appears in *FRUS: 1946*, VI,
696–709. The "X" article appeared as "The Sources of Soviet Conduct," *Foreign Affairs*,
XXV(July, 1947), 566–82.

31. NSC 68, "United States Objectives and Policies for National Security," April
14, 1950, appears in *FRUS: 1950*, I, 235–92.

32. For the individuals involved, see Gregg Herken, "The Great Foreign Policy
Fight," *American Heritage*, XXXVII(April-May, 1986), 65–80. The difficulties are covered in Gaddis, *Strategies of Containment, passim.*

33. Kennan to State Department, February 22, 1946, *FRUS: 1946*, VI, 700. See
also Kennan's dispatch of March 20, 1946, *ibid.*, pp. 721–23.

34. NSC 20/1, August 18, 1948, in Etzold and Gaddis, eds., *Containment*,
p. 187.

35. Joint Orientation Conference lecture, September 19, 1949, George F. Kennan
Papers, Box 17, Seeley Mudd Library, Princeton University.

36. Kennan unpublished paper, "The Soviet Way of Thought and Its Effect on
Foreign Policy," January 24, 1947, *ibid.*, Box 16.

37. NSC 68, April 14, 1950, *FRUS: 1950*, I, 242, 247.

38. For Nitze's agreement with the overall objective of containment as Kennan
had framed it, see Paul H. Nitze, *From Hiroshima to Glasnost: At the Center of
Decision* (New York: Grove Weidenfeld, 1989), pp. 51–52, 97.

39. I have discussed this problem in greater detail in John Lewis Gaddis, "Containment and the Logic of Strategy," *The National Interest*, #10(Winter, 1987/88),
27–38.

40. See Schlesinger, *The Cycles of American History*, pp. 141–62; also Chapter
Three of this book.

41. The classic discussion is, of course, Coral Bell, *Negotiation from Strength: A Study in the Politics of Power* (New York: Chatto and Windus, 1963).

42. Kennan did comment, in 1949, that "I would rather wait thirty years for a defeat of the Kremlin brought about by the tortuous and exasperatingly slow devices of diplomacy than to see us submit to the test of arms a difference so little susceptible to any clear and happy settlement by those means." [National War College lecture, "Where Do We Stand?" December 21, 1949, George F. Kennan Papers, Box 17, Seeley Mudd Library, Princeton University]. But this remark suggests that thirty years represented the outer limit of the time Kennan thought would be necessary. Nitze has also acknowledged having failed to anticipate how long containment would take to work. See *From Hiroshima to Glasnost*, p. 52.

43. Or so I have argued in *Strategies of Containment*, pp. 352–57.

44. See Georgii Arbatov, "The Limited Power of an Ordinary State," *New Perspectives Quarterly*, V(Summer, 1988), 31.

45. George F. Kennan, *Memoirs: 1925–1950* (Boston: Atlantic Little, Brown, 1967), pp. 365–67.

46. NSC-68, April 14, 1950, *FR: 1950*, I, 272–76. See also Nitze, *From Hiroshima to Glasnost*, p. 52; and Strobe Talbott, *The Master of the Game: Paul Nitze and the Nuclear Peace* (New York: Knopf, 1988), p. 72. For a more skeptical view of Nitze's interest in negotiations, see David Callahan, *Dangerous Capabilities: Paul Nitze and the Cold War* (New York: HarperCollins, 1990), p. 143.

47. Stephen E. Ambrose, *Eisenhower: The President* (New York: Simon and Schuster 1984), pp. 38, 93, 122–23, 148, 169, 206, 248, 295, 313.

48. Gaddis, *Strategies of Containment*, pp. 132–36.

49. Eisenhower press conference, February 2, 1955, *Public Papers of the Presidents of the United States: Dwight D. Eisenhower, 1955* (Washington: Government Printing Office, 1959), p. 235.

50. See, on this point, David Allan Mayers, *Cracking the Monolith: U. S. Policy Against the Sino-Soviet Alliance, 1949–1955* (Baton Rouge: Louisiana State University Press, 1986), especially pp. 115–25.

51. Gaddis, *Strategies of Containment*, p. 135.

52. Charles E. Bohlen, *Witness to History: 1929–1969* (New York: Norton, 1973), pp. 309–36. See also T. Michael Ruddy, *The Cautious Diplomat: Charles E. Bohlen and the Soviet Union, 1929–1969* (Kent, Ohio: Kent State University Press, 1986), pp. 109–24.

53. Gaddis, *Strategies of Containment*, p. 228.

54. Roger Hilsman, *To Move a Nation: The Politics of Foreign Policy in the Administration of John F. Kennedy* (New York: Doubleday, 1967), pp. 344–57.

55. Rostow draft, "Basic National Security Policy," March 26, 1962, Lyndon B. Johnson Papers, Vice Presidential-Security File, Box 7, Lyndon B. Johnson Library.

56. Kennedy American University address, June 10, 1963, *Public Papers of the Presidents of the United States: John F. Kennedy, 1963* (Washington: Government Printing Office, 1964), pp. 461–62.

57. See, on this point, Gerald M. Steinberg, *Satellite Reconnaissance: The Role of Informal Bargaining* (New York: Praeger, 1983), pp. 39–70; and Paul B. Stares, *The Militarization of Space: U.S. Policy, 1945–1984* (Ithaca: Cornell University Press, 1985), pp. 62–71.

58. For an interesting argument to this effect, see Janos Radvanyi, *Delusion and Reality: Gambits, Hoaxes, and Diplomatic One-Upmanship in Vietnam* (South Bend, Ind.: Gateway Editions, 1978).

59. John Newhouse, *Cold Dawn: The Story of SALT* (New York: Holt, Rinehart and Winston, 1973), pp. 130–32.

60. Maddux, *Years of Estrangement*, pp. 13–15; Bennett, *Franklin D. Roosevelt and the Search for Security*, pp. 21–24. Litvinov's reports are printed in the Soviet Foreign Ministry publication, *Dokumenty vneshnei politiki SSSR* (Moscow: 1957–), XVI, especially pp. 658–59.

61. See Bohlen, *Witness to History*, pp. 39–41; also Kennan, *Memoirs: 1925–1950*, pp. 82–85.

62. Thomas R. Maddux, "United States-Soviet Naval Relations in the 1930's: The Soviet Union's Efforts to Purchase Naval Vessels," *Naval War College Review*, XXIX(Fall, 1976), 28–37.

63. For Roosevelt's wartime policy toward the Soviet Union, see Gaddis, *Russia, the Soviet Union, and the United States*, pp. 144–67.

64. See, on these points, Gaddis, *Strategies of Containment*, pp. 4–13.

65. Dallek, *Franklin D. Roosevelt and American Foreign Policy*, pp. 533–34.

66. See, on this point, Vojtech Mastny, *Russia's Road to the Cold War: Diplomacy, Warfare, and the Politics of Communism, 1941–1945* (New York: Columbia University Press, 1979), especially p. 306.

67. Gaddis, *Strategies of Containment*, pp. 285–86.

68. Peter Schmeisser, "Taking Stock: Is America in Decline?" *New York Times Magazine*, April 18, 1988, provides a good introduction to the "declinist" literature. See also, on detente as declinism, Gray, *The Geopolitics of Super Power*, pp. 24–24; also Henry R. Nau, *The Myth of America's Decline: Leading the World Economy into the 1990s* (New York: Oxford University Press, 1990), especially 131–88.

69. Raymond L. Garthoff, *Detente and Confrontation: American-Soviet Relations from Nixon to Reagan* (Washington: Brookings Institution, 1985), pp. 41–42.

70. Garthoff argues strongly (if, to my mind, somewhat unconvincingly) in *Detente and Confrontation* that for these reasons the United States bears the chief responsibility for the collapse of detente.

71. For more on this, see Chapter One of this book.

72. Robert Dallek, *The American Style of Foreign Policy: Cultural Politics and Foreign Affairs* (New York: Knopf, 1983), pp. 62–91, stresses the interrelationship of domestic and foreign policy in Wilson's administration.

73. For Roosevelt's realism, see Dallek, *Franklin D. Roosevelt and American Foreign Policy*, pp. 321, 533–34.

74. John Lewis Gaddis, *The United States and the Origins of the Cold War* (New York: Columbia University Press, 1972), pp. 34–42.

75. Quoted in Keith David Eagles, "Ambassador Joseph E. Davies and American-Soviet Relations, 1937–1941" (Ph. D. Dissertation, University of Washington, 1966), p. 328.

76. Stimson's brief flirtation with "atomic reform" can be traced in Henry L. Stimson and McGeorge Bundy, *On Active Service in Peace and War* (New York: Harper, 1948), pp. 638–46. See also Godfrey Hodgson, *The Colonel: The Life and Wars of Henry Stimson, 1867–1950* (New York: Knopf, 1990), pp. 342–65.

77. See Henry A. Kissinger, *American Foreign Policy*, 3rd ed. (New York: Norton, 1977), pp. 124–26, 158–59, 172–73; also Stanley Hoffmann, *Primacy or World Order: American Foreign Policy since the Cold War* (New York: McGraw-Hill, 1978), pp. 57–58.

78. "We were convinced that Jackson was acting like a man who, having won once at roulette, organizes his yearly budget in anticipation of a recurrence. Inevitably,

his approach would backfire sooner or later." [Henry A. Kissinger, *Years of Upheaval* (Boston: Little, Brown, 1982), p. 987].

79. Garthoff, *Detente and Confrontation*, pp. 412, 456.

80. *Ibid.*, pp. 563–58. For an alternative point of view, see Gaddis Smith, *Morality, Reason and Power: American Diplomacy in the Carter Years* (New York: 1986), pp. 67–68.

81. Gaddis, *Russia, the Soviet Union, and the United States*, pp. 295–313.

82. Seweryn Bialer and Joan Afferica, "Reagan and Russia," *Foreign Affairs*, LXI(Winter, 1982/83), especially 261–67.

83. See, for example, Geoffrey Hosking, *The Awakening of the Soviet Union* (Cambridge: Harvard University Press, 1990), p. 2; and Jerry Hough, *Russia and the West: Gorbachev and the Politics of Reform*, 2nd ed. (New York: Simon and Schuster), p. 119. Obviously much else apart from SDI also contributed to the rise of Gorbachev. It will be a long time—and it will require much greater access to Soviet sources than we have now—before we can sort out just how much weight to give to each of the many circumstances that led to this development. But there are moments in history when a single dramatic development can galvanize a country into taking action—*Sputnik* had this effect on the United States in 1957—and the reaction to SDI inside the Soviet Union may have been an example of that.

84. See Steven Merritt Miner, "Military Crisis and Social Change in Russian and Soviet History," in George E. Hudson, ed., *Soviet National Security Policy Under Perestroika* (Boston: Unwin Hyman, 1989), pp. 29–46.

85. For more on this, see Chapter Nine, below.

86. This parallels Marshal Ferdinand Foch's favorite military question during World War I: "De quoi s'agit-il?" See Bernard Brodie, *War and Politics* (New York: Macmillan, 1973), p. 1.

THREE

Morality and the American Experience in the Cold War

This essay originally appeared in a different form in Kenneth W. Thompson, ed., *Ethics and International Relations* (New Brunswick: Transaction Books, 1985), pp. 109–26, and is included in this collection with the permission of the Carnegie Council on Ethics and International Affairs. I am grateful to Kenneth W. Thompson and Campbell Craig for critical comments.

1. Arthur M. Schlesinger, Jr., *The Cycles of American History* (Boston: Houghton Mifflin, 1986), p. 80.

2. See also Norman A. Graebner's distinction between the "analytical" and the "ideological" traditions in American diplomatic history in the introduction to his edited collection, *Ideas and Diplomacy: Readings in the Intellectual Tradition of American Foreign Policy* (New York: Oxford University Press, 1964), pp. vii-viii.

3. "X" [George F. Kennan], "The Sources of Soviet Conduct," *Foreign Affairs*, XXV(July, 1947), 582.

4. For three recent attempts to re-create the mood at the time, see Alan Bullock, *Ernest Bevin: Foreign Secretary, 1945–1951* (New York: Norton, 1983), pp. 6–19; John Lewis Gaddis, *The Long Peace: Inquiries into the History of the Cold War* (New York: Oxford University Press, 1987), pp. 20–47; and all of Hugh Thomas, *Armed Truce: The Beginnings of the Cold War, 1945–46* (London: Hamish Hamilton, 1986).

5. See John Lewis Gaddis, "The Emerging Post-Revisionist Synthesis on the Origins of the Cold War," *Diplomatic History*, VII(Summer, 1983), especially pp. 180–81. Today Soviet historians, relishing their new-found freedom to criticize their own country's policies, are more likely than their American counterparts to assume American innocence.

6. Lord Inverchapel to Ernest Bevin, May 22, 1947, FO 371/61048/AN1986, Public Record Office, London.

7. Truman speech in Rio de Janeiro, September 2, 1947, *Public Papers of the Presidents: Harry S. Truman, 1947* (Washington: Government Printing Office, 1963), p. 429. For Kennan's contribution to the drafting of this speech, see Kennan to Robert Lovett, August 1, 11, 18, 19, 1947, Policy Planning Staff Files, Box 33, "Chronological-1947," Department of State Records, National Archives.

8. The Marshall Plan's multiple advantages are made clear in Michael J. Hogan, *The Marshall Plan: America, Britain, and the Reconstruction of Western Europe, 1947–1952* (Cambridge: Cambridge University Press, 1987).

9. Niebuhr to James Conant, March 12, 1946, Reinhold Niebuhr Papers, Box 3, Library of Congress. See also Richard Fox, *Reinhold Niebuhr: A Biography* (New York: Pantheon, 1985), pp. 224–25.

10. Truman speech to Congress, March 12, 1947, *Truman Public Papers, 1947*, pp. 178–79. The most recent account of the Truman Doctrine, its origins, and its consequences, is Howard Jones, *"A New Kind of War": America's Global Strategy and the Truman Doctrine in Greece* (New York: Oxford University Press, 1989).

11. Inverchapel to Bevin, January 29, 1948, FO 371/68025/AN593, and May 5, 1948, FO 371/68014/AN1914, Public Record Office.

12. Dean Acheson, *Present at the Creation: My Years in the State Department* (New York: Norton, 1969), p. 375.

13. See, on this, J. Samuel Walker, "'No More Cold War': American Foreign Policy and the 1948 Soviet Peace Offensive," *Diplomatic History*, V(Winter, 1981), 75–91.

14. Geir Lundestad, "Empire by Invitation? The United States and Western Europe, 1945–1952," *Journal of Peace Research*, XXIII(September, 1986), 263–77; also Lundestad, *The American "Empire" and Other Studies of US Foreign Policy in a Comparative Perspective* (New York: Oxford University Press, 1990), pp. 54–62.

15. *The Journals of David E. Lilienthal: The Atomic Energy Years, 1945–1950* (New York: Harper & Row, 1964), p. 161.

16. The most detailed account is in the Central Intelligence Agency's own internal history of these developments, Arthur B. Darling, *The Central Intelligence Agency as Instrument of Government, to 1950* (University Park: Pennsylvania State University Press, 1990 [originally issued in 1953 and declassified in 1989]), pp. 245–81. See also John Ranelagh, *The Agency: The Rise and Decline of the CIA* (New York: Simon and Schuster, 1986), pp. 132–38; George F. Kennan, *Memoirs: 1950–1963* (Boston: Atlantic Little, Brown, 1972), pp. 202–3; and, for events in Italy, James Edward Miller, *The United States and Italy, 1940–1950: The Politics and Diplomacy of Stabilization* (Chapel Hill: University of North Carolina Press, 1986), pp. 243–49.

17. See Cord Meyer, *Facing Reality: From World Federalism to the CIA* (New York: Harper and Row, 1980); also Peter Coleman, *The Liberal Conspiracy: The Congress for Cultural Freedom and the Struggle for the Mind of Postwar Europe* (New York: Free Press, 1989).

18. George F. Kennan, *Memoirs: 1925–1950* (Boston: Little, Brown, 1967), pp. 406–14.

19. Kennan memorandum, "International Control of Atomic Energy," January 20,

1950, U.S. Department of State, *Foreign Relations of the United States [hereafter FRUS]: 1950* (Washington: Government Printing Office, 1977), I, 39.

20. We now know that the Russians had already begun work on a thermonuclear weapon at this time. See McGeorge Bundy, *Danger and Survival: Choices About the Bomb in the First Fifty Years* (New York: Random House, 1988), pp. 197–98.

21. Quoted in Gregg Herken, *The Winning Weapon: The Atomic Bomb in the Cold War, 1945–1950* (New York: Knopf, 1980), pp. 316–17, 321.

22. NSC-68, "United States Objectives and Programs for National Security," April 14, 1950, *FRUS: 1950* (Washington: Government Printing Office, 1977), I, 234–92. The quotations that follow are from pp. 238–44.

23. There are obvious echoes here to "just war" tradition. For a discussion, see Michael Walzer, *Just and Unjust Wars: A Moral Argument with Historical Illustrations* (New York: Basic Books, 1977); also James Turner Johnson, *Just War Tradition and the Restraint of War: A Moral and Historical Inquiry* (Princeton: Princeton University Press, 1981).

24. *The Federalist Papers* (New York: New American Library, 1961), p. 178.

25. Thomas Powers, *The Man Who Kept the Secrets: Richard Helms and the CIA* (New York: Knopf, 1979), is particularly good on the dilemmas, both moral and constitutional, raised by service in the intelligence establishment.

26. Eisenhower to Lewis Douglas, March 29, 1955, Dwight D. Eisenhower Papers, Whitman File, "DDE Diary," Box 6, "Mar. 55(1)," Dwight D. Eisenhower Library. Emphasis in the original. See also H. W. Brands, Jr., *Cold Warriors: Eisenhower's Generation and American Foreign Policy* (New York: Columbia University Press, 1988), pp. 48, 67.

27. Gaddis, *The Long Peace*, pp. 174–94. See also Chapter Four of this book.

28. See Charles R. Morris, *Iron Destinies, Lost Opportunities: The Arms Race Between the U.S.A. and the U.S.S.R., 1945–1987* (New York: Harper and Row, 1988), pp. 183–92.

29. For more on shifting official rationales for the American involvement in Vietnam, see John Lewis Gaddis, *Strategies of Containment: A Critical Appraisal of Postwar American National Security Policy* (New York: Oxford University Press, 1982), pp. 238–43.

30. A good discussion is D. Michael Shafer, *Deadly Paradigms: The Failure of U. S. Counterinsurgency Policy* (Princeton: Princeton University Press, 1988).

31. Powers, *The Man Who Kept the Secrets*, and Ranelagh, *The Agency*, provide the best accounts.

32. Note the tortured efforts of the Catholic bishops to wrestle with this question in *The Challenge of Peace: God's Promise and Our Response* (Washington: National Conference of Catholic Bishops, 1983).

33. It is worth noting that some strong critics of the Eisenhower "massive retaliation" strategy—notably Dean Acheson, Walt Rostow, and Henry Kissinger—would later support the war in Vietnam.

34. Gaddis, *Strategies of Containment*, pp. 174–75. See also Chapter Four of this book.

35. Robert W. Tucker, *The Radical Left and American Foreign Policy* (Baltimore: Johns Hopkins University Press, 1971), provides a succinct summary and evaluation of the "realist" and the "radical" positions on Vietnam.

36. Ole R. Holsti and James N. Rosenau, *American Leadership in World Affairs: Vietnam and the Breakdown of Consensus* (Boston: Allen and Unwin, 1984), documents this development.

37. Rex Harry Davis and Robert Crocker Good, eds., *Reinhold Niebuhr on Politics* (New York: Scribners, 1960), p. 65.

38. Barton Gellman, *Contending with Kennan: Toward a Philosophy of American Power* (New York: Praeger, 1984), pp. 64–65. As Gellman and many other critics have pointed out, it is difficult to discern a consistent Kennan position over the years on the relationship of morality to foreign policy. Kennan himself admitted this in a response to Gellman, "Morality and Foreign Policy," *Foreign Affairs*, LXIV(Winter, 1985/86), 205. But I am not aware of any point in Kennan's career at which he would have endorsed disorder as the path to justice.

39. Henry A. Kissinger, *American Foreign Policy*, 3rd ed. (New York: Norton, 1977), pp. 218–19; Henry A. Kissinger, *White House Years* (Boston: Little, Brown, 1979), p. 55.

40. Quoted in Gaddis Smith, *Morality, Reason, and Power: American Diplomacy in the Carter Years* (New York: Hill and Wang, 1986), p. 28. Carter frequently quoted Niebuhr during the presidential campaign, but as Smith points out, it is not at all clear that he ever grasped Niebuhr's point about the need for those in government to do evil at times to accomplish good.

41. Raymond L. Garthoff, *Detente and Confrontation: American-Soviet Relations from Nixon to Reagan* (Washington: Brookings Institution, 1985), pp. 1005–8.

42. Daniel Patrick Moynihan, *On the Law of Nations* (Cambridge, Massachusetts: Harvard University Press, 1990), p. 160. For the Helsinki Conference, see Garthoff, *Detente and Confrontation*, pp. 473–79.

43. See Gerald R. Ford, *A Time to Heal* (New York: Harper and Row, 1979), p. 398.

44. For a good summary of the difficulties, see Geoffrey Hosking, *The Awakening of the Soviet Union* (Cambridge, Massachusetts: Harvard University Press, 1990), pp. 1–18.

45. State of the Union Address, February 6, 1985, *Public Papers of the Presidents of the United States: Ronald Reagan, 1985* (Washington: Government Printing Office, 1987), p. 135. For the origins—and amorphousness—of the Reagan Doctrine, see Lou Cannon, *President Reagan: The Role of a Lifetime* (New York: Simon and Schuster, 1991), pp. 369–70.

46. Ronald Reagan, *National Security Strategy of the United States* (Washington: Government Printing Office, 1987), p. 5.

47. Martin Anderson, *Revolution* (New York: Harcourt Brace Jovanovich, 1988), pp. 63–73. There was an interesting parallel, on this point, between Reagan's views and those of George Kennan, who in 1981 called for a 50 precent reduction in strategic arms. See George F. Kennan, *The Nuclear Delusion: Soviet-American Relations in the Atomic Age* (New York: Pantheon, 1982), pp. 174–82.

48. Ronald Reagan, *An American Life* (New York: Simon and Schuster, 1990), p. 547. See also Cannon, *President Reagan*, pp. 319–22.

49. See Chapter Two of this book.

50. Coral Bell, *The Reagan Paradox: American Foreign Policy in the 1980s* (New Brunswick: Rutgers University Press, 1989), pp. 66–67. See also Reagan, *An American Life*, p. 294; and Cannon, *President Reagan*, pp. 298–300.

51. Although Coral Bell points out that the Reagan Doctrine— perhaps in another example of expediency becoming conviction—did come to be applied against authoritarians on the right as well as on the left: witness Washington's role in unseating Ferdinand Marcos in the Philippines, and "Baby Doc" Duvalier in Haiti in 1986 [*The Reagan Paradox*, pp. 105–8, 114–15].

52. Joseph E. Persico, *Casey: From the OSS to the CIA* (New York: Viking, 1990), pp. 371–80.

53. Bell, *The Reagan Paradox*, p. 150. See also the "Roundtable Discussion" in David E. Kyvig, ed., *Reagan and the World* (New York: Greenwood Press, 1990), pp. 151–81.

54. As Schlesinger acknowledges. See *The Cycles of American History*, pp. 293–96.

55. Kennan to State Department, February 22, 1946, *FRUS: 1946* (Washington: Government Printing Office, 1969), VI, 709.

56. George Orwell, *1984* (New York: Harcourt, Brace, 1949).

FOUR
The Unexpected John Foster Dulles

This essay was originally published in a slightly different form in Richard H. Immerman, ed., *John Foster Dulles and the Diplomacy of the Cold War* (Princeton: Princeton University Press, 1990), pp. 47–77, and is included here with the permission of the Princeton University Press. I wish to thank Richard Immerman and Fred Greenstein for their helpful comments on earlier drafts.

1. The cartoons in question are reproduced in Townsend Hoopes, *The Devil and John Foster Dulles* (Boston: Atlantic Little, Brown, 1973), pp. 292, 309, 416, 447.

2. Louis L. Gerson, *John Foster Dulles* (New York: Cooper Square, 1968); Michael A. Guhin, *John Foster Dulles: A Statesman and His Times* (New York: Columbia University Press, 1972).

3. Hoopes, *The Devil and John Foster Dulles*, passim.

4. Ronald W. Pruessen, *John Foster Dulles: The Road to Power* (New York: Free Press, 1982).

5. Immerman, ed., *John Foster Dulles and the Diplomacy of the Cold War*, comes closest.

6. See, for example, Fred I. Greenstein, *The Hidden-Hand Presidency: Eisenhower as Leader* (New York: Basic Books, 1982), pp. 87–90; also Richard A. Melanson and David Mayers, eds., *Reevaluating Eisenhower: American Foreign Policy in the Fifties* (Urbana: University of Illinois Press, 1987), especially pp. 1–10.

7. For an excellent example of how "unexpected" or "hidden" characteristics can affect leadership, see Greenstein, *The Hidden-Hand Presidency*, passim.

8. John Foster Dulles, "A Policy of Boldness," *Life*, XXXII(May 19, 1952), 146–60.

9. See, on this point, John Lewis Gaddis, *The Long Peace: Inquiries Into the History of the Cold War* (New York: Oxford University Press, 1987), pp. 124–29.

10. Minutes, National Security Council meeting of February 11, 1953, U. S. Department of State, *Foreign Relations of the United States* [hereafter *FRUS*]: *1952–54* (Washington: Government Printing Office, 1984), XV, 770. See also the NSC minutes for October 7, 1953, *ibid.*, II, 533.

11. Minutes, NSC meeting of March 31, 1953, *ibid.*, pp. 265–66.

12. Minutes, NSC meeting, June 5, 1953, *ibid.*, pp. 374–75.

13. Dulles to Eisenhower, September 6, 1953, *ibid.*, pp. 458–59.

14. Phyllis D. Bernau memorandum of Dulles-Strauss telephone conversation, March 29, 1954, *ibid.*, pp. 1379–80.

15. Minutes, NSC meeting, May 16, 1954, *ibid.*, pp. 1424–28. Eisenhower in this case appeared to agree with Dulles's strongly expressed views: he commented during the course of the meeting that "everybody seems to think that we're skunks, saber-rattlers and warmongers." [*Ibid.*, p. 1428].

16. Livingston Merchant to Robert R. Bowie, May 25, 1954, *ibid.*, p. 1448; minutes, NSC meeting, May 27, 1954, *ibid*, pp. 1453–54; Dulles to James S. Lay, Jr., June 23, 1954, *ibid.*, pp. 1463–67.

17. Minutes, NSC meeting, June 23, 1954, *ibid.*, pp. 1468–69. Eisenhower accepted the conclusions upon which Dulles and the committee he headed on this subject had agreed, but dissented vigorously from the proposition that nuclear abolition required total disarmament: "if he knew any way to abolish atomic weapons which would ensure the certainty that they would be abolished, he would be the very first to endorse it, regardless of general disarmament." Surely the United States, with its vast resources, could "whip the Soviet Union in any kind of war that had been fought in the past or any other kind of war than an atomic war." The difficulty was not morality, the President insisted: "the real thing was that the advantage of surprise almost seemed the decisive factor in an atomic war, and we should do anything we could to remove this factor." [*Ibid.*, p. 1469].

18. Minutes, NSC meeting, June 24, 1954, *ibid.*, pp. 694–95.

19. Minutes, NSC meeting, August 5, 1954, *ibid.*, pp. 706–7. Eisenhower qualified Dulles's generalization by pointing out that the Russians had, from time to time, boasted that the United States no longer had an atomic monopoly.

20. Minutes, NSC meeting, August 12, 1954, *ibid.*, p. 1485.

21. Speech to the Council on Foreign Relations, January 12, 1954, *Department of State Bulletin* [hereafter *DSB*], XXX(January 25, 1954), 108.

22. John Foster Dulles, "Policy for Security and Peace," *Foreign Affairs*, XXXII(April, 1954), 353–64.

23. Dulles statement to closed NATO ministerial meeting, Paris, April 23, 1954, *FRUS: 1952–54*, V, 512.

24. "Basic National Security Policy (Suggestions of the Secretary of State)," November 15, 1954, *ibid.*, II, 772–75.

25. Minutes, NSC meeting, November 24, 1954, *ibid.*, pp. 789–90, 794–95.

26. Minutes, NSC meeting, December 21, 1954, *ibid*, pp. 833–836. Issuing ultimata to the Russians to refrain from further attempts to expand their influence beyond their borders, Dulles argued, would probably also alienate the allies; moreover, "the remaining areas into which the Soviets could expand their powers were not areas—except perhaps in the case of the Middle East—whose acquisition would notably increase the actual power of the Soviet bloc, although the prestige of the latter might gain." The NATO area was secure, as was Latin America. The situation in the Pacific was "pretty well in hand," except for Indonesia. South and Southeast Asia remained areas of concern, but the countries in question "lie so close to the orbit of the USSR and China, and all of the countries in question are so weak themselves, that they cannot but pose very serious problems to us.... Yet if one looked at the other side of the picture, these countries are not really of great significance to us, other than from the point of view of prestige, except that they must be regarded as staging grounds for further forward thrusts by the Communist powers." Only the Middle East and Indonesia remained as areas both vulnerable to Soviet expansion and vital to the interests of the United States. [*Ibid.*]

27. Howard Meyers notes, Dulles conversation with State Department advisers, December 29, 1954, *ibid.*, pp. 1585–86. It is worth noting that Eisenhower had made a similar argument in a meeting with Dulles and other advisers on January 16, 1954. [*Ibid.*, pp. 1342–43].

28. Dulles memorandum of conversation with Eisenhower, December 26, 1955, John Foster Dulles Papers, White House memoranda, Box 3, "Meetings with the President, 1955 (1)," Dwight D. Eisenhower Library. Eisenhower added that perhaps the sequence should be reversed: the Russians could be asked to give up the right of veto in the Security Council, and then if they refused, the forty-two nation group could be formed. [*Ibid.*]

29. Untitled Dulles memorandum, January 28, 1956, *ibid.*, Subject series, Box 4, "Papers on Nuclear Weapons 1/56 (1)."

30. Dulles memorandum of conversation with Eisenhower, December 3, 1956, *ibid.*, White House memoranda, Box 4, "Meetings with the President, August-December, 1956 (2)."

31. Dulles memorandum of conversation with Eisenhower, November 7, 1957, *ibid.*, Box 5, "Meetings with the President, 1957 (2)."

32. Dulles memorandum of conversation with Eisenhower, April 1, 1958, *ibid.*, Box 6. I am indebted to Fred Greenstein for this reference.

33. Dulles radio-television address, January 27, 1953, *DSB*, XXVIII (February 9, 1953), 211–13.

34. Dulles speech at Colgate University, July 7, 1950, *ibid.*, XXIV(July 17, 1950), 88.

35. Andrew H. Berding, *Dulles on Diplomacy* (Princeton: Princeton University Press, 1965), pp. 7–8, 30–31.

36. Dulles speech at Geneva Conference on Korea, April 28, 1954, *DSB*, XXX(May 10, 1954), 706.

37. Dulles radio-television address, January 27, 1953, *DSB*, XXVIII (February 9, 1953), 215–16. The term "gastronomic" imagery was first suggested to me by Professor John F. Zeugner of Worcester Polytechnic Institute.

38. Untitled memorandum, June 16, 1949, John Foster Dulles Papers, Box 40, "Council of Foreign Ministers" folder, Seeley Mudd Library, Princeton University.

39. Dulles to Homer Ferguson, June 28, 1949, *ibid.*, Box 41, "Ferguson" folder.

40. Dulles to Acheson, November 30, 1950, *ibid.*, Box 48, "Korea" folder.

41. For details, see Gaddis, *The Long Peace*, pp. 170–73.

42. Dulles to Bowles, March 25, 1952, Dulles Papers (Princeton), Box 58, "Bowles" folder. See also the transcript of a Dulles interview on "Meet the Press," February 10, 1952, as quoted in David Allan Mayers, *Cracking the Monolith: U. S. Policy Against the Sino-Soviet Alliance, 1949–1955* (Baton Rouge: Louisiana State University Press, 1986), p. 119.

43. John Foster Dulles, *War or Peace* (New York: Macmillan, 1950), p. 242.

44. Minutes, NSC meeting, March 31, 1953, *FRUS: 1952–54*, II, 267–68.

45. U. S. delegation minutes, Eisenhower-Churchill-Bidault meeting, Bermuda, December 7, 1953, *ibid.*, V, 1809–14. See also NSC 166/1, approved by Eisenhower on November 6, 1953, which noted: "As the inevitable differences in interest, viewpoint, or timing of actions develop between the Russians and the Chinese; as the Chinese tend to become importunate in their demands for Russian assistance or support; or as the role of the Chinese as viceregents for international communism in the Far East becomes too independent and self reliant—there will be strong temptation for the Russians to attempt to move in the direction of greater disciplinary control over the

Chinese Communists. If the time ever comes when the Russians feel impelled to contest with the Chinese Communist leaders for primacy in the domestic apparatus of control of the Chinese regime, the alliance will be critically endangered. For . . . the Chinese Communist leaders are Chinese as well as Communists." [NSC 166/1, "U. S. Policy Towards Communist China," November 6, 1953, *ibid.*, XIV, 281.]

46. See Hoopes, *The Devil and John Foster Dulles*, pp. 262–63, 268.

47. Dulles memorandum, September 12, 1954, *FRUS: 1952–54*, XIV, 612. During the previous summer, Dulles had received from Senator William F. Knowland information purporting to come from Beijing indicating that the Russians were less than enthusiastic about supporting the Chinese if they got into a war with the United States, and that the Chinese had expressed "mild resentment" over this. ["Information from Peiping Concerning the Geneva Conference," attached to Dulles to Knowland, June 30, 1954, Dulles Papers (Princeton), Box 79, "China, People's Republic" folder. Early in 1955, U. N. Secretary-General Dag Hammarskjöld, with Washington's approval, invited representatives from the PRC to participate in a Security Council debate on the offshore islands crisis, but the Chinese refused to do so. [Editorial notes, *FRUS: 1955–57*, II, 178–79, 202–3.]

48. Minutes, NSC meeting, November 24, 1954, *FRUS: 1952–54*, II, 789.

49. Livingston Merchant notes, Dulles conversation with Sir Roger Makins, February 7, 1955, *FRUS: 1955–57*, II, 236.

50. Walter McConaughy notes, Dulles-Yeh conversation, February 10, 1955, *ibid.*, pp. 253–58. See also Dulles memoranda of conversations with Chiang Kai-shek, March 4, 1955, and with Australian Prime Minister Robert Menzies, March 14, 1955, *ibid.*, pp. 323, 369.

51. *Ibid.*, p. 254.

52. Minutes, NSC meeting, August 18, 1954, *FRUS: 1952–54*, XIV, 534. Dulles had noted in an earlier NSC meeting on August 5 that "there should be long-range plans for a rollback in the satellites, in Iran, etc., but . . . these plans would have to be very long-range indeed." [*Ibid*, II, 711.]

53. Memorandum, Dulles-Lloyd conversation, January 31, 1956, *FRUS: 1955–57*, III, 292. See also Dulles's speech at San Francisco, June 28, 1957, *ibid.*, p. 564.

54. See Kenneth T. Young, *Negotiating with the Chinese Communists: The United States Experience, 1953–1967* (New York: McGraw-Hill, 1968), pp. 91–128.

55. Dulles-Yeh conversation, February 10, 1955, *ibid.*, II, 258.

56. Minutes, NSC meeting, December 21, 1954, *ibid.*, p. 836. Dulles records himself the following day as having told the President that, "in my opinion, the possibilities of change which would be in the interest of the United States would come from either (a) the traditional tendency of the Chinese to be individualistic or (b) the traditional Chinese dislike of foreigners which was bound in the long run to impair relations with Russia." Dulles notes Eisenhower as responding that "under present conditions, no change of our attitude was possible, but that if the Chinese Communists met certain quite obvious requirements, then the situation might be different." [Dulles memorandum of conversation with Eisenhower, December 22, 1954, *FRUS: 1952–54*, XIV, 1048].

57. See John Ranelagh, *The Agency: The Rise and Decline of the CIA* (New York: Simon and Schuster, 1986), pp. 285–88.

58. "Notes for Foreign Relations Committee Appearance," June 26, 1956, Dulles Papers (Princeton), Box 109, "Soviet Union" folder.

59. Dulles memorandum of conversation with Eisenhower, July 13, 1956, Dulles

Papers (Eisenhower Library), White House Memoranda, Box 4, "Meetings with the President, January-July, 1956 (1)."

60. Dulles to Eisenhower, September 9, 1956, *ibid.*, Box 3, "Correspondence-General 1956 (2)."

61. Dulles memorandum of conversation with Eisenhower, September 17, 1956, *ibid.*, Box 4, "Meetings with the President, August-December, 1956 (5)." Dulles made these points in the context of discussing Soviet-Egyptian relations during the Suez Canal crisis.

62. Dulles memorandum of conversation with Eisenhower, December 15, 1956, *ibid.*, Box 4, "Meetings with the President, August-December, 1956 (2)."

63. Dulles memorandum of conversation with Eisenhower, December 22, 1956, *ibid.*, Box 4, "Meetings with the President, August-December, 1956 (1)."

64. State Department transcript, Dulles interview with William D. Clark of British Independent Television, October 23, 1958, Dulles Papers (Princeton), Box 127, "Deterrent Strategy" folder.

65. Dulles speech at San Francisco, December 4, 1958, *ibid.*, Box 132, "Massive Retaliation" folder.

66. Undated speech fragment, *ibid.*, Box 143, "Soviet Union" folder.

67. Hoopes, *The Devil and John Foster Dulles*, p. 171.

68. Dulles remarks to New York State Republican dinner, New York, May 7, 1953, *DSB*, XXVIII(May 18, 1953), 707.

69. Dulles undated draft, "Estimate of Prospects of Soviet Union Achieving Its Goals," Dulles Papers (Princeton), Box 89, "Atomic Energy" folder.

70. Dulles memorandum, September 6, 1953, *FRUS: 1952–54*, II, 459.

71. See George F. Kennan, *Memoirs: 1950–1963* (Boston: Atlantic Little, Brown, 1972), pp. 229–61. Kennan had, of course, put forward a similar proposal within the government in 1948–49, known as "Program A." See his *Memoirs: 1925–1950* (Boston: Atlantic Little, Brown, 1967), pp. 421–26; also PPS 37/1, "Position To Be Taken by the U. S. at a CFM Meeting," November 15, 1948, *FRUS: 1948*, II, 1320–38.

72. Dulles memorandum, September 6, 1953, *FRUS: 1952–54*, II, 459. Dulles brought up the example of Finland as a model for future Soviet-East European relations several months later in a conversation with Churchill and Eden, but Eden pointed out that "considerable autonomy was permissible to Finland from Russia because Finland was 'the road to nowhere,' but the satellite countries were 'the road to somewhere else'." [Dulles memorandum of conversation with Churchill and Eden, April 12, 1954, Dulles Papers (Eisenhower Library), White House Memoranda, Box 1, "Meetings with the President 1954 (4)"].

73. Eisenhower to Dulles, September 8, 1953, *FRUS: 1952–54*, II, 460.

74. Dulles to Bowie, September 8, 1953, Dulles Papers (Eisenhower Library), White House Memoranda, Box 1, "Correspondence 1953 (2)."

75. See C. D. Jackson to Eisenhower, October 2, 1953, *FRUS: 1952–54*, II, 1224–26.

76. "Summary of Discussion of State Draft of Part Two of Presidential Speech," October 19, 1953, *ibid.*, p. 1228.

77. Dulles to Eisenhower, October 23, 1953, *ibid.*, p. 1234.

78. Dulles to Eisenhower, May 12, 1954, Dulles Papers (Eisenhower Library), White House Memoranda, Box 1, "Correspondence 1954 (2)." This memorandum was written in reply to one from Eisenhower, enclosing—as was often the President's

habit—an unsigned proposal for Dulles's comments, in this case one advocating a "really grand effort to achieve whole peace for the whole world." The proposed package included a mutual withdrawal of Soviet and American forces in Europe, an agreement on free elections in Korea and Indochina, and a worldwide reduction in military forces. [Eisenhower to Dulles, May 6, 1954, *ibid.*]

79. Stephen E. Ambrose, *Eisenhower: The President* (New York: Simon and Schuster, 1984), p. 132.

80. Minutes, NSC meeting, October 7, 1953, *FRUS: 1952–54*, II, 529–30. Although it is worth noting that Eisenhower, somewhat surprised by Dulles's tone, observed "with a smile" that "this was not the way that the Secretary of State usually talked to him about this problem." [*Ibid.*, p. 529]. No one had the right to assume, Dulles argued in a May, 1954, public address, "that he sees the future so clearly that he is justified in concluding either that war is inevitable or that methods of conciliation are futile. Efforts for honorable peace are required out of a decent respect for the opinion of mankind." [Dulles speech at Williamsburg, Virginia, May 15, 1954, *DSB*, XXX(May 24, 1954), 780]. Negotiations had the additional advantage, the Secretary of State noted pragmatically, that "they clarify the issues."

81. Minutes, NSC meeting, December 21, 1954, *FRUS: 1952–54*, II, 842–43. It had been true, Dulles added, that the State Department had been reluctant to participate in the Berlin foreign ministers' conference or in the Geneva conference on Korea and Indochina, held earlier in the year. But it had done so in order to secure allied cooperation in the rearmament of Germany, and because "world opinion demanded that the United States participate in these negotiations with the Communists." [*Ibid.*, p. 844].

82. Dulles remarks at Advertising Club of New York, March 31, 1955, *DSB*, XXXII(April 4, 1955), 552.

83. Dulles press conference, April 5, 1955, *ibid.*, XXXII(April 18, 1955), 642.

84. Dulles press conference, July 26, 1955, *ibid.*, XXXIII(August 8, 1955), 218.

85. Dulles press conference, August 10, 1955, *ibid.*, XXXIII(August 22, 1955), 299.

86. Dulles speech to the American Legion, Miami, October 10, 1955, *ibid.*, XXXIII(October 24, 1955), 639. See also Dulles's memorandum of a conversation with Eisenhower, October 11, 1955, Dulles Papers (Eisenhower Library), White House Memoranda, Box 3, "Meetings with the President 1955 (2)."

87. Minutes, NSC meeting, February 7, 1956, Dwight D. Eisenhower Papers, Ann Whitman File, NSC Series, Box 7, Dwight D. Eisenhower Library.

88. Dulles radio-television address, July 22, 1957, *DSB*, XXVII(August 12, 1957), 267–72.

89. Dulles press conference, April 24, 1956, *DSB*, XXXIV(May 7, 1956), 749. See also Dulles's press conference of May 15, 1956, *ibid.*, (May 28, 1956), 885.

90. Dulles to Eisenhower, May 18, 1956, Dulles Papers (Eisenhower Library), White House Memoranda, Box 3, "Correspondence-General 1956 (4)."

91. Dulles press conference, July 17, 1957, *DSB*, XXXVII(August 5, 1957), 228–29. Dulles did note, during a Cabinet meeting several months later, that in a recent hard-line speech Khrushchev had seemed to be "moving in two opposite directions at the same time," but Ambassador Llewellyn Thompson speculated that "much of the fanatical was done by Khrushchev because of being under pressure internally." [Cabinet Minutes, February 7, 1958, Eisenhower Papers, Whitman File, DDE Diary, Box 18, "Staff Notes, February, 1958."]

92. Dulles to Eisenhower, March 25, 1958, Dulles Papers (Eisenhower Library), White House Memoranda, Box 6, "Correspondence-General 1958 (6)."

93. Dulles to Adenauer, June 30, 1958, Dulles Papers (Princeton), Box 125, "Atomic weapons (1)."

94. Dulles BBC interview, December 3, 1957, *DSB*, XXXVII(December 23, 1957), 988.

95. See note 93.

96. Dulles memorandum of conversation with Eisenhower, August 3, 1958, Dulles Papers (Eisenhower Library), White House Memoranda, Box 7, "Meetings with the President, July-December, 1958 (9)."

97. Minutes, Bipartisan Congressional Meeting, January 5, 1959, Eisenhower Papers, Whitman File, DDE Diary, Box 24, "Staff Notes, January, 1959 (2)."

98. Eisenhower dictated note, *ibid.*, Box 17, "DDE Diary January, 1958."

99. Pruessen, *John Foster Dulles*, p. xii.

100. See Greenstein, *The Hidden-Hand Presidency*, *passim*.

101. See, on this point, Gaddis, *Strategies of Containment*, pp. 174–75.

102. See David Alan Rosenberg, "The Origins of Overkill: Nuclear Weapons and American Strategy, 1945–1960," *International Security*, VII(Spring, 1983), 3–71.

103. For the "peak danger" concept, see Gaddis, *Strategies of Containment*, pp. 96–97.

FIVE
Intelligence, Espionage, and Cold War History

This essay originally appeared in a different form in *Diplomatic History*, XIII(Spring, 1989), 191–212, and is included in this collection by permission of Scholarly Resources Inc. I would like to thank Alan Booth and D. C. Watt for their critical comments on that earlier version.

1. See—by no means an exhaustive list—Sir John Masterman, *The Double-Cross System in the War of 1939–1945* (New Haven: Yale University Press, 1972); F. W. Winterbotham, *The Ultra Secret* (New York: Harper and Row, 1974); William Stephenson, *A Man Called Intrepid: The Secret War* (New York: Harcourt Brace Jovanovich, 1976); R. V. Jones, *The Wizard War: British Scientific Intelligence, 1939–1945* (New York: Coward, McCann and Geoghegan, 1978); Ralph F. Bennett, *Ultra in the West: The Normandy Campaign* (London: Hutchinson, 1979); Ronald Lewin, *Ultra Goes to War: The First Account of World War II's Greatest Secret Based on Official Documents* (New York: McGraw-Hill, 1979); F. H. Hinsley, *et al.*, *British Intelligence in the Second World War: Its Influence on Strategy and Operations*, 3 vols. (London: H. M. S. O., 1979–1988); Peter Calvocoressi, *Top Secret Ultra* (New York: Pantheon, 1980); Stephen E. Ambrose and Richard H. Immerman, *Ike's Spies: Eisenhower and the Espionage Establishment* (Garden City, N. Y.: Doubleday, 1981); Anthony Cave Brown, *The Last Hero: Wild Bill Donovan* (New York: Random House, 1982) and *Bodyguard of Lies* (New York: Harper & Row, 1985); Ronald Lewin, *The American Magic: Codes, Ciphers, and the Defeat of Japan* (New York: Farrar Straus Giroux, 1982); Bradley F. Smith, *The Shadow Warriors: O.S.S. and the Origins of the C.I.A.* (New York: Basic Books, 1983); Edwin T. Layton, with Roger Pineau and John Costello, *"And I Was There": Pearl Harbor and Midway—Breaking the Secrets* (New York: Morrow, 1985); Barry M. Katz, *Foreign Intelligence: Research and Analysis in the Office of Strategic Services, 1942–1945* (Cambridge: Harvard University Press, 1989);

also special issues on "Intelligence Services during the Second World War," *Journal of Contemporary History*, XXII(April and October, 1987).

2. For example, Ernest R. May, ed., *Knowing One's Enemies: Intelligence Assessment Before the Two World Wars* (Princeton: Princeton University Press, 1984); Christopher Andrew, *Her Majesty's Secret Service: The Making of the British Intelligence Community* (New York: Viking, 1985); Wesley K. Wark, *The Ultimate Enemy: British Intelligence and Nazi Germany, 1933–1939* (Ithaca: Cornell University Press, 1985); Philip J. Knightly, *The Second Oldest Profession* (New York: Norton, 1987). Nor should one neglect a classic book on this subject whose appearance anticipated the upsurge of interest in intelligence studies, David Kahn, *The Codebreakers: The Story of Secret Writing* (New York: Macmillan, 1967). Among the journals now exclusively devoted to this field are the *Foreign Intelligence Literary Scene, Intelligence and National Security, Intelligence Quarterly, Cryptologia*, and the *International Journal of Intelligence and Counterintelligence*. My Ohio University colleague Alan Booth has for some years now offered a well-subscribed course, "Espionage and History."

3. Smith, *The Shadow Warriors*, pp. 402–7. For a more optimistic view of the possibilities, see D. Cameron Watt, "Intelligence and the Historian," *Diplomatic History*, XIV(Spring, 1990), 199–204.

4. The Central Intelligence Agency does now have a Historical Review Program charged with the task of reviewing for declassification historically significant records. This program has resulted in the release of two sanitized internal histories of the Agency, Arthur B. Darling, *The Central Intelligence Agency: An Instrument of Government, to 1950* (Washington: Central Intelligence Agency, declassified 1989), and Ludwell Lee Montague, *General Walter Bedell Smith as Director of Central Intelligence, October, 1950-February, 1953* (Washington: Central Intelligence Agency, declassified 1990). These volumes have since been published by the Pennsylvania State University Press. It is not yet clear, though, whether the guidelines under which this program operates will allow the release of documentary material comparable to what is already available on the OSS.

5. A point made with great force by Roberta Wohlstetter in her pioneering work, *Pearl Harbor: Warning and Decision* (Stanford: Stanford University Press, 1962).

6. Kahn, *The Codebreakers*, pp. 650–54.

7. See Brown, *The Last Hero*, pp. 417–18; and Anthony Glees, *The Secrets of the Service: A Story of Soviet Subversion of Western Intelligence* (New York: Carroll and Graf, 1987), pp. 247–52. It is interesting to note that where information about the Russians could be gleaned from ULTRA or MAGIC—in the form of intercepted German or Japanese reports about the Soviet Union—these were carefully deciphered. See Lewin, *The American Magic*, p. 238.

8. Jeffrey Richelson, *American Espionage and the Soviet Target* (New York: Morrow, 1987), pp. 43–45, 196.

9. Brown, *The Last Hero*, pp. 417, 419.

10. Glees, *The Secrets of the Service*, p. 246.

11. Martin Gilbert, *Winston Churchill: Finest Hour, 1939–1941* (Boston: Houghton Mifflin, 1983), p. 1209. See also Robert Chadwell Williams, *Klaus Fuchs, Atom Spy* (Cambridge: Harvard University Press, 1987), pp. 56–59. As Williams points out, the Russians would, of course, through their spy, Kim Philby, have had some idea about the source of this information. See also Christopher Andrew and Oleg Gordievsky, *KGB: The Inside Story* (New York: HarperCollins, 1990), pp. 302–6, in which Gordievsky, a KGB defector who had access to that organization's historical archives,

emphasizes the role of the alleged "fifth man" in the Cambridge spy ring, John Cairn-cross, in passing unadulterated ULTRA information to the Russians.

12. See Bradley F. Smith, "Sharing Ultra in World War II," *International Journal of Intelligence and Counterintelligence*, II(Spring, 1988), 59–72.

13. Brown, *The Last Hero*, pp. 422–25; Smith, *The Shadow Warriors*, pp. 330–59. See also Smith, "Sharing Ultra in World War II," p. 61; and John Ranelagh, *The Agency: The Rise and Decline of the CIA* (New York: Simon and Schuster, 1986), p. 71.

14. Glees, *Secrets of the Service*, p. 294; Richard Rhodes, *The Making of the Atomic Bomb* (New York: Simon and Schuster, 1986), pp. 525–38.

15. John R. Deane, *The Strange Alliance: The Story of Our Efforts at Wartime Co-operation with Russia* (New York: Viking, 1947). See also John Lewis Gaddis, *The United States and the Origins of the Cold War, 1941–1947* (New York: Columbia University Press, 1972), pp. 80–85.

16. Andrew and Gordievsky, *KGB*, pp. 225, 271. See Geoff Jukes, "The Soviets and Ultra," *Intelligence and National Security*, III(April, 1988), 233–47.

17. The most comprehensive account, on the British side, is Andrew Boyle, *The Fourth Man: The Definitive Account of Kim Philby, Guy Burgess, and Donald Maclean and Who Recruited Them to Spy for Russia* (New York: Dial/James Wade, 1979). For the American side, see Allen Weinstein, *Perjury: The Hiss-Chambers Case* (New York: Knopf, 1978), especially pp. 112–57. Andrew and Gordievsky, *KGB*, pp. 184–232, adds new information to the story from Soviet sources.

18. See Andrew, *Her Majesty's Secret Service*, p. 408. For such rudimentary efforts as the British did attempt prior to June, 1941, see *ibid.*, pp. 355–57; and Glees, *Secrets of the Service*, pp. 92–94, 280. Jonathan Haslam, *The Soviet Union and the Struggle for Collective Security in Europe, 1933–39* (New York: St. Martin's, 1984), p. 155, points out that, whatever the truth was, the Soviet government must have assumed foreign embassies in Moscow were running spies.

19. For speculation as to why the Russians enjoyed such success in Great Britain, see Glees, *Secrets of the Service*, pp. 132–33.

20. Williams, *Klaus Fuchs*, pp. 47, 60.

21. *Ibid.*, pp. 65–69. Roosevelt and Churchill had agreed in August, 1943, not to communicate information about the bomb "to third parties except by mutual consent." But it was not until September, 1944, that Roosevelt and Churchill, in rejecting a proposal from Niels Bohr, explicitly ruled out sharing information about the bomb with the Russians. [Rhodes, *The Making of the Atomic Bomb*, pp. 523–38]. For concern about Soviet espionage, see Martin J. Sherwin, *A World Destroyed: Hiroshima and the Origins of the Arms Race* (New York: Random House, 1987), pp. 62–63, 82–83, 100–2, 112.

22. Andrew and Gordievsky, *KGB*, pp. 299–300, 304–5, provides some informa-tion on what the British spies conveyed. David C. Martin, *Wilderness of Mirrors* (New York: Harper and Row, 1980), pp. 29–30, reports that the Russians abruptly contracted their North American espionage activities after the September, 1945, defection in Ottawa of Soviet embassy code-clerk Igor Guzenko. The flow of information from British sources apparently continued until the defection of Guy Burgess and Donald Maclean in 1951.

23. Martin, *Wilderness of Mirrors*, pp. 1–9; Weinstein, *Perjury*, pp. 328–31.

24. Glees, *Secrets of the Service*, pp. 279–88; Andrew and Gordievsky, *KGB*, p. 214.

25. J. Edgar Hoover to Harry Vaughan, October 19 and November 8, 1945, Harry S. Truman Papers, PSF, Box 167, "FBI-C" and Box 169, "FBI-S," Harry S. Truman

Library. See also Robert J. Lamphere and Tom Schachtman, *The FBI-KGB War: A Special Agent's Story* (New York: Random House, 1986), pp. 32–41; Weinstein, *Perjury*, pp. 356–57; and Ronald Radosh and Joyce Milton, *The Rosenberg File: A Search for the Truth* (New York: Holt, Rinehart and Winston, 1983), pp. 224–34.

26. Canadian Prime Minister William L. Mackenzie King's first reaction, on learning of Guzenko's defection, was that "we should be extremely careful in becoming a party to any course of action which would link the Government of Canada up with this matter in a manner which might cause Russia to feel that we had performed an unfriendly act. . . . For us to come into possession of a secret code book—of a Russian secret code book—would be a source of major complications." [J. W. Pickersgill and D. F. Foster, *The Mackenzie King Record: Volume 3, 1945–1946* (Toronto: University of Toronto Press, 1970), pp. 8, 10].

27. Lamphere and Schachtman, *The FBI-KGB War*, pp. 40–41; Weinstein, *Perjury*, pp. 357–59.

28. As late as September, 1946, Truman could order that a report on Soviet intentions prepared by his aide, Clark Clifford, not be circulated within the government even on a top-secret basis for fear of what the consequences of a leak might be. See John Lewis Gaddis, *The Long Peace: Inquiries into the History of the Cold War* (New York: Oxford University Press, 1987), p. 33.

29. Glees, *Secrets of the Service*, pp. 309–313; Anthony Cave Brown, *"C": The Secret Life of Sir Stewart Graham Menzies, Spymaster to Winston Churchill* (New York: Macmillan, 1987), pp. 692–94. Speculation about why nothing was done can be found in Chapman Pincher, *Too Secret Too Long* (New York: St. Martin's, 1984), and Peter Wright with Paul Greenglass, *Spycatcher: The Candid Autobiography of a Senior Intelligence Officer* (New York: Viking Penguin, 1987). For a critical evaluation of this argument, see Glees, *Secrets of the Service*, pp. 318–99.

30. For an estimate of the kind of material the British spies provided, see Andrew and Gordievsky, *KGB*, pp. 377, 389–95. A particularly ironic incident occurred in connection with a September 20, 1946, dispatch from the British Embassy in Washington to the Foreign Office on the subject of President Truman's firing of Henry Wallace. The dispatch, which among other things referred to "the President, the frail barque of whose judgment has been tossed hither and yon by the swirling eddies of circumstance," was sent by mistake *en clair*. T. A. D. Wilson-Young of the North American Department alerted the Embassy to this gaffe, noting: "We were rather worried at the possible uses to which the Russian and perhaps French Governments might have put your telegram. But we have since been relieved to learn that the telegram was not . . . automatically repeated *en clair*. As the result of the commendable initiative of the duty officer in charge of the Communications Department, it was encyphered before onward despatch." "We were indeed aghast when we saw what had happened," Embassy First Secretary D. D. Maclean contritely replied. [Foreign Office Records, FO 371/51626/AN2886, Public Record Office, London].

31. Soviet sources suggest that the Truman administration's decision to break up the OSS late in 1945 did seriously disrupt Moscow's intelligence-gathering operations inside the United States, since the KGB was much less successful in penetrating the CIA after its creation in 1947 than the NKVD had been in infiltrating its predecessor agency. [Andrew and Gordievsky, *KGB*, p. 367]. It is also the case that the Congress, in 1946, severely restricted the extent to which information on the production of atomic weapons could be shared with the British, and the Truman administration acquiesced in these restrictions. [Timothy J. Botti, *The Long Wait: The Forging of the*

Anglo-American Nuclear Alliance, 1945–1958 (Westport, Conn.: 1987), pp. 17–24.] These measures were taken, though, largely for domestic political reasons; there is no evidence that concern over lax security practices had anything to do with them.

32. Martin, *Wilderness of Mirrors*, pp. 39–43; Lamphere and Schachtman, *The FBI-KGB War*, pp. 126–227; Radosh and Milton, *The Rosenberg File*, pp. 7–9, 140–41; Williams, *Klaus Fuchs*, p. 6.

33. William Weisband, an employee of the Armed Forces Security Agency, apparently informed the Russians in 1948 that the United States was in the process of breaking these Soviet codes; moreover in 1949 Kim Philby was given access to the information derived from them. [Martin, *Wilderness of Mirrors*, pp. 43–44; Lamphere and Schachtman, *The FBI-KGB War*, pp. 130–31].

34. Glees, *Secrets of the Service*, pp. 307.

35. Martin, *Wilderness of Mirrors*, pp. 72–75; Ranelagh, *The Agency*, pp. 138–42.

36. William E. Burrows, *Deep Black: Space Espionage and National Security* (New York: Random House, 1986), pp. 55–69. See also John Prados, *The Soviet Estimate: U. S. Intelligence Analysis and Russian Military Strength* (New York: Dial Press, 1982), pp. 26–30; and Richelson, *American Espionage and the Soviet Target*, pp. 73–126.

37. Ranelagh, *The Agency*, pp. 137, 156–57, 226–28; Andrew and Gordievsky, *KGB*, pp. 383–90. See also John Prados, *Presidents' Secret Wars: CIA and Pentagon Covert Operations Since World War II* (New York: Morrow, 1986), pp. 30–60; and, on Albania, Nicholas Bethell, *Betrayed* (New York: Times Books, 1984). Vojtech Mastny has pointed out, though, that Stalin's 1949–50 purges of his own loyal supporters in Eastern Europe on false charges of treason may have been an indirect response to American covert operations there. ["Europe in US-USSR Relations: A Topical Legacy," *Problems of Communism*, XXXVII(January- February, 1988), 27–28].

38. See James Edward Miller, *The United States and Italy, 1940–1950: The Politics and Diplomacy of Stabilization* (Chapel Hill: University of North Carolina Press, 1986), pp. 243–49; Ranelagh, *The Agency*, pp. 137–38, 216, 248–52. Peter Coleman, *The Liberal Conspiracy: The Congress for Cultural Freedom and the Struggle for the Mind of Postwar Europe* (New York: Free Press, 1989), provides a more general account of early CIA activities in this area.

39. Early CIA assessments can most easily be sampled in the Harry S. Truman Papers, PSF, Boxes 255–57, but many have also been published in the U. S. Department of State series, *Foreign Relations of the United States* [hereafter *FRUS*]. Walter Laqueur, *A World of Secrets: The Uses and Limits of Intelligence* (New York: Basic Books, 1985), pp.110–22, provides the most comprehensive overall evaluation of this material; see also Matthew A. Evangelista, "Stalin's Postwar Army Reappraised," *International Security*, VII(Winter, 1982/1983), 110–138. For the early estimate-making process, see Prados, *The Soviet Estimate* pp. 4–14; and Lawrence Freedman, *U. S. Intelligence and the Soviet Strategic Threat*, 2nd ed. (Princeton: Princeton University Press, 1986), pp. 30–32.

40. Ranelagh, *The Agency*, pp. 186–88; Prados, *The Soviet Estimate*, pp. 19–20; Robert M. Blum, "Surprised by Tito: The Anatomy of an Intelligence Failure," *Diplomatic History*, XII(Winter, 1988), 39–57.

41. The point is made, in a more general way, by former FBI agent Robert Lamphere in his useful memoir, *The FBI-KGB War*, pp. 136–37, 201; see also Andrew and Gordievsky, *KGB*, pp. 380–81.

42. These books are all cited in the notes above.

43. Chapman Pincher's *Too Secret Too Long* and Peter Wright's *Spycatcher* set off major controversies when they were published in Great Britain. See Watt, "Intelligence and the Historian," pp. 203–4.

44. Robin W. Winks, *Cloak and Gown: Scholars in the Secret War, 1939–1961* (New York: Morrow, 1987), p. 63. Recent research suggests that the rumor about Hitler was Soviet disinformation, the purpose of which remains unclear. See Glees, *Secrets of the Service*, p. 292.

45. One can get some sense of the unease that comes with such a revelation by examining the agitated marginal markings someone in the White House—it is not clear who—made on FBI Director J. Edgar Hoover's initial report on what Donald Maclean and Guy Burgess might have known. [Hoover to Sidney W. Souers, June 18, 1951, Truman Papers, Box 169, "FBI-S].

46. Laqueur, *A World of Secrets*, pp. 99–100. For an interesting example of what the report of a "mole" to his "handlers" might look like—one that suggests something of the difficulties an analyst might encounter in making sense of such information— see Weinstein, *Perjury*, p. 239.

47. Roy A. Medvedev, *Let History Judge: The Origins and Consequences of Stalinism*, rev. and expanded ed., translated by George Shriver (New York: Columbia University Press, 1989), pp. 735–47; Adam Ulam, *Stalin: The Man and His Era* (New York: Viking, 1973), pp. 532–38. See also Kahn, *The Codebreakers*, pp. 655, 659; and John Erickson, "Threat Identification and Strategic Appraisal by the Soviet Union, 1930–1941," in May, ed., *Knowing One's Enemies*, p. 420.

48. Milovan Djilas, *Conversations with Stalin*, translated by Michael B. Petrovich (New York: Harcourt Brace and World, 1962), p. 73. William Taubman has commented, with regard to Stalin's view of his wartime allies, that "[t]o one accustomed to Kremlin politics, apparent generosity meant either deviousness or infirmity or both." [*Stalin's American Policy: From Entente to Detente to Cold War* (New York: Norton, 1982), p. 32.]

49. John Russell to Paul Mason, October 2, 1952, Foreign Office Records, FO 371/100826/NS1023/29. See also H. A. F. Hohler to P. F. Grey, December 15, 1952, *ibid.*, FO 371/100826/NS1023/34.

50. Masterman, *The Double-Cross System*, *passim*.

51. But see Brown, "C", pp. 694–712, for speculation that Philby may have been run as an unwitting double-agent.

52. The possibility is made at least plausible by fragmentary evidence that the Americans, at least, by 1949, were in fact funneling disinformation to the Russians. See Alan Kirk to Dean Acheson, October 1, 1949, *FRUS: 1949*, V, 147.

53. It is interesting to note that, even with the relatively full information Klaus Fuchs provided on the atomic bomb, Stalin did not order full-scale bomb development until after Truman had informed him of the successful Trinity test in July, 1945. See David Holloway, *The Soviet Union and the Arms Race* (New Haven: Yale University Press, 1983), pp. 19–20.

54. Kahn, *The Codebreakers*, p. 638; Weinstein, *Perjury*, pp. 132–55. Allegations have also been made that some documents compromised in 1940 by a code-clerk in the American Embassy in London may have found their way to the Russians. See Warren F. Kimball and Bruce Bartlett, "Roosevelt and Prewar Commitments to Churchill: The Tyler Kent Affair," *Diplomatic History*, V(Fall, 1981), 296n.

55. For a quick overview, see John Lewis Gaddis, *Russia, the Soviet Union, and the United States: An Interpretive History*, 2nd ed. (New York: McGraw-Hill, 1990),

pp. 159–67. Roosevelt's statement about withdrawing troops from Europe is in *FRUS: The Conferences at Malta and Yalta, 1945* (Washington: Government Printing Office, 1955), p. 617. It has become increasingly evident with the passage of time that Churchill's hopes for postwar cooperation with the Russians were much greater than he implies in his wartime memoirs. See, for example, John Colville, *The Fringes of Power: 10 Downing Street Diaries, 1939–1955* (New York: Norton, 1985), p. 593.

56. For Roosevelt's peculiar approach to management, see William E. Leuchtenburg, "Franklin D. Roosevelt: The First Modern President," in Fred I. Greenstein, ed., *Leadership in the Modern Presidency* (Cambridge: Harvard University Press, 1988), pp. 28–30.

57. Glees, *The Secrets of the Service*, pp. 200–203.

58. Vojtech Mastny, *Russia's Road to the Cold War: Diplomacy, Warfare, and the Politics of Communism, 1941–1945* (New York: Columbia University Press, 1979), p. 194.

59. Glees, *The Secrets of the Service*, pp. 43–44, 58, 62, 180–81.

60. See Mastny, *Russia's Road to the Cold War*, especially pp. 43, 71–72. Taubman, *Stalin's American Policy*, especially pp. 7–8, 10, 74, 78, acknowledges that Stalin's long-term objective was to dominate Europe, but like Mastny sees no clearly worked-out plan for accomplishing this. For Glees's defense of his argument, which leaves me unconvinced, see *The Secrets of the Service*, pp. 181–91.

61. See Gaddis, *The Long Peace*, pp. 25–29.

62. Andrew and Gordievsky, *KGB*, pp. 287–90, 332–33, 349–50. For more on this issue, see Arthur Schlesinger, Jr., "The Harry Hopkins Affair," *The Atlantic*, CCLXVII(March, 1991), 126–30.

63. Weinstein, *Perjury*, pp. 237–40.

64. See Warren F. Kimball, *Swords or Ploughshares? The Morgenthau Plan for Defeated Nazi Germany, 1943–1946* (Philadelphia: Lippincott, 1976), pp. 25–26; also Gaddis, *The United States and the Origins of the Cold War*, p. 128. White did, however, apparently play an important role in seeing to it that the Russians obtained plates that allowed them to duplicate—without American control—the occupation currency used in Germany after that country's surrender. See Andrew and Gordievsky, *KGB*, pp. 336–37.

65. Weinstein, *Perjury*, pp. 351–64, 510. See also the most recent assessement of the Yalta Conference, Russell D. Buhite, *Decisions at Yalta: An Appraisal of Summit Diplomacy* (Wilmington, Delaware: Scholarly Resources, 1986), pp. 129–30.

66. Andrew and Gordievsky, *KGB*, pp. 367, 375–76, present a good account of the difficulties Soviet intelligence faced in the United States immediately after the war.

67. Hoover to Souers, June 18, 1951, Truman Papers, PSF, Box 169, "FBI-S". See also Lamphere and Schachtman, *The FBI-KGB War*, pp. 234–35. Both Maclean and Klaus Fuchs represented the British in top secret discussions with the Americans on nuclear cooperation in 1949; there is some reason to believe, though, that neither man, by this time, was telling the Russians everything they knew about nuclear matters. See Williams, *Klaus Fuchs*, pp. 101–2; Glees, *Secrets of the Service*, pp. 354. The Anglo-American negotiations are discussed in Botti, *The Long Wait*, pp. 47–64.

68. Williams, *Klaus Fuchs*, pp. 148–49; Lamphere and Schachtman, *The FBI-KGB War*, pp. 237–38; Ranelagh, *The Agency*, p. 149.

69. See, for example, Burgess's comment on the February, 1950, Sino-Soviet Friendship Treaty, quoted in Gaddis, *The Long Peace*, p. 166n.

70. Lamphere and Schachtman, *The FBI-KGB War*, pp. 238–39. See also, on the

general question of what the British spies knew, Peter Hennessy and Kathleen Townsend, "The Documentary Spoor of Burgess and Maclean," *Intelligence and National Security*, II(April, 1987), 291–301.

71. Martin, *Wilderness of Mirrors*, pp. 21–23; Andrew and Gordievsky, *KGB*, pp. 371–72.

72. Such is the major argument of Bethell's account of the Albanian operation, *Betrayed*, especially pp. 191–92, although Bethell considers the entire initiative ill-conceived and is careful not to blame its demise entirely on Philby. See also Andrew and Gordievsky, *KGB*, pp. 383–90.

73. Information on CIA operations in Afghanistan is still thin, but see Bob Woodward, *Veil: The Secret Wars of the CIA, 1981–1987* (New York: Simon and Schuster, 1987), pp. 316–18, 372–73; and Joseph E. Persico, *Casey: From the OSS to the CIA* (New York: Viking, 1990), pp. 309–13.

74. Lamphere and Schachtman, *The FBI-KGB War*, p. 157.

75. See Rhodes, *The Making of the Atomic Bomb*, p. 750.

76. Hoover to Sidney W. Souers, February 21, 1950, Truman Papers, PSF Box 168, "FBI-F". See also Williams, *Klaus Fuchs*, pp. 7, 131; Radosh and Milton, *The Rosenberg File*, pp. 20–21; and Daniel Hirsch and William G. Mathews, "The H-Bomb: Who Really Gave Away the Secret?" *Bulletin of the Atomic Scientists*, XLVI(January/February, 1990), 22–30, which suggests that Soviet scientists would have learned more by analyzing atmospheric debris from the first American H-bomb tests than from Fuchs' espionage.

77. See, on these points, Gaddis, *The Long Peace*, pp. 110–12. One of my former students, Neal Rosendorf, has pointed out that any reader of *Aviation Week* in August, 1948, would have learned that the B–29s were not atomic-capable. ["Perceptions and Realities: The Deployment of B–29s to England during the Berlin Crisis of 1948," (Rutgers University Honors Thesis, April, 1987)].

78. Ranelagh, *The Agency*, pp. 154–55; Andrew and Gordievsky, *KGB*, pp. 394–95.

79. See, on Stalin's behavior during the Berlin crisis, Hannes Adomeit, *Soviet Risk-Taking and Crisis Behavior: A Theoretical and Empirical Analysis* (London: Allen & Unwin, 1982), p. 143.

80. Botti, *The Long Wait*, pp. 65–70; Williams, *Klaus Fuchs*, pp. 100, 138.

81. The lofty contempt for British intelligence on the part of its American "cousins" is a recurring theme in John LaCarré's "Smiley" novels. See also Ranelagh, *The Agency*, pp. 157–58.

82. Glees, *Secrets of the Service*, pp. 398–99.

83. See J. Samuel Walker, "'No More Cold War': American Foreign Policy and the 1948 Soviet Peace Offensive," *Diplomatic History*, V(Winter, 1981), 75–91.

84. Glees, *Secrets of the Service*, pp. 214–16.

85. See Robert Messer, *The End of an Alliance: James F. Byrnes, Roosevelt, Truman and the Origins of the Cold War* (Chapel Hill: University of North Carolina Press, 1982), pp. 185–86. Although Truman may also have suffered from a certain amount of "information overload" on this subject, given the extent to which FBI Director Hoover by 1946 had begun to inundate him with wildly inaccurate information on Soviet activities. This included, among other things, a November, 1945, report alleging that Stalin had been deposed, and a May, 1946, report that linked Dean Acheson and John J. McCloy to a Soviet spy ring. Hoover also warned the State Department in May, 1947, that the Soviet government had never recognized the purchase of Alaska, and was contemplating holding a plebiscite within the U.S.S.R. to determine

whether it should be returned. [Hoover to Vaughan, November 19, 1945, and to George E. Allen, May 29, 1946, Truman Papers, PSF, Box 169 "FBI-S, Box 167 "FBI-Atomic Bomb"; Hoover to Jack D. Neal, March 18, 1947, Department of State Decimal File, Box 3429, 711.61/3/1847, Diplomatic Branch, National Archives. See also Richard Gid Powers, *Secrecy and Power: The Life of J. Edgar Hoover* (New York: Macmillan, 1987), pp. 280–82].

86. "No one who has lived through these postwar years can be sanguine about reaching agreements in which reliance can be placed and which will be observed by the Soviet leaders in good faith. We must not, in our yearning for peace, allow ourselves to be betrayed by vague generalities or beguiling proffers of peace which are unsubstantiated by good faith solidly demonstrated in daily behavior. We are always ready to discuss, to negotiate, to agree, but we are understandably loath to play the role of international sucker." [Dean Acheson speech at Berkeley, California, March 16, 1950, *Department of State Bulletin*, XXII(March 27, 1950), 477]. See also Coral Bell, *Negotiation from Strength: A Study in the Politics of Power* (New York: Knopf, 1963).

87. See Marshall D. Shulman, *Stalin's Foreign Policy Reappraised* (Cambridge, Massachusetts: Harvard University Press, 1963).

88. Quoted in Glees, *Secrets of the Service*, p. 252.

89. See Taubman, *Stalin's American Policy*, p. 8–9.

90. William Yandell Elliott told students at the Naval War College in 1949: "If you had been playing the Russian line after this war, would you have made the incredible mistakes that the Politburo and the Kremlin have? You might have had the world on a silver platter if your manners had been good. Roosevelt had dished it all out to them. It was theirs for the taking. All that they had to do was to avoid showing this offensive, aggressive and uproarious kind of condemnation of all the outside world that Mr. Vishinsky and Molotov have treated us to ever since, and that Stalin has underlined from his base back home.... It is natural, I think, that the rulers who are educated and chosen this way have a stupid set of responses.... They are victims of their own lines and of their own method of propaganda." [Elliott lecture, "Vital U. S. Commercial and Economic Problems," September 22, 1949, Naval War College Archives, Record Group 15]. The point is also nicely made by Vojtech Mastny, "Stalin and the Militarization of the Cold War," *International Security*, IX(Winter, 1984–85), 109–29.

91. See Laqueur, *A World of Secrets*, pp. 11–12. Note also the convincing argument, in Andrew and Gordievsky, *KGB*, pp. 386–87, that the KGB failed to take maximum advantage of the intelligence coups it achieved.

92. Soviet sources have now confirmed that such authorization was given. See Alexander Makhov, "Stalin Approved Kim Il Sung's Order," *Moscow News Weekly*, #27(July 15–22, 1990), 12.

93. I heard Mastny make this observation at a meeting of Soviet and American historians in Moscow in 1987. The proposition was not challenged from the Soviet side.

94. Gaddis, *Russia, the Soviet Union, and the United States*, pp. 295–98.

95. That would appear to have been the case in Operation RYAN, a massive KGB effort during the early 1980s to detect Western preparations—nonexistent as it turned out—for a nuclear attack on the Soviet Union. See Andrew and Gordievsky, *KGB*, pp. 581–605. The KGB was perceptive, however, in naming the operation for the hero of several Tom Clancy novels that had not yet been written.

96. Alain C. Enthoven and K. Wayne Smith, *How Much Is Enough? Shaping the Defense Program, 1961–1969* (New York: Harper and Row, 1971), pp. 132–42.

97. Raymond L. Garthoff, *Detente and Confrontation: American-Soviet Relations from Nixon to Reagan* (Washington: Brookings Institution, 1985), pp. 551, 795–96; Daniel Patrick Moynihan, *On the Law of Nations* (Cambridge: Harvard University Press, 1990), p. 158.

98. Laqueur, *A World of Secrets*, pp. 42–43. This proposition seems confirmed by a report that reached the State Department in May, 1948, on the contents of a Soviet diplomatic pouch intercepted—under circumstances not specified—by Canadian authorities. Francis B. Stevens of the Department noted that "the pouch contained coverage of the Canadian press which consisted exclusively of quotations from extreme and obscure Party line newspapers and violent and slanderous conservative editorials. While this evidence is by no means conclusive, it is a straw in the wind to support the thesis we have long held that the press reporting received by the Soviet Foreign Office from its missions abroad is anything but objective." [Stevens to Llewellyn Thompson, George F. Kennan, and Charles E. Bohlen, May 7, 1948, Department of State Decimal File, Box 6463, 861.00/5–748]. Ambassador Alan Kirk reported after meeting Stalin in August, 1949, that "he certainly dominates the situation here, and Vyshinski was hopping around like a pea on a hot griddle to do his slightest wish." [Kirk to Acheson, August 23, 1949, *FRUS: 1949*, V, 654].

99. Jack Snyder's forthcoming book, *Myths of Empire*, suggests that the domestic political "log-rolling" that is characteristic of democracies contributes to this tendency.

100. For more on this, see Gaddis, *The Long Peace*, pp 195–214.

101. For an example of an egregiously irresponsible way of approaching this problem, see the recently released volume on Iran, 1951–54, in the Department of State's documentary series, *Foreign Relations of the United States*. By entirely excluding documentation on the 1953 CIA-organized coup against the Mosadeq government, those responsible for this volume have not only distorted the truth; they have called into question the reputation for objectivity long enjoyed by this venerable and once distinguished historical source. For more on this, see Bruce R. Kuniholm, "Foreign Relations, Public Relations, Accountability, and Understanding," *Perspectives* [newsletter of the American Historical Association], XXVIII(May/June, 1990), 1, 11–12; and Warren I. Cohen, "Gaps in the Record: How State Has Allowed History To Be Incomplete," *Foreign Service Journal*, LXVII (August, 1990), 27–29.

102. See Ranelagh, *The Agency*, 552–77, 584–603; also Thomas Powers, *The Man Who Kept the Secrets: Richard Helms and the CIA* (New York: Knopf, 1979), pp. 347–95; and Loch K. Johnson, *A Season of Inquiry: The Senate Intelligence Investigation* (Lexington: University Press of Kentucky, 1985).

103. Although Andrew and Gordievsky claim to have cleared up the matter once and for all. See *KGB*, p. 216.

104. Good models to follow would be the oral history programs at the presidential libraries, and the Foreign Affairs Oral History Program at Georgetown University, which concentrates on interviews with retired Foreign Service officers.

105. It is by no means beyond the realm of possibility that retired KGB operatives might be willing to take part in such sessions.

106. See, especially, Robert Jervis, *Perception and Misperception in International Politics* (Princeton: Princeton University Press, 1976); Richard Ned Lebow, *Between War and Peace: The Nature of International Crisis* (Baltimore: Johns Hopkins University Press, 1981); Deborah Welch Larson, *Origins of Containment* (Princeton: Princeton University Press, 1985); Robert Jervis, Richard Ned Lebow, and Janice Gross

Stein, *Psychology and Deterrence* (Baltimore: Johns Hopkins University Press, 1985). See also Robert Jervis, "Intelligence and Foreign Policy: A Review Essay," *International Security*, XI(Winter, 1986–87), 141–61.

107. I have in mind here the examples of Roosevelt's and Stalin's "administrative" styles, cited in the text.

108. Ernest R. May, "Conclusions: Capabilities and Proclivities," in May, ed., *Knowing One's Enemies*, p. 532. May does add, though, that continuity in organizational structure—whatever its faults—appears to correlate with successful assessment.

SIX
The Essential Relevance of Nuclear Weapons

This essay is to appear in a slightly different form in Patrick J. Garrity and Steven Maaranen, eds., *The Future of Nuclear Weapons*, forthcoming from the Center for National Security Studies at the Los Alamos National Laboratories. My thanks to Garrity, John Mueller, Philip Nash, and David Broscious for commenting on earlier drafts.

1. Thucydides, *History of the Peloponnesian War*, translated by Rex Warner (New York: Penguin Books, 1954), p. 48.

2. *New York Times*, May 25, 1946.

3. (New York: Basic Books, 1989). See also Mueller's article, "The Essential Irrelevance of Nuclear Weapons: Stability in the Postwar World," *International Security*, XIII(Fall, 1988), 55–79.

4. *Ibid.*, pp. 62–75.

5. See, on this point, John Lewis Gaddis, "Expanding the Data Base: Historians, Political Scientists, and the Enrichment of Security Studies," *International Security*, XII(Summer, 1987), 17–19; also Coral Bell, *The Reagan Paradox: American Foreign Policy in the 1980s* (New Brunswick: Rutgers University Press, 1989), especially pp. 6, 16–17.

6. These methodological techniques are discussed in greater detail in John Lewis Gaddis, "Nuclear Weapons and International Systemic Stability," Emerging Issues Occasional Papers Series #2, January, 1990, American Academy of Arts and Sciences. See also, on the uses of counterfactual analysis, James D. Fearon, "Counterfactuals and Hypothesis Testing in Political Science," *World Politics*, XLIII(January, 1991), 169–95.

7. For the parallel between historical and scientific reasoning, see E. H. Carr, *What Is History?* (New York: Random House, 1961), p. 136.

8. Which has already been written. See McGeorge Bundy, *Danger and Survival: Choices About the Bomb in the First Fifty Years* (New York: Random House, 1988).

9. Carl Kaysen, "Is War Obsolete? A Review Essay," *International Security* XIV(Spring, 1990), 61.

10. See Michael S. Sherry, *Preparing for the Next War: American Plans for Postwar Defense, 1941–45* (New Haven: Yale University Press, 1977).

11. See John Gimbel, "Project Paperclip: German Scientists, American Policy, and the Cold War," *Diplomatic History*, XIV(Summer, 1990), 343–65.

12. For the "crystal ball" effect, see Albert Carnesale, *et al.*, *Living with Nuclear Weapons* (New York: Bantam Books, 1983), p. 44.

13. See Paul Boyer, *By the Bomb's Early Light: American Thought and Culture at the Dawn of the Atomic Age* (New York: Pantheon, 1985); and Spencer Weart, *Nuclear Fear: A History of Images* (Cambridge, Massachusetts: Harvard University Press, 1988). We now have evidence that Soviet observers too found the effects of the atomic bombings impressive. See Nikita Moiseyev, "The Hiroshima and Nagasaki Tragedy in Documents," *International Affairs*, #8(August, 1990), 122–39, which reproduces reports received by Stalin on the physical damage at Hiroshima and Nagasaki.

14. Niles Eldredge, *Time Frames: The Evolution of Punctuated Equilibria* (Princeton: Princeton University Press, 1985). See also Stephen Jay Gould, *Time's Arrow, Time's Cycle: Myth and Metaphor in the Discovery of Geological Time* (Cambridge, Massachusetts: Harvard University Press, 1987), pp. 2–3.

15. For more on the concept of "stability," see S. David Broscious, "Approaches to International Systemic Stability," a working paper in the Nuclear History Program.

16. It has, for years, been generally accepted that Israel possesses nuclear weapons, and it probably did in 1973. See Bundy, *Danger and Survival*, pp. 505–12.

17. One estimate places total deaths—military and civilian— from World Wars I and II alone at 70 million. ["The Self-Purged Century," *The Economist*, CCCXII(August 12, 1989), 13.] Post-1945 combat deaths in interstate wars for the major nations that participated in the world wars total approximately 1.6 million, of which 900,000 were Chinese battle deaths in the Korean War. [Melvin Small and J. David Singer, *Resort to Arms: International and Civil Wars, 1816–1980* (Beverly Hills: Sage, 1982), pp. 89–95.] I have used the estimate of 15,000 for Soviet battle deaths in Afghanistan. I have also assumed post–1945 civilian war deaths for the principal World War I and II belligerents to be negligible, since no interstate wars have been fought on their territory during that period.

18. There is no standard list of diplomatic crises, but World War I is generally regarded as having broken out after six crises—Morocco (1905), Bosnia and Herzegovina (1908–09), Morocco (1910), the First Balkan War (1912), the Second Balkan War (1913), and Sarajevo (1914). World War II broke out in Europe after five crises—Ethiopia (1935–36), the Rhineland (1936), Austria (1938), Czechoslovakia (1938–39), and Poland (1939); World War II in Asia also after five—Manchuria (1931–32), Shanghai (1932), China (1937), Indochina (1940–41), Oil Embargo (1941). But since 1945 there have been at least thirty-seven major crises—Iran (1946), Greece (1947), Czechoslovakia (1948), Berlin (1948), Korea (1950–53), East Berlin (1953), Indochina (1954), Quemoy-Matsu (1954–55), Hungary (1956), Suez (1956), Lebanon (1958), Quemoy-Matsu (1958), Berlin (1958–59), U-2 incident (1960), Bay of Pigs (1961), Berlin (1961), Sino-Indian conflict (1962), Cuba (1962), Dominican Republic (1965); India-Pakistan War (1965), Vietnam (1965–75), Six-Day War (1967), Czechoslovakia (1968), Sino-Soviet border incidents (1969), India-Pakistan War (1971), Yom Kippur War (1973), Iran (1978–81), Afghanistan (1979–88), Sino-Vietnamese War (1979), Nicaragua/El Salvador (1979–1990), Iran-Iraq War (1980–88), Falklands War (1982), Lebanon (1982–84), Korean airliner incident (1983), Panama (1989), Iraqi invasion of Kuwait (1990), Persian Gulf War (1991)—not one of which has led to a world war.

19. See, on this point, Gaddis, *The Long Peace*, pp. 104–46.

20. This process of nuclear "learning" can be traced in Bundy, *Danger and Survival*, especially pp. 463–516. But see also John Wilson Lewis and Xue Litai, *China*

Builds the Bomb (Stanford: Stanford University Press, 1988); Joseph S. Nye, Jr., "Nuclear Learning and U.S.-Soviet Security Regimes," *International Organization*, XLI(Summer, 1987), 371–402; also an unpublished paper on Soviet nuclear learning, Vladislav M. Zubok, "Learning Against the Grain: Nuclear Weapons in Soviet Military Doctrine and Diplomacy, 1953–55."

21. See Thomas C. Schelling, *Arms and Influence* (New Haven: Yale University Press, 1966), pp. 132–34.

22. I would differentiate here between risk-taking that led to crises involving nuclear threats, on the one hand, and the issuance of nuclear threats during those crises once they had developed, on the other. Richard K. Betts has argued that nuclear superiority did make the United States more willing to engage in the latter category of activity. [*Nuclear Blackmail and Nuclear Balance* (Washington: Brookings Institution, 1987), p. 178.]

23. For a good overview of pre–1945 international systems, see Gordon A. Craig and Alexander L. George, *Force and Statecraft: Diplomatic Problems of Our Time* 2nd ed. (New York: Oxford University Press, 1990).

24. See Arno J. Mayer, *Political Origins of the New Diplomacy, 1917–1918: Wilson vs. Lenin* (New Haven: Yale University Press, 1959).

25. Paul Kennedy, *The Rise and Fall of the Great Powers: Economic Change and Military Conflict from 1500 to 2000* (New York: Random House, 1987), traces this process of "relative decline"in chapters 7 and 8.

26. See Bundy, *Danger and Survival*, p. 502.

27. Robert O. Keohane, *After Hegemony: Cooperation and Discord in the World Political Economy* (Princeton: Princeton University Press, 1984), especially pp. 182–216.

28. Kenneth N. Waltz, *Theory of International Politics* (New York: Random House, 1979), pp. 132–38.

29. Robert Axelrod, *The Evolution of Cooperation* (New York: asic Books, 1984).

30. I have discussed this dilemma at greater length in John Lewis Gaddis, "Containment and the Logic of Strategy," *The National Interest*, #10(Winter, 1987/8), 27–38.

31. See John Lewis Gaddis, *Strategies of Containment: A Critical Appraisal of Postwar American National Security Policy* (New York: Oxford University Press, 1982).

32. Colin S. Gray, *The Geopolitics of Super Power* (Lexington: University Press of Kentucky, 1988), pp. 18–19, 56.

33. I am indebted to Aaron Friedberg for this insight.

34. See Lawrence S. Kaplan, *NATO and the United States: The Enduring Alliance* (Boston: Twayne, 1988), pp. 58–62.

35. The term "trading" state comes from Richard Rosecrance, *The Rise of the Trading State: Commerce and Conquest in the Modern World* (New York: Basic Books, 1986).

36. See, on this, Bundy, *Danger and Survival*, pp. 427–36.

37. For one interesting possibility, see the discussion of "passive deterrence" in Patrick J. Garrity, "The Future of Nuclear Weapons: Final Study Report," Report No. 8 (February, 1990), Center for National Security Studies, Los Alamos National Laboratories.

38. For a strongly worded but, I think, profoundly wrong argument that we should, see John J. Mearsheimer, "Back to the Future: Instability in Europe after the Cold War," *International Security*, XV(Summer, 1990), 5–56.

39. I discuss some alternative explanations in *The Long Peace,* pp. 215–45.

40. Mueller acknowledges the point somewhat cryptically in *Retreat from Doomsday,* p. 219.

SEVEN
The Unexpected Ronald Reagan

This essay originally appeared in a slightly different form and under a different title in David E. Kyvig, ed., *Reagan and the World* (New York: Greenwood Press, 1990), pp. 17–38. I also used portions of it in my chapter on the Reagan administration in the second edition of my book, *Russia, the Soviet Union, and the United States: An Interpretive History* (New York: McGraw-Hill, 1990). It appears here with the permission of Greenwood Press and McGraw-Hill.

1. The best overall treatment of Carter administration foreign policy is Gaddis Smith, *Morality, Reason, and Power: American Diplomacy in the Carter Years* (New York: Hill and Wang, 1986).

2. News conference, January 29, 1981, *Public Papers of the Presidents of the United States: Ronald Reagan, 1981* (Washington: Government Printing Office, 1982), p. 57.

3. Haig statement to the Senate Foreign Relations Committee, January 9, 1981, U. S. Department of State, *American Foreign Policy: Current Documents, 1981* (Washington: Government Printing Office, 1984), p. 3. The comment about Carter is in Alexander M. Haig, Jr., *Caveat: Realism, Reagan, and Foreign Policy* (New York: Macmillan, 1984), p. 29.

4. Weinberger address, American Newspaper Publishers Association, Chicago, May 5, 1981, *American Foreign Policy, 1981,* p. 39. See also Caspar Weinberger, *Fighting for Peace: Seven Critical Years in the Pentagon* (New York: Warner Books, 1990), pp. 39–79. For the Navy's "maritime" strategy, see Robert W. Komer, *Maritime Strategy or Coalition Defense?* (Cambridge, Mass.: Abt Books, 1984), especially pp. 55–63.

5. See Strobe Talbott, *The Master of the Game: Paul Nitze and the Nuclear Peace* (New York: Knopf, 1988), p. 168; also Jerry W. Sanders, *Peddlers of Crisis: The Committee on the Present Danger and Containment* (Boston: South End Press, 1983), pp. 281–89.

6. Strobe Talbott, *Deadly Gambits: The Reagan Administration and the Stalemate in Arms Control* (New York: Knopf, 1984), pp. 15–18.

7. Reagan speech at Eureka College, Eureka, Illinois, May 9, 1982, *Public Papers of the Presidents of the United States: Ronald Reagan, 1982* (Washington: Government Printing Office, 1983), p. 585. For the origins of START, see Talbott, *Deadly Gambits,* pp. 222–23.

8. See Stephen S. Rosenfeld, "Testing the Hard Line," *Foreign Affairs,* LXI("America and the World, 1982"), 492, 504. For warhead figures, see George E. Hudson and Joseph Kruzel, eds., *American Defense Annual: 1985–1986* (Lexington, Mass.: Lexington Books, 1985), p. 93. Reagan himself later admitted that he had not realized at the time of the May, 1982, speech that the Russians relied primarily on land-based ICBMs. [Talbott, *Deadly Gambits,* p. 263.]

9. *Ibid.,* pp. 224–26, 287. See also Rosenfeld, "Testing the Hard Line," pp. 504–8; and, for a catalogue of such statements, Robert Scheer, *With Enough Shovels: Reagan, Bush, and Nuclear War* (New York: Random House, 1983).

10. Spencer R. Weart, *Nuclear Fear: A History of Images* (Cambridge, Mass.: Harvard University Press, 1988), pp. 375–88; William Schneider, "Rambo and Reality: Having It Both Ways," in Kenneth A. Oye, Robert J. Lieber, and Donald Rothchild, eds., *Eagle Resurgent? The Reagan Era in American Foreign Policy* (Boston: Little, Brown, 1987), pp. 42–44. See also Jonathan Schell, *The Fate of the Earth* (New York: Knopf, 1982), a book that contributed powerfully to fueling this concern; and the 1983 American Catholic bishops' pastoral letter, *The Challenge of Peace: God's Promise and Our Response* (Washington: National Conference of Catholic Bishops, 1983), which attempted to address the moral dimensions of the issue.

11. Speech to the National Association of Evangelicals, Orlando, Florida, March 8, 1983, *Public Papers of the Presidents of the United States: Ronald Reagan, 1983* (Washington: Government Printing Office, 1984), pp. 363–64. For an attempt to place this speech in a broader philosophical context, see William K. Muir, Jr., "Ronald Reagan: The Primacy of Rhetoric," in Fred I. Greenstein, ed., *Leadership in the Modern Presidency* (Cambridge, Mass.: Harvard University Press, 1988), pp. 271–78.

12. Radio-television address, March 23, 1983, *Reagan Public Papers: 1983*, pp. 442–43.

13. Speech at Notre Dame University, May 17, 1981, *Reagan Public Papers: 1981*, p. 434. See also Reagan's speech to the British Parliament, London, June 8, 1982, *Reagan Public Papers: 1982*, pp. 742–48; and Lou Cannon, *President Reagan: The Role of a Lifetime* (New York: Simon and Schuster, 1991), pp. 315–18.

14. Karen Dawisha, "The U. S. S. R. in the Middle East: Superpower in Eclipse?" *Foreign Affairs*, LXI(Winter, 1982/83), 438–52. For events in Poland, see Charles Gati, "Polish Futures, Western Options," *ibid.*, pp. 292–308; and Seweryn Bialer, *The Soviet Paradox: External Expansion, Internal Decline* (New York: Knopf, 1986), pp. 213–31.

15. For overviews of Soviet economic problems, see *ibid.*, pp. 47–50, 165; also Robert W. Campbell, "The Economy," in Robert F. Byrnes, ed., *After Brezhnev: The Sources of Soviet Conduct in the 1980s* (Bloomington: Indiana University Press, 1983), pp. 68–124. For the growing gap between Soviet and Chinese agriculture, see Paul Kennedy, *The Rise and Fall of the Great Powers: Economic Change and Military Conflict from 1500 to 2000* (New York: Random House, 1987), p. 492.

16. Francis Fukuyama, "Gorbachev and the Third World," *Foreign Affairs*, LXIV(Spring, 1986), especially pp. 721–21. For the efforts of Soviet analysts to come to grips with this phenomenon, see Jerry F. Hough, *The Struggle for the Third World: Soviet Debates and American Options* (Washington: Brookings Institution, 1986).

17. For the Reagan Doctrine, see Cannon, *President Reagan*, pp. 369–70; also Stephen S. Rosenfeld, "The Guns of July," *Foreign Affairs*, LXIV(Spring, 1986), 698–714; and Alexander Dallin and Gail W. Lapidus, "Reagan and the Russians: American Policy Toward the Soviet Union," in Oye, Lieber and Rothchild, eds., *Eagle Resurgent?*, pp. 223–26. Unlike the Truman, Eisenhower, and Carter doctrines, the Reagan Doctrine formalized a strategy that was already under way. The closest thing to a definitive statement of it would not come until President Reagan's 1985 State of the Union address, delivered on February 6, 1985. [*Public Papers of the Presidents of the United States: Ronald Reagan, 1985* (Washington: Government Printing Office, 1988), p. 135].

18. *New York Times*, January 22, 1989.

19. For a sophisticated effort to analyze differences among the President's advisers, see Dallin and Lapidus, "Reagan and the Russians," pp. 199–202.

20. Reagan press conference, January 29, 1981, *Reagan Public Papers, 1981*, p. 57.

21. Cannon, *President Reagan*, pp. 297–98.

22. Except on one occasion in 1984, when the President, while testing what turned

out to be an open microphone, jovially announced that he had outlawed Russia forever, and was about to begin bombing it. [*New York Times*, August 13, 1984].

23. Reagan television address, January 16, 1984, *Public Papers of the Presidents of the United States: Ronald Reagan, 1984* (Washington: Government Printing Office, 1986), pp. 40–44.

24. Cannon, *President Reagan*, p. 300.

25. For these developments, see Talbott, *Deadly Gambits*, pp. 350–56.

26. *London Times*, December 18, 1984.

27. MacNeil-Lehrer News Hour, December 21, 1988, Public Broadcasting System.

28. Mikhail Gorbachev, *Perestroika: New Thinking for Our Country and the World* (New York: Harper and Row, 1987), p. 51.

29. Georgii Arbatov, Director of the Institute for the Study of the USA and Canada in Moscow, suggested—perhaps only half whimsically—that this was the strategy. See his "The Limited Power of an Ordinary State," *New Perspectives Quarterly*, V(Summer, 1988), 31.

30. White House announcement, July 2, 1985, U. S. Department of State, *American Foreign Policy: 1985* (Washington: Government Printing Office, 1987), p. 402n. For Reagan's comment, see his reply to questions from members of the Magazine Publishing Association, March 14, 1985, *Reagan Public Papers: 1985*, p. 285.

31. Donald T. Regan, *For the Record: From Wall Street to Washington* (New York: Harcourt Brace Jovanovich, 1988), p. 351.

32. Talbott, *The Master of the Game*, pp. 285–88.

33. *Ibid.*, pp. 289–90.

34. See Nicholas Daniloff, *Two Lives, One Russia* (Boston: Houghton Mifflin, 1988).

35. Regan, *For the Record*, pp. 376–81.

36. Quoted in *ibid.*, p. 390. See also Talbott, *The Master of the Game*, pp. 315–25.

37. John Newhouse, *War and Peace in the Nuclear Age* (New York: Knopf, 1989), pp. 394–98. See also Regan, *For the Record*, pp. 391–96; and Cannon, *President Reagan*, pp. 768–70.

38. Michael Balfour, *The Kaiser and His Times* (Boston: Houghton Mifflin, 1964), p. 257. For post-mortems on Reykjavik, see Stanley Hoffmann, "An Icelandic Saga," *New York Review of Books*, XXXIII (November 28, 1986), 15–17; and James Schlesinger, "Reykjavik and Revelations: A Turn of the Tide?" *Foreign Affairs*, LXV("America and the World, 1986"), 426–46.

39. Michael Mandelbaum, "The Reagan Administration and the Nature of Arms Control," in Joseph Kruzel, ed., *American Defense Annual: 1988–89* (Lexington, Mass.: Lexington Books, 1988), pp. 204–8.

40. *New York Times*, December 6, 1988. For the Moscow summit, see Cannon, *President Reagan*, pp. 783–89.

41. See McGeorge Bundy, *Danger and Survival: Choices About the Bomb in the First Fifty Years* (New York: Random House, 1988), p. 583.

42. See, on this point, Kenneth N. Waltz, *Theory of International Relations* (New York: Random House, 1979), p. 61.

43. See Lou Cannon's account of a secret Reagan meeting with Soviet Ambassador Anatolii Dobrynin in February, 1983. [*President Reagan*, pp. 311–12].

44. A typical example is Garry Wills, "Mr. Magoo Remembers," *New York Review of Books*, XXXVII(December 20, 1990), 3–4.

45. Reagan's most perceptive biographer has pointed out that he was guided "both

by extraordinary vision and by remarkable ignorance." [Cannon, *President Reagan*, p. 290]. The implication is that the ignorance may have made possible the vision.

46. Or so it appeared at the time. Whether these principles will survive the pressures that now threaten to break up the Soviet Union remains to be seen.

EIGHT
How the Cold War Might End

1. "How the Cold War Might End," *The Atlantic*, CCLX(November, 1987), 88–100, included in this collection with the permission of *The Atlantic*.

2. Barry Lopez, *Arctic Dreams: Imagination and Desire in a Northern Landscape* (New York: Scribner's, 1986), pp. 211–13.

3. James Schlesinger, "Reykjavik and Revelations: A Turn of the Tide?" *Foreign Affairs*, LXV("America and the World, 1986"), 437.

4. See, on this point, Peter G. Feaver, "Does Moscow Know Where Its Nukes Are?" *Los Angeles Times*, December 22, 1990.

5. Lou Cannon, *President Reagan: The Role of a Lifetime* (New York: Simon and Schuster, 1991), pp. 62–64.

6. Radio-television address, April 30, 1970, *Public Papers of the Presidents of the United States: Richard M. Nixon, 1970* (Washington: Government Printing Office, 1971), p. 409.

7. "[T]here is nothing in the character or tradition of the Russian state to suggest that it could ever accept imperial decline gracefully. Indeed, historically, *none* of the overextended, multinational empires with have been dealt with in this survey—the Ottoman, the Spanish, the Napoleonic, the British—ever retreated to their own ethnic base until they had been defeated in a Great Power war, or (as with Britain after 1945) were so weakened by war that an imperial withdrawal was politically unavoidable. Those who rejoice at the present-day difficulties of the Soviet Union and who look forward to the collapse of that empire might wish to recall that such transformations normally occur at very great cost, and not always in a predictable fashion." [Paul Kennedy, *The Rise and Fall of the Great Powers: Economic Change and Military Conflict from 1500 to 2000* (New York: Random House, 1987), p. 514.]

8. Michael Doyle, "Kant, Liberal Legacies, and Foreign Affairs," *Philosophy and Public Affairs*, XII(Summer and Fall, 1983), 205–35, 323–53.

9. For an excellent discussion of why, see Geoffrey Hosking, *The Awakening of the Soviet Union* (Cambridge, Massachusetts: Harvard University Press, 1990), pp. 19–36.

10. Robert Axelrod, *The Evolution of Cooperation* (New York: Basic Books, 1984).

11. See Kenneth A. Oye, ed., *Cooperation Under Anarchy* (Princeton: Princeton University Press, 1986).

12. Kenneth N. Waltz, *Theory of International Politics* (New York: Random House, 1979); Robert Gilpin, *War and Change in World Politics* (Cambridge: Cambridge University Press, 1981).

13. Peter Stein and Peter Feaver, "Assuring Control of Nuclear Weapons: The Evolution of Permissive Action Links," Occasional Paper No. 2, Center for Science and International Affairs, Harvard University, 1987, pp. 83–84.

14. See Chapter Ten.

15. For a rather desperate attempt to find a future for the Warsaw Pact, see John Lewis Gaddis, "One Germany—in Both Alliances," *New York Times*, March 21, 1990.

16. See Rex Harry Davis and Robert Crocker Good, eds., *Reinhold Niebuhr on Politics* (New York: Scribners, 1960), p. 65.

17. Crane Brinton, *The Anatomy of Revolution* (New York: Prentice-Hall, 1952), p. 189.

18. Stephen Jay Gould provides a fine discussion of the nature of contingency in *Wonderful Life: The Burgess Shale and the Nature of History* (New York: Norton, 1989).

NINE
Tectonics, History, and the End of the Cold War

This essay was originally prepared for the project on "Alternative Futures for Soviet-American Relations" at the Mershon Center of the Ohio State University, and has not been previously published. The participants in that project, especially Charles and Margaret Hermann, have provided helpful suggestions on earlier drafts.

1. Although he does not use the term "tectonic" to describe them, Stanley Hoffmann provides an excellent description of these forces in "International Relations: The Long Road to Theory," in James N. Rosenau, ed., *International Politics and Foreign Policy: A Reader in Research and Theory* (New York: Free Press, 1961), p. 432.

2. See Chapter Eight of this book.

3. William H. McNeill, *The Pursuit of Power: Technology, Armed Force, and Society since A. D. 1000* (Chicago: University of Chicago Press, 1982), p. 143.

4. Paul Kennedy, *The Rise and Fall of the Great Powers: Economic Change and Military Conflict from 1500 to 2000* (New York: Random House, 1987), p. xvi.

5. See, for example, Jonathan Schell, *The Fate of the Earth* (New York: Knopf, 1982).

6. Carl von Clausewitz, *On War*, edited and translated by Michael Howard and Peter Paret (Princeton: Princeton University Press, 1976). It is important to note that Clausewitz did foresee, and warned strongly against, the possibility that war could become an act of pure violence, uninformed by reason.

7. For a retrospective argument to this effect, see David Kaiser, *Politics and War: European Conflict from Philip II to Hitler* (Cambridge, Massachusetts: Harvard University Press, 1990).

8. John Mueller, *Retreat From Doomsday: The Obsolescence of Major War* (New York: Basic Books, 1989), especially pp. 17–77.

9. McGeorge Bundy, *Danger and Survival: Choices About the Bomb in the First Fifty Years* (New York: Random House, 1988), pp. 324, 374.

10. Kennedy, *The Rise and Fall of the Great Powers*, pp. xx–xxi.

11. For a discussion of technological advance as a linear force in history, see Martin Van Creveld, *Technology and War: From 2000 B.C. to the Present* (New York: Free Press, 1989), pp. 314–16.

12. See John A. Hall, *Liberalism: Politics, Ideology, and the Market* (Chapel Hill: University of North Carolina Press, 1987), pp. 78, 82–83.

13. A recent example—perhaps written with tongue slightly in cheek—is Francis Fukuyama, "The End of History," *The National Interest*, #16(Summer, 1989), 3–18.

14. S. Frederick Starr, "The Changing Nature of Change in the USSR," in Seweryn Bialer and Michael Mandelbaum, eds., *Gorbachev's Russia and American Foreign Policy* (Boulder: Westview Press, 1988), pp. 6–8, 16–17; Jerry Hough, *Russia and the*

West: Gorbachev and the Politics of Reform, 2nd ed. (New York: Simon and Schuster, 1990), pp. 74–76.

15. William H. McNeill, "Winds of Change," in Nicholas X. Rizopolous, ed., *Sea-Changes: American Foreign Policy in a World Transformed* (New York: Council on Foreign Relations Press, 1990), pp. 168–71; Theodore S. Hamerow, *From the Finland Station: The Graying of Revolution in the Twentieth Century* (New York: Basic Books, 1990), pp. 210–25, 302–9; Timothy Garton Ash, *The Magic Lantern: The Revolution of '89 Witnessed in Warsaw, Budapest, Berlin, and Prague* (New York: Random House, 1990), p. 147.

16. See, for example, Walter L. Dorn, *Competition for Empire: 1740–1763* (New York: Harper and Row, 1940), pp. 80–84.

17. A particularly vivid account is Simon Schama, *Citizens: A Chronicle of the French Revolution* (New York: Knopf, 1989).

18. The most eloquent account of this intensification of military violence is John Keegan, *The Face of Battle* (New York: Viking, 1976). But see also his *The Mask of Command* (New York: Viking, 1987).

19. Japan's brutality before and during World War II—and the brutality it quickly provoked from its adversaries—has been too easily forgotten. For a valuable corrective, see John W. Dower, *War Without Mercy: Race and Power in the Pacific War* (New York: Pantheon, 1986). I have also benefited from conversations with Akira Iriye relating to the general phenomenon of transnational brutality in the 1930s.

20. Stalin is alleged to have said this to Pierre Laval in Moscow in 1935, but the original published source for the story appears to be Winston S. Churchill, *The Gathering Storm* (New York, Bantam Books, 1961), p. 117.

21. I mean by this, in particular, the extensive bombing of predominantly civilian targets, both by conventional means and, in Japan, through the use of the atomic bomb.

22. John Lewis Gaddis, *The Long Peace: Inquiries into the History of the Cold War* (New York: Oxford University Press, 1987), pp. 118–20.

23. See Garton Ash, *The Magic Lantern*, pp. 133–34.

24. *Ibid.*, 142.

25. I have put the word "defeat" in quotation marks to make the point that a defeat for authoritarianism could well be a "victory" for those who have had to endure it. See, on this point, John Lewis Gaddis, "Coping With Victory," *The Atlantic*, CCLXV(May, 1990), 60.

TEN

Great Illusions, the Long Peace, and the Future of the International System

This essay appears in a different form in Charles W. Kegley, Jr., ed., *The Long Postwar Peace: Contending Explanations and Projections* (New York: HarperCollins, 1990), pp. 25–55, and is included here with the permission of HarperCollins Publishers. I wish to thank Karin Wright and Philip Nash for research assistance; also, for critical suggestions, Emanuel Adler, Erik Hagerman, Chaim Kaufmann, Melvyn Leffler, Ralph Levering, Geir Lundestad, Sean Lynn-Jones, David Nixon, John Ruggie, Steven Van Evera, Fareed Zakaria, and, not least, Erik Yesson, who asked the question.

1. Norman Angell, *The Great Illusion: A Study of the Relationship of Military Power in Nations to Their Economic and Social Advantage* (London: Heinemann, 1910). It is important to note that Angell never ruled out the possibility of war itself;

his argument rather was that, once involved in war, modern industrial states would not be able to sustain it. See, on this point, J. D. B. Miller, *Norman Angell and the Futility of War: Peace and the Public Mind* (New York: St. Martin's, 1986), pp. 42, 51.

2. See, on the state of international relations theory, K. J. Holsti, *The Dividing Discipline: Hegemony and Diversity in International Theory* (Boston: Allen and Unwin, 1985); Patrick M. Morgan, *Theories and Approaches to International Politics: What Are We To Think?* 4th ed. (New Brunswick: Transaction Books, 1987); and Ole R. Holsti, "Models of International Relations and Foreign Policy," *Diplomatic History*, XIII(Winter, 1989), 15–43.

3. I am following here a suggestion advanced in Carey B. Joynt and Nicholas Rescher, "The Problem of Uniqueness in History," *History and Theory*, I(1961), 154.

4. For some defenses of utilitarian standards in explanation, see E. H. Carr, *What Is History?* (New York: Knopf, 1961), pp. 140–41; Stanley Hoffmann, "International Relations: The Long Road to Theory," in James Rosenau, ed., *International Politics and Foreign Policy: A Reader in Research and Theory* (New York: Free Press, 1961), p. 429; Raymond Aron, "What Is a Theory of International Relations?" *Journal of International Affairs*, XXII(1967), 206; Robert Jervis, *Perception and Misperception in International Politics* (Princeton: Princeton University Press, 1976), p. 6; and, for prediction, Alexander L. George, "Problem-Oriented Forecasting," in Nazli Choucri and Thomas W. Robinson, eds., *Forecasting in International Relations: Theory, Method, Problems, Prospects* (San Francisco: W. H. Freeman, 1978), p. 336. International relations theorists may object to my characterization of what they produce as "merchandise," or "commodities"; nor are they likely to welcome my suggestion that historians in search of theoretical explanations should "shop around." I will cheerfully apologize to any theorist who has not, at one time or another, "shopped around" in historical accounts for data to support hypotheses.

5. Holsti, *The Dividing Discipline*, pp. vii–viii, 73–74, 80. As Thomas Kuhn points out, however, the existence of multiple paradigms is often what brings about transitions from one dominant paradigm to another. [*The Structure of Scientific Revolutions*, 2ne ed., enlarged (Chicago: University of Chicago Press, 1970), p. 150.]

6. I am aware of the impropriety involved, strictly speaking, in equating "theories" with "paradigms." However, the terms "paradigm redundancy" and "paradigm fratricide" seem to me preferable to the alternatives, which would be the inelegant "theory redundancy" and "theory fratricide." Convinced that the field of international security studies needs no new infusion of graceless jargon, I have here exercised the historian's prerogative of preferring style over fussiness.

7. Several political scientists, perhaps knowing more than they care to admit, have quietly suggested this possibility to me.

8. See, for example, Kenneth Waltz, *Theory of International Politics* (New York: Random House, 1979), pp. 186, 188; Michael Mandelbaum, *The Nuclear Revolution: International Politics Before and After Hiroshima* (Cambridge: Cambridge University Press, 1981), especially pp. 58–77; Gordon A. Craig and Alexander L. George, *Force and Statecraft: Diplomatic Problems of Our Time* (New York: Oxford University Press, 1983), pp. 117–20; Joseph S. Nye, Jr., "Nuclear Learning and U.S.-Soviet Security Regimes," *International Organization*, XLI(Summer, 1987), 371–402; and, for the "crystal ball" effect, Albert Carnesale, *et al.*, *Living with Nuclear Weapons* (New York: Bantam Books, 1983), p. 44.

9. McGeorge Bundy, *Danger and Survival: Choices About the Bomb in the First Fifty Years* (New York: Random House, 1988), p. 592; see also pp. 584–86, 597. Richard

K. Betts assesses the effectiveness of nuclear threats in *Nuclear Blackmail and Nuclear Balance* (Washington: Brookings Institution, 1987). For the size of the nuclear arsenal, see David Alan Rosenberg, "The Origins of Overkill: Nuclear Weapons and American Strategy, 1945–1960," *International Security*, VII(Spring, 1983), 3–71.

10. Kenneth N. Waltz, *The Spread of Nuclear Weapons: More May Be Better*, Adelphi Papers, No. 171 (London: International Institute of Strategic Studies, 1981), p. 28. See also Kenneth N. Waltz, "Nuclear Myths and Political Realities," *American Political Science Review*, LXXXIV(September, 1990), 733–34.

11. John J. Mearsheimer, "Back to the Future: Instability in Europe After the Cold War," *International Security*, XV(Summer, 1990), 54.

12. The point is more fully elaborated in Geoffrey Blainey, *The Causes of War*, 3rd ed. (New York: Free Press, 1988), pp. 53–54.

13. Waltz, "Nuclear Myths and Political Realities," p. 734.

14. Alexander L. George, Philip J. Farley, and Alexander Dallin, eds., *U.S.-Soviet Security Cooperation: Achievements, Failures, Lessons* (New York: Oxford University Press, 1988), pp. 6–7.

15. As I tried to do in putting forward the original "long peace" thesis. See John Lewis Gaddis, *The Long Peace: Inquiries into the History of the Cold War* (New York: Oxford University Press, 1987), especially pp. 229–232. I use the term "stability" in this paper in Kenneth Waltz's sense: "A system is stable as long as its structure endures. In self-help systems, a structure endures as long as there is no consequential change in the number of principal units." [*Theory of International Politics*, p. 135n.]

16. Although he accepts the argument that nuclear weapons "have had a profound effect on the conduct of statecraft," Robert Gilpin is careful to note that "[t]he thesis that nuclear weapons have made hegemonic war or a system-changing series of limited wars an impossibility must remain inconclusive." [*War and Change in World Politics* (Cambridge: Cambridge University Press, 1981), pp. 215, 218.] See also George Modelski and Patrick M. Morgan, "Understanding Global War," *Journal of Conflict Resolution*, XXIX(September, 1985), 406–12.

17. John Mueller, *Retreat from Doomsday: The Obsolescence of Major War* (New York: Basic Books, 1989), pp. 110–15. I discuss the Mueller thesis in greater detail in Chapter Six of this book.

18. Waltz, *Theory of International Politics*, especially pp. 121, 173.

19. The most obvious previous examples of bipolarity—Athens versus Sparta, Rome versus Carthage—were in fact regional rivalries; and although European competition for colonial empire in the 16th through the 19th century at times took on the appearance of worldwide bipolarity, it would be difficult to find instances in which the power gradient separating the two predominant states from their nearest rivals was as great as it would be for the United States and the Soviet Union after World War II. See also, on this point, Joseph S. Nye, Jr., "Old Wars and Future Wars: Causation and Prevention," *Journal of Interdisciplinary History*, XVIII(Spring, 1988), 585.

20. Waltz, *Theory of International Politics*, pp. 173–74. See also pp. 180–81; and "Reflections on *Theory of International Politics*: A Response to My Critics," in Robert O. Keohane, ed., *Neorealism and Its Critics* (New York: Columbia University Press, 1986) pp. 327–28.

21. By far the most influential of these studies is Paul Kennedy, *The Rise and Fall of the Great Powers: Economic Change and Military Conflict from 1500 to 2000* (New York: Random House, 1987). But see also David P. Calleo, *Beyond American Hegemony: The Future of the Western Alliance* (New York: Basic Books, 1987); Michael W. Doyle, *Empires* (Ithaca: Cornell University Press, 1986); Aaron L. Friedberg,

The Weary Titan: Britain and the Experience of Relative Decline, 1895–1905 (Princeton: Princeton University Press, 1988); Walter Russell Mead, *Mortal Splendor: The American Empire in Transition* (Boston: Houghton Mifflin, 1987); and Mancur Olson, *The Rise and Decline of Nations: Economic Growth, Stagflation, and Social Rigidities* (New Haven: Yale University Press, 1982).

22. Kennedy, *The Rise and Fall of the Great Powers*, p. 48.

23. Examples, for the Russians, would include Yugoslavia, Albania, China, Egypt, and Somalia; for the Americans, France (under DeGaulle), Cuba, Iran, and Nicaragua.

24. Robert Gilpin, "American Policy in the Post-Reagan Era," *Daedalus*, CXVI(Summer, 1987), 33–67.

25. See, on this point, Zbigniew Brzezinski, *The Grand Failure: The Birth and Death of Communism in the Twentieth Century* (New York: Scribner's, 1989); also Robert Heilbroner, "The Triumph of Capitalism," *New Yorker*, LXV(January 23, 1989), 98–109.

26. For an elaboration of this argument, see Chapter Six of this book.

27. Bundy, *Danger and Survival*, pp. 502–3. See also Waltz's helpful distinction between the "usefulness" and "usability" of force in *Theory of International Relations*, p. 185.

28. See especially, on battleships, Martin van Creveld, *Technology and War: From 2000 B.C. to the Present* (New York: Free Press, 1989), p. 207.

29. Gilpin, *War and Change in World Politics*, pp. 30–31, provides a good discussion of prestige as a form of power.

30. See, for the complexities involved in deciding *not* to become a nuclear power, Bundy, *Danger and Survival*, pp. 513–16.

31. See Peter D. Feaver, "Does Moscow Know Where Its Nukes Are?" *Los Angeles Times*, December 22, 1990; also William J. Broad, "Guarding the Bomb: A Perfect Record, But Can It Last?" *New York Times*, January 29, 1991.

32. This summary of "hegemonic stability" theory is based on Robert Gilpin, *The Political Economy of International Relations* (Princeton: Princeton University Press, 1987), pp. 72–73. But see also Robert O. Keohane and Joseph S. Nye, *Power and Interdependence: World Politics in Transition* (Boston: Little, Brown, 1977), pp. 42–46; and, for a critique of the theory, Robert O. Keohane, *After Hegemony: Cooperation and Discord in the World Political Economy* (Princeton: Princeton University Press, 1984), pp. 32–39.

33. See Charles P. Kindleberger, *The World in Depression, 1929–1939* (Berkeley: University of California Press, 1973), especially p. 28. Henry R. Nau, *The Myth of America's Decline: Leading the World Economy into the 1990s* (New York: Oxford University Press, 1990), pp. 89–91, questions the frequently made assertion that the Bretton Woods system played a critical role in promoting post-World War II prosperity.

34. Keohane, *After Hegemony*, especially pp. 243–47. See also Calleo, *Beyond American Hegemony*, especially pp. 215–17.

35. Gilpin's *War and Change in World Politics* remains the most sophisticated effort to relate hegemonic stability theory to Cold War history, but that is not the main purpose of the book; nor has his more recent work expanded on the connection.

36. See Kindleberger, *The World in Depression*, pp. 26–28.

37. Gilpin, *The Political Economy of International Relations*, pp. 74–75, makes the point that hegemony can have geopolitical as well as economic dimensions.

38. See Waltz's chapter on "The Management of International Affairs" in *Theory of International Politics*, pp. 194–210; also Gilpin, *War and Change in World Politics*, p. 237.

39. For more on dual hegemonic crisis management, see Gaddis, *The Long Peace*, pp. 238–43; also Chapter Nine of this book.

40. See also Gilpin, *War and Change in World Politics*, p. 237.

41. Keohane, *After Hegemony*, pp. 54–55, 62, 88. Regime theory is examined in detail in Stephen Krasner, ed., *International Regimes* (Ithaca: Cornell University Press, 1983).

42. For some of the problems involved, see Robert Jervis, "Security Regimes," in *ibid.*, pp. 173–94; also Charles Lipson, "International Cooperation in Economic and Security Affairs," *World Politics*, XXXVII(October, 1984), especially pp. 12–18.

43. Robert Axelrod, *The Evolution of Cooperation* (New York: Basic Books, 1984); Kenneth A. Oye, ed., *Cooperation Under Anarchy* (Princeton: Princeton University Press, 1986).

44. See George, Farley, and Dallin, eds., *U.S.-Soviet Security Cooperation*, especially pp. 13–14; also Nye, "Nuclear Learning and U.S.-Soviet Security Regimes," especially pp. 371–78.

45. See Geir Lundestad, "Empire by Invitation? The United States and Western Europe, 1945–1952," *Journal of Peace Research*, XXIII(1986), 263–77; also G. John Ikenberry, "Rethinking the Origins of American Hegemony," *Political Science Quarterly*, CIX(Fall, 1989), 375–400.

46. Even tyrants, Waltz points out, need cooperation if they are to rule. [*Theory of International Politics*, pp. 188–89.] See also Gilpin, *War and Change in World Politics*, p. 16.

47. Calleo, *Beyond American Hegemony*, pp. 34–36. My own attempt to deal with this issue is in *The Long Peace*, pp. 61–71. See also, for the propensity of nations to "balance" against threats rather than to "bandwagon" before them, see Stephen M. Walt, *The Origins of Alliances* (Ithaca: Cornell University Press, 1987).

48. An interesting problem for historians would be to show just when this pattern of cooperative management began.

49. I owe this insight to one of my students, Ed Merta, who discusses this historical pattern in "Fallen Empires and the Origins of the Persian Gulf Crisis," Ohio University Contemporary History Institute *Thinkpiece* #4(January, 1991).

50. See Joseph S. Nye, Jr., "Neorealism and Neoliberalism," *World Politics*, XL(January, 1988), 249. In his more recent writing, Waltz does acknowledge the possibility—and begins to discuss the mechanisms of—further systemic change. See "Reflections on *Theory of International Politics*," pp. 327–28.

51. I am using the term "environment" here in the sense that Gilpin does: "A state system, like any other political system, exists in a technological, military, and economic environment that both restricts the behavior of its members and provides opportunities for policies of aggrandizement." [*War and Change in World Politics*, p. 53.] I would add, though, that moral environments can also affect the behavior of states, and that the opportunities provided need not be limited to aggrandizement.

52. See, on this point, Robert W. Cox, "Social Forces, States and World Orders: Beyond International Relations Theory," in Keohane, ed., *Neorealism and Its Critics*, p. 245. John Ruggie comments, in the same volume, on the difficulty "structural realism" would have in explaining how the modern state system evolved out of the medieval period. ["Continuity and Transformation in the World Polity," *ibid.*, pp. 142–43.] A related criticism appears in Alexander E. Wendt, "The Agent-Structure Problem in International Relations Theory," *International Organization*, XLI(Summer, 1987), especially pp. 342–44.

53. Mueller, *Retreat From Doomsday*, pp. 11–12; also James Lee Ray, "The Ab-

olition of Slavery and the End of International War," *International Organization*, XLIII(Summer, 1989), 405–39. Something similar happened on a smaller scale, Mueller points out, to dueling: in 1804 it was possible for a sitting vice president of the United States and a former secretary of the treasury— fearing ridicule if they did not—to agree to settle their differences by firing pistols at one another, with lethal results for Alexander Hamilton. But by the late 19th century any public figure who proposed resolving a quarrel in this way would have been ridiculed for doing so: social customs had shifted, and a procedure once considered the only way to preserve honor now had come to seem dishonorable, even silly. [*Retreat from Doomsday*, pp. 9–11.]

54. See Stephen Kern, *The Culture of Time and Space, 1880–1914* (Cambridge, Massachusetts: Harvard University Press, 1983), especially pp. 65–70.

55. Waltz argues, correctly in my view, that they have long had such an interest. [*Theory of International Politics*, p. 203.]

56. For more on these trends, see Chapter Nine of this book.

57. Francis Fukuyama, "The End of History?" *National Interest*, #16(Summer, 1989), 3. See also, on the reception of this article, James Atlas, "What Is Fukuyama Saying and to Whom Is He Saying It?" *New York Times Magazine*, October 22, 1989, pp. 38–42, 54–55.

58. For more on this consensus, see Samuel P. Huntington, "No Exit: The Errors of Endism," *National Interest*, #17(Fall, 1989), 3–11.

59. Mueller, *Retreat from Doomsday*, especially pp. 60–77, 217–19.

60. My objections to it are set out in Chapter Six of this book.

61. A proposition amply confirmed by the "new" social history. See, for examples, Lawrence Stone, *The Family, Sex and Marriage in England, 1500–1800* (New York: Harper and Row, 1979); Robert Darnton, *The Great Cat Massacre and Other Episodes in French Cultural History* (New York: Basic Books, 1984); and John Boswell, *The Kindness of Strangers: The Abandonment of Children in Western Europe from Late Antiquity to the Renaissance* (New York: Pantheon, 1989).

62. See on this point, in addition to Mueller, Ray, "The Abolition of Slavery and the End of International War," pp. 438–39. John Ruggie notes the difficulty "structural realism" has in dealing with the consequences of social change in "Continuity and Transformation in the World Polity," pp. 148–52.

63. See Gaddis, *The Long Peace*, pp. 104–46.

64. I am indebted to James Lee Ray for these points, which appear in "The Abolition of Slavery and the End of International War," pp. 431–34.

65. Note the emergence of something approaching a new "never again" school within the American military establishment, together with Soviet Foreign Minister Eduard Shervardnadze's recent characterization of the invasion of Afghanistan as "illegal" and "immoral." [See Philip Taubman, "The Shultz-Weinberger Feud," *New York Times Magazine*, April 14, 1985, pp. 51, 91–108; Edward Luttwak, "Do the Joint Chiefs Fear All Risks?" *New York Times*, October 27, 1989; and, for the Shevardnadze speech, *ibid.*, October 23, 1989].

66. The most influential work in this field was Keohane and Nye, *Power and Interdependence*; but see also, among many others, James N. Rosenau, *The Study of Global Interdependence* (London: Pinter, 1980); and Richard W. Mansbach and John A. Vasquez, *In Search of Theory: A New Paradigm for Global Politics* (New York: Columbia University Press, 1981). Few if any "neo-liberals" would have gone so far as to claim that "realism" was totally outmoded: security was still a concern of states; military strength did still count for something. But they did assert that the international system no longer functioned solely as a "self-help" arrangement in which each

nation was responsible for ensuring its own security; rather, common interests in certain areas had emerged, and that in turn implied the concept of *mutual* security, a phenomenon for which traditional "realism" was ill-equipped to account.

67. Nye, "Neorealism and Neoliberalism," p. 239. See also Holsti, "Models of International Relations and Foreign Policy," pp. 26–27. The narrowness with which the recent Canadian-American free trade agreement escaped being wrecked on the shoals of *Canadian* [sic!] nationalism suggests how precariously based the idea of interdependence continues to be.

68. Waltz, for example, cites economic indicators to argue that they are not. [*Theory of International Politics*, pp. 141, 151, 168–69.]

69. "The Russians Are Coming," *The Economist*, CCCXVII(October 20, 1990), 11–12.

70. See, for example, a recent statement of this thesis, Richard Rosecrance, *The Rise of the Trading State: Commerce and Conquest in the Modern World* (New York: Basic Books, 1986), especially pp. 78–79, 212–13.

71. Waltz, *Theory of International Politics*, pp. 138–39; Gaddis, *The Long Peace*, p. 224. Michael Doyle accepts this generalization, but is careful to confine it to relations between liberal and non-liberal states. ["Kant, Liberal Legacies, and Foreign Affairs, Part 2," *Philosophy and Public Policy*, XII(Fall, 1983), 326.]

72. Gaddis, *The Long Peace*, pp. 195–214. Satellites do not, of course, reveal enemy intentions. But they can reveal a good deal about the physical deployments that are necessary before one can act on one's intentions.

73. *Ibid.*, p. 208. See also the *New York Times*, November 23, 1988.

74. I have in mind here the Salman Rushdie affair, in which the Ayatollah managed, by getting *The Satanic Verses* temporarily removed from bookstore shelves while simultaneously getting it on the best seller lists, to shape the reading habits of several million Americans. For a good account of how Western influences helped set off the Iranian revolution, see Roy Mottahedeh, *The Mantle of the Prophet: Religion and Politics in Iran* (New York: Pantheon, 1985).

75. For one scholar's anticipation of such a backlash, see Harry Harding, *China's Second Revolution: Reform After Mao* (Washington: Brookings Institution, 1987), pp. 134–35, 157, 282.

76. See John Lewis Gaddis, *Russia, the Soviet Union, and the United States: An Interpretive History*, 2nd ed. (New York: McGraw-Hill, 1990), pp. 339–41.

77. Fukuyama, "The End of History?" pp. 3, 9–14. See also the *New Republic*'s 75th anniversary editorial, "After the Revolutions," CCI(November 6, 1989), 11–14; also an *Economist* editorial, "The Self-Purged Century," CCCXII(August 12, 1989), 13–14.

78. See John A. Hall, *Liberalism: Politics, Ideology and the Market* (Chapel Hill: University of North Carolina Press, 1987), pp. 119, 199; also Hall's *Powers and Liberties: The Causes and Consequences of the Rise of the West* (Berkeley: University of California Press, 1985), pp. 203–9; Heilbroner, "The Triumph of Capitalism," *passim.*; and, for the distinction between extensive utilization and intensive exploitation, S. Frederick Starr, "The Changing Nature of Change in the USSR," in Seweryn Bialer and Michael Mandelbaum, eds., *Gorbachev's Russia and American Foreign Policy* (Boulder: Westview Press, 1988), especially pp. 7–8.

79. "The broader the scope of the work and the deeper the reform, the greater the need to increase the interest in it and convince millions and millions of people of its necessity. This means that if we have set out for a radical and all-round restructuring, we must also unfold the entire potential of democracy." [Mikhail S. Gorbachev, *Per-*

estroika: New Thinking for Our Country and for the World (New York: Harper and Row, 1987), p. 32.] That Gorbachev attributed these thoughts to Lenin, who, we are told, saw "socialism and democracy as indivisible," shows that the Soviet leader was not above bending a little history to make a point.

80. See Harding, *China's Second Revolution*, especially pp. 274–77.

81. The best preliminary accounts of these still quite recent developments are Timothy Garton Ash, *The Uses of Adversity: Essays on the Fate of Central Europe* (New York: Random House, 1989); and *The Magic Lantern: The Revolution of '89 Witnessed in Warsaw, Budapest, Berlin and Prague* (New York: Random House, 1990).

82. Doyle's argument appears in full in "Kant, Liberal Legacies, and Foreign Affairs," *Philosophy and Public Affairs*, XII(Summer and Fall, 1983), 205–35, 323–53, and is summarized in Michael W. Doyle, "Liberalism and World Politics," *American Political Science Review*, LXXX(December, 1986), 1151–62.

83. See Gaddis, *The Long Peace*, p. 239.

84. Fukuyama, "The End of History?" p. 18.

85. I have adapted this image from Stephen J. Pyne's *The Ice: A Journey to Antarctica* (New York: Ballantine Books, 1986), especially chapter one. An irreverent student has pointed out to me that historians seem to find it easier to think of dependent variables as small animals. He is probably right.

86. See Herbert Butterfield, *The Origins of History* (New York: Basic Books, 1981), pp. 121–26.

87. Consider the remarkable response, during 1988, to Paul Kennedy's *The Rise and Fall of the Great Powers: Economic Change and Military Conflict from 1500 to 2000*.

88. As, for example, presidential "death cycles": every American president elected in a year ending in zero from 1840 through 1960 died in office. The pattern held through seven iterations, but without any credible causal mechanism to explain it. And yet, with the retirement in good health of Ronald Reagan, the oldest of all the presidents broke the pattern. For more on the confusion of correlation with cause, see David Hackett Fischer, *Historians' Fallacies: Toward a Logic of Historical Thought* (New York: Harper and Row, 1970), pp. 167–69.

89. A point elegantly made in Stephen Jay Gould, *Time's Arrow, Time's Cycle: Myth and Metaphor in the Discovery of Geological Time* (Cambridge, Massachusetts: Harvard University Press, 1987), pp. 48–49. See also Joynt and Rescher, "The Problem of Uniqueness in History," p. 159.

90. See R. Damian Nance, Thomas R. Worsley and Judith R. Moody, "The Supercontinent Cycle," *Scientific American*, CCLIX(July, 1988), 72–79.

91. There is, of course, the whole separate and tangled subject of Kondratieff cycles in economics, from which source much of long cycle theory originally developed. See Joshua A. Goldstein, *Long Cycles: Prosperity and War in the Modern Age* (New Haven: Yale University Press, 1988), pp. 25–39; and, for a good introduction to long-cycle theory in general, George Modelski, ed., *Exploring Long Cycles* (Boulder: Lynne Rienner, 1987).

92. *War and Change in World Politics*, especially pp. 9–15; Goldstein, *Long Cycles*, pp. 15–17; Modelski and Morgan, "Understanding Global War," pp. 391–417; and Olson, *The Rise and Decline of Nations*, pp. 36–73. Kennedy's *The Rise and Fall of the Great Powers* also follows this general line of reasoning, although his terminology does not always follow that of the above-mentioned works.

93. Gilpin, *War and Change in World Politics*, p. 93.

94. Kennedy, *The Rise and Fall of the Great Powers*, pp. 436–37.

95. Goldstein, *Long Cycles*, pp. 260, 282. Mancur Olson provides a slightly different explanation, which focuses on the way "distributional coalitions slow down a society's capacity to adopt new technologies and to reallocate resources in response to changing conditions, and thereby reduce the rate of economic growth." It follows from this, he notes, that "countries whose distributional coalitions have been emasculated or abolished by totalitarian government or foreign occupation should grow relatively quickly after a free and stable legal order is established." [*The Rise and Decline of Nations*, pp. 74–75.]

96. See, for example, Modelski and Morgan, "Understanding Global War," p. 394; Goldstein, *Long Cycles*, p. 285; Kennedy, *The Rise and Fall of the Great Powers*, pp. 16–30.

97. Gilpin, *War and Change in World Politics*, pp. 7, 213–19. The quotation is from p. 215. It should be pointed out that Gilpin differentiates between "cycles of empire," which precede the modern state system, and the hegemonic cycles that characterize it today. [*Ibid.*, pp. 110–145.] See also, on the effect of nuclear weapons on long cycles, Gilpin, *The Political Economy of International Relations*, p. 351; and Kennedy, *The Rise and Fall of the Great Powers*, p. 537.

98. *Ibid.*, p. xx.

99. Although, to my knowledge, no one has worked out a method by which we might measure rates of technological innovation. How would the past forty years compare, for example, with 1870–1910, which saw the development of the telephone, the phonograph, the automobile, electric power, the motion picture, radio, the airplane, and the submarine? Or compare progress in aviation between 1940 and 1965—where one advanced from the B-17 to manned orbiting satellites—as against 1965 to the present.

100. Such is the conclusion—misunderstood by many of his critics— of Kennedy's *Rise and Fall of the Great Powers*, especially p. 514.

101. Joseph S. Nye, Jr., *Bound to Lead: The Changing Nature of American Power* (New York: Basic Books, 1990).

102. Gilpin, *War and Change in World Politics*, p. 49.

103. Waltz, *Theory of International Politics*, p. 68.

104. Gould's *Time's Arrow, Time's Cycle* is a brilliant commentary on this point. See also, on the notion of complementarity, John Gerard Ruggie, "Changing Frameworks of International Collective Behavior: On the Complementarity of Contradictory Tendencies," in Choucri and Robinson, eds., *Forecasting in International Relations*, pp. 384–406; Richard Rhodes, *The Making of the Atomic Bomb* (New York: Simon and Schuster, 1986), pp. 131–32; and, intriguingly, Strobe Talbott, *The Master of the Game: Paul Nitze and the Nuclear Peace* (New York: Knopf, 1988), p. 36.

105. See Richard Fox, *Reinhold Niebuhr: A Biography* (New York: Pantheon, 1985), pp. 290–91.

106. See Heinz R. Pagels, *The Dreams of Reason: The Computer and the Rise of the Sciences of Complexity* (New York: Bantam, 1988), pp. 226–27. James Gleick's best-seller, *Chaos: The Making of a New Science* (New York: Viking, 1987), is the best general introduction to this field.

107. "Any generalization about the thinking of an age is the more persuasive the greater the conceptual distance between the sources on which it is based." [Kern, *The Culture of Time and Space*, p. 7].

108. Although one cannot rule out altogether the possibility that developments in one area could affect others: it is not too difficult to conceive of a form of "liberalism" that seeks to abolish nuclear deterrence, bipolarity, and hegemonic management.

ELEVEN
Toward the Post-Cold War World

This essay was originally prepared for the 1991–1992 edition of the *American Defense Annual*, and an abbreviated version of it appeared in the Spring, 1991, issue of *Foreign Affairs*. It appears here in revised form with the permission of Lexington Books and the Council on Foreign Relations. My thanks, for critical suggestions, to Alfred Eckes, Aaron Friedberg, Michael Gaddis, Joseph Kruzel, Philip Nash, and Richard Vedder.

1. Speech to the House of Commons, March 1, 1848, quoted in Jasper Ridley, *Lord Palmerston* (London: Constable, 1970), p. 334.

2. An unpublished paper by Professor Terry L. Deibel of the National War College, "Strategies Before Containment—Patterns for the Future," has influenced my thinking on this point.

3. See Felix Gilbert, *To the Farewell Address: Ideas of Early American Foreign Policy* (Princeton: Princeton University Press, 1961), especially pp. 19–43.

4. Gordon S. Wood, *The Creation of the American Republic, 1776–1787* (Chapel Hill: University of North Carolina Press, 1969), pp. 135–36, 448–49, 548–49.

5. Americans were quick to react to the possibility of British and French expansion into Texas and California in the 1840s; they deliberately "tilted" toward Russia during the Crimean War; Lincoln's Emancipation Proclamation can be understood as a successful attempt, by moral means, to turn the European balance of power against the Confederacy; and Theodore Roosevelt played an explicit balancing role in the diplomacy of the Russo-Japanese War, first favoring Japan, and then Russia.

6. For more on these points, see Chapter One of this book.

7. See John Mueller, *Retreat From Doomsday: The Obsolescence of Major War* (New York: Basic Books, 1989); also Chapter Six.

8. I have adapted this analogy from Heinz R. Pagels, *The Dreams of Reason: The Computer and the Rise of the Sciences of Complexity* (New York: Simon and Schuster, 1988), p. 227. See also on the concept of geopolitical maps, Hans J. Morgenthau, "Refections on the State of Political Science," *Review of Politics*, XVII(October, 1955), 455–56.

9. *Public Papers of the Presidents of the United States: Harry S. Truman, 1947* (Washington: Government Printing Office, 1963), p. 178. See also John Lewis Gaddis, *Strategies of Containment: A Critical Appraisal of Postwar American National Security Policy* (New York: Oxford University Press, 1982), pp. 65–66.

10. Or, as the editors of *The Economist* recently put it, "the trend is towards both fission and fusion, with plenty of tension between the two." ["Go Forth and Unify," *The Economist*, CCCLXVII(October 6, 1990), 16.] I am indebted to Geoffrey Dabelko for bringing this reference to my attention.

11. For example, Wendell L. Willkie, *One World* (New York: Simon and Schuster, 1943).

12. On the importance of communications in the collapse of communism, see Zbigniew Brzezinski, *The Grand Failure: The Birth and Death of Communism in the Twentieth Century* (New York: Charles Scribner's Sons, 1989), pp. 254–55.

13. See, on this point, Gaddis, *Strategies of Containment*, pp. 28–29, 58–61.

14. To be sure, General Charles DeGaulle terminated France's formal military association with NATO in 1966. But by that time, it had become clear that West Germany was so firmly linked to NATO that it could pose no future threat. And we

now know that, in certain areas at least, informal French military cooperation with NATO members has never ceased. See especially, on this last point, Richard H. Ullman, "The Covert French Connection," *Foreign Policy*, #75(Summer, 1989), 3–33.

15. The term "soft power" comes from Joseph S. Nye, Jr., *Bound to Lead: The Changing Nature of American Power* (New York: Basic Books, 1990), especially p. 188. See also Nye, "Soft Power," *Foreign Policy*, #80(Fall, 1990), 153–71.

16. Theodore S. Hamerow, *From the Finland Station: The Graying of Revolution in the Twentieth Century* (New York: Basic Books, 1990), pp. 210–25, 300–309. See also Chapters Ten and Eleven of this book.

17. See the *New York Times*, February 22, 1990; also Timothy Garton Ash, *The Uses of Adversity: Essays on the Fate of Central Europe* (New York: Random House, 1989), pp. 191–93.

18. Michael Doyle, "Kant, Liberal Legacies, and Foreign Affairs," *Philosophy and Public Affairs*, XII(Summer and Fall, 1983), 205–35, 323–53; also Doyle, "Liberalism and World Politics," *American Political Science Review*, LXXX(December, 1987), 1151–69.

19. See, for example, A. W. DePorte, *Europe Between the Super-Powers: The Enduring Balance*, second edition (New Haven: Yale University Press, 1986), pp. 186–87; also Michael Howard, "1989: A Farewell to Arms?" *International Affairs*, LXV(Summer, 1989), especially pp. 409–10. But lots of authors have found events to be moving faster than their word processors recently: an obvious example is John Lewis Gaddis, "One Germany—in Both Alliances," *New York Times*, March 21, 1990.

20. Celestine Bohlen, "Ethnic Rivalries Revive in East Europe," *ibid*, November 12, 1990.

21. John F. Burns, "In Quebec, Yet Another Splintering," *ibid.*, July 29, 1990.

22. See Bernard Lewis, "The Roots of Muslim Rage," *The Atlantic*, CCLXVI (September, 1990), 47–60.

23. For an excellent account, see Thomas L. Friedman, *From Beirut to Jerusalem* (New York: Farrar, Straus and Giroux, 1989).

24. See Allen Bloom, *The Closing of the American Mind* (New York: Simon and Schuster, 1987), pp. 68–88; also William H. McNeill, "Winds of Change," in Nicholas X. Rizopolous, ed., *Sea-Changes: American Foreign Policy in a World Transformed* (New York: Council on Foreign Relations Press, 1990), p. 176. The nation did, after all, survive the infatuation of successive earlier generations with Frank Sinatra, Elvis Presley, and the Beatles.

25. There is growing evidence, as well, that the standard of living for the middle class in the United States is no longer improving. See "American Living Standards: Running to Stand Still," *The Economist*,CCCXVII(November 10, 1990), 19–22.

26. See the special issue, "Race on Campus," *New Republic*, CCIV(February 19, 1991); also Dinesh D'Souza, "Illiberal Education," *The Atlantic*, CCLXVII(March, 1991), 51–79.

27. See William F. Buckley, Jr., *Gratitude: Reflections On What We Owe To Our Country* (New York: Random House, 1990).

28. One of the best explications of Smith's ideas occurs in Robert L. Heilbroner's *The Worldly Philosophers: The Lives, Times, and Ideas of the Great Economic Thinkers*, 6th ed. (New York: Simon and Schuster, 1986), pp. 42–74. For a recent update, see Robert L. Heilbroner, "Economic Predictions," *New Yorker*, LXVII(July 8, 1991), 70–77.

29. Most of the Germans who voted for Hitler in the early 1930s probably thought they were voting for freedom, as they understood it; some Russians today, as they

contemplate the complications of life under *perestroika*, would just as soon have Stalin back.

30. Lou Cannon, *President Reagan: The Role of a Lifetime* (New York: Simon and Schuster, 1991), pp. 62–64. See also Chapter Eight of this book.

31. Joseph S. Nye, Jr., "Nuclear Learning and U.S.-Soviet Security Regimes," *International Organization*, XVI(Summer, 1987), 371–402; Robert Jervis, *The Meaning of the Nuclear Revolution: Statecraft and the Prospect of Armageddon* (Ithaca: Cornell University Press, 1989).

32. Alfred E. Eckes, Jr., *A Search for Solvency: Bretton Woods and the International Monetary System, 1941–1971* (Austin: University of Texas Press, 1975); Robert A. Pollard, *Economic Security and the Origins of the Cold War, 1945–1950* (New York: Columbia University Press, 1985); G. John Ikenberry, "Rethinking the Origins of American Hegemony," *Political Science Quarterly*, CIV(Fall, 1989), 375–400.

33. Henry R. Nau, *The Myth of America's Decline: Leading the World Economy into the 1990s* (New York: Oxford University Press, 1990), pp. 77–128, makes a strong argument that it was really the Marshall Plan that created the system of price stability, liberalized trade, and minimally-regulated markets from which postwar prosperity resulted.

34. See Bruce G. Blair and Henry W. Kendall, "Accidental Nuclear War," *Scientific American*, CCLXIII(December, 1990), 53–58.

35. McNeill, "Winds of Change," pp. 187–92.

36. See, on this point, Chapter Six of this book.

37. See John Lewis Gaddis, *The Long Peace: Inquiries Into the History of the Cold War* (New York: Oxford University Press, 1987), pp. 215–45.

38. For example, Paul Kennedy, *The Rise and Fall of the Great Powers: Economic Change and Military Conflict from 1500 to 2000* (New York: Random House, 1987); David P. Calleo, *Beyond American Hegemony: The Future of the Western Alliance* (New York: Basic Books, 1987); Clyde V. Prestowitz, Jr., *Trading Places: How We Are Giving Our Future to Japan and How to Reclaim It* (New York: Basic Books, 1989).

39. The dangers are bluntly stated in two recent articles by John J. Mearsheimer, "Why We Will Soon Miss the Cold War," *The Atlantic*, CCLXVI(August, 1990), 35–50; and "Back to the Future: Instability in Europe After the Cold War," *International Security*, XV(Summer, 1990), 5–56.

40. An extreme, but prominent, example of such celebration is Francis Fukuyama, "The End of History?" *The National Interest*, #16(Summer, 1989), 3–18.

41. Seweryn Bialer, "Russia vs. the Soviet Union," *U.S. News*, CIX(November 5, 1990), 46–47.

42. See, on this point, George F. Kennan, "Communism in Russian History," *Foreign Affairs*, LXIX(Winter, 1990/91), especially pp. 181–84.

43. Preoccupation with European developments prior to August, 1990, may well have prevented the U. S. and the U. S. S. R. from sending sufficiently discouraging signals to Saddam Hussein.

44. W. W. Rostow, *The Stages of Economic Growth: A Non-Communist Manifesto* (New York: Cambridge University Press, 1962), p. 164. For a strong critique of this theory, see D. Michael Shafer, *Deadly Paradigms: The Failure of U.S. Counterinsurgency Policy* (Princeton: Princeton University Press, 1988).

45. See Hamerow, *From the Finland Station*, especially pp. 349–53; also Brzezinski, *The Grand Failure*, pp. 250–51.

46. Doyle, "Kant, Liberal Legacies, and Foreign Affairs," pp. 351–53.

47. Which would be a pattern consistent with Doyle's reminder that although democracies tend not to fight one another, they do not shrink from using force against undemocratic states. [*Ibid.*, pp. 323–37].

48. James Chace has suggested, persuasively in my view, that this attitude goes back to Lyndon Johnson's attempt to fight the Vietnam War without asking for sacrifices on the home front. [*Solvency: The Price of Survival* (New York: Random House, 1981), p. 15.]

49. See Robert Gilpin, *The Political Economy of International Relations* (Princeton: Princeton University Press, 1987), pp. 334–37. It is worth noting that, with all their complaints about taxes, Americans still pay far less than do the citizens of most other industrial countries. For 1989 comparisons, see *The Economist*, CCCXVII(October 27, 1990), 24.

50. Richard Lacayo, "Why No Blue Blood Will Flow," *Time*, CXXXVI(November 26, 1990), 34.

51. Not the least of the unfortunate consequences of the Persian Gulf crisis is the extent to which it distracted attention from the problems of the Soviet Union and Eastern Europe.

52. See the editorial, "The Russians Are Coming," *The Economist*, CCCXVII(October 20, 1990), 11–12.

53. Nau, *The Myth of America's Decline*, pp. 340–42, provides a good discussion of the Marshall Plan's relevance to the problem of maintaining global prosperity in the 1990s. The best assessment of the Marshall Plan's impact in the late 1940s is Michael J. Hogan, *The Marshall Plan: America, Britain, and the Reconstruction of Western Europe, 1947–1952* (Cambridge: Cambridge University Press, 1987), especially pp. 430–45.

54. See Timothy Garton Ash, "Germany Unbound," *New York Review of Books*, XXXVIII(November 22, 1990), pp. 11–15. The Conference on Security and Cooperation in Europe, which is now little more than a framework for negotiations, suffers from a deficiency opposite to that of NATO and the European Community: it includes *all* of the states of Europe, from the largest to the most microscopic, and it requires unanimity in order to act, which in most cases ensures that it will not.

55. See Gaddis, *The Long Peace*, especially pp. 222–23, 239–40; also Mueller, *Retreat from Doomsday*, pp. 217–44.

56. For an eloquent explanation of the advantages adherence to international law can offer, see Daniel Patrick Moynihan, *On the Law of Nations* (Cambridge, Massachusetts: Harvard University Press, 1990).

57. See Gina Kolata, "Japanese Labs in U.S. Luring America's Computer Experts," *New York Times*, November 11, 1990.

58. McNeill, "Winds of Change," pp. 184–87, sets this problem within a long-term historical context.

59. See note 52, above. Recent large increases in the emigration of Soviet Jews to Israel have, of course, already increased tensions in the Middle East.

60. For a more pessimistic view, see McNeill, "Winds of Change," pp. 178–79. Alan Wolfe, "The Return of the Melting Pot," *New Republic*, CCIII(December 31, 1990), 27–34, is an excellent discussion of both the advantages and the problems that new waves of immigration are creating for the United States.

61. See Chapter Ten of this book.

62. My understanding of "solvency" here echoes that of Walter Lippmann: "If its expenditures are safely within its assured means, a family is solvent when it is poor,

or is well-to-do, or is rich. The same principle holds true of nations." [*U. S. Foreign Policy: Shield of the Republic* (Boston: Little, Brown, 1943), p. 10.] For a thoughtful elaboration of this principle, see Chace, *Solvency, passim.*

63. Gaddis, *Strategies of Containment*, pp. 135–6. Emphasis added.

64. Eisenhower's "Farewell Address," delivered on January 17, 1961, and printed in the *Public Papers of the Presidents of the United States: Dwight D. Eisenhower, 1960* (Washington: Government Printing Office, 1961), pp. 1035–40, is well worth regular re-reading.

65. One striking indication of this lack of consensus is the current polarization of the international studies community into optimistic and pessimistic schools of thought regarding the nature of the post-Cold War world. The optimists include Francis Fukuyama, Richard Rosecrance, Joseph S. Nye, Jr., and John Mueller; but there is an equally conspicuous and equally influential group of pessimists, among them Paul Kennedy, David Calleo, Clyde Prestowitz, and John Mearsheimer. (Specific references to the work of all of these individuals appear elsewhere in these notes.) To oversimplify, the optimists tend to give greater weight to the forces of integration in current world politics, while the pessimists stress the forces of fragmentation. The differences between them are so stark, though, that the proverbial man from Mars might reasonably wonder whether these two groups of analysts are writing about the same planet.

66. *The Federalist Papers*, (New York: New American Library, 1961), p. 320.

Bibliography

MANUSCRIPT COLLECTIONS

Dulles, John Foster. Papers. Dwight D. Eisenhower Library.
————. Papers. Seeley Mudd Library, Princeton University.
Eisenhower, Dwight D. Papers. Dwight D. Eisenhower Library.
Great Britain. Foreign Office Records. Public Record Office, London.
Johnson, Lyndon B. Papers. Lyndon B. Johnson Library.
Kennan, George F. Papers. Seeley Mudd Library, Princeton University.
Niebuhr, Reinhold. Papers. Library of Congress.
Truman, Harry S. Papers. Harry S. Truman Library.
U. S. Department of State. Decimal File. Diplomatic Branch, National Archives.
————, Policy Planning Staff Records. Diplomatic Branch, National Archives.
U. S. Naval War College. Archives. Naval War College.

UNPUBLISHED MATERIALS

Deibel, Terry L., "Strategies Before Containment—Patterns for the Future."
Eagles, Keith David, "Ambassador Joseph E. Davies and American- Soviet Relations, 1937–1941" (Ph. D. Dissertation, University of Washington, 1966).
Rosendorf, Neal M., "Perceptions and Realities: The Deployment of B-29s to England during the Berlin Crisis of 1948" (Rutgers University Honors Thesis, April, 1987).
Zubok, Vladislav M., "Learning Against the Grain: Nuclear Weapons in Soviet Military Doctrine and Diplomacy, 1953–55." (Paper prepared for an Ohio University conference on "Soviet-American Relations, 1950–55," October, 1988).

PUBLISHED DOCUMENTS

Etzold, Thomas H., and John Lewis Gaddis, eds., *Containment: Documents on American Policy and Strategy, 1945–1950* (New York: Columbia University Press, 1978).

Kimball, Warren F., ed., *Churchill and Roosevelt: The Complete Correspondence* (Princeton: Princeton University Press, 1984). 3 vols.
Public Papers of the Presidents of the United States: Dwight D. Eisenhower, 1955, 1960 (Washington: Government Printing Office, 1959, 1961).
Public Papers of the Presidents of the United States: Harry S. Truman, 1947 (Washington: Government Printing Office, 1963).
Public Papers of the Presidents of the United States: John F. Kennedy, 1963 (Washington: Government Printing Office, 1964).
Public Papers of the Presidents of the United States: Richard M. Nixon, 1970 (Washington: Government Printing Office, 1971).
Public Papers of the Presidents of the United States: Ronald Reagan, 1981–85 (Washington: Government Printing Office, 1982–88).
U. S. Bureau of the Census. *Statistical History of the United States from Colonial Times to the Present* (Washington: Government Printing Office, 1960).
U. S. Department of State. *American Foreign Policy: Current Documents, 1981, 1985* (Washington: Government Printing Office, 1984, 1987).
———, *Department of State Bulletin.*
———. *Foreign Relations of the United States [hereafter FRUS]: 1920,* III (Washington: Government Printing Office, 1936).
———. *FRUS: 1946,* VI (Washington: Government Printing Office, 1969).
———. *FRUS: 1948,* II (Washington: Government Printing Office, 1973).
———. *FRUS: 1949,* V (Washington: Government Printing Office, 1976).
———. *FRUS: 1950,* I (Washington: Government Printing Office, 1977).
———. *FRUS: 1952–54,* II, V, XIV, XV (Washington: Government Printing Office, 1983–85).
———. *FRUS: 1955–57,* II, III (Washington: Government Printing Office, 1986).
———. *FRUS: The Conferences at Malta and Yalta, 1945* (Washington: Government Printing Office, 1955).
U. S. S. R. Ministerstvo innostrannykh del. *Dokumenty vneshnei politiki SSSR.*

BOOKS

Acheson, Dean, *Present at the Creation: My Years in the State Department* (New York: Norton, 1969).
Adomeit, Hannes, *Soviet Risk-Taking and Crisis Behavior: A Theoretical and Empirical Analysis* (London: Allen & Unwin, 1982).
Ambrose, Stephen E., *Eisenhower: The President* (New York: Simon and Schuster 1984).
———, and Richard H. Immerman, *Ike's Spies: Eisenhower and the Espionage Establishment* (Garden City, N. Y.: Doubleday, 1981).
Anderson, Martin, *Revolution* (New York: Harcourt Brace Jovanovich, 1988).
Andrew, Christopher, *Her Majesty's Secret Service: The Making of the British Intelligence Community* (New York: Viking, 1985).
———, and Oleg Gordievsky, *KGB: The Inside Story* (New York: HarperCollins, 1990).
Angell, Norman, *The Great Illusion: A Study of the Relationship of Military Power in Nations to Their Economic and Social Advantage* (London: Heinemann, 1910).
Axelrod, Robert, *The Evolution of Cooperation* (New York: Basic Books, 1984).
Balfour, Michael, *The Kaiser and His Times* (Boston: Houghton Mifflin, 1964).

Beisner, Robert L., *From the Old Diplomacy to the New, 1865–1900*, 2nd ed. (Arlington Heights, Ill.: Harlan-Davidson, 1986).

Bell, Coral, *Negotiation from Strength: A Study in the Politics of Power* (New York: Chatto and Windus, 1963).

———, *The Reagan Paradox: American Foreign Policy in the 1980s* (New Brunswick: Rutgers University Press, 1989).

Bennett, Edward M., *Franklin D. Roosevelt and the Search for Security: American-Soviet Relations, 1933–1939* (Wilmington, Del.: Scholarly Resources, 1985).

Bennett, Ralph F., *Ultra in the West: The Normandy Campaign* (London: Hutchinson, 1979).

Berding, Andrew H., *Dulles on Diplomacy* (Princeton: Princeton University Press, 1965).

Bethell, Nicholas, *Betrayed* (New York: Times Books, 1984).

Betts, Richard K., *Nuclear Blackmail and Nuclear Balance* (Washington: Brookings Institution, 1987).

Bialer, Seweryn, *The Soviet Paradox: External Expansion, Internal Decline* (New York: Knopf, 1986).

———, and Michael Mandelbaum, eds., *Gorbachev's Russia and American Foreign Policy* (Boulder: Westview Press, 1988).

Blainey, Geoffrey, *The Causes of War*, 3rd ed. (New York: Free Press, 1988).

Bloom, Allen, *The Closing of the American Mind* (New York: Simon and Schuster, 1987).

Bohlen, Charles E., *Witness to History: 1929–1969* (New York: Norton, 1973).

Boswell, John, *The Kindness of Strangers: The Abandonment of Children in Western Europe from Late Antiquity to the Renaissance* (New York: Pantheon, 1989).

Botti, Timothy J., *The Long Wait: The Forging of the Anglo-American Nuclear Alliance, 1945–1958* (Westport, Conn.: 1987).

Boyer, Paul, *By the Bomb's Early Light: American Thought and Culture at the Dawn of the Atomic Age* (New York: Pantheon, 1985).

Boyle, Andrew, *The Fourth Man: The Definitive Account of Kim Philby, Guy Burgess, and Donald Maclean and Who Recruited Them to Spy for Russia* (New York: Dial/James Wade, 1979).

Brands, H. W., Jr., *Cold Warriors: Eisenhower's Generation and American Foreign Policy* (New York: Columbia University Press, 1988).

Brinton, Crane, *The Anatomy of Revolution* (New York: Prentice-Hall, 1952).

Brodie, Bernard *War and Politics* (New York: Macmillan, 1973).

Brown, Anthony Cave, *Bodyguard of Lies* (New York: Harper & Row, 1985).

———, *"C": The Secret Life of Sir Stewart Graham Menzies, Spymaster to Winston Churchill* (New York: Macmillan, 1987).

———, *The Last Hero: Wild Bill Donovan* (New York: Random House, 1982).

Buckley, William F., Jr., *Gratitude: Reflections On What We Owe To Our Country* (New York: Random House, 1990).

Buhite, Russell D., *Decisions at Yalta: An Appraisal of Summit Diplomacy* (Wilmington, Delaware: Scholarly Resources, 1986).

Bullock, Alan, *Ernest Bevin: Foreign Secretary, 1945–1951* (New York: Norton, 1983).

Bundy, McGeorge, *Danger and Survival: Choices About the Bomb in the First Fifty Years* (New York: Random House, 1988).

Burrows, William E., *Deep Black: Space Espionage and National Security* (New York: Random House, 1986).

Butterfield, Herbert, *The Origins of History* (New York: Basic Books, 1981).

Byrnes, Robert F., ed., *After Brezhnev: The Sources of Soviet Conduct in the 1980s* (Bloomington: Indiana University Press, 1983).

Brzezinski, Zbigniew, *The Grand Failure: The Birth and Death of Communism in the Twentieth Century* (New York: Scribners,1989).

Callahan, David, *Dangerous Capabilities: Paul Nitze and the Cold War* (New York: HarperCollins, 1990).

Calleo, David P., *Beyond American Hegemony: The Future of the Western Alliance* (New York: Basic Books, 1987).

Calvocoressi, Peter, *Top Secret Ultra* (New York: Pantheon, 1980).

Campbell, Charles S., *The Transformation of American Foreign Relations, 1865–1900* (New York: Harper and Row, 1976).

Cannon, Lou, *President Reagan: The Role of a Lifetime* (New York: Simon and Schuster, 1991).

Carnesale, Albert, *et al.*, *Living with Nuclear Weapons* (New York: Bantam Books, 1983).

Carr, E. H., *What Is History?* (New York: Random House, 1961).

Chace, James. *Solvency: The Price of Survival* (New York: Random House, 1981).

Chang, Gordon H., *Friends and Enemies: The United States, China, and the Soviet Union, 1948–1972* (Stanford: Stanford University Press, 1990).

Chomsky, Noam, *Towards a New Cold War: Essays on the Current Crisis and How We Got There* (New York: Pantheon, 1982).

Choucri, Nazli, and Thomas W. Robinson, eds., *Forecasting in International Relations: Theory, Method, Problems, Prospects* (San Francisco: W. H. Freeman, 1978).

Churchill, Winston S., *The Gathering Storm* (New York, Bantam Books, 1961).

Clausewitz, Carl von, *On War*, edited and translated by Michael Howard and Peter Paret (Princeton: Princeton University Press, 1976).

Coleman, Peter, *The Liberal Conspiracy: The Congress for Cultural Freedom and the Struggle for the Mind of Postwar Europe* (New York: Free Press, 1989).

Colville, John, *The Fringes of Power: 10 Downing Street Diaries, 1939–1955* (New York: Norton, 1985).

Cooper, John Milton, Jr., *The Warrior and the Priest: Woodrow Wilson and Theodore Roosevelt* (Cambridge: Harvard University Press, 1983).

Craig, Gordon A., and Alexander L. George, *Force and Statecraft: Diplomatic Problems of Our Time*, 2nd ed. (New York: Oxford University Press, 1990).

———, and Felix Gilbert, eds., *The Diplomats: 1919–1939* (Princeton: Princeton University Press, 1953). 2 vols.

Crook, D. P., *The North, the South, and the Powers, 1861–1865* (New York: John Wiley, 1974).

Dallek, Robert, *The American Style of Foreign Policy: Cultural Politics and Foreign Affairs* (New York, Knopf, 1983).

———. *Franklin D. Roosevelt and American Foreign Policy, 1932–1945* (New York: Oxford University Press, 1979).

Daniloff, Nicholas, *Two Lives, One Russia* (Boston: Houghton Mifflin, 1988).

Darling, Arthur B., *The Central Intelligence Agency as Instrument of Government, to 1950* (University Park: Pennsylvania State University Press, 1990 [originally published as a CIA classified document in 1953]).

Darnton, Robert, *The Great Cat Massacre and Other Episodes in French Cultural History* (New York: Basic Books, 1984).

Davis, Rex Harry, and Robert Crocker Good, eds., *Reinhold Niebuhr on Politics* (New York: Scribners, 1960).

Deane, John R., *The Strange Alliance: The Story of Our Efforts at Wartime Co-operation with Russia* (New York: Viking, 1947).

DePorte, A. W., *Europe Between the Super-Powers: The Enduring Balance,* 2nd ed. (New Haven: Yale University Press, 1986).

Devlin, Patrick, *Too Proud to Fight: Woodrow Wilson's Neutrality* (New York: Oxford University Press, 1975).

Djilas, Milovan, *Conversations with Stalin,* translated by Michael B. Petrovich (New York: Harcourt Brace and World, 1962).

Dorn, Walter L., *Competition for Empire: 1740–1763* (New York: Harper and Row, 1940).

Dower, John W., *War Without Mercy: Race and Power in the Pacific War* (New York: Pantheon, 1986).

Doyle, Michael W., *Empires* (Ithaca: Cornell University Press, 1986).

Dulles, John Foster, *War or Peace* (New York: Macmillan, 1950).

Eckes, Alfred E., Jr., *A Search for Solvency: Bretton Woods and the International Monetary System, 1941–1971* (Austin: University of Texas Press, 1975).

Eldredge, Niles, *Time Frames: The Evolution of Punctuated Equilibria* (Princeton: Princeton University Press, 1985).

Enthoven, Alain C., and K. Wayne Smith, *How Much Is Enough? Shaping the Defense Program, 1961–1969* (New York: Harper and Row, 1971).

The Federalist Papers (New York: New American Library, 1961).

Fischer, David Hackett, *Historians' Fallacies: Toward a Logic of Historical Thought* (New York: Harper and Row, 1970).

Ford, Gerald R., *A Time to Heal* (New York: Harper and Row, 1979).

Fowler, W. B., *British-American Relations, 1917–1918: The Role of Sir William Wiseman* (Princeton: Princeton University Press, 1969).

Fox, Richard, *Reinhold Niebuhr: A Biography* (New York: Pantheon, 1985).

Freedman, Lawrence, *U. S. Intelligence and the Soviet Strategic Threat,* 2nd ed. (Princeton: Princeton University Press, 1986).

Friedberg, Aaron L., *The Weary Titan: Britain and the Experience of Relative Decline, 1895–1905* (Princeton: Princeton University Press, 1988).

Friedman, Thomas L., *From Beirut to Jerusalem* (New York: Farrar, Straus and Giroux, 1989).

Gaddis, John Lewis, *The Long Peace: Inquiries into the History of the Cold War* (New York: Oxford University Press, 1987).

———. *Russia, the Soviet Union, and the United States: An Interpretive History,* 2nd ed. (New York: McGraw-Hill, 1990).

———. *Strategies of Containment: A Critical Appraisal of Postwar American National Security Policy* (New York: Columbia University Press, 1982).

———. *The United States and the Origins of the Cold War, 1941–1947* (New York: Columbia University Press, 1972).

Garthoff, Raymond L., *Detente and Confrontation: American-Soviet Relations from Nixon to Reagan* (Washington: Brookings Institution, 1985).

Garton Ash, Timothy, *The Magic Lantern: The Revolution of '89 Witnessed in Warsaw, Budapest, Berlin, and Prague* (New York: Random House, 1990).

———, *The Uses of Adversity: Essays on the Fate of Central Europe* (New York: Random House, 1989).

Geduld, Harry M., ed., *The Definitive Time Machine: A Critical Edition of H. G. Wells' Scientific Romance* (Bloomington: Indiana University Press, 1987).

Gellman, Barton, *Contending with Kennan: Toward a Philosophy of American Power* (New York: Praeger, 1984).

George, Alexander L., Philip J. Farley, and Alexander Dallin, eds., *U.S.-Soviet Security Cooperation: Achievements, Failures, Lessons* (New York: Oxford University Press, 1988).

Gerson, Louis L., *John Foster Dulles* (New York: Cooper Square, 1968).

Gilbert, Felix, *To the Farewell Address: Ideas of Early American Foreign Policy* (Princeton: Princeton University Press, 1961).

Gilbert, Martin, *Winston Churchill: Finest Hour, 1939–1941* (Boston: Houghton Mifflin, 1983).

Gilpin, Robert, *The Political Economy of International Relations* (Princeton: Princeton University Press, 1987).

———, *War and Change in World Politics* (Cambridge: Cambridge University Press, 1981).

Glees, Anthony, *The Secrets of the Service: A Story of Soviet Subversion of Western Intelligence* (New York: Carroll and Graf, 1987).

Gleick, James, *Chaos: The Making of a New Science* (New York: Viking, 1987).

Goldstein, Joshua A., *Long Cycles: Prosperity and War in the Modern Age* (New Haven: Yale University Press, 1988).

Gorbachev, Mikhail S., *Perestroika: New Thinking for Our Country and for the World* (New York: Harper and Row, 1987).

Gould, Stephen Jay, *Time's Arrow, Time's Cycle: Myth and Metaphor in the Discovery of Geological Time* (Cambridge, Mass.: Harvard University Press, 1987).

———, *Wonderful Life: The Burgess Shale and the Nature of History* (New York: Norton, 1989).

Graebner, Norman A., ed., *Ideas and Diplomacy: Readings in the Intellectual Tradition of American Foreign Policy* (New York: Oxford University Press, 1964).

Gray, Colin S., *The Geopolitics of Super Power* (Lexington: University Press of Kentucky, 1988).

Greenstein, Fred I., *The Hidden-Hand Presidency: Eisenhower as Leader* (New York: Basic Books, 1982).

———, ed., *Leadership in the Modern Presidency* (Cambridge, Mass.: Harvard University Press, 1988).

Guhin, Michael A., *John Foster Dulles: A Statesman and His Times* (New York: Columbia University Press, 1972).

Haig, Alexander M., Jr., *Caveat: Realism, Reagan, and Foreign Policy* (New York: Macmillan, 1984).

Hall, John A., *Liberalism: Politics, Ideology, and the Market* (Chapel Hill: University of North Carolina Press, 1987).

———, *Powers and Liberties: The Causes and Consequences of the Rise of the West* (Berkeley: University of California Press, 1985).

Halle, Louis J., *The Cold War as History* (New York: Harper and Row, 1967).

Hamerow, Theodore S., *From the Finland Station: The Graying of Revolution in the Twentieth Century* (New York: Basic Books, 1990).

Harding, Harry, *China's Second Revolution: Reform After Mao* (Washington: Brookings Institution, 1987).

Haslam, Jonathan, *The Soviet Union and the Struggle for Collective Security in Europe, 1933–39* (New York: St. Martin's, 1984).

Heilbroner, Robert L., *The Worldly Philosophers: The Lives, Times, and Ideas of the Great Economic Thinkers*, 6th ed. (New York: Simon and Schuster, 1986).

Heinrichs, Waldo, *Threshold of War: Franklin D. Roosevelt and American Entry into World War II* (New York: Oxford University Press, 1988).

Herken, Gregg, *The Winning Weapon: The Atomic Bomb in the Cold War, 1945–1950* (New York: Knopf, 1980).

Hilsman, Roger, *To Move a Nation: The Politics of Foreign Policy in the Administration of John F. Kennedy* (New York: Doubleday, 1967).

Hinsley, F. H., *et al.*, *British Intelligence in the Second World War: Its Influence on Strategy and Operations*, 3 vols. (London: H. M. S. O., 1979–1988).

Hodgson, Godfrey, *The Colonel: The Life and Wars of Henry Stimson, 1867–1950* (New York: Knopf, 1990).

Hoffmann, Stanley, *Primacy or World Order: American Foreign Policy since the Cold War* (New York: McGraw-Hill, 1978).

Hogan, Michael J., *Informal Entente: The Private Structure of Cooperation in Anglo-American Economic Diplomacy, 1918–1928* (Columbia: University of Missouri Press, 1977).

————, *The Marshall Plan: America, Britain, and the Reconstruction of Western Europe, 1947–1952* (Cambridge: Cambridge University Press, 1987).

Holloway, David, *The Soviet Union and the Arms Race* (New Haven: Yale University Press, 1983).

Holsti, K. J., *The Dividing Discipline: Hegemony and Diversity in International Theory* (Boston: Allen and Unwin, 1985).

Holsti, Ole R., and James N. Rosenau, *American Leadership in World Affairs: Vietnam and the Breakdown of Consensus* (Boston: Allen and Unwin, 1984).

Hoopes, Townsend., *The Devil and John Foster Dulles* (Boston: Atlantic Little, Brown, 1973).

Hosking, Geoffrey, *The Awakening of the Soviet Union* (Cambridge: Harvard University Press, 1990).

Hough, Jerry, *Russia and the West: Gorbachev and the Politics of Reform*, 2nd ed. (New York: Simon and Schuster, 1990).

————, *The Struggle for the Third World: Soviet Debates and American Options* (Washington: Brookings Institution, 1986).

Hudson, George E., ed., *Soviet National Security Policy Under Perestroika* (Boston: Unwin Hyman, 1989).

————, and Joseph Kruzel, eds., *American Defense Annual: 1985–1986* (Lexington, Mass.: Lexington Books, 1985).

Hunt, Michael H., *Ideology and U.S. Foreign Policy* (New Haven: Yale University Press, 1987).

Immerman, Richard H., ed., *John Foster Dulles and the Diplomacy of the Cold War* (Princeton: Princeton University Press, 1990).

James, D. Clayton, *The Years of MacArthur: Triumph and Disaster, 1945–1964* (Boston: Houghton Mifflin, 1985).

Jervis, Robert, *The Meaning of the Nuclear Revolution: Statecraft and the Prospect of Armageddon* (Ithaca: Cornell University Press, 1989).

————, *Perception and Misperception in International Politics* (Princeton: Princeton University Press, 1976).

————, Richard Ned Lebow, and Janice Gross Stein, *Psychology and Deterrence* (Baltimore: Johns Hopkins University Press, 1985).

Johnson, James Turner, *Just War Tradition and the Restraint of War: A Moral and Historical Inquiry* (Princeton: Princeton University Press, 1981).

Johnson, Loch K., *A Season of Inquiry: The Senate Intelligence Investigation* (Lexington: University Press of Kentucky, 1985).

Jones, Howard, *"A New Kind of War": America's Global Strategy and the Truman Doctrine in Greece* (New York: Oxford University Press, 1989).

Jones, R. V., *The Wizard War: British Scientific Intelligence, 1939–1945* (New York: Coward, McCann and Geoghegan, 1978).

Kahn, David, *The Codebreakers: The Story of Secret Writing* (New York: Macmillan, 1967).

Kaiser, David, *Politics and War: European Conflict from Philip II to Hitler* (Cambridge, Mass.: Harvard University Press, 1990).

Kaplan, Lawrence S., *NATO and the United States: The Enduring Alliance* (Boston: Twayne, 1988).

Katz, Barry M., *Foreign Intelligence: Research and Analysis in the Office of Strategic Services, 1942–1945* (Cambridge: Harvard University Press, 1989).

Keegan, John, *The Face of Battle* (New York: Viking, 1976).

———, *The Mask of Command* (New York: Viking, 1987).

Kegley, Charles W., Jr., ed., *The Long Postwar Peace: Contending Explanations and Projections* (New York: HarperCollins, 1990).

Kennan, George F., *American Diplomacy: 1900–1950* (Chicago: University of Chicago Press, 1951).

———, *Memoirs: 1925–1950* (Boston: Atlantic Little, Brown, 1967).

———, *Memoirs: 1950–1963* (Boston: Atlantic Little, Brown, 1972).

———, *The Nuclear Delusion: Soviet-American Relations in the Atomic Age* (New York: Pantheon, 1982).

———, *Soviet-American Relations, 1917–1920: The Decision to Intervene* (Princeton: Princeton University Press, 1958).

Kennedy, Paul, *The Rise and Fall of the Great Powers: Economic Change and Military Conflict from 1500 to 2000* (New York: Random House, 1987).

Keohane, Robert O., *After Hegemony: Cooperation and Discord in the World Political Economy* (Princeton: Princeton University Press, 1984).

———, ed., *Neorealism and Its Critics* (New York: Columbia University Press, 1986).

———, and Joseph S. Nye, *Power and Interdependence: World Politics in Transition* (Boston: Little, Brown, 1977).

Kern, Stephen, *The Culture of Time and Space, 1880–1914* (Cambridge, Mass.: Harvard University Press, 1983).

Kimball, Warren F., *Swords or Ploughshares? The Morgenthau Plan for Defeated Nazi Germany, 1943–1946* (Philadelphia: Lippincott, 1976).

Kindleberger, Charles P., *The World in Depression, 1929–1939* (Berkeley: University of California Press, 1973).

Kissinger, Henry A., *American Foreign Policy*, 3rd ed. (New York: Norton, 1977).

———, *White House Years* (Boston: Little, Brown, 1979).

———, *Years of Upheaval* (Boston: Little, Brown, 1982).

Khrushchev, Nikita S., *Khrushchev Remembers: The Last Testament*, translated and edited by Strobe Talbott (Boston: Little, Brown, 1974).

Knightley, Philip J., *The Second Oldest Profession* (New York: Norton, 1987).

Komer, Robert W., *Maritime Strategy or Coalition Defense?* (Cambridge, Mass.: Abt Books, 1984).

Krasner, Stephen, ed., *International Regimes* (Ithaca: Cornell University Press, 1983).

Kruzel, Joseph, ed., *American Defense Annual: 1988–89* (Lexington, Mass.: Lexington Books, 1988).

Kuhn, Thomas, *The Structure of Scientific Revolutions*, 2nd ed., enlarged (Chicago: University of Chicago Press, 1970).

Kyvig, David E., ed., *Reagan and the World* (New York: Greenwood Press, 1990).

Lamphere, Robert J., and Tom Schachtman, *The FBI-KGB War: A Special Agent's Story* (New York: Random House, 1986).

Langer, William L., and S. Everett Gleason, *The Challenge to Isolation: The World Crisis of 1937–1940 and American Foreign Policy* (New York: Harper and Row, 1952).

Laqueur, Walter, *A World of Secrets: The Uses and Limits of Intelligence* (New York: Basic Books, 1985).

Larson, Deborah Welch, *Origins of Containment* (Princeton: Princeton University Press, 1985).

Layton, Edwin T., with Roger Pineau and John Costello, *"And I Was There": Pearl Harbor and Midway—Breaking the Secrets* (New York: Morrow, 1985).

Lebow, Richard Ned, *Between War and Peace: The Nature of International Crisis* (Baltimore: Johns Hopkins University Press, 1981).

Leffler, Melvyn P., *The Elusive Quest: America's Pursuit of European Stability and French Security, 1919–1933* (Chapel Hill: University of North Carolina Press, 1979).

Levin, N. Gordon, *Woodrow Wilson and World Politics: America's Response to War and Revolution* (New York: Oxford University Press, 1968).

Lewin, Ronald, *The American Magic: Codes, Ciphers, and the Defeat of Japan* (New York: Farrar Straus Giroux, 1982).

———, *Ultra Goes to War: The First Account of World War II's Greatest Secret Based on Official Documents* (New York: McGraw-Hill, 1979).

Lewis, John Wilson, and Xue Litai, *China Builds the Bomb* (Stanford: Stanford University Press, 1988).

Lilienthal, David E., *The Journals of David E. Lilienthal: The Atomic Energy Years, 1945–1950* (New York: Harper & Row, 1964).

Link, Arthur S., *Woodrow Wilson: Revolution, War, and Peace* (Arlington Heights, Ill.: Harlan-Davidson, 1979).

Lippmann, Walter, *U. S. Foreign Policy: Shield of the Republic* (Boston: Little, Brown, 1943).

Lopez, Barry, *Arctic Dreams: Imagination and Desire in a Northern Landscape* (New York: Scribner's, 1986).

Lundestad, Geir, *The American "Empire" and Other Studies of US Foreign Policy in a Comparative Perspective* (New York: Oxford University Press, 1990).

Maddux, Thomas R., *Years of Estrangement: American Relations with the Soviet Union, 1933–1941* (Tallahassee: University Presses of Florida, 1980).

Mandelbaum, Michael, *The Nuclear Revolution: International Politics Before and After Hiroshima* (Cambridge: Cambridge University Press, 1981).

Mansbach, Richard W. and John A. Vasquez, *In Search of Theory: A New Paradigm for Global Politics* (New York: Columbia University Press, 1981).

Marks, Frederick W., III, *Wind over Sand: The Diplomacy of Franklin D. Roosevelt* (Athens: University of Georgia Press, 1988).

Martin, David C., *Wilderness of Mirrors* (New York: Harper and Row, 1980).

Masterman, Sir John, *The Double-Cross System in the War of 1939–1945* (New Haven: Yale University Press, 1972).

Mastny, Vojtech, *Russia's Road to the Cold War: Diplomacy, Warfare, and the Politics of Communism, 1941–1945* (New York: Columbia University Press, 1979).

May, Ernest R., ed., *Knowing One's Enemies: Intelligence Assessment Before the Two World Wars* (Princeton: Princeton University Press, 1984).

Mayer, Arno J., *Political Origins of the New Diplomacy, 1917–1918: Wilson vs. Lenin* (New Haven: Yale University Press, 1959).

Mayers, David Allan, *Cracking the Monolith: U.S. Policy Against the Sino-Soviet Alliance, 1949–1955* (Baton Rouge: Louisiana State University Press, 1986).

McCormick, Thomas J., *America's Half Century: United States Foreign Policy in the Cold War* (Baltimore: Johns Hopkins University Press, 1989).

McNeill, William H., *The Pursuit of Power: Technology, Armed Force, and Society since A. D. 1000* (Chicago: University of Chicago Press, 1982).

Mead, Walter Russell, *Mortal Splendor: The American Empire in Transition* (Boston: Houghton Mifflin, 1987).

Medvedev, Roy A., *Let History Judge: The Origins and Consequences of Stalinism*, rev. and expanded ed., translated by George Shriver (New York: Columbia University Press, 1989).

Melanson, Richard A., and David Mayers, eds., *Reevaluating Eisenhower: American Foreign Policy in the Fifties* (Urbana: University of Illinois Press, 1987).

Messer, Robert, *The End of an Alliance: James F. Byrnes, Roosevelt, Truman and the Origins of the Cold War* (Chapel Hill: University of North Carolina Press, 1982).

Meyer, Cord, *Facing Reality: From World Federalism to the CIA* (New York: Harper and Row, 1980).

Miller, J. D. B., *Norman Angell and the Futility of War: Peace and the Public Mind* (New York: St. Martin's, 1986).

Miller, James Edward, *The United States and Italy, 1940–1950: The Politics and Diplomacy of Stabilization* (Chapel Hill: University of North Carolina Press, 1986).

Modelski, George, ed., *Exploring Long Cycles* (Boulder: Lynne Rienner, 1987).

Montague, Ludwell Lee, *General Walter Bedell Smith as Director of Central Intelligence, October, 1950-February, 1953* (University Park, Pennsulvania: Pennsylvania State University Press, 1991 [originally published as a CIA classified document in 1971]).

Morgan, Patrick M., *Theories and Approaches to International Politics: What Are We To Think?* 4th ed. (New Brunswick: Transaction Books, 1987).

Morris, Charles R., *Iron Destinies, Lost Opportunities: The Arms Race Between the U,S.A. and the U.S.S.R., 1945–1987* (New York: Harper and Row, 1988).

Mottahedeh, Roy, *The Mantle of the Prophet: Religion and Politics in Iran* (New York: Pantheon, 1985).

Moynihan, Daniel Patrick, *On the Law of Nations* (Cambridge, Mass.: Harvard University Press, 1990).

Mueller, John, *Retreat from Doomsday: The Obsolescence of Major War* (New York: Basic Books, 1989).

National Conference of Catholic Bishops. *The Challenge of Peace: God's Promise and Our Response* (Washington: National Conference of Catholic Bishops, 1983).

Nau, Henry R., *The Myth of America's Decline: Leading the World Economy into the 1990s* (New York: Oxford University Press, 1990).

Newhouse, John, *Cold Dawn: The Story of SALT* (New York: Holt, Rinehart and Winston, 1973).

———, *War and Peace in the Nuclear Age* (New York: Knopf, 1989).

Ninkovich, Frank, *Germany and the United States: The Transformation of the German Question Since 1945* (Boston: Twayne, 1988).

Nitze, Paul H., *From Hiroshima to Glasnost: At the Center of Decision* (New York: Grove Weidenfeld, 1989).

Nye, Joseph S., Jr., *Bound to Lead: The Changing Nature of American Power* (New York: Basic Books, 1990).

Olson, Mancur, *The Rise and Decline of Nations: Economic Growth, Stagflation, and Social Rigidities* (New Haven: Yale University Press, 1982).

Orwell, George, *1984* (New York: Harcourt, Brace, 1949).

Oye, Kenneth A., ed., *Cooperation Under Anarchy* (Princeton: Princeton University Press, 1986).

———, Robert J. Lieber, and Donald Rothchild, eds., *Eagle Resurgent? The Reagan Era in American Foreign Policy* (Boston: Little, Brown, 1987).

Pagels, Heinz R., *The Dreams of Reason: The Computer and the Rise of the Sciences of Complexity* (New York: Bantam, 1988).

Persico, Joseph E., *Casey: From the OSS to the CIA* (New York: Viking, 1990).

Pickersgill, J. W., and D. F. Foster, eds., *The Mackenzie King Record: Volume 3, 1945–1946* (Toronto: University of Toronto Press, 1970).

Pincher, Chapman, *Too Secret Too Long* (New York: St. Martin's, 1984).

Pipes, Richard, *The Russian Revolution* (New York: Knopf, 1990).

Pollard, Robert A., *Economic Security and the Origins of the Cold War, 1945–1950* (New York: Columbia University Press, 1985).

Powers, Richard Gid, *Secrecy and Power: The Life of J. Edgar Hoover* (New York: Macmillan, 1987).

Powers, Thomas, *The Man Who Kept the Secrets: Richard Helms and the CIA* (New York: Knopf, 1979).

Prados, John, *Presidents' Secret Wars: CIA and Pentagon Covert Operations Since World War II* (New York: Morrow, 1986).

———, *The Soviet Estimate: U. S. Intelligence Analysis and Russian Military Strength* (New York: Dial Press, 1982).

Prestowitz, Clyde V., Jr., *Trading Places: How We Are Giving Our Future to Japan and How to Reclaim It* (New York: Basic Books, 1989).

Pruessen, Ronald W., *John Foster Dulles: The Road to Power* (New York: Free Press, 1982).

Pyne, Stephen J., *The Ice: A Journey to Antarctica* (New York: Ballantine Books, 1986).

Radosh, Ronald, and Joyce Milton, *The Rosenberg File: A Search for the Truth* (New York: Holt, Rinehart and Winston, 1983).

Radvanyi, Janos, *Delusion and Reality: Gambits, Hoaxes, and Diplomatic One-Upmanship in Vietnam* (South Bend, Ind.: Gateway Editions, 1978).

Ranelagh, John, *The Agency: The Rise and Decline of the CIA* (New York: Simon and Schuster, 1986).

Reagan, Ronald, *An American Life* (New York: Simon and Schuster, 1990).

———, *National Security Strategy of the United States* (Washington: Government Printing Office, 1987).

Regan, Donald T., *For the Record: From Wall Street to Washington* (New York: Harcourt Brace Jovanovich, 1988).

Rhodes, Richard, *The Making of the Atomic Bomb* (New York: Simon and Schuster, 1986).

Richelson, Jeffrey, *American Espionage and the Soviet Target* (New York: Morrow, 1987).

Ridley, Jasper, *Lord Palmerston* (London: Constable, 1970).

Rizopolous, Nicholas X., ed., *Sea-Changes: American Foreign Policy in a World Transformed* (New York: Council on Foreign Relations Press, 1990).

Rosecrance, Richard, *The Rise of the Trading State: Commerce and Conquest in the Modern World* (New York: Basic Books, 1986).

Rosenau, James N., *The Study of Global Interdependence* (London: Pinter, 1980).

———, ed., *International Politics and Foreign Policy: A Reader in Research and Theory* (New York: Free Press, 1961).

Rostow, W. W., *The Stages of Economic Growth: A Non-Communist Manifesto* (New York: Cambridge University Press, 1962).

Ruddy, T. Michael, *The Cautious Diplomat: Charles E. Bohlen and the Soviet Union, 1929–1969* (Kent, Ohio: Kent State University Press, 1986).

Sanders, Jerry W., *Peddlers of Crisis: The Committee on the Present Danger and Containment* (Boston: South End Press, 1983).

Schama, Simon, *Citizens: A Chronicle of the French Revolution* (New York: Knopf, 1989).

Scheer, Robert, *With Enough Shovels: Reagan, Bush, and Nuclear War* (New York: Random House, 1983).

Schell, Jonathan, *The Fate of the Earth* (New York: Knopf, 1982).

Schelling, Thomas C., *Arms and Influence* (New Haven: Yale University Press, 1966).

Schilling, Warner R., Paul Y. Hammond, and Glenn H. Snyder, *Strategy, Politics, and Defense Budgets* (New York: Columbia University Press, 1962).

Schlesinger, Arthur M., Jr., *The Cycles of American History* (Boston: Houghton Mifflin, 1986).

Schwabe, Klaus, *Woodrow Wilson, Revolutionary Germany, and Peacemaking, 1918–1919: Missionary Diplomacy and the Realities of Power*, translated by Robert and Rita Kimber (Chapel Hill: University of North Carolina Press, 1985).

Shafer, D. Michael, *Deadly Paradigms: The Failure of U.S. Counterinsurgency Policy* (Princeton: Princeton University Press, 1988).

Sherry, Michael S., *Preparing for the Next War: American Plans for Postwar Defense, 1941–45* (New Haven: Yale University Press, 1977).

Sherwin, Martin J., *A World Destroyed: Hiroshima and the Origins of the Arms Race* (New York: Random House, 1987).

Shulman, Marshall D., *Stalin's Foreign Policy Reappraised* (Cambridge, Mass.: Harvard University Press, 1963).

Sipols, Vilnis, *The Road to Great Victory: Soviet Diplomacy, 1941–1945*, translated by Lev Bobrov (Moscow: Progress Publishers, 1985).

Sivachev, Nikolai V., and Nikolai N. Yakovlev, *Russia and the United States*, translated by Olga Adler Titelbaum (Chicago: University of Chicago Press, 1979).

Small, Melvin, and J. David Singer, *Resort to Arms: International and Civil Wars, 1816–1980* (Beverly Hills: Sage, 1982).

Smith, Bradley F., *The Shadow Warriors: O.S.S. and the Origins of the C.I.A.* (New York: Basic Books, 1983).

Smith, Daniel M., *The Great Departure: The United States and World War I, 1914–1918* (New York: John Wiley, 1965).

Smith, Gaddis, *Morality, Reason and Power: American Diplomacy in the Carter Years* (New York: 1986).

Stares, Paul B., *The Militarization of Space: U.S. Policy, 1945–1984* (Ithaca: Cornell University Press, 1985).

Steinberg, Gerald M., *Satellite Reconnaissance: The Role of Informal Bargaining* (New York: Praeger, 1983).

Stephenson, William, *A Man Called Intrepid: The Secret War* (New York: Harcourt Brace Jovanovich, 1976).

Stimson, Henry L., and McGeorge Bundy, *On Active Service in Peace and War* (New York: Harper, 1948).

Stone, Lawrence, *The Family, Sex and Marriage in England, 1500–1800* (New York: Harper and Row, 1979).

Talbott, Strobe, *Deadly Gambits: The Reagan Administration and the Stalemate in Arms Control* (New York: Knopf, 1984).

———, *The Master of the Game: Paul Nitze and the Nuclear Peace* (New York: Knopf, 1988).

Taubman, William, *Stalin's American Policy: From Entente to Detente to Cold War* (New York: Norton, 1982).

Thomas, Hugh, *Armed Truce: The Beginnings of the Cold War, 1945–46* (London: Hamish Hamilton, 1986).

Thucydides, *History of the Peloponnesian War*, translated by Rex Warner (New York: Penguin Books, 1954).

Tucker, Robert W., *The Radical Left and American Foreign Policy* (Baltimore: Johns Hopkins University Press, 1971).

Ulam, Adam, *Stalin: The Man and His Era* (New York: Viking, 1973).

Utley, Jonathan G., *Going to War with Japan, 1937–1941* (Knoxville: University of Tennessee Press, 1985).

Van Creveld, Martin, *Technology and War: From 2000 B.C. to the Present* (New York: Free Press, 1989).

Walt, Stephen M., *The Origins of Alliances* (Ithaca: Cornell University Press, 1987).

Waltz, Kenneth N., *The Spread of Nuclear Weapons: More May Be Better*, Adelphi Papers, No. 171 (London: International Institute of Strategic Studies, 1981).

———, *Theory of International Politics* (New York: Random House, 1979).

Walzer, Michael, *Just and Unjust Wars: A Moral Argument with Historical Illustrations* (New York: Basic Books, 1977).

Wark, Wesley K., *The Ultimate Enemy: British Intelligence and Nazi Germany, 1933–1919* (Ithaca: Cornell University Press, 1985).

Watt, Donald Cameron, *How War Came: The Immediate Origins of the Second World War, 1938–1939* (New York: Pantheon, 1989).

Weart, Spencer, *Nuclear Fear: A History of Images* (Cambridge, Mass.: Harvard University Press, 1988).

Weinberger, Caspar, *Fighting for Peace: Seven Critical Years in the Pentagon* (New York: Warner Books, 1990).

Weinstein, Allen, *Perjury: The Hiss-Chambers Case* (New York: Knopf, 1978).

Williams, Robert Chadwell, *Klaus Fuchs, Atom Spy* (Cambridge: Harvard University Press, 1987).

Williams, William Appleman, *The Tragedy of American Diplomacy* (New York: Norton, 1988 [first published in 1959]).

Willkie, Wendell L., *One World* (New York: Simon and Schuster, 1943).

Winks, Robin W., *Cloak and Gown: Scholars in the Secret War, 1939–1961* (New York: Morrow, 1987).

Winterbotham, F. W., *The Ultra Secret* (New York: Harper and Row, 1974).

Woodward, Bob, *Veil: The Secret Wars of the CIA, 1981–1987* (New York: Simon and Schuster, 1987).

Wright, Peter, with Paul Greenglass, *Spycatcher: The Candid Autobiography of a Senior Intelligence Officer* (New York: Viking Penguin, 1987).

Wohlstetter, Roberta, *Pearl Harbor: Warning and Decision* (Stanford: Stanford University Press, 1962).

Wood, Gordon S., *The Creation of the American Republic, 1776–1787* (Chapel Hill: University of North Carolina Press, 1969).

Young, Kenneth T., *Negotiating with the Chinese Communists: The United States Experience, 1953–1967* (New York: McGraw-Hill, 1968).

ARTICLES

"After the Revolutions," *New Republic*, CCI(November 6, 1989), 11–14.

"American Living Standards: Running to Stand Still," *The Economist*, CCCXVII(November 10, 1990), 19–22.

Apple, R. W., Jr., "The New Embrace: U. S. Moves to Help Cold War Rival Much as It Aided World War II Foes," *New York Times*, December 13, 1990.

Arbatov, Georgii, "The Limited Power of an Ordinary State," *New Perspectives Quarterly*, V(Summer, 1988), 28–32.

Aron, Raymond, "What Is a Theory of International Relations?" *Journal of International Affairs*, XXII(1967), 185–206.

Atlas, James, "What Is Fukuyama Saying and to Whom Is He Saying It?" *New York Times Magazine*, October 22, 1989, pp. 38–42, 54–55.

Bialer, Seweryn, "Russia vs. the Soviet Union," *U.S. News*, CIX(November 5, 1990), 46–47.

———, and Joan Afferica, "Reagan and Russia," *Foreign Affairs*, LXI(Winter, 1982/83), 249–71.

Blair, Bruce G., and Henry W. Kendall, "Accidental Nuclear War," *Scientific American*, CCLXIII(December, 1990), 53–58.

Blum, Robert M., "Surprised by Tito: The Anatomy of an Intelligence Failure," *Diplomatic History*, XII(Winter, 1988), 39–57.

Bohlen, Celestine, "Ethnic Rivalries Revive in East Europe," *New York Times*, November 12, 1990.

Broad, William J., "Guarding the Bomb: A Perfect Record, But Can It Last?" *New York Times*, January 29, 1991.

Broscious, S. David, "Approaches to International Systemic Stability," Nuclear History Program Working Paper, September, 1990.

Buhite, Russell D., and Wm. Christopher Hamel, "War for Peace: The Question of an American Preventive War Against the Soviet Union, 1945–1955," *Diplomatic History*, XIV(Summer, 1990), 367–84.

Burns, John F., "In Quebec, Yet Another Splintering," *New York Times*, July 29, 1990.

Campbell, Robert W., "The Economy," in Robert F. Byrnes, ed., *After Brezhnev: The Sources of Soviet Conduct in the 1980s* (Bloomington: Indiana University Press, 1983), pp. 68–124.

Cohen, Warren I., "Gaps in the Record: How State Has Allowed History To Be Incomplete," *Foreign Service Journal*, LXVII (August, 1990), 27–29.

Cox, Robert W., "Social Forces, States and World Orders: Beyond International Relations Theory," in Robert O. Keohane, ed., *Neorealism and Its Critics* (New York: Columbia University Press, 1986), pp. 204–54.

Dallin, Alexander, and Gail W. Lapidus, "Reagan and the Russians: American Policy

Toward the Soviet Union," in Kenneth A. Oye, Robert J. Lieber, and Donald Rothchild, eds., *Eagle Resurgent? The Reagan Era in American Foreign Policy* (Boston: Little, Brown, 1987), pp. 193–254.

Dawisha, Karen, "The U. S. S. R. in the Middle East: Superpower in Eclipse?" *Foreign Affairs*, LXI(Winter, 1982/83), 438–52.

Doyle, Michael, "Kant, Liberal Legacies, and Foreign Affairs," *Philosophy and Public Affairs*, XII(Summer and Fall, 1983), 205–35, 323–53.

———, "Liberalism and World Politics," *American Political Science Review*, LXXX(December, 1986), 1151–62.

D'Souza, Dinesh, "Illiberal Education," *The Atlantic*, CCLXVII(March, 1991), 51–79.

Dulles, John Foster, "A Policy of Boldness," *Life*, XXXII(May 19, 1952), 146–60.

———, "Policy for Security and Peace," *Foreign Affairs*, XXXII(April, 1954), 353–64.

Erickson, John, "Threat Identification and Strategic Appraisal by the Soviet Union, 1930–1941," in Ernest R. May, ed., *Knowing One's Enemies: Intelligence Assessment Before the Two World Wars* (Princeton: Princeton University Press, 1984), pp. 375–423.

Evangelista, Matthew A., "Stalin's Postwar Army Reappraised," *International Security*, VII(Winter, 1982/83), 110–38.

Fearon, James D., "Counterfactuals and Hypothesis Testing in Political Science," *World Politics*, XLIII(January, 1991), 169–95.

Feaver, Peter G., "Does Moscow Know Where Its Nukes Are?" *Los Angeles Times*, December 22, 1990.

Fukuyama, Francis, "The End of History," *The National Interest*, #16(Summer, 1989), 3–18.

———, "Gorbachev and the Third World," *Foreign Affairs*, LXIV(Spring, 1986), 715–31.

Gaddis, John Lewis, "Containment and the Logic of Strategy," *The National Interest*, #10(Winter, 1987/88), 27–38.

———, "Coping With Victory," *The Atlantic*, CCLXV(May, 1990), 49–60.

———, "The Emerging Post-Revisionist Synthesis on the Origins of the Cold War," *Diplomatic History*, VII(Summer, 1983), 171–90.

———, "Expanding the Data Base: Historians, Political Scientists, and the Enrichment of Security Studies," *International Security*, XII(Summer, 1987), 3–21.

———, "Nuclear Weapons and International Systemic Stability," Emerging Issues Occasional Papers Series #2, January, 1990, American Academy of Arts and Sciences.

———, "One Germany—in Both Alliances," *New York Times*, March 21, 1990.

Garrity, Patrick J., "The Future of Nuclear Weapons: Final Study Report," Report No. 8 (February, 1990), Center for National Security Studies, Los Alamos National Laboratories.

Garton Ash, Timothy, "Germany Unbound," *New York Review of Books*, XXXVII(November 22, 1990), pp. 11–15.

Gati, Charles, "Polish Futures, Western Options," *Foreign Affairs*, LXI(Winter, 1982/83), 292–308.

George, Alexander L., "Problem-Oriented Forecasting," in Nazli Choucri and Thomas W. Robinson, eds., *Forecasting in International Relations: Theory, Method, Problems, Prospects* (San Francisco: W. H. Freeman, 1978), 329–36.

Gilpin, Robert, "American Policy in the Post-Reagan Era," *Daedalus*, CXVI(Summer, 1987), 33–67.

Gimbel, John, "Project Paperclip: German Scientists, American Policy, and the Cold War," *Diplomatic History*, XIV(Summer, 1990), 343–65.

"Go Forth and Unify," *The Economist*, CCCLXVII(October 6, 1990), 16.

Heilbroner, Robert, "Economic Predictions," *New Yorker*, LXVII(July 8, 1991), 70–77."

———, The Triumph of Capitalism," *New Yorker*, LXV(January 23, 1989), 98–109.

Hennessy, Peter, and Kathleen Townsend, "The Documentary Spoor of Burgess and Maclean," *Intelligence and National Security*, II(April, 1987), 291–301.

Herken, Gregg, "The Great Foreign Policy Fight," *American Heritage*, XXXVII(April-May, 1986), 65–80.

Hirsch, Daniel, and William G. Mathews, "The H-Bomb: Who Really Gave Away the Secret?" *Bulletin of the Atomic Scientists*, XLVI(January/February, 1990), 22–30.

Hoffmann, Stanley, "An Icelandic Saga," *New York Review of Books*, XXXIII(November 28, 1986), 15–17.

———, "International Relations: The Long Road to Theory," in James N. Rosenau, ed., *International Politics and Foreign Policy: A Reader in Research and Theory* (New York: Free Press, 1961), pp. 421–37.

Holsti, Ole R., "Models of International Relations and Foreign Policy," *Diplomatic History*, XIII(Winter, 1989), 15–43.

Huntington, Samuel P., "No Exit: The Errors of Endism," *National Interest*, #17(Fall, 1989), 3–11.

Ikenberry, G. John, "Rethinking the Origins of American Hegemony," *Political Science Quarterly*, CIX(Fall, 1989), 375–400.

Jervis, Robert, "Intelligence and Foreign Policy: A Review Essay," *International Security*, XI(Winter, 1986–87), 141–61.

———, "Security Regimes," in Stephen Krasner, ed., *International Regimes* (Ithaca: Cornell University Press, 1983). pp. 173–94.

Joynt, Carey B., and Nicholas Rescher, "The Problem of Uniqueness in History," *History and Theory*, I(1961), 150–62.

Jukes, Geoff, "The Soviets and Ultra," *Intelligence and National Security*, III(April, 1988), 233–47.

Kaufmann, William W., "Two American Ambassadors: Bullitt and Kennedy," in Gordon A. Craig and Felix Gilbert, eds., *The Diplomats: 1919–1939* (Princeton: Princeton University Press, 1953), pp. 649–81.

Kaysen, Carl, "Is War Obsolete? A Review Essay," *International Security* XIV(Spring, 1990), 42–64.

Kennan, George F., "Communism in Russian History," *Foreign Affairs*, LXIX(Winter, 1990/91), 168–86.

———, "Morality and Foreign Policy," *Foreign Affairs*, LXIV(Winter, 1985/86), 205–18.

———, "The Sources of Soviet Conduct," *Foreign Affairs*, XXV(July, 1947), 566–82.

Kimball, Warren F., and Bruce Bartlett, "Roosevelt and Prewar Commitments to Churchill: The Tyler Kent Affair," *Diplomatic History*, V(Fall, 1981), 291–311.

Kirkpatrick, Jeane J., "Dictatorships and Double Standards," *Commentary*, LXVIII(November, 1979), 34–45.

Kolata, Gina, "Japanese Labs in U.S. Luring America's Computer Experts," *New York Times*, November 11, 1990.

Krakau, Knud, "American Foreign Relations: A National Style?" *Diplomatic History*, VIII(Summer, 1984), 253–72.

Kuniholm, Bruce R., "Foreign Relations, Public Relations, Accountability, and Understanding," *Perspectives* [newsletter of the American Historical Association], XXVIII(May/June, 1990), 1, 11–12.

Lacayo, Richard, "Why No Blue Blood Will Flow," *Time*, CXXXVI (November 26, 1990), 34.

Leuchtenburg, William E., "Franklin D. Roosevelt: The First Modern President," in Fred I. Greenstein, ed., *Leadership in the Modern Presidency* (Cambridge, Mass.: Harvard University Press, 1988), pp. 7–40.

Lewis, Bernard, "The Roots of Muslim Rage," *The Atlantic*, CCLXVI (September, 1990), 47–60.

Lipson, Charles, "International Cooperation in Economic and Security Affairs," *World Politics*, XXXVII(October, 1984), 1–23.

Lundestad, Geir, "Empire by Invitation? The United States and Western Europe, 1945– 1952," *Journal of Peace Research*, XXIII(September, 1986), 263–77.

Luttwak, Edward, "Do the Joint Chiefs Fear All Risks?" *New York Times*, October 27, 1989.

Maddux, Thomas R., "United States-Soviet Naval Relations in the 1930's: The Soviet Union's Efforts to Purchase Naval Vessels," *Naval War College Review*, XXIX(Fall, 1976), 28–37.

Makhov, Alexander, "Stalin Approved Kim Il Sung's Order," *Moscow News Weekly*, #27(July 15–22, 1990), 12.

Mandelbaum, Michael, "The Reagan Administration and the Nature of Arms Control," in Joseph Kruzel, ed., *American Defense Annual: 1988–89* (Lexington, Mass.: Lexington Books, 1988), pp. 193–208.

Mastny, Vojtech, "Europe in US-USSR Relations: A Topical Legacy," *Problems of Communism*, XXXVII(January-February, 1988), 16–29.

———, "Stalin and the Militarization of the Cold War," *International Security*, IX(Winter, 1984–85), 109–29.

May, Ernest R., "Conclusions: Capabilities and Proclivities," in May, ed., *Knowing One's Enemies: Intelligence Assessment Before the Two World Wars* (Princeton: Princeton University Press, 1984), pp. 503–42.

McNeill, William H., "Winds of Change," in Nicholas X. Rizopolous, ed., *Sea-Changes: American Foreign Policy in a World Transformed* (New York: Council on Foreign Relations Press, 1990), pp. 163–203.

Mearsheimer, John J., "Back to the Future: Instability in Europe after the Cold War," *International Security*, XV(Summer, 1990), 5–56.

———, "Why We Will Soon Miss the Cold War," *The Atlantic*, CCLXVI(August, 1990), 35–50.

Merta, Ed, "Fallen Empires and the Origins of the Persian Gulf Crisis," Ohio University Contemporary History Institute *Thinkpiece* #4(January, 1991).

Miner, Steven Merritt, "Military Crisis and Social Change in Russian and Soviet History," in George E. Hudson, ed., *Soviet National Security Policy Under Perestroika* (Boston: Unwin Hyman, 1989), pp. 29–46.

Modelski, George, and Patrick M. Morgan, "Understanding Global War," *Journal of Conflict Resolution*, XXIX(September, 1985), 391–417.

Moiseyev, Nikita, "The Hiroshima and Nagasaki Tragedy in Documents," *International Affairs*, #8(August, 1990), 122–39.

Morgenthau, Hans J., "Reflections on the State of Political Science," *Review of Politics*, XVII(October, 1955), 455–56.

Mueller, John, "The Essential Irrelevance of Nuclear Weapons: Stability in the Postwar World," *International Security*, XIII(Fall, 1988), 55–79.

Muir, William K., Jr., "Ronald Reagan: The Primacy of Rhetoric," in Fred I. Greenstein, ed., *Leadership in the Modern Presidency* (Cambridge, Mass.: Harvard University Press, 1988), pp. 260–95.

Nance, R. Damian, Thomas R. Worsley and Judith R. Moody, "The Supercontinent Cycle," *Scientific American*, CCLIX(July, 1988), 72–79.

Nye, Joseph S., Jr., "Neorealism and Neoliberalism," *World Politics*, XL(January, 1988), 235–51.

——, "Nuclear Learning and U.S.-Soviet Security Regimes," *International Organization*, XLI(Summer, 1987), 371–402.

——, "Old Wars and Future Wars: Causation and Prevention," *Journal of Interdisciplinary History*, XVIII(Spring, 1988), 581–90.

——, "Soft Power," *Foreign Policy*, #80(Fall, 1990), 153–71.

"Race on Campus," *New Republic*, CCIV(February 19, 1991) [special issue].

Ray, James Lee, "The Abolition of Slavery and the End of International War," *International Organization*, XLIII(Summer, 1989), 405–39.

Rosenberg, David Alan, "The Origins of Overkill: Nuclear Weapons and American Strategy, 1945–1960," *International Security*, VII(Spring, 1983), 3–71.

Rosenfeld, Stephen S., "The Guns of July," *Foreign Affairs*, LXIV(Spring, 1986), 698–714.

——, "Testing the Hard Line," *Foreign Affairs*, LXI("America and the World, 1982"), 489–510.

Ruggie, John Gerard, "Continuity and Transformation in the World Polity," in Robert O. Keohane, ed., *Neorealism and Its Critics* (New York: Columbia University Press, 1986), pp. 131–57.

——, "Changing Frameworks of International Collective Behavior: On the Complementarity of Contradictory Tendencies," in Nazli Choucri and Thomas W. Robinson, eds., *Forecasting in International Relations: Theory, Method, Problems, Prospects* (San Francisco: W. H. Freeman, 1978), pp. 384–406.

"The Russians Are Coming," *The Economist*, CCCXVII(October 20, 1990), 11–12.

Schilling, Warner R., "The Politics of National Defense: Fiscal 1950," in Warner R. Schilling, Paul Y. Hammond, and Glenn H. Snyder, *Strategy, Politics, and Defense Budgets* (New York: Columbia University Press, 1962), pp. 1–266.

Schlesinger, Arthur, Jr., "The Harry Hopkins Affair," *The Atlantic*, CCLXVII(March, 1991), 126–30.

Schlesinger, James, "Reykjavik and Revelations: A Turn of the Tide?" *Foreign Affairs*, LXV("America and the World, 1986"), 426–46.

Schmeisser, Peter, "Taking Stock: Is America in Decline?" *New York Times Magazine*, April 18, 1988, pp. 24–27, 66–68, 96.

Schneider, William, "Rambo and Reality: Having It Both Ways," in Kenneth A. Oye, Robert J. Lieber, and Donald Rothchild, eds., *Eagle Resurgent? The Reagan Era in American Foreign Policy* (Boston: Little, Brown, 1987), pp. 41–72.

"The Self-Purged Century," *The Economist*, CCCXII(August 12, 1989), 13.

Smith, Bradley F., "Sharing Ultra in World War II," *International Journal of Intelligence and Counterintelligence*, II(Spring, 1988), 59–72.

Starr, S. Frederick, "The Changing Nature of Change in the USSR," in Seweryn Bialer and Michael Mandelbaum, eds., *Gorbachev's Russia and American Foreign Policy* (Boulder: Westview Press, 1988), pp. 3–35.

Stein, Peter, and Peter Feaver, "Assuring Control of Nuclear Weapons: The Evolution of Permissive Action Links," Occasional Paper No. 2, Center for Science and International Affairs, Harvard University, 1987.

Tatu, Michel, "U.S.-Soviet Relations: A Turning Point?" *Foreign Affairs*, LXI(America and the World, 1982), 591–610.

Taubman, Philip, "The Shultz-Weinberger Feud," *New York Times Magazine*, April 14, 1985, pp. 51, 91–108.

Ullman, Richard H., "The Covert French Connection," *Foreign Policy*, #75(Summer, 1989), 3–33.

Walker, J. Samuel, " 'No More Cold War': American Foreign Policy and the 1948 Soviet Peace Offensive," *Diplomatic History*, V(Winter, 1981), 75–91.

Waltz, Kenneth N., "Nuclear Myths and Political Realities," *American Political Science Review*, LXXXIV(September, 1990), 731–45.

———, "Reflections on *Theory of International Politics*: A Response to My Critics," in Robert O. Keohane, ed., *Neorealism and Its Critics* (New York: Columbia University Press, 1986), pp. 322–45.

Watt, D. Cameron, "Intelligence and the Historian," *Diplomatic History*, XIV(Spring, 1990), 199–204.

Wendt, Alexander E., "The Agent-Structure Problem in International Relations Theory," *International Organization*, XLI(Summer, 1987), 335–70.

White, Donald W., "The Nature of World Power in American History: An Evaluation at the End of World War II," *Diplomatic History*, XI(Summer, 1987), 181–202.

Wills, Garry, "Mr. Magoo Remembers," *New York Review of Books*, XXXVII(December 20, 1990), 3–4.

Wolfe, Alan, "The Return of the Melting Pot," *New Republic*, CCIII(December 31, 1990), 27–34.

Index